DEFENSE MANAGEMENT REFORM

PETER LEVINE

DEFENSE MANAGEMENT REFORM

How to Make the Pentagon Work Better and Cost Less

STANFORD UNIVERSITY PRESS

STANFORD, CALIFORNIA

Stanford University Press

Stanford, California

©2020 by the Board of Trustees of the Leland Stanford Junior University. All rights reserved.

No part of this book may be reproduced or transmitted in any form or by any means, electronic or mechanical, including photocopying and recording, or in any information storage or retrieval system without the prior written permission of Stanford University Press.

Printed in the United States of America on acid-free, archival-quality paper

Library of Congress Cataloging-in-Publication Data is available upon request.

ISBN 978-1-5036-1046-0 (cloth)

ISBN 978-1-5036-1184-9 (paperback)

ISBN 978-1-5036-1185-6 (electronic)

Cover design: Alan Smithee

Typeset by Newgen in 10.75/15 pt Adobe Caslon Pro

CONTENTS

Foreword by Carl Levin ... vii

Acknowledgments ... ix

Introduction:
The Problem of Defense Management ... 1
Finding a Targeted Solution to the Right Set of Problems ... 5
Getting the Initiative Approved ... 11
Getting the Initiative Implemented on a Lasting Basis ... 17
The Case Studies ... 22

1 Civilian Personnel Reform at the Department of Defense ... 26
 The Civil Service Demonstration Projects ... 30
 The Enactment of NSPS Legislation ... 37
 The Implementation of NSPS ... 44
 The NSPS Pay-for-Performance System ... 52
 Labor Relations and the Collapse of the NSPS ... 67
 The Road Forward ... 77

2 Lessons from the Never-Ending Search for Acquisition Reform ... 82
 The Need for Acquisition Reform ... 87
 1981–1982: The Carlucci Initiatives ... 93
 1983–1985: The Era of Waste, Fraud, and Abuse ... 99
 1986–1992: The Packard Commission ... 107
 1993–2004: Reinventing Government ... 116
 2007–2014: The WSARA Era ... 129

	Assessment	137
	The Road Forward	143
3	Auditing the Pentagon	149
	The Road to the CFO Act and the Goal of a Clean Audit	156
	The 1990s: The Bush I and Clinton Administrations	164
	The 2000s: The Bush II and Obama Administrations	186
	Assessment	216
	Afterword	224
	Notes	229
	Index	321

FOREWORD

Rarely a month goes by without a stream of articles detailing waste and mismanagement in the Pentagon. On December 1, 2018, a *New York Times* editorial proclaimed that "The Pentagon Doesn't Know Where Its Money Goes." Later that month, an op-ed piece in the same newspaper stated that "These Toilet Seat Lids Aren't Gold-Plated, but They Cost $14,000," while a commentary published by the Heritage Foundation brashly asserted, "Pentagon Waste Shouldn't Stop Congress from Fully Equipping the Military."

Peter Levine's book explains in clear detail why the Pentagon has failed a long-required audit and why its acquisition system continues to produce examples of overspending, along with other management failures. That much has been done before. Peter's book, however, looks not just at Pentagon failures, but also at real-world examples of reforms that have worked. He builds on the DOD's mixed history of failure and success to describe the path that needs to be followed to achieve lasting management reforms. By showing not only where and why Pentagon management has fallen short, but where it can succeed, Peter has delivered an optimistic and realistic way forward.

Throughout the book and its case studies, Peter combines careful detailed analysis with common sense and an awareness of human aspects of reform efforts in the legislative and executive branches. For instance, rather than beating up on a Pentagon bureaucracy stereotypically accused of defending its own turf, Peter sees a natural testing of ideas by people of good will who offer important institutional perspectives. A process that allows those views and experiences to be voiced, he concludes, provides greater legitimacy and, if it is well organized, can promote more successful and lasting reform.

Driving the story of this book is an appreciation of the Pentagon's vital purpose of helping to defend our nation and the importance of sound management for the Pentagon's $700 billion budget and trillions of dollars of assets. When that management falls short, the result is not only a waste of the taxpayers' dollars, but a trail of negative stories that can undermine our nation's security and our people's belief in a democratic government.

Peter Levine's years on the front lines of government management make him the ideal person to tell this story. Peter served on my staff for twenty-eight years—first at the Senate Governmental Affairs Committee and then at the Senate Armed Services Committee, where he became general counsel and then staff director. In this time, Peter saw reforms that successfully leapt legislative hurdles, and others that went nowhere. He saw that for legislated reform to be effective, it must be the product of a deliberative process and a collaborative development of solutions, and—equally importantly—it must be received, understood, and executed in the federal agencies. Peter's knowledge and commitment to defense management issues was so deep and objective that his counsel was sought out by members and staff of both parties.

After leaving my staff, Peter was appointed as the Defense Department's deputy chief management officer (DCMO)—the senior DOD official in charge of management reform. He did so well in that job that he was soon asked to step into the vacant position of under secretary of defense for personnel and readiness, with policy responsibility for a military and civilian workforce of more than 2.2 million. This experience served to deepen his understanding of the obstacles to reform and the paths to success.

The result is a book that is the product of a unique combination of legislative and executive branch background. Our country is the beneficiary of Peter Levine's public service and will benefit from the practical wisdom he gained, as chronicled in this book. It will serve for years to come as a primer both for those who seek to understand how the Department of Defense works, and for those who accept management responsibility and strive to help the department to effectively fulfill its vital role.

Carl Levin
U.S. Senator from Michigan, 1977–2015
Chair, Senate Armed Services Committee, 2001–2003 and 2007–2015

ACKNOWLEDGMENTS

When I was preparing to leave the Pentagon at the end of 2016, Dr. David Chu, the president of the Institute for Defense Analyses (IDA), invited me to come to the IDA and write a book on defense management reform. This book would not exist without Dr. Chu's advocacy and support.

Defense Management Reform is rooted in the experiences of my thirty-year career in the legislative and executive branches of government—a career that was made possible when Senator Carl Levin brought me onto his staff in 1987. Those of us who had the privilege of working for Senator Levin know that he was not only an energetic and intelligent public servant but also a wonderful person. He also showed us the importance of working across the aisle, forming enduring partnerships with many outstanding Republican senators, including John Warner, John McCain, and Bill Cohen.

I learned almost as much from the many talented professional staff members with whom I worked over the years. I am particularly grateful to my three Democratic staff directors—Linda Gustitus, David Lyles, and Rick DeBobes, and to my Republican partners of many years—John Bonsell, Pablo Carrillo, and Bill Greenwalt, for their friendship and support. There are too many others to thank by name, but I believe that if the American people could see the hard work and civic spirit shown on a daily basis by congressional staff, they would have a much higher opinion of their Congress.

After eighteen years with the Senate Armed Services Committee, I moved to the Pentagon when Senator Levin retired at the end of the 113th Congress. Secretary of Defense Ash Carter and Deputy Secretary Bob Work not only brought me onto their team but also taught me important lessons about effective leadership in the executive branch. I am also indebted to my two Pentagon deputies—Stephanie Barna at

USD(P&R) and Dave Tillotson at DCMO—who provided untiring support and showed me how to make things work in the Pentagon.

I would also like to thank the former government officials who agreed to be interviewed in the course of my research, the IDA reviewers who provided so many constructive comments, and my fantastic editors—Chuck Everett of IDA and Leah Pennywark of Stanford University Press. This book is better for their efforts.

Finally, neither this book nor my career in public service would have been possible without the constant love and support of my wife, Mary Ellen, and our son Daniel. They are the loves of my life, and everything I do is better because of them.

DEFENSE MANAGEMENT REFORM

INTRODUCTION
The Problem of Defense Management

ON February 9, 2015, the Defense Business Board (DBB)—a panel of corporate business leaders established to provide independent advice to the secretary of defense—reported that it had found a way to slash waste in the Department of Defense (DOD). "We see a clear path to saving over $125 billion over the next five years," the DBB reported.[1] The projected savings were the product of a simple mathematical calculation. Savings of $125 billion would be achieved, the DBB declared, if the DOD met a "realistic goal" of 7 percent annual productivity gains in six "Core Business Processes."[2] Moreover, nobody would have to be fired. The department could achieve the savings by just not replacing the 25 to 30 percent of the DOD civilian workforce that was projected to retire or leave over a five-year period.[3]

The report was much less clear on how the 7 percent productivity gains necessary to meet the savings targets could be achieved, suggesting timelines to "stand up and train teams," "design initiatives," "deploy productivity initiatives," and "track savings."[4] Approaches to be considered included more efficient use of service contracts, streamlined organizational structures, and rationalized business systems.[5] None of these approaches was particularly revolutionary. The DOD had tried all of them before, with significant investments of time and effort leading to marginal success. The DBB had said, in effect, "We gave you the dollar amount, now *you* go and find the savings."

For almost two years, the report sat on the shelf, ignored by the DOD, the press, and the public. Then, in December 2016, the report was thrust back into the spotlight with a *Washington Post* article by Craig Whitlock and Bob Woodward under the headline "Pentagon Buries Evidence of $125 Billion in Bureaucratic Waste."[6] The article pointed out that DBB chair Robert Stein had been replaced three months after the study was completed. "They're all complaining that they don't have any money," Stein was quoted as saying. "We proposed a way to save a ton of money."[7] The implication was clear: senior DOD officials could easily have saved $125 billion dollars if they had only wanted to—they just didn't have the guts to go after waste and inefficiency.

On May 23, 2015, one month after Stein was replaced as DBB chair, I was confirmed by the Senate to serve as the DOD's deputy chief management officer (DCMO). The DCMO was established in 2007 to ensure that a senior official had formal, full-time responsibility to oversee DOD management—including the issues that the DBB claimed the DOD had been neglecting. Unfortunately, there is a huge gap between the objectives of the DCMO and the capabilities and authorities of the office. Before I was confirmed, the position of DCMO had been vacant for the better part of two years, and it was not clear that anybody in the department had even noticed.

Some of my colleagues felt that I deserved what I got in the new assignment. For the previous twenty-eight years, I had worked for Senator Carl Levin on the staffs of the Senate Armed Services Committee (SASC) and the Senate Governmental Affairs Committee (SGAC). In these positions, I advised senators on defense management issues and advocated the more efficient use of service contracts, workforce improvements, the rationalization of business systems and processes, and other reforms. In fact, I had recommended the legislation that established the position of DCMO, out of a sincere belief that a greater focus on management issues was needed at senior levels of the Pentagon. It seemed only fair that I should be the one to try to make the office work.

After I had been on the job for a few weeks, Deputy Secretary of Defense Bob Work called me into his office and told me that because of the strict budget caps imposed by the Budget Control Act of 2011, the DOD needed to look for money anywhere it could be found. "How much money can you save through management efficiencies?" he asked. I guessed about $5 billion over the five years of the Future Years Defense Program (FYDP), and he told me to get to work. Over the next year, most of my time was directed toward achieving those savings.

With the deputy secretary's support, we put together a proposal to reduce the size of the department's management headquarters, cut low-priority service contracts, and reap savings from fielding new business systems. We incorporated proposals from the department's chief information officer to achieve additional savings by rationalizing the department's information technology (IT) applications through enterprise licensing and data center consolidation. We established working groups, review boards, and other consultative mechanisms to ensure that the projected management changes were actually implemented and achieved the projected savings.

Over the course of the year, our projected savings went as high as $10 billion, before dropping back to $7 billion as we came to grips with the real world in which our plans would have to be implemented. Even though our initiatives covered much of the same ground as the DBB (service contract reviews, organizational delayering, and IT rationalization), however, we never thought that it was remotely possible that we could achieve overhead savings anywhere close to the $125 billion proposed by the board's January report.

Why not?

First, the DOD budget does not have a line item for waste. Inefficiency is embedded in thousands of different work processes and organizational structures throughout the department. As tempting as it may be to seek "quick wins" and immediate savings, there are few shortcuts, and easy solutions rarely result in long-term improvements. Across-the-board reductions cut good programs and bad programs alike, adding to bottlenecks, slow-downs, and backlogs. If you really want to root out waste and inefficiency, you have to go through the painstaking process of reviewing processes and organizations one step at a time. Since the easiest savings are identified first, it gets harder and harder as you go. Defense dollars may be spent in large buckets, but savings are typically identified and implemented in small spoonfuls.

As former secretary of defense Robert Gates explained in 2015, trying to achieve savings through "mindless salami slicing of programs and organizations" is tempting but amounts to "managerial and political cowardice." "True reform," he said, "requires making trades and choices and tough decisions, recognizing that some activities are more important than others. It is hard to do, but essential if you are to reshape any organization into a more effective and efficient enterprise."[8] He added, "At the end of the day, re-drawing the organization chart or enacting new acquisitions laws and rules will matter less than leaders skilled enough to execute programs effectively, willing to make tough, usually unpopular choices, and establish strong measures of accountability."[9]

Second, many of the good ideas have already been tried. For example, the 2015 DBB report suggested that the department could save between $46 and $89 billion through "optimization" of service contract spending. However, every specific idea proposed by the DBB with regard to service contracts had already been tried. As early as 2001 and 2002, SASC required the department to adopt private sector practices, including "conducting spending analyses, rationalizing supplier bases, and expanding the use of cross-functional, commodity-based teams."[10] Over the years that followed, the department went through round after round of service contract reviews and reductions. There is still money to be saved, but it is fanciful to believe that the DOD could suddenly save tens of billions of dollars by reviewing spending that it has already been squeezing for years.

Third, any significant change in DOD organizations or processes is likely to encounter significant institutional resistance. For example, when the department first took on defense commissary reform, it ran into a wall of opposition from military and veterans service organizations, which viewed any reduction in the commissary subsidy as a cut in military compensation. When I took over the effort as DCMO, we developed an approach that would save money by making the commissaries more efficient without reducing benefits to service members, retirees, and their families. Congress became more supportive, but we continued to encounter resistance from commissary suppliers who benefitted from the old, inefficient system.

Finally, real reform requires an up-front investment of time and resources. The DBB projected that the department would achieve 9 percent savings in the first year of the program. We knew that it would take at least a year to identify needed changes, get policies in place, and start drilling down to implement them through the department. Thus, the first year would likely require a net expenditure, not a net saving. Too often in the past, the DOD has made the mistake of assuming that efficiencies would be easily achieved and locking early savings into the budget. When the savings did not materialize, the bills had to be paid by cutting operational accounts, which undermines military capabilities. There are no easy victories in defense management: you get what you pay for, in both money and time.

So what makes a defense management reform initiative successful? I break success down into three steps.

- First, the initiative has to provide a targeted solution to the right set of problems. The resources that the department can devote to reform are limited, so focusing on low-priority problems or on too many problems at the same time can be counterproductive.
- Second, the initiative has to be enacted or approved. Even a well-designed and targeted management reform cannot be effective if it is never tried. A major initiative is most likely to gain traction if it has support from both political parties, from the executive branch and Congress, and from the interested public.
- Third, the initiative has to be effectively implemented on a lasting basis. Successful implementation requires strong leadership and continuous engagement with the affected components and functional communities across the department.

FINDING A TARGETED SOLUTION TO THE RIGHT SET OF PROBLEMS

Early in my Senate career, I learned that progress comes best in bite-sized chunks, with focused solutions to clearly defined problems. Just six months after I started work for Senator Levin, we held hearings on efforts to protect employees who blow the whistle on waste, fraud, and abuse in the federal government. We learned that although the Civil Service Reform Act of 1978 had established a legal mechanism for protecting whistleblowers, the mechanism was not effective. At that time, the government was pursuing only 5 percent of the cases in which whistleblowers sought relief, and even those cases were rarely successful because of unfavorable legal standards. As a result, 70 percent of government employees who had knowledge of waste, fraud, and abuse said that they would not report it, and the number of employees who feared reprisal had almost doubled—from 20 percent to 37 percent—in less than five years.[11]

Senator Levin responded with a carefully targeted approach to the problem. He introduced a bill that established new, more favorable legal standards for whistleblower cases and authorized whistleblowers who were not satisfied with the government's actions on their behalf to bring an individual right of action. It took two years of work, but the Whistleblower Protection Act of 1989[12] was the first major piece of legislation signed by President George H. W. Bush, and the standard of proof that we developed for the bill has since been replicated in other whistleblower protection statutes across the federal government.

Other projects followed, addressing issues such as the DOD's excess inventory of obsolete and unneeded spare parts; the department's reliance on elaborate military specifications instead of simplified commercial item descriptions; the improper use of inside information in the procurement process; the use of interagency contracting mechanisms to avoid competition requirements; the acquisition of contract services; the impact of deep cuts to the acquisition workforce; the mismanagement of wartime contracting; the need for rapid acquisition authority to meet battlefield needs; and problems with counterfeit parts and lack of security in the DOD supply chain.

One of my proudest moments came in 2009, when Senator Levin determined that we had to do something about excessive cost growth in the DOD's biggest weapons programs. We drafted a bill that focused relentlessly on improving the front end of the acquisition process, which experts told us drove higher acquisition costs. The Weapon Systems Acquisition Reform Act of 2009[13] was approved unanimously by both houses of Congress and made a real difference in controlling weapon systems cost growth.

Along the way, I learned the risk of relying on one-size-fits-all solutions in circumstances where they do not fit. A warranty or a fixed-price contract that protects the buyer's interest when a consumer purchases a television set or a car may not be effective for the purchase of an advanced aircraft or missile system. Streamlined commercial purchasing techniques that reduce overhead in the purchase of off-the-shelf items may undermine important government interests when applied to the acquisition of military-unique weapon systems. And an audited financial statement that provides important information about the value of a commercial enterprise may have no similar use when applied to a federal agency.

An even greater risk is the failure to consider not only what is broken but what is *not* broken. For example, the "up-or-out" policy that serves as the basis for officer personnel management in today's military has been criticized for being out of step with the demographics of the twenty-first-century job market, for pushing highly trained officers with critical skills into premature retirement, and for limiting the department's access to talent that will be needed to respond to emerging threats. Respected experts have advocated eliminating the up-or-out policy, scrapping mandatory promotion timelines and mandatory retirement dates, and applying market-based solutions to officer assignments and career advancement.

While the diagnosis has much truth, some of the prescriptions would be worse than the disease. The up-or-out policy helps shape the military by ensuring that the officer corps is continually refreshed and by providing a competitive environment in which it is possible to provide responsibility to developing leaders at an early age. In a culture that finds it difficult to say "no" to anybody, this system also provides an essential forcing function to remove weaker performers from the force. When I served as the under secretary of defense for personnel and readiness (USD[P&R]), I sought to address shortcomings in officer career patterns by adding needed flexibility to a working system—not by tearing that system down.

The Goldwater-Nichols Department of Defense Reorganization Act of 1986 ("Goldwater-Nichols")[14] is often considered to be the gold standard of defense reform. Goldwater-Nichols, which was enacted over the strong objections of the secretary of defense and the joint chiefs of staff, sought to address organizational weaknesses that made it difficult for the services to work together, undermining military operations. As a result of Goldwater-Nichols, "jointness" is now widely accepted throughout the DOD as an operating concept and as a key to military advancement—significantly enhancing the operational effectiveness of our armed forces.

Some have argued that the Goldwater-Nichols experience shows that the Pentagon cannot reform itself because "there are too many conflicting interests and priorities and parochial interests that just can't be overcome from within. They're going to have to be addressed from an external source."[15] Others have pointed to the long deliberative period before the statute was enacted and have argued that "possibly the most important factor in passing the Goldwater-Nichols Act was the relentless bipartisan effort of its sponsors over the course of nearly five years to methodically study relevant issues and build consensus reform, even in the face of strong opposition from the Department."[16]

It is certainly true that outside pressure—in the form of legislation or adverse publicity—can play an important role in helping DOD leaders overcome internal opposition to undertake needed reforms. Congress devoted unparalleled attention to Goldwater-Nichols, with five years of hearings and consensus building preceding the enactment of the statute and continuous oversight for decades thereafter. When I became SASC staff director more than twenty-five years later, the first question that the committee asked of every nominee for a senior military position was still, "Do you support the Goldwater-Nichols organizational reforms?"

However, three other factors contributed greatly to the success of the legislation. First was a specific, well-defined problem: a series of operational failures experienced by the US military. Second was an identified root cause: the inability of the military services to function as a unified force. Third was a course of action that directly addressed the root cause. As Senator Sam Nunn explained while Goldwater-Nichols was under consideration, "Every time we've failed or performed poorly—such as Vietnam, *Mayaguez*, *Pueblo*, Beirut, Grenada—it can be traced to the lack of unity of command.... We must give [our commanders] the authority they need to meld units from all services into an effective fighting force."[17]

By the time Goldwater-Nichols was enacted, it ran to a hundred pages and touched major parts of the defense organization. However, the singular purpose of the act was to strengthen field commanders by establishing unity of command. The critical provision required that all forces operating within the geographic area of a combatant command be under the control of a single combatant commander and that the chain of command for those forces—regardless of military service involved—runs from the president to the secretary of defense and from the secretary to the combatant commander.[18] Other provisions reinforced the unity of command by eliminating the role of the military departments in operational matters and establishing joint officer personnel policies to break down the old, service-centric culture.

In essence, Goldwater-Nichols successfully changed the way the military operated because it was a powerful hammer blow delivered with precision aim to the head of a single nail.

By contrast, when Senator John McCain set out to reform DOD organization and management in 2015, he identified problems ranging from a declining force structure, aging equipment, and cost overruns to the quality of military advice to civilian leaders and the effectiveness of civilian oversight of the military.[19] SASC heard from dozens of witnesses at hearings addressing Goldwater-Nichols, defense reform, defense organization, defense strategy and force structure, the future of warfare, the roles and missions of the armed forces, obstacles to effective management, acquisition reform, personnel reform, and the development of policy, strategy, and plans.[20]

One year later, Congress produced the most voluminous National Defense Authorization Act (NDAA) ever, with a record 1,545-page conference report.[21] With regard to DOD organization and management, however, the bill was remarkably thin. A new requirement for a National Defense Strategy replaced the Quadrennial Defense Review; the department was directed to establish a unified combatant command for cyber operations; and the Office of the Under Secretary of Defense for Acquisition, Technology, and Logistics (USD[AT&L]) was split in two.

Reasonable observers will debate the usefulness of these organizational reforms. It is unlikely, however, that any of them will fundamentally change the Pentagon bureaucracy or make the DOD a more innovative, agile, efficient, or effective organization.

My former colleagues on the SASC staff hoped to address the department's management problems with a provision requiring the secretary to establish a set of "cross-functional mission teams" to "produce comprehensive and fully integrated policies, strategies, plans, and resourcing decisions."[22] The new cross-functional teams, the committee report asserted, would fill in "an unfinished goal of the original Goldwater-Nichols reform agenda" by "correcting the mission integration problems in the Washington headquarters organizations" of the Pentagon.[23] The result would be "the best possible policy, strategy, planning, and resource allocation decision making."[24]

In contrast to the original Goldwater-Nichols Act, which provided a targeted set of solutions to a single, well-defined problem, this provision offered a single solution for the widest possible array of problems. Indeed, while the law spelled out the structure of cross-functional teams in exquisite detail, it was notably silent on the problems that these teams were to address. The SASC report provided only that the secretary of defense would be required to "identify the missions, other high-priority outputs, and important activities of the Department of Defense" for which mission teams would be established.[25]

The SASC report asserted that the cross-functional teams would be able to overcome the department's parochial bureaucratic structures and develop "clear, coherent, efficacious courses of action" rather than a "lowest-common-denominator consensus" because they would work directly for the secretary of defense.[26] This view was based on two fundamental misunderstandings. First, the department's functional communities speak for important institutional interests that do not disappear just because they are ignored. Second, the time and energy of the secretary of defense is a scarce and finite resource that cannot be increased by law. Legislating that the secretary will give his personal time and attention to a set number of mission teams established by congressional directive does not make it so.

The new administration did its best to comply with the legislation, dutifully designating working groups on major issues as "cross-functional teams." In the summer of 2017, the department established cross-functional teams to address IT systems, logistics and supply chain management, real property management, community services, human resource management, financial management, acquisition and procurement, and health care management. The teams were directed to develop detailed work plans within sixty days and then turn immediately to the development and deployment of revised business processes and procedures.[27]

Two years later, there was no evidence that the new cross-functional teams had been any more decisive, innovative, or effective than working groups previously used in the department. In January 2019, the Government Accountability Office reported that only a handful of business reform initiatives developed by the cross-functional teams had been handed off to the military services for implementation. The department estimated that it would need at least $6.7 billion to implement the initiatives, but no funding had been identified.[28] Congress has an important role to play in setting priorities and establishing ground rules for DOD operations and activities, but good management is impossible to legislate.

GETTING THE INITIATIVE APPROVED

Even a well-designed and targeted management reform cannot be effective if it is never tried. For a legislative initiative, a bill has to be enacted. A statute can be enacted in a single day or it can be the product of years of effort. The strongest legislative products, however, are the result of a deliberative process that begins with the exploration of problems, continues with the development of solutions, and concludes with the building of consensus. In legislative terms, these steps often take the form of staff investigation and oversight hearings, the drafting of legislation and legislative hearings, and then committee markup and floor consideration.

My first major legislative experience followed this classic pattern. We started with an investigation of the Wedtech scandal—the case of a small business in the Bronx that used political connections to skirt procurement rules and obtain large Army and Navy contracts that it was incapable of performing. Our Wedtech report found that loopholes in the federal lobbying laws had enabled the company's influence-peddling activities to proceed undiscovered for years.[29] We then investigated the lobbying disclosure laws themselves, learning that they were so dysfunctional that lobbyists were choked by paperwork without providing any useful information at all.

The Lobbying Disclosure Act was signed into law in 1995, cleaning up a problem that we had identified and addressed through the course of eight years of investigation, hearings, and legislative effort.[30] The key to the enactment of the legislation—beyond the obvious doggedness of its chief sponsor—was the strong bipartisan support it received in both houses. The importance of bipartisanship was drummed into me from the time I first arrived on Capitol Hill. If a Democratic senator wanted to get legislation enacted, I learned that the first step was always to find a Republican cosponsor. A bill that had only Democrats or only Republicans as sponsors was unlikely to get out of committee, and if it did, it would probably not be taken up on the Senate floor.

The Federal Acquisition Streamlining Act (FASA) provided an even better model of bipartisan legislation in this period. In the early 1990s, Congress received an eight-volume, 1,800-page report from the "Section 800" independent acquisition advisory commission.[31] The report included a detailed prescription for streamlining the acquisition system, including recommendations to amend or repeal nearly three hundred laws—far more than congressional committees could hope to sort through in the normal course of business. Moreover, some of the recommendations were controversial, threatening a negative reaction to the whole project.

A bipartisan, multicommittee staff working group was established to break through the potential gridlock. Over the next eight months, the staff group met every week to review the Section 800 report line-by-line and develop provision-by-provision recommendations. In these discussions, as in most of our staff work, it was never relevant who was a Republican or who was a Democrat—we were all just working to get the legislation right. After joint hearings by SASC and the SGAC, the bill passed the Senate by unanimous consent and was eventually approved by the House 425–0.[32] The legislative process took two years, but the result was a piece of landmark legislation that dramatically streamlined the procurement system and that has stood the test of time.[33]

When I moved from SGAC to SASC staff in 1996, I found an equally constructive approach. The tenor was set from the top. Senator Levin always had an excellent working relationship with his Republican counterpart, regardless whether we were in the majority or the minority and whether his opposite number was Strom Thurmond, John Warner, John McCain, or Jim Inhofe. The committee was rightly proud of its bipartisan tradition, which had resulted in the enactment of an NDAA every year since 1962. Most of these bills were reported unanimously out of committee, and, when there was a record vote on final passage, they often had the support of ninety or more senators.

The close relationship between the chairs and ranking minority members was reflected in the staff. Unlike other Senate committees, the majority and minority staffs of SASC shared office space, which facilitated friendship and teamwork. The general rule was that all meetings included majority and minority staff, so that both parties could work from a common set of information. During my eighteen years with the committee, I found that my closest working relationships were often with my Republican counterparts, because we attended all of the same meetings and worked together on a daily basis.

The committee had to address highly contentious issues every year: missile defense, base closures, funding for the Iraq War, Guantánamo detainees, the prohibition on torture, sexual assault, cuts to major weapons programs, and changes in military compensation—the list goes on and on. Nonetheless, bipartisanship was expected when it came to the committee's legislative business. The working documents for committee markups had places for sign-off by the majority and the minority staff. Likewise, the conference working documents called for four-way sign-off by the two staffs of the House and Senate committees. It was understood that the majority could override the minority if necessary, but it was in everybody's interest that this happen as infrequently as possible.

The few cases in which the committee's bipartisan model broke down show the importance of this model. In 2003, confronted by a controversial proposal to overhaul the defense civilian personnel system, Senator Levin worked with Senator Susan Collins, the Republican chair of the Homeland Security and Governmental Affairs Committee (HSGAC), to develop a bipartisan compromise. The Collins-Levin bill was approved by the HSGAC on a near-unanimous 10–1 vote. As described later in this book, however, the Bush administration rejected the compromise and insisted on a hard-edged, single-party approach that strengthened opposition and led to the eventual collapse of the reform effort.

Three years later, Senator Levin worked with senators John Warner, John McCain, and Lindsey Graham to develop a bipartisan approach to codify in statute the military commission system for trying Guantánamo detainees.[34] Once again, the administration rejected the bipartisan compromise and insisted on a single-party solution. The administration's version of the Military Commissions Act of 2006 was enacted on a party-line vote[35] and lasted barely three years before a new president and a new Congress replaced it with the Military Commissions Act of 2009[36]—essentially the original Warner-Levin-McCain-Graham proposal. By that time, however, the military commission system was mired in constitutional challenges and procedural litigation. If military commissions ever had a chance of working, it was already long gone.

Bipartisanship may be easier for SASC and the HSGAC than for other committees because national defense and government management issues tend to enjoy broad support in both parties. In today's Congress, however, almost any issue can become tinged with partisanship. That lack of cooperation is unfortunate. It is occasionally possible to enact a statute with the support of only a single party, but doing so is rarely a road to lasting reform.

Surprisingly, gaining approval for a management reform initiative in the executive branch can be just as hard as getting legislation enacted. You might think that the advance approval of the secretary or the deputy secretary would be enough to get the job done, but that is not the way the DOD works. While the operational chain of command in the military is simple and direct, administrative decision-making authority is diffused in a hundred directions and has as many different power centers. The direction of the secretary or the deputy secretary can be used to leverage favorable outcomes, but nothing is final until formal guidance documents are signed and funding is provided through the programming and budgeting processes.

For example, the deputy secretary liked the new business model that I proposed for the defense commissaries and exchanges and told me to go forward with it. I soon learned, however, that each of the commissaries and exchanges was a separate business unit with its own leadership, its own board of directors, and its own support from the services. Moving forward meant establishing a working group to give these groups an opportunity to express their views and concerns. I could draft a formal policy and a legislative proposal authorizing the policy, but these documents had to be "coordinated" with the leadership of the commissaries and exchanges, the military departments, and other interested DOD officials.

Even that was not all. On top of the policy approval process, reform proposals had to go through a separate programming and budget process that required the approval or acquiescence of an entirely different set of DOD officials—the service programmers and budgeters, the comptroller, and the lead DOD programmer (the director of cost accounting and program evaluation). The policy process and the programming process culminated in separate presentations to the senior leadership of the department, through the secretary's Senior Leadership Council (SLC)[37] for the policy approval and through the deputy's Management Action Group (DMAG)[38] for program and budget approval.

This process is burdensome but appropriate. Our proposed headquarters reductions, for example, had an impact on every part of the department. As smart as my staff was, they could not be expected to understand the full range of organizations, functions, and activities covered by the proposal. It took months of consultation and communication to devise a consistent set of targets and definitions and provide appropriate flexibility and exclusions. This process also helped to build a consensus in favor of the proposal. If we had failed to coordinate in this manner, we would have encountered unintended side effects and opposition from leaders whose organizations and missions were unnecessarily compromised.

My predecessor at USD(P&R) learned this lesson the hard way. On March 30, 2015, Secretary of Defense Ash Carter called for the department to "think hard about how to attract, inspire, and excite" young Americans to help build the Force of the Future (FotF).[39] Assuming the secretary's support, Acting Under Secretary Brad Carson initiated a secretive and lightning-fast review and circulated a 120-page memorandum containing dozens of far-reaching proposals, including the elimination of the long-standing "up-or-out" system for military promotions, the replacement of the existing civil service system with a new pay-for-performance approach, and the creation of an array of new personnel benefits and organizations.[40]

The proposals hit like a lead balloon. The military services saw the up-or-out proposal as a threat to undermine a system that had long ensured the continuous refreshment and renewal of military leadership. The federal employee unions saw the civil service proposals as an effort to slash workers' rights and undermine the department's civilian workforce. Republicans in Congress saw the new benefits as an effort at social engineering and a wasteful expenditure of scarce defense dollars. The opposition was fierce and quickly became personal—even growing to include unfortunate and unfounded allegations about Carson's conduct in office.

"What the building thinks" is a phrase voiced in the Pentagon that describes the kind of concerns that can arise in opposition to proposals that have not been adequately vetted. The views of "the building" are often discounted by those who see them as nothing more than the rigid inflexibility of small-minded bureaucrats who are protecting their turf. There is no question that the Pentagon can be resistant to change, but in many cases there is good reason for the resistance. DOD officials care deeply about the mission of the department and are naturally concerned by proposals for disruptive changes that threaten to restructure organizations, unsettle existing relationships, and reduce resources in a manner that could compromise that mission.

In some cases, it is necessary to override parochial concerns in the broader interest of the department, but failure to engage and at least understand the motivation for the concerns is never a good option. Senior officials can ignore what the building thinks, but they do so at their own peril. No matter how important these officials may think they are, the building will be around a lot longer than they will. Executive branch management reform initiatives, like legislative initiatives, are most likely to succeed when their proponents invest the time and effort needed to build a broad base of support.

GETTING THE INITIATIVE IMPLEMENTED ON A LASTING BASIS

Early in my tenure on Capitol Hill, I learned that the enactment of a statute, while it might be a major achievement, is rarely sufficient to accomplish significant change. It does not do much good to get a statute enacted (or an executive branch initiative approved) if it is never successfully implemented. The struggle to get an initiative implemented can be every bit as much of a battle—and every bit as political—as the effort to achieve enactment or approval.

One of the first issues I worked on after joining Senator Levin's staff in the late 1980s was the DOD's acquisition of off-the-shelf products—then known as "non-developmental items" or "NDIs." For years, independent reviews had criticized the department for its continued reliance on military-unique products even when its needs could have been met by existing commercial products at a fraction of the cost. Finally, in 1986, Congress enacted a statutory preference for the purchase of NDIs and required the department to identify and remove impediments to such purchases.[41]

Two years later, we revisited the issue, holding hearings and interviewing procurement specialists at the DOD and in the contractor community. What we learned really opened my eyes as a young lawyer getting a first look at the inner workings of government. Virtually nothing had been done to implement the statute! Far from ramping up the use of commercial items and off-the-shelf products, the department had largely abandoned an earlier effort to replace detailed military specifications with simplified commercial item descriptions.[42]

More laws were enacted, but things really began to change only when Secretary of Defense William Perry issued a memorandum that directed changes to military specifications and made the acquisition of commercial items his highest priority.[43] The department tasked teams of acquisition officials to review and rewrite military specifications and began an active effort to include commercial technology in military systems. It turns out that the actions of a determined secretary can make far more difference than the enactment of a statute or two.

In my experience, a statute can spur the department to action, but it is the department's action—not the statute—that determines whether a management reform is successful. This appears to be the case regardless of whether the statute establishes aspirational goals or changes binding rules. For example, the Chief Financial Officers Act of 1990 (CFO Act), was a largely aspirational statute, establishing the goal of making federal agencies auditable but providing few tools with which to accomplish this objective.[44] With a boost from years of congressional oversight, the CFO Act has driven the DOD to spend billions of dollars in pursuit of auditability, but the objective is little closer today than it was when the statute was enacted. The success or failure of this effort has been largely a matter of executive branch performance.

The Competition in Contracting Act of 1984 (CICA) also established an aspirational goal—increasing competition in federal agency procurements. Unlike the CFO Act, CICA also changed the contracting rules of the road to promote this objective, requiring the use of competitive procedures except in limited circumstances and establishing public notice requirements, justification requirements for sole-source awards, and bid protest procedures to provide enforcement.[45] Even with these new rules, however, individual competition decisions remained entirely in the hands of executive branch officials, who retained broad discretion over each individual procurement. Competition levels are considerably higher today than they were in 1984 but continue to fluctuate as the DOD's management focus ebbs and flows over the years.

Without political commitment and active follow-up, some statutes have no impact at all. In 2001, for example, the Bush administration sought to address problems in the acquisition of major weapon systems by placing a new emphasis on "evolutionary acquisition" and "spiral development." Bill Greenwalt and I, who then handled acquisition policy issues on the SASC staff, supported the concept of incremental acquisition but were concerned by vague descriptions of how it would work, which appeared to indicate that defense programs would no longer be held to a defined baseline, potentially giving the contractors a "blank check."

We recommended two elegant legislative provisions that laid out how acquisition programs could be held to firm baselines even as new technologies were incorporated. Both provisions were enacted as part of the Fiscal Year (FY) 2003 NDAA,[46] but nobody in the department ever lifted a finger to implement either one. The department continued to propose the acquisition programs that DOD officials wanted, and Congress continued to approve funding for these programs. This was a classic case of staff-driven legislation: without any effective follow-up, the department felt free to ignore it.

This may sound like a cavalier approach to statutory requirements, but, given the ever-growing volume of the annual NDAAs, the department cannot possibly give its full attention to every provision. The conference report on the FY 2008 NDAA, for example, was 1,364 pages long[47]—a dramatic contrast to the first NDAA, enacted in 1962, which takes less than a page in the volume of collected US statutes.[48] Before 1980, the annual defense bills rarely included any acquisition policy provisions. By the time I arrived in 1987, each bill included a separate title dedicated to acquisition provisions—typically about 20 to 30 acquisition policy provisions. More recently, the number of acquisition provisions has exploded, with 66 provisions enacted in 2008, 77 in FY 2016, and 88 in FY 2017—many of them making major changes to the acquisition system.[49]

When I was writing those provisions, I did not fully appreciate—and I do not think that the staffs of the armed services committees appreciate today—how the volume of these provisions undermines their effectiveness. Senior DOD officials have limited bandwidth and cannot reasonably be expected to devote a significant personal effort to the implementation of more than a handful of legislative provisions a year. The lesson that the committees have yet to learn is that a focus on everything can often be the same thing as a focus on nothing. This notion is particularly true in a time of limited budgets, when the same Congress that imposes a multitude of new requirements is also cutting the headquarters workforce that is responsible for implementing these requirements.

In fairness, some senior DOD officials have failed to grasp the same point. At the end of the 1980s, Deputy Secretary Donald Atwood issued hundreds of "Defense Management Review Decisions," or DMRDs, that addressed virtually every aspect of DOD management and diluted the department's management attention to such an extent that few of the initiatives were likely to be effectively implemented. In the 1990s, the Clinton administration's acquisition reform efforts suffered a similar fate, as the department cranked out more major initiatives than a rapidly shrinking acquisition workforce could hope to absorb. A senior acquisition official later told RAND that acquisition reform "has been good at cranking out policies, but hasn't made anything faster, better, or cheaper."[50]

The FotF initiatives that I inherited when I became acting USD(P&R) faced the same potential pitfall, with far more proposals than we could hope to implement in the few months remaining in the Obama administration. I made it a priority to winnow out less-important proposals and focus on obtaining buy-in from the military services for the remaining efforts. Because the services had a strong interest in initiatives to enhance recruiting efforts, make military careers more attractive and productive by adding flexibility to the officer promotion system, and strengthen the civilian workforce through the increased use of direct hiring authority and highly qualified experts, we hoped that they would continue to work on them even after we left—and they appear to have done so.

In addition to Secretary Carter's FotF initiative, I was responsible for implementing a new policy to allow service by transgender service members, and I had to handle the inevitable "pop-up" crises that every senior DOD manager must face. In my case, the biggest crisis was caused by the California National Guard's unfortunate decision to try to force soldiers to repay reenlistment bonuses for which they were technically ineligible, years after they had reenlisted and served with honor in Iraq and Afghanistan. A close second was Senator McCain's insistence that my office had acted improperly in suspending the University of Phoenix from the DOD tuition assistance program due to repeated violations of its agreement with the department and complaints about its deceptive practices.

These issues left me with limited time to take on the myriad of other personnel and readiness issues facing the department. A few months after I took office, the armed services committees proposed dozens of new statutory provisions addressing military and civilian personnel policy. I tried to weigh in on these provisions so that the department's views would be heard. However, I was never going to be able to devote significant time or effort to more than a handful. Somebody somewhere in the Pentagon would be responsible for implementing each one of them, but there was no way that they could all get the senior leadership attention that would be needed to make them work best. No matter how hard I tried, I knew that Congress could write more legislative provisions than I could possibly implement.

In other cases, Congress does not seem to understand what is and is not possible to implement. The biggest legislative issue that I had to address as DCMO was a proposed 30 percent cut to DOD headquarters activities (on top of a 20 percent cut previously imposed by Secretary of Defense Hagel).[51] The proposal was so poorly drafted that it would have resulted in the virtual elimination of important organizations like the Washington Headquarters Services, Defense Contract Management Agency, the Defense POW/MIA Accounting Agency, the Defense Security Cooperation Agency, and the Defense Threat Reduction Agency. Unfortunately, the elimination of a defense agency does not eliminate the need to do its work.

Over a period of months, I worked with Congress and senior leaders in the department to establish a more achievable reduction.[52] It was then my job to make sure that the cuts really happened. Even before the final bill was enacted, we had countless meetings to nail down exactly what was covered by new definitions of management headquarters and the credit that would be provided for cuts already achieved pursuant to Secretary Hagel's earlier requirement. Additional meetings were needed to define new data elements for the department's programming and budgeting systems to ensure that our progress toward the goal could be tracked. We even required the under secretaries of defense and heads of defense agencies to present specific plans showing which positions would be cut and when, and we recorded the elimination of the positions in the department's authoritative manpower systems to ensure that the cuts were enforceable.

The committee staff viewed the reductions as a success, seeing them as a vindication for the original proposal, without understanding the hard work that went into making the cuts a reality. Three years later, legislation was once again proposed requiring the elimination of entire defense agencies without the recognition that their functions would have to be performed somewhere and by someone.[53] As important as it is to cut bureaucracy at the DOD, Congress does not have an easy time distinguishing between dispensable overhead and important value-added activities and determining which functions can be cut without undermining the mission. This work is the hard work of implementation, and it takes place in the executive branch, not in the legislative branch.

THE CASE STUDIES

The balance of this book presents case studies of three defense management reform issues, each of which has been the focus of significant attention from Congress and DOD leadership over a period of several decades: civilian personnel reform, acquisition reform, and financial management reform. These issues were selected not just because of my personal participation in them but also because they demonstrate the wide array of hurdles faced by reformers and the critical elements of success. Other issues could have been chosen—for example, military personnel reform, health care reform, service contract reform, or logistics reform. It is my hope that the lessons learned from the selected case studies may also be found applicable to these areas.

I group the lessons into a substantive and a political dimension. On the political side, the case studies show that a management reform initiative is most likely to be adopted and implemented if it has solid support from both political parties, the executive branch and the Congress are working together toward a common objective, and the affected organizational and functional communities are supportive. In cases where the initiative seeks to overcome established incentives, effective organizational enforcement mechanisms are also essential to ensure implementation.

For example, the Bush administration's legislative proposal for the National Security Personnel System (NSPS) was enacted and the new system was implemented for a short period of time. However, the administration made a series of political mistakes, passing up a legislative compromise that could have provided a broad base of bipartisan support, excluding Congress from the design of the new system, and insisting upon far-reaching labor relations and appeals provisions that undermined workforce support and were anathema to the federal employee unions. As a result, the new civilian personnel system proved to be unsustainable when Congress and the presidency changed hands, and it was overturned a few short years after it had been implemented.

Similarly, the Carlucci acquisition reforms of the early 1980s lacked an organizational structure to ensure action and were never fully implemented because of Secretary Weinberger's decision to delegate acquisition authority to the military services; the spare parts reforms of the late 1980s were launched entirely by Congress in the face of DOD opposition and were implemented only for as long as members of Congress continued to pay attention; and defense-wide organizations established to reform business and accounting practices in the 1990s and 2000s failed because the military services retained control over their own business systems and processes and were unwilling or unable to support the changes.

By contrast, more targeted civilian personnel reforms undertaken over the last decade have had bipartisan support in Congress, did not provoke an adverse reaction from the workforce, and appear to have been implemented successfully. The Packard Commission reforms of the late 1980s and the Weapon Systems Acquisition Reform Act (WSARA)–era reforms of the 2000s were also endorsed by the DOD leadership and received bipartisan support in Congress. Both reforms included organizational mechanisms to help them overcome parochial incentives in the acquisition process, and both were successfully implemented.

On the substantive side, the case studies show that management reform initiatives are most likely to achieve positive results when they prioritize critical tasks, clearly define the problem to be solved, tailor the solution to the problem, and assign responsibility to those best equipped to act. For example, NSPS risked multiple points of failure because it attempted to address the full range of civilian personnel issues at the same time. Similarly, the Corporate Information Management program of the 1990s and the Business Enterprise Architecture program of the 2000s tried to develop a grand design that would solve all of the financial management problems of the DOD, and, in each case, the effort failed because it was far beyond the capacity and patience of the department.

Other management reform efforts have suffered from a lack of focus. For example, the department's effort in the 1990s and 2000s to audit its way to auditability identified pervasive problems with virtually every aspect of DOD business systems and processes but failed to prioritize solutions, sending senior officials off in too many fruitless directions at the same time. Similarly, the 1980s spare parts scandals led to the enactment of dozens of disparate legislative provisions that required added resources to implement and produced limited results. Recently enacted NDAAs also have overwhelmed the absorption capacity of the acquisition system, calling for too many initiatives chasing too few implementation resources, and yielding diminishing returns.

In general, focused, bite-sized reforms have been the most enduring. In the personnel arena, these reforms include the civilian personnel flexibilities enacted in the last few years and special authorities provided for the workforce of the defense laboratories, the acquisition workforce, the intelligence workforce, and the cyber workforce. In the acquisition arena, successful reforms include the establishment of the independent director of operational test and evaluation in the early 1980s and Secretary Perry's directive to replace military specifications with commercial item descriptions in the 1990s. In the financial management arena, the establishment of the Defense Finance and Accounting Service in the 1990s and the efforts of the military services and the Defense Logistics Agency to develop enterprise resource programs to manage their own finances in the 2000s were markedly more successful than efforts to impose comprehensive solutions from the outside.

The most successful acquisition reform initiatives of recent years were the Packard Commission recommendations of the late 1980s and the WSARA changes of the 2000s. These acquisition reform efforts shared a clear problem definition (overly optimistic cost estimates, gold-plated requirements, and immature technologies at the front end of weapons programs), and a focused set of solutions (improved cost estimating, early tradeoffs between cost and performance, and risk reduction through increased front-end investment in engineering and testing). Neither reform "fixed" the acquisition system, but each left its mark with enduring improvements.

Senator John Glenn identified a fundamental truth in 1994, when he called management reform "the grunt work of government."[54] It is hard work and never glamorous, and it goes on and on without end, but everybody benefits if it is successful. New challenges, new tools, and new opportunities present themselves every year. DOD officials can improve management outcomes by changing incentives, streamlining organizations and reengineering processes, improving systems, and eliminating unneeded programs. Congress can help by establishing goals, providing needed authorities, and removing statutory impediments. No magic fixes will "solve" management problems, but more can always be done to make the organization work better.

I spent a career on Capitol Hill and in the Pentagon, working to make needed improvements to the department's business systems, processes, and organizations. Generations of leaders and staff before me pursued similar objectives. Generations of leaders and staff after me will do the same. In an organization as large and complex as the Pentagon, it would be unreasonable to expect management problems to go away. Still, our national defense is at stake, as is the expenditure of billions of dollars, and leadership can make a real difference for better or for worse. I hope that readers of this book will gain some understanding of what makes a management reform initiative more likely to succeed. Most of all, I hope that those readers will find, as I have, that the challenge is worth undertaking and the effort is worth making.

CHAPTER 1

CIVILIAN PERSONNEL REFORM AT THE DEPARTMENT OF DEFENSE

ON June 4, 2003, Secretary of Defense Donald H. Rumsfeld appeared before the Senate Governmental Affairs Committee (SGAC), accompanied by the chairman of the Joint Chiefs of Staff, to launch a full-court legislative pitch for civilian personnel reform. "In an age when terrorists move information at the speed of an E-mail or money at the speed of a wire transfer and fly around in commercial jetliners," the secretary argued, the "lives of the men and women in uniform and, indeed, the American people" required a more effective and responsive civilian personnel system.[1]

Five months later, President George W. Bush signed the National Defense Authorization Act for Fiscal Year 2004, authorizing the secretary to establish a new DOD civilian human resources system, known as the National Security Personnel System (NSPS). Secretary Rumsfeld celebrated the legislation as "the most significant improvement to civilian personnel management since the [1978] Civil Service Reform Act."[2]

The DOD launched an intensive effort to implement the new authority, mobilizing a program office that reported directly to the deputy secretary. Final regulations were issued in late 2005, and the first 11,000 DOD civilian employees were trained and moved into the new system a few months later. Successive spirals of employees followed, with 211,000 making the switch by early 2009. Countless hours were spent reclassifying positions into the new system, developing written performance objectives and performance plans, and administering the new performance appraisal and pay-for-performance systems.

The NSPS effort was initiated at a time of consensus among current and former DOD officials and outside experts that the old civil service system was overly bureaucratic, inflexible, and in need of reform. It drew on the experience of a series of successful demonstration programs run by the department. It benefited from political momentum generated by the attacks of September 11, 2001, and the successful march to Baghdad. It received an unprecedented level of resources, including staff assignments, training budgets, prompt funding for information technology systems and solutions, and senior-level attention and commitment.

The NSPS, during the period that it was in effect, delivered on its promise in important ways. Managers devoted more time and attention to performance management than ever before. The new performance management system did a significantly better job of distinguishing among employees on the basis of their contribution to the department's mission than the old system. Strong performers were rewarded with pay increases and new levels of recognition and responsibility, and significantly more employees were terminated or otherwise penalized for poor performance.

Despite these achievements, however, the reform effort failed. Just five years after its enactment, the NSPS legislation was repealed, and the department began to convert NSPS employees back into the old General Schedule (GS) system. The experience was so painful that even though the new legislation directed continued reform efforts, including new performance management and workforce incentive systems, this authority went largely unused.

The failure was both substantive and political. On the substantive side, the reform effort failed to clearly define the problem to be solved and tailor the solution to that problem.

First, the NSPS effort was based on demonstration programs that had worked in the defense laboratories but failed to recognize that a reform that addresses the problems of scientists and engineers in defense laboratories might not meet the needs of a workforce that includes receptionists, security guards, nurses, counselors, and contract auditors. Even in the private sector, pay band systems like the one included in the NSPS were rarely applied to nonmanagerial employees and hourly workers and almost never applied to union employees. Yet, the NSPS sought to apply a single pay-for-performance system to the entire department, lumping all DOD employees together into just four career fields and three pay bands. Such one-size-fits-all solutions are unlikely to meet the needs of an institution as large and diverse as the Department of Defense.

Second, rather than adopting targeted solutions for discrete problems, the NSPS sought to replace—in their entirety—the hiring, classification, pay, performance management, employee discipline, dispute resolution, and labor relations systems of the department. The scope of this effort not only created a massive workload that saturated the human resources capacity of the department, it also created multiple points of failure. The federal civil service system is incredibly complex. It has thousands of rules—not just because it is overly bureaucratic (which it is), but also because there are thousands of issues that human resource managers are unlikely to address successfully without guidance. The NSPS threw out not only rules that needed to change, but also processes that served useful purposes—taking on the thankless task of rewriting the entire rulebook at the same time.

Despite these substantive challenges, the NSPS would likely be the DOD civilian personnel system today if the administration had not also failed to build effective coalitions and unnecessarily stoked opposition forces, leading to the political collapse of the reform effort just five years after it was initiated. The most successful defense reform efforts almost always have support from both political parties, from the executive branch and Congress, and from a significant part of the affected population. The NSPS effort—although it successfully drew on national security concerns arising out of the attacks of September 11, 2001, and the global war on terrorism—failed on all three accounts.

At the time that the NSPS legislation was prepared, the administration already knew—based on the prior experience of civilian personnel legislation for the Department of Homeland Security (DHS)—that the proposal was likely to draw determined opposition from the federal employee unions and their allies in Congress. Faced with this challenge, the administration could have attempted to soften, co-opt, or split the opposition through compromise and conciliation. Instead, the administration chose a hard-edged approach that strengthened the opposition and led to the eventual collapse of the reform effort.

The Bush administration was offered a bipartisan approach to civilian personnel reform when Senator Susan Collins introduced a version of the NSPS-authorizing legislation that was cosponsored by three Republicans and two Democrats. The bill was reported out of the SGAC on a near-unanimous 10–1 vote. However, the administration rejected the bipartisan approach, choosing instead a single-party strategy that relied on getting "the last Republican vote." The absence of any Democratic support helped make the NSPS unsustainable when Congress and the presidency changed hands a few years later.

The single-party legislative approach made it possible to enact legislation that maximized the authority and flexibility of the department to establish the new personnel system. Only the barest features of the new system were outlined in statute. Every aspect was left to be detailed in DOD regulations and issuances. The decision to minimize the role of Congress was also shortsighted. Because Congress was not a full partner in the design of the NSPS, it had no investment in the new system. When questions of fairness and equity were raised, the executive branch found itself defending the system on its own. Reform with staying power needs support in the executive branch and the legislative branch.

Finally, successful personnel reform should be conscious of the interests and needs of affected constituencies, including the federal employee unions. The administration helped strengthen opposition to the proposed reform by insisting on comprehensive changes to the collective bargaining and employee appeals systems that were largely unrelated to the reform's core purpose of linking pay to performance. Civilian personnel reform was never likely to get union support since the federal employee unions had long opposed pay-for-performance systems. However, the administration turned this opposition into an all-out, life-and-death matter for the unions by seeking to undermine the labor relations system in a way that challenged the unions' very purpose of existence.

The NSPS made changes to parts of the system that probably needed to be changed, but it also changed parts of the system that were working reasonably well. In the end, it failed because of the controversy generated by parts of the new system that may not have been necessary at all, and this failure dragged down the prospect of constructive reform—in areas where it remains very much needed—for at least another decade.

Today, as the NSPS experience fades in the memory of Congress and the DOD workforce, reform again seems possible. In recent years, Congress has enacted a number of targeted reforms intended to address ongoing deficiencies in the department's hiring, performance management, and pay systems. Additional incremental reforms of this kind could bring about measurable improvements in the defense civilian personnel system—and could do so without imposing a massive one-size-fits-all solution or triggering the kind of political problems—including all-out opposition by the federal employee unions—that NSPS was unable to overcome.

THE CIVIL SERVICE DEMONSTRATION PROJECTS

The DOD civilian workforce is an essential pillar of the department on which our military relies to perform its critical missions around the world every day. DOD civilians run training and education programs, manage travel and change of duty stations, and provide security, support, and facilities sustainment on military bases. They help address problems like sexual assault, suicides, bullying and hazing, and drug abuse. They provide financial advice, voting assistance, and family life counseling to service members around the world. They play key roles in running 664 hospitals and clinics, 172 schools, 1,880 retail stores, and 2,390 restaurants for our men and women in uniform and for their families.

DOD civilians also serve as operational enablers in the intelligence and cyber domains and are essential to warfighter training and combat system and equipment readiness. They help manage and oversee more than $200 billion a year in acquisition spending and operate depots and arsenals that maintain and recapitalize a huge inventory of the most complex and advanced fighting equipment in human history. They are also the lifeblood of a logistics system that works 24 hours a day, 365 days a year to ensure that military equipment and supplies are ready when and where needed, anywhere in the world, and often with little or no notice.

In many parts of the DOD, career civilians are the repository of essential institutional knowledge that members of the military lack, due to the rotation of military assignments. In 2000, the Defense Science Board (DSB) found that the department's civilian personnel "are indispensable in managing the Department's budgeting, legal, logistics, acquisition, information systems, research and development, and other programs."[3] Comptroller General David Walker said, "Federal employees represent an asset that needs to be valued, not a cost that needs to be cut."[4]

Despite the value that civilian employees provide to the department, the civilian workforce has been widely disparaged in recent years. Part of the problem is that the laws, rules, and practices governing the civil service system have become overly bureaucratic and stultified over the years. As a result, the reputation of the federal civilian workforce has been tarred by deficiencies in the system within which it is required to work.

The competitive civil service system was first established by the Pendleton Act of 1883 to replace the so-called spoils system that had been used for more than a hundred years by federal officials to place friends, family members, and political cronies into federal office. It was most recently overhauled by the Civil Service Reform Act of 1978 (CSRA), which established statutory merit principles as the basis of federal employment. The merit principles provide that federal hiring decisions will be made solely on the basis of merit, employees and applicants for employment will receive fair and equitable treatment in all aspects of employment, equal pay will be provided for work of equal value, and employees will be protected against arbitrary action, personal favoritism, and political coercion.

The employment system built around these principles was designed to ensure against a return to the abuses that characterized the nineteenth-century patronage system. In this regard, it has been strikingly successful. In a time of heightened political partisanship, the federal civilian workforce has shown an ability to transition seamlessly from one administration to the next, without regard to changes in party control. Also, while improprieties occur from time to time, the civil service system remains remarkably free of the favoritism, nepotism, and corruption that have marked many other public employment systems around the globe and across time.

Over time, however, many have come to view the civil service system as bureaucratic and inefficient. The Clinton administration's National Performance Review argued in 1993, "Over time, the ideal of internal equity has emerged as the supreme goal of the system," to such an extent that it "worked against ... more effective government."[5] In 2003, the second Volcker Commission on Public Service found that the civil service system provided "too few rewards for those who do their jobs well and too few penalties for those who perform poorly," and discouraged many potential employees "who are reluctant to enter a field where there are so few financial rewards for their hard work, where mediocrity and excellence yield the same pay check."[6]

Some inflexible requirements, such as the maddeningly detailed requirements for job classifications, are required by statute or regulation. Others, like the persistent grade inflation that has undermined DOD performance appraisal systems for years, are the product of a culture in which it is easier and more comfortable for managers to avoid confrontation than to make meaningful distinctions among their employees. The interconnected nature of law, regulation, practice, and culture have created a complex ecosystem that remains resistant to change.

The CSRA itself included a mechanism to enable the civil service system to evolve over time. Section 601 of the CSRA authorized the Office of Personnel Management (OPM) to establish "demonstration projects" under which the application of the civil service laws and regulations to an agency could be waived or modified. This provision was intended to provide a testbed for the purpose of determining "whether a specified change in personnel policies or procedures would result in improved Federal personnel management."[7]

The seminal demonstration project was established in 1980 at the Naval Weapons Center, China Lake, and the Naval Oceans Systems Center, San Diego. The China Lake project was designed to address the concern that the rigid GS classification system and tenure-based statutory pay tables were making it difficult for Navy laboratories to attract and retain the highly skilled scientists and engineers that they needed. The China Lake project replaced the GS system with a limited number of career paths and pay bands that enabled higher than usual starting salaries and recruiting bonuses for new hires and made it possible to reward top performers with higher pay. The solution was designed specifically to address the identified problem. Employee rights, hiring processes, leave policies, disciplinary mechanisms, dispute resolution processes, labor relations systems, and retirement systems were left untouched by the demonstration program.

The China Lake project was widely viewed as a success. The Packard Commission concluded that the innovation helped attract high-quality personnel to entry-level positions, reduced separation rates for scientists and engineers, improved employee morale, and lowered management costs.[8] The General Accounting Office (GAO)[9] confirmed that turnover among scientists was lower at China Lake than at other defense laboratories, retention was strong among highly rated employees, and managers and employees gave the system high ratings.[10] The Merit Systems Protection Board (MSPB) reported that starting salaries for scientists had increased substantially, that larger pay increases were available for good performance, and that turnover among top performers decreased.[11] Employee approval of the system grew from 29 percent at the outset to 70 percent by year fourteen.[12]

The demonstration project was not budget neutral—higher starting salaries and larger salary increases in the early years of the project meant that China Lake employees were paid, on average, 6 percent more than their counterparts in other laboratories. For this reason, the GAO concluded that while the project showed that pay-for-performance could be implemented to the satisfaction of managers and employees, it was not possible to determine whether a budget-neutral system would have a positive effect on recruiting and retention[13] or whether the China Lake approach could be successfully transferred to other, larger organizations.[14] Moreover, the DOD was never able to demonstrate that the project improved the quality of laboratory research.[15]

Nonetheless, other parts of the DOD scientific and engineering community hoped for similar flexibility to address their own hiring and retention problems. In 1987, the Army reported difficulty hiring electronic engineers, general physicists, and computer scientists; the Navy indicated that lower salary levels were impeding recruitment of scientists and engineers; and the Air Force indicated that it was having difficulty competing for the graduates of the best schools—even with special pay rates.[16] A DSB study on technology base management concluded that "with a few exceptions, DOD laboratories cannot compete for top technical people and the laboratories lose good people quickly."[17]

For more than a decade, the OPM resisted requests to extend the China Lake demonstration program to other defense laboratories. By 1987, twenty-six federal agencies had contacted the OPM to inquire about demonstration projects, but only two projects had been approved and implemented.[18] DOD officials complained that the OPM wanted extensive justification for every proposed project, and was unwilling to accept "duplication of features tested in 'China Lake' or other demos."[19] The OPM reportedly believed that demonstration projects like China Lake "were of little potential value from a research point of view and discouraged agencies from pursuing the proposals or disapproved them."[20]

In 1994, Congress overruled the OPM concerns, making the China Lake project permanent and authorizing other defense laboratories to undertake similar demonstration projects.[21] The laboratory demonstration (Lab Demo) provision authorized the laboratories to institute policies that were "generally similar in nature to the China Lake demonstration project," so each of them mimicked the China Lake pay-banding system, converging on a single approach to pay-for-performance.[22] However, each of the laboratory demonstration programs developed its own tailored performance management system, method for translating employee performance ratings into pay increases and awards, approach to managing pay costs, and transparency mechanisms for performance and pay decisions.[23]

Over the next decade, the OPM found that the Lab Demo programs were successfully achieving their goals and that managers and employees were generally satisfied with the programs.[24] The OPM reported the following:

- Overall support for the projects increased gradually in all but one of the Lab Demos.
- Implementation of pay-for-performance systems increased job satisfaction in most of the Lab Demos and was impact-neutral in the rest.

- Increases in individual effort and motivation were found.
- The flexibility to pay higher starting salaries and reward high performers was helpful in attracting and retaining talent.
- There was no overall negative impact on perceived fairness of pay administration.
- Perceived accuracy and fairness of ratings tended to drop following implementation but gradually rose after that.
- The perception that managers addressed poor performers effectively increased.
- Pay satisfaction increased for all of the Lab Demos.[25]

In addition, annual turnover rates for top performers dropped dramatically after the Lab Demo programs were introduced.[26]

While the Lab Demo programs were "certainly an improvement over the previous system,"[27] the DSB found in 1998 that the program was "simply not sufficient to solve the problem of providing adequate numbers of capable scientists and engineers to the DOD and the Services."[28] The DSB identified the cap on federal employee pay as the source of the problem. Even with the new flexibility provided by the Lab Demo program, the DSB reported, the salaries that the DOD laboratories could offer were "still not competitive with those offered by industry."[29] For this reason, the DSB recommended an entirely new model for the defense laboratories, with extensive use of private sector scientists and engineers on a rotational basis.[30]

In 1995, Congress extended Lab Demo authority beyond the science and technology community for the first time, establishing the acquisition demonstration (Acq Demo) program. While the statutory authority for the Acq Demo program was open ended, the provision was widely understood as an authorization to extend the China Lake pay-banding approach to the acquisition workforce.[31] When the Acq Demo program was finally implemented in February 1999, its key feature was a pay-for-performance approach that replaced the fifteen GS grades with four new pay bands.[32]

Despite its potentially broad scope, the Acq Demo program was largely limited to employees in headquarters organizations, covering only about 5 percent of the defense civilian acquisition workforce. The problem was union opposition. Under Secretary of Defense for Acquisition, Technology, and Logistics Jacques Gansler later explained: "The law allowed me to have a much larger experiment, but because of union opposition it ended up being a much smaller number. . . . They lobbied very strongly against even the experiment and lobbied their people against joining the experiment."[33]

A 2006 evaluation of the Acq Demo program concluded that the new performance management system resulted in higher retention levels for "high contributors" and increased separation rates for "low contributors."[34] Acq Demo employees believed that the program resulted in a stronger connection between pay and performance,[35] and that the streamlined classification system substantially reduced paperwork in the new system.[36] On the other hand, employees in the control group felt that they were treated more fairly than Acq Demo employees,[37] and the pay experimentation appears to have had no demonstrable impact on the effectiveness of Acq Demo organizations.[38]

Many observers saw the Lab Demo and Acq Demo programs as the first step toward a performance-based approach that would eventually replace the seniority-based civil service system. The GAO and the National Academy of Public Administration endorsed the expansion of pay-for-performance throughout the federal government.[39] The DSB concluded: "It is time for the Department . . . to start extending successful reforms across DoD and converting them into personnel policies and programs."[40] Although limitations on the scope of the Lab Demo and Acq Demo programs raised questions about their scalability,[41] the consensus seemed to be that such problems could be addressed by gradually phasing in new authorities.[42]

Union officials were less enthusiastic, contending that performance-based bonuses and retention allowances authorized in the existing law provided federal agencies all the authority they needed.[43] These officials vehemently opposed a "zero sum model" of pay-for-performance that would "take from one person or group in order to fund an increase for another."[44] The president of the DOD's largest union argued against the return of the "favoritism and the suspicion of corruption" that had "bedeviled the majority of performance-based award systems that focus exclusively on individual contributions."[45]

Members of Congress were skeptical as well. The skepticism was bipartisan: one representative expressed concern about "pay parity issues"; another said that "some smaller version or pilot program" was needed to discover mistakes before moving forward; a third called for getting a performance management system in place before trying to tie in pay; a fourth warned that "'flexibility' should not mean undermining basic civil service job protections"; a fifth stated that "there is no infrastructure in place to really do pay for performance"; and a sixth agreed that "we are getting the cart before the horse" in pushing for new pay systems.[46] Despite the success of the Lab Demo and Acq Demo programs, department-wide civilian personnel reform appeared to remain in the far-off future.

THE ENACTMENT OF NSPS LEGISLATION

The September 11, 2001, attacks on the World Trade Center and the Pentagon shook the American political system. Within little more than a month, the president announced the creation a new Office of Homeland Security, an Office of Combating Terrorism, a Critical Infrastructure Protection Board, and a Homeland Security Council. On September 18, an Authorization for Use of Military Force against the perpetrators of the attacks was signed into law. Five weeks later, the USA Patriot Act was enacted.

A year later, Congress enacted the most extensive reorganization of the federal government in the last fifty years—the integration of parts of twenty-two different federal agencies into a single new entity, the DHS. The most controversial provision in the Homeland Security Act of 2002 authorized the secretary of homeland security to waive large parts of the civil service laws for the purpose of establishing a "flexible" and "contemporary" new human resources management system in the department.[47]

At the time, the argument was made that the new authority was needed to enable the secretary to bring together the employees of twenty-two disparate federal agencies into a single workforce with a single set of rules. Lurking under the surface was an additional agenda: the national security arguments for the creation of a DHS civilian personnel system created political momentum that could be used to put into motion a broader personnel reform agenda that had long been stymied by institutional resistance.

As the DOD began the next legislative cycle, Secretary of Defense Donald Rumsfeld directed his staff to come up with transformation initiatives that were as bold as possible. The under secretary for personnel and readiness, Dr. David Chu, proposed DOD-wide civilian personnel reform using the pay-banding approach of the demonstration programs.[48] Secretary Rumsfeld embraced the concept and urged even bolder action. One former DOD official remembers the secretary reacting to the initial proposal by saying, "Is that all there is? Are you kidding me? Is this all you guys want to change?" Chu recalls the secretary instructing him to "go for everything you can."[49]

The DOD's aggressive approach met some resistance within the administration. The department initially sought unilateral authority for the secretary of defense to act on his own in developing a new human resources system, without any role for the OPM.[50] Senior DOD officials thought that the OPM was resistant to change, while the OPM believed that outside oversight was needed to ensure that the DOD's actions were consistent with the merit principles. The conflict became so intense that it had to be resolved by the White House.[51]

At the same time, the DOD proposal quickly encountered opposition from the federal employee unions. In January 2003, Chu made an effort to convince the union leadership that a new personnel system was in the best interest of federal employees and, by extension, in the interest of the unions themselves. "If we don't change this system," he argued, "the civilian workforce of this Department is slowly going out of business because the rules are so cumbersome."[52] Union officials, who were suspicious of the DOD's motives and resentful of earlier actions taken by the Bush administration, were not convinced.

Both sides saw the meeting as unproductive. DOD officials felt that "there was not much to discuss with union officials," because there was no common ground. The union representatives believed that the DOD had no real intention of engaging but wanted to tell Congress that the unions had been consulted.[53] Comptroller General David Walker told the

SGAC: "There was basically no consultation—of unions, of employees, of their executives."[54] OPM representatives remember that with Republican majorities in both houses, DOD and administration officials "put no real effort" into working with the unions, because they were not going to be able to prevent the enactment of legislation.[55]

On April 10, 2003, the administration submitted the Defense Transformation for the 21st Century Act to Congress.[56] The DOD proposal, like the Homeland Security Act, authorized the establishment of a new human relations system that would be "flexible" and "contemporary," without defining the salient features of the proposed system.[57] Both bills authorized the waiver of existing provisions of law addressing the classification of jobs, performance management, and employee pay.[58] Both bills also authorized the development of alternative systems for labor relations and employee appeals.[59]

Unlike the Homeland Security Act, the DOD draft included the authority to waive provisions of law addressing hiring, training, pay administration, and allowances.[60] It authorized the secretary of defense to exclude the OPM from the decision-making process and act on his own when he determined that it was in the interest of national security.[61] It also provided that the implementation of the new authority would be exercised in the "sole, exclusive, and unreviewable discretion" of the secretary.[62]

Other provisions in the bill sought broad authorities unrelated to civilian personnel. The bill proposed to give the secretary power to override legislative limitations on the use of personal services contracts,[63] unilaterally extend the terms of the service chiefs[64] and reassign senior general and flag officers without Senate confirmation.[65] The bill proposed to repeal congressional reporting requirements for major defense acquisition[66] and major automated information system programs.[67] It authorized the secretary to waive key requirements of the environmental laws.[68] It provided the secretary carte blanche to reorganize the department,[69] and it authorized the secretary to transfer billions of dollars from one program to another without the approval of Congress.[70]

Most of the bill hit the cutting room floor as soon as it arrived on Capitol Hill. The civilian personnel provisions, by contrast, were put on a fast track toward enactment. "I was knocking on an open door" with Representatives Duncan Hunter and Tom Davis—the new chairs of the House Armed Services Committee and the Government Reform Committee—Chu recalled.[71] On April 29, 2003, the two chairs made their endorsement public, introducing the NSPS proposal as a House bill without any modification to the administration language.[72] The proposal was also introduced in the Senate by Senators John Warner and Carl Levin, the SASC chair and ranking member, but the Senate bill was introduced "by request," indicating that the senators did not endorse the proposal by introducing it.[73]

The two House committees held hearings and voted favorably on the bill just a month after it was submitted. A Democratic amendment to require the department to submit a legislative proposal detailing the new personnel system before any authorities were granted was defeated on a party-line vote of 28–32.[74] Additional amendments to build protections into the new personnel system and restore collective bargaining rights were also rejected on party-line votes. It helped that the NSPS proposal had been briefed to Vice President Cheney, who supported the effort, and that the White House lobbying team was present for the markup.[75] The administration did not get everything it asked for—a few minor amendments were accepted in the markup[76]—but all of the key elements of the legislation were intact.

This success came at a price. Twenty Democratic members of the committee signed Minority views arguing that the enactment of the NSPS would strip away fundamental rights from DOD employees, risking a return to the patronage system that had resulted in so much incompetence and corruption in the federal workforce in the nineteenth century.[77] When the legislation came to the House floor as part of the Fiscal Year (FY) 2004 NDAA, Democrats were blocked by rule from offering amendments to modify the civilian personnel provisions. As a result, the only House vote on the issue came on a procedural motion, which was defeated on a near party-line vote of 204–224.[78] On May 22, just six weeks after the legislation was first received in Congress, it was approved by the full House.

As is often the case, the Senate undertook a slower and more bipartisan approach. SASC, which marked up its version of the FY 2004 NDAA on May 9, excluded the NSPS proposal on the ground that senators had not yet had time to review the legislation.[79] On June 2, 2003, after several weeks of bipartisan discussions, Senator Susan Collins—the Republican SGAC chair—introduced a version of the legislation that was cosponsored by three Republicans and two Democrats.[80]

Like the administration proposal and the House bill, the Collins bill authorized the DOD to waive existing civil service statutes to establish a flexible and contemporary new personnel system. Like the administration proposal and the House bill, it authorized new classification, performance management, and pay-for-performance systems, new employee appeals processes, and national-level collective bargaining. Moreover, the Collins bill, like the administration proposal and the House bill, would have authorized the secretary to implement the new personnel system across the department after consultation with employee unions but without collective bargaining.[81]

However, the Collins bill differed from the administration and House bills in several respects. For example, it required that the new system be phased in over several years[82] and that overall levels funding for civilian pay not be reduced.[83] Most significantly, the Collins bill endeavored to maintain employee due process and labor relations protections. With regard to due process, the bill maintained an appellate role for the independent MSPB and provided that MSPB precedents would remain in place except to the extent that the secretary established new and different standards.[84] With regard to labor relations, the bill did not authorize the DOD to waive the "Chapter 71" collective bargaining rights of federal employees.[85] The bill provided for bargaining to be conducted at the national level as requested by the administration and placed time limits on the dispute resolution process,[86] but otherwise left collective bargaining rights unchanged.

Some DOD officials saw merit in the Collins bill. When the proposal was presented to Secretary Rumsfeld, however, he rejected it on the spot. Principal Deputy Under Secretary of Defense Charles Abell, who made the presentation, reports that the secretary did not see Senator Collins as a friend of the administration and believed that if Democrats supported her bill, it could not be a very strong approach. From his point of view, bipartisanship was a weakness, not a strength. Bipartisanship required compromise, and the secretary was more interested in retaining as much as possible of his original proposal.[87]

At a SGAC hearing on the bill, the administration showed little interest in the Collins bill. Secretary Rumsfeld testified that the administration language was not intended to end collective bargaining, but merely to bring collective bargaining to the national level "so that the Department could negotiate with national unions instead of dealing with more than 1,300 different union locals."[88] The secretary did not explain why the Collins bill—which expressly authorized collective bargaining at the national level—was inadequate to achieve this purpose.

On June 17, 2003, the Collins bill was reported out of the SGAC on a near-unanimous 10–1 vote. With this action, a strong bipartisan coalition lined up behind the comprehensive reform of the DOD personnel system, endorsing the waiver of civil service statutes governing classification, pay, performance management, and employee appeals, making a significant change to labor relations requirements in the form of the authorization of national-level collective bargaining, and providing for the implementation of the new system without collective bargaining. Such bipartisan legislative branch support for comprehensive civilian personnel reform would have been unthinkable even six months earlier.

Far from accepting the bipartisan Senate approach and claiming victory, the administration dug in to fight for the House legislation, endeavoring to make the House approach a matter of party loyalty for Republicans. For DOD officials, the fundamental issue was the authority of the department to manage its civilian workforce. This authority was undermined by outside entities that could challenge or overrule DOD positions: the OPM, the MSPB, the Federal Labor Relations Authority, and the federal employee unions. Negotiation with these outside parties would slow the implementation of a new personnel management system and undermine its purpose.[89]

From the union perspective, the proposed waiver of Chapter 71 posed an existential threat. These provisions were the basic charter for their existence, giving them a position in the federal system as a protector of employee rights. If the provisions were waived, not only would employee protections be removed, but it is not clear that the unions would continue to serve any purpose at all.[90] To the DOD leadership, outside guarantors of employee rights impeded effective management of the workforce with burdensome procedures and misguided precedents. To employee representatives, the absence of outside guarantors meant the absence of employee rights.

The administration strategy was to build a Republican-only majority among the Senate conferees by persuading Senator Collins to support the DOD position.[91] As a result, the real negotiations over the civilian personnel provisions took place between Senator Collins and administration officials in a series of meetings at the White House.

The issues of phase-in and pay comparability were addressed first. In lieu of the Senate provision limiting the new system to 240,000 employees in the first two years, the conferees agreed that no more than 300,000 employees could be included until the department had an effective performance management system in place.[92] The Senate provisions designed to ensure that overall funding for civilian pay kept pace with funding levels under the GS system were modified by adding the words "to the maximum extent practicable"—making them a statement of aspiration rather than a legal requirement.[93]

With regard to employee appeals, the conference report included language from the Collins bill that applied existing MSPB standards and precedents except to the extent specifically overruled in DOD implementing regulations.[94] It provided for review of DOD decisions by the MSPB and in the courts, but only in the case of employee dismissals and reductions in pay.[95] It also provided that the requirement for MSPB review would sunset after seven years unless renewed by Congress.[96]

There is a good chance that these compromises would have held bipartisan support among Senate conferees. However, the most difficult issue—collective bargaining—was still outstanding. Senator Collins had indicated that she was not going to give in on this issue, and she knew that if she did so she would lose Democratic support for her bipartisan approach. The administration and the House conferees were equally locked in to their insistence on a completely new labor relations system for the department. Collective bargaining became the last issue—not only on the NSPS legislation, but in the entire defense authorization conference.

In the end, an agreement was reached that included *both* the administration position *and* the Collins position in the legislation. The agreement included the provision upon which Senator Collins had insisted, making the existing labor relations laws "non-waivable."[97] However, it also included a second section, providing that "notwithstanding" the first provision, the secretary was authorized to establish "a labor relations system to address the unique role that the Department's civilian workforce plays in supporting the Department's national security mission."[98] The compromise also included a six-year sunset—an aspect of the provision that senior DOD officials viewed as a "poison pill," requiring them to race toward implementation.[99]

It was never clear what the two provisions meant. Was the new labor relations system supposed to be consistent with the requirements of Chapter 71, or did it override that law? If it had to be consistent with Chapter 71, what did the new authority accomplish? If it did override Chapter 71, what was the meaning of the statement that the law was "non-waivable"? This ambiguity may have been the worst of both worlds for the department. The language was sufficiently threatening to collective bargaining rights that it lost all bipartisan support for the NSPS legislation. At the same time, it was sufficiently vague that it placed administration efforts to address the issue of collective bargaining under a legal cloud.

The DOD had captured a political moment of opportunity and pushed hard for as much authority as it could get. This strategy looked like a political success story: a deal had been struck, and the legislation was enacted. However, the department had missed the opportunity to build a broad base of support through its unwillingness to give ground, and, as a result, the legislation carried the seeds of its own destruction.

THE IMPLEMENTATION OF THE NSPS

During the NSPS hearings, Comptroller General David Walker laid out his vision for the implementation of federal pay-for-performance systems. The likelihood of success would be greatest, the comptroller general said, if the reform effort involved employees, their representatives, and other stakeholders in the design of the system.[100] Moving too quickly would raise the risk of "doing it wrong" and setting back the effort to move toward performance-based management, not only at the DOD, but in the federal government as a whole.[101] No matter what the DOD might want to do, Walker concluded from a practical standpoint that the department would not be able to adopt the new system with anything other than a phased approach.[102]

The DOD chose to ignore the comptroller general's advice.

After President Bush signed the bill into law on November 24, 2003, the department moved to implement the new authority as quickly as possible. Chu announced an intent to bring the first 300,000 DOD employees—about half of the civilian workforce—into the NSPS before the beginning of the next fiscal year. "We are counting on the powers in this act to be effective immediately. These are authorities for the here and now," he stated.[103] This decision to act fast was a conscious choice. House Government Reform Committee Chair Davis had advised that it would be a good idea to have as much of the system as possible in place before the 2004 elections to make it difficult for a new Congress or a new administration to change it.[104]

Chu believed that the opportunity for reform would be fleeting and that swift action was the key to success.[105] Accordingly, he developed a strategy of "race across the bridge and burn it behind you," hoping to get the new system developed before institutional resistance could build up.[106] In line with this view, the director of the NSPS Implementation Office determined that extensive coordination within the department would take too much time, undermining the prospects of success.[107] "Too much cooperation, at too early a stage," the director believed, "would blunt the system's transformative edge and delay its rollout."[108] Her preferred plan was "to present a fait accompli quickly, then persuade or pressure others to accept the system."[109]

Senior DOD officials believed that the major design work for the NSPS had already been essentially completed. A DOD task force had conducted a comprehensive review of the Lab Demo and Acq Demo programs and made recommendations for compensation, recruitment, and performance management systems.[110] A model regulation bringing together those recommended best practices[111] was expected to serve as the basis for the new NSPS system. For this reason, the department expected its efforts to focus largely on implementation, rather than policy.[112]

On December 1, 2003, the department established the NSPS Implementation Office. On December 19, the implementation team met and agreed to the objective of moving all DOD civilians into the NSPS within a two-year period. The DOD timeline called for developing proposals, meeting with the unions, and notifying Congress of final NSPS plans by August 6. Implementation would commence with the beginning of the new fiscal year on October 1.[113] The department, in its effort to move as quickly as possible, did not intend to publish regulations for public notice and comment, even though that would make them more vulnerable to legal challenge.[114]

On January 22, 2004, DOD officials met with union representatives and agreed to provide a written outline of the proposed system.[115] Two weeks later, the department began its first substantive public engagement of the implementation phase by providing the unions a comprehensive outline of a new labor relations system.

The February 6, 2004, labor relations paper outlined fundamental changes not only to what collective bargaining was and what it would cover, but also to what a federal employee union was and who it could represent. For example, the paper suggested

- changing unions into fee-for-service organizations, with an obligation to provide services to employees who chose not to become dues-paying members;
- providing that unions would be recognized only if a majority of the bargaining unit members (not just those who choose to vote) supported union representation;
- excluding significant new categories of employees from union representation;
- giving the DOD unilateral authority to decide which issues were "significant" enough to merit collective bargaining;

- providing that DOD-wide and component-wide "issuances" would automatically override collective bargaining agreements; and
- redefining collective bargaining as a sixty-day "consultation," after which management could implement any proposed changes.[116]

This was the area in which the administration's position was the weakest. None of these proposals had been publicly discussed in any phase of the hearings or discussions leading up to the enactment of the NSPS legislation. The department had insisted that it would protect collective bargaining rights and had not asked publicly for any changes beyond the use of national-level bargaining. Democrats were united against changes in collective bargaining, and critical Republicans had been convinced to vote for the final legislation only with promises that the department did not plan significant change. Moreover, the department had not done any significant advance work—like the best practices work on compensation and performance management—to consider what a new collective bargaining system might look like.[117]

The union reaction was predictably swift and outraged. Within a week, the unions initiated a campaign of demonstrations and grassroots lobbying efforts, beginning with a rally at the Capitol and the circulation of a pledge to fight against the DOD proposal.[118] On February 11, 2004, the new president of the American Federation of Government Employees (AFGE) told Congress that the "system outlined by DOD will be management by fear, intimidation, and coercion, and the resulting loss to the public's interest will be discrimination, cronyism, favoritism, and patronage."[119] At a two-day meeting between the DOD and the federal employee unions, the two sides proved unable to even discuss the issue.[120] By the end of the meeting, DOD officials reported, the unions "were downright hostile and inflammatory."[121]

Congressional Democrats, most of whom had opposed the NSPS labor relations provisions from the outset, were quick to join the criticism. On February 25, the top Democrats on the key House and Senate committees sent a joint letter to the secretary of defense complaining that the February 6 outline contained "wholesale changes to the current federal employee labor relations system, including changes to internal union procedures, which have no relation to the department's national security mission" and urging that the proposal be immediately withdrawn.[122] Letters urging the withdrawal of the proposal followed, carrying the signatures of 145 members of the House[123] and 17 senators.[124]

Senator Carl Levin, who had worked with Senator Collins on the bipartisan bill in the previous Congress, confronted Chu with his concerns at a SASC hearing. The DOD proposal, Levin argued, "is that it will talk to the unions if it wants to, but doesn't have to listen to what the unions have to say, and it won't be bound by any agreement that may be reached." In his view, this approach was "needlessly confrontational" and risked undermining the department's relationship with its own employees.[125] Chu replied by emphasizing that the DOD proposal was only the start of the process: "These are concepts," he stated. "This is not an answer, not a solution, not a decision."[126]

On March 2, Senators Warner and Collins, the Republican chairs of SASC and the SGAC, made the concerns bipartisan, telling the DOD that collaboration with the employee unions was vital and that they would be providing "constant oversight."[127] The next day, four Republican members of the SGAC joined with Senator Levin in a letter stating that "full collaboration with the Office of Personnel Management and the federal employee unions" was critical to the "ultimate acceptance and successful implementation" of the NSPS.[128] Senator George Voinovich, a long-time advocate of civilian personnel reform in the federal government, went to the Pentagon to personally express his concerns about the "hasty" and "unrealistic" manner in which the department proposed to move forward.[129]

At the same time, dissent grew within the administration itself. The DOD team, in its haste to roll out NSPS proposals and begin the implementation process, had not consulted with the OPM despite the statutory requirement to do so. DOD officials felt that they had a depth of personnel expertise and knew what to do without the need for the OPM's assistance.[130] Beyond that, Secretary Rumsfeld resented the role of the OPM, believing that it undermined his authority over his own department.[131] Now, however, congressional concerns about the department's implementation approach were heightened by reports that the OPM had been cut out of the process.[132]

On March 9, 2004, OPM director Kay Cole James urged Secretary Rumsfeld to reconsider his implementation approach. Director James identified a series of critical legal, policy, and technical issues that "have profound tactical and strategic implications" for the DOD, the Office of Management and Budget (OMB), and the administration. The labor relations proposal, in particular, appeared to be "contrary to law, insofar as it attempts to replace collective bargaining with 'consultation' and eliminate collective bargaining agreements altogether" and contained many elements that "lack a clear and defensible national security nexus."[133] Failure to correct these problems, the director concluded, "could undermine everything we are trying to achieve with NSPS."[134]

Worse still, senior managers in the military departments who would be responsible for implementing the NSPS rebelled, complaining that they could not successfully implement a new personnel system on the proposed schedule.[135] The proposal had been developed with "no partnership, no teamwork, no deep understanding of the complexity of this, no real appreciation for the nature of the transformational change involved," they observed. It just wasn't realistic to assume that the organizations that would have to live with the new system were just going to accept and implement it without "a serious effort at building a partnership."[136] One DOD official remembers: "It was like a small nuclear device went off"— the military departments "saw that this was going to just blow up in our face, and we were all going to lose something that had good in it."[137]

In March 2004, Secretary Rumsfeld directed a freeze in NSPS development, while the department conducted a strategic review of the effort.[138] He asked Navy Secretary Gordon England to work with the unions to make sure that the transition to the NSPS was handled in a fair and transparent manner.[139] Five working groups were established to conduct the review, with the OPM and military services as full partners. Chu and Secretary England jointly published an open letter assuring DOD employees that the department understood the need to treat workers fairly and protect their rights and that the process for developing the NSPS would be "inclusive and comprehensive."[140]

On April 13, the recommendations of the strategic review were presented to the senior leaders of the department, including Secretary

Rumsfeld. The recommendations called for abandoning earlier implementation plans and undertaking a slower, more inclusive process that would be driven by the achievement of milestones rather than arbitrary timelines.[141] As Secretary England later explained, "There was no possible way of implementing this in the Department the way it was being approached, and . . . Congress wasn't going to let us do it anyway, and therefore, you'd better stop what's doing and recreate a whole new process of the National Security Personnel System."[142]

The department's initial attempt at implementation was officially dead, but serious damage had been done. Key members of Congress—Democrats and Republicans—were now skeptical of the department's ability to implement the new system in a fair and efficient manner. Federal employee unions were emboldened by their success.[143] As a DOD labor relations official later recalled, "We united [the] unions."[144] Having never liked the idea of pay-for-performance in the first place, the unions were now on an all-out war footing, believing that they had been confirmed in their view that the primary goal of the NSPS was "to destroy collective bargaining, marginalize the unions, and weaken employee protections, not to create a better personnel system for civilian employees and improve the Department's ability to protect national security."[145]

Given a second chance, the department took a new approach. Secretary England, who was designated to lead the effort, took the view that process was as important as substance. "If we're not seen as being thoughtful about people's input, reaching out and talking to stakeholders, hearing what people's concerns are, hearing what people have to say," he said, "then it doesn't matter how good the system is, you'll lose people."[146] The new implementation model was based on the department's experience with implementing major acquisition programs, with a program executive office (PEO) headed by a veteran Navy acquisition program manager establishing key performance parameters (KPPs) for the project.[147] As Secretary England explained, designing and implementing the NSPS was "far more complex than an aircraft carrier. With a lot more people involved."[148]

While the previous implementation program had called for covering half the DOD workforce in less than a year, the department's new approach was "event-driven" rather than "calendar-driven."[149] The political drive to implement as soon as possible was replaced by a determination not to put the NSPS into place before it was ready—"meaning all stakeholders have been adequately trained, the IT systems and policies and procedures have been developed and tested, and organizations are ready to make the cultural change to NSPS."[150] Secretary England brought in managers from large organizations who "actually owned the civilian[s]" and understood the practical management problems involved in building a new personnel system from the ground up.[151] The OPM and the military departments were made full partners in the effort, co-leading meetings and helping to staff the working groups and an overarching integrated product team.[152]

The DOD also made new efforts to involve the workforce. A new NSPS website received more than 100 million visits. The DOD convened 106 focus groups, held more than fifty town hall meetings,[153] and conducted a series of leadership conferences.[154] Over a period of just over a year, the department conducted roughly half a million training events. As Principal Under Secretary of Defense Michael Dominguez explained, "In addition to training on NSPS mechanics, supervisors were trained in soft skills, how to coach, monitor, and build a team. Employees also were offered soft-skill training, how to communicate, improve writing skills, and interact with their supervisor."[155]

The department also initiated a comprehensive communication program directed at the unions and Congress. Secretary England, who had a long and generally positive track record with the unions, reached out to key members of Congress of both parties and held a series of lunches, dinners, and other meetings with labor leaders.[156] Mary Lacey, the NSPS program executive, did the same.[157] While Secretary England was unable to breach the unions' opposition to the NSPS, his outreach efforts lowered the temperature substantially. Meetings with the unions were still contentious, but the openness of the new leadership "had a calming effect on the unions, particularly during [the] early meetings."[158]

The DOD took a spiral approach to implementation that allowed time to correct mistakes before they undermined the system with the entire workforce. For example, the department delayed the rollout of the first spiral of the NSPS and reduced the number of employees included from 65,000 to 11,000 when it appeared that more training was needed before implementation.[159] Lacey explained that she called for the delay because the department needed "more time to focus on simplifying the performance management design, getting performance objectives right, and ensuring the system is simple, clear and understandable."[160]

The department subsequently made changes to training, information systems, and guidance materials in response to problems experienced in the first spiral.[161] Secretary England explained: "We piloted, launched it, learned from that spiral, the next spiral, incorporated the improvements. . . . Like you would turn a weapon system to the warriors, we would turn a new personnel system to the personnel community."[162]

The more deliberative process was time consuming. Draft regulations were not published until February 2005, final regulations were not issued until November 2005, and the initial spiral of 11,000 DOD employees did not enter the NSPS until May 2006. By the end of 2008, the NSPS was fully launched, with more than 200,000 DOD employees in the new system, but five years had already passed since the enactment of the statute. The department had developed a model system for the implementation of major reform in the department, but the Bush administration was coming to an end without having built the support necessary to ensure that the NSPS would survive without it.

THE NSPS PAY-FOR-PERFORMANCE SYSTEM

The benefits of pay-for-performance systems are often assumed. A widely available private sector compensation guide reports: "Everyone seems to agree that linking employee pay to performance is the most effective compensation structure to encourage organizational improvement efforts."[163] One professor testifying on the NSPS told senators that pay-for-performance systems "can and do increase employee understanding of what is required of them and increase both their performance and organizational outcomes"[164] Another asserted that "financial incentives may work more strongly in the public sector."[165] He concluded: "If you are in the private sector and don't use pay for performance, they will look at you like you are crazy."[166] A 2004 report concluded that "money is a motivator," and that "research over the years confirms that people—and ultimately the organizations themselves—perform better when they are rewarded for performance."[167]

However, the evidence is not so clear. As one article notes, basic assumptions about financial incentives "are just that—assumptions. They are usually taken on faith rather than based on evidence."[168] A 2004 study by Harvard's Kennedy School of Government concluded that performance pay is likely to work as an effective motivator only in circumstances where organizational goals are clear, employees work on a few well-defined tasks, results can easily be measured and attributed to one person's effort, and employees are motivated primarily by money rather than other goals and values.[169] These conditions for success, the study concludes, "are generally not met in the private sector, even less so in the public sector."[170]

In fact, performance pay may even undercut employees' "intrinsic motivation" based on "factors like the meaning of the job, a sense of satisfaction at the accomplishment of valued tasks, and the engagement with one's values."[171] Others have warned that federal employees tend to be motivated primarily by factors other than pay,[172] a point that has been repeatedly documented in employee surveys conducted by MSPB.[173]

Perhaps for this reason, the architects of the NSPS avoided narrow reliance on employee motivation as a justification for the new pay-for-performance system. The Preamble to the Final Rule implementing the NSPS states: "This system does not assume that individuals are motivated by pay, but rather that we have an obligation as an employer to reward the highest performers with additional compensation—however they may be motivated to achieve excellence."[174] The Operational Requirements Document for the NSPS established five KPPs for the new system: (1) develop a high-performing workforce for the department, (2) provide for agile and responsive workforce and management, (3) ensure a credible and trusted system, (4) operate on a fiscally sound basis, and (5) include effective information technology and infrastructure support.[175]

The new pay and performance management systems, in particular, were intended to achieve multiple objectives:

- reduce paperwork by simplifying the job classification system[176]
- bring in new talent by providing more flexibility on starting salaries[177]
- motivate employees to achieve mission objectives by better linking pay to performance[178]
- empower supervisors to manage their own workforces by establishing goals and rewarding employees who achieve them[179]
- enhance efficiency by making employee compensation more sensitive to market forces[180]
- increase retention of top performers by rewarding excellence and removing artificial barriers on upward pay mobility[181]
- identify poor performers to encourage them to leave the workforce by denying them automatic pay raises[182]
- increase workforce agility by simplifying the process for reassignment, deployment, and new duties[183]

Performance Management
An effective pay-for-performance system requires performance measurement to differentiate between successful and unsuccessful employees. Until an agency has "modern, effective, credible, and, as appropriate, validated performance management systems in place with adequate safeguards, including reasonable transparency and appropriate accountability mechanisms, to ensure fairness and prevent politicization and abuse,"[184] Comptroller General David Walker explained, it is not ready to institute pay-for-performance. Following this advice, Secretary England made the establishment of a new performance management system the centerpiece of NSPS implementation, saying, "Get the performance management system right, and everything else would follow."[185]

The Civil Service Reform Act already required federal agencies to maintain performance appraisal systems to serve "as a basis for training, rewarding, reassigning, promoting, reducing in grade, retaining, and removing employees."[186] However, these systems were not working as intended. The Clinton administration's National Performance Review asserted that the existing, government-wide system was not responsive to the varying needs and cultures of diverse federal agencies, failed to provide adequate feedback on expectations and performance, and was threatening to employee and supervisor alike.[187] These problems were exacerbated by a common view that performance ratings were inflated almost to the point of being meaningless.[188]

As a result, federal employees and managers had little confidence in performance appraisals. In the early 1990s, the GAO reported that 20 of 21 supervisors surveyed said that the existing system did not improve performance, and the OPM reported that only 19 percent of 31,000 employees surveyed believed that the system motivated employees to perform well.[189] Ten years later, MSPB found the situation essentially unchanged: only 20 percent of employees surveyed reported that the performance appraisal system motivated them to do a good job.[190]

The NSPS replaced the CSRA evaluation process with a new performance management system that required the establishment of an annual performance plan for every employee,[191] linked employee objectives to the DOD's overall mission and strategic goals,[192] and rated performance on a five-point scale, based on the manner and extent to which employees achieved their objectives.[193] Raters could also consider "contributing factors"—such as technical proficiency, critical thinking, cooperation and teamwork, leadership, consumer focus, resource management, and communication—that could raise or lower an employee's score.[194]

The NSPS rating system, by itself, was not necessarily better or worse than other performance appraisal systems used in the federal government. The DOD's mission is not easily quantified, making the work objectives of individual DOD employees difficult to measure as well.[195] Moreover, any performance measurement system must balance individual achievements against organizational achievements, short-term goals against long-term goals, technical proficiency against hard work, and best efforts against actual outcomes achieved. For this reason, the success or failure of any performance evaluation system in the department depends almost entirely on the work of those who are charged with implementing it.

What distinguished the NSPS system from its predecessors was the degree of effort that went into engaging managers and employees. The NSPS performance management system was founded on continual engagement between supervisors and employees,[196] including a dialog over performance objectives and expectations,[197] periodic feedback and interim reviews of employee performance,[198] employee self-assessments,[199] supervisory assessments,[200] communication of ratings results,[201] and ratings appeals.[202] The NSPS required managers "to do the hard work of coaching, mentoring, performance feedback and importantly, setting goals and objectives that are clear, understandable, compelling to people."[203]

In fact, the managers and employees complained that the labor-intensive NSPS performance management system detracted from mission productivity and impinged on personal time, with supervisors required to spend forty to sixty hours per year per employee to make the system work. "There are not enough hours in a day," one supervisor complained.[204] Despite these demands, a plurality of NSPS supervisors believed that the time required to develop good performance plans, discuss and assess performance, and give feedback to employees was worthwhile.[205]

This managerial focus resulted in a more credible distribution of employee ratings. In contrast to the grade inflation in prior performance evaluation systems, only 5 percent of NSPS employees received "outstanding" ratings, while 57 percent received the median rating of 3 for "valued performers."[206] The reduction in grade inflation did not come without pain, however, since employees who had routinely received ratings of 4 or 5 under the previous system did not react well to the lower ratings. In 2008, the NSPS PEO reported that employees who received lower ratings under the NSPS worried about the consequences of the rating if they tried to move to a non-NSPS organization.[207] The overall effect of the change was "a decrease in morale" and a threat to the "self-esteem and identity as professionals" of previous high-mark performers.[208]

Pay Banding
With the success of the Lab Demo and Acq Demo programs, pay banding had come to be seen as *the* approach to pay reform for federal civil-

ians. In August 2003, the National Academy for Public Administration (NAPA) reported that "broadbanding and pay-for-performance currently are in the forefront of federal compensation discussions."[209] The report did not identify or discuss any approach to pay-for-performance other than pay banding.[210]

Advocates for federal pay-for-performance systems argued that pay banding was the wave of the future in the private sector as well. For example, the IBM Center for the Business of Government contended that major corporations were abandoning traditional pay-for-performance models in favor of pay bands because more traditional pay-for-performance systems (which used narrower job classifications and pay ranges) did not provide sufficient flexibility to respond market pressures and reward individual skills and contributions. The report concluded, "It seems at this point that the trend to adopt banded salary systems will continue."[211]

As is too often the case, the federal government jumped onto a bandwagon just as it began to lose momentum, and remained on the same course when other organizations had already begun to move on. In July 2003, NAPA reported that enthusiasm for pay banding had diminished as companies saw that they were stuck with "a 'hodge-podge' of jobs in each band," making it hard for managers and employees to understand the grouping of jobs or the basis for pay limits.[212] By 2017, a survey of the compensation practices of 7,700 private sector companies characterized remaining broadband pay systems as a "remnant of early compensation structures" and "a dying breed." For companies "wondering how to be more nimble," the survey concluded, "the message is simple: ditch the broadbands."[213]

Some experts warned that private sector pay bands typically covered "homogeneous workforces"[214] that were "relatively small in scale,"[215] and that scaling the system up to cover the DOD's diverse 700,000 employee civilian workforce would be difficult.[216] Private sector pay bands were carefully tailored to the needs of the company, with large companies using ten or more pay bands to accommodate workforce diversity.[217] Pay band systems focused predominantly on executives and officer workers, with few covering "nonexempt" hourly workers, and virtually none covering union employees.[218]

The DOD, by contrast, designed a system that lumped the entire GS workforce of the department into just four career groups: standard, scientific and engineering, medical, and investigative and protective services. Each career group was subdivided into three or four pay schedules (reflecting career stages) and three or four overlapping pay bands. In practice, the vast majority of DOD employees fell into just a few categories: 72 percent were in the "standard" career group;[219] 60 percent were in the "professional" pay schedule;[220] and 69 percent were in pay band 2.[221]

Collapsing so many employees into just a handful of pay categories ensured flexibility for DOD managers, but provided little structure for career and compensation decisions. In contrast to the private sector experience, the department intended eventually to include even wage-grade employees—whose hourly rates were set on the basis of market surveys—in the new system. As one pay-for-performance advocate later noted, the DOD "is a unique conglomerate; its many units have different missions, cultures, and management styles. . . . No large, highly diversified company," he concluded, "would try to force-fit a uniform, rigid salary system in every business unit."[222]

The department attempted to address the issue of overly broad pay bands by authorizing its components to develop unique "business rules" to manage occupations and positions within a single pay band in light of the complexity of the work, the scope and duties of positions, mission criticality, difficulty filling positions, and external market salary levels.[223] Internal business rules could establish pay ceilings and floors (known as "control points") for a set of occupations or positions within a pay band.[224] They could also establish criteria for new-hire salaries, promotions, reassignments, and reductions in force (RIFs) for such occupations or positions.[225]

The use of business rules allowed local managers to make decisions about compensation and rewards that were best suited for their own workforces, but could be frustrating to employees, some of whom felt that key elements of the process were hidden from them. Indeed, the preamble to the final rule implementing the NSPS noted that a number of commenters had "likened control points to 'invisible barriers that prevent most employees from ever reaching the top of their band.'"[226]

Pay Pools

In an organization the size of the DOD, individual supervisors have different standards. Many incline toward inflated ratings that, if left unchecked, could push employees toward the top of pay bands, raising the overall cost of civilian personnel compensation to the department.[227] Others might abuse the flexibility afforded by the system and give in to personal and cultural biases in favor of friends or people who are more like them.

The department sought to address equity and affordability concerns by establishing calibration committees, known as "pay pools," to ensure the consistency of employee ratings and pay decisions. Pay pools grouped employees together into organizational units, with an average size of 112 employees and a median size of 85 employees.[228] Each pay pool was run by a "pay pool panel"—a board of management officials with responsibility for the organizations and functions in the pay pool—under the oversight of a more senior "pay pool manager."[229] Higher-level "performance review authorities" were established to review multiple pay pools within a DOD component, command, or field activity.[230]

Each pay pool received a set amount of money to allocate for performance-based pay raises and bonuses. Pay pool funds came from three sources: (1) the amount historically spent in the GS system for within-grade increases, step increases, and promotions between grades; (2) the amount that would have been available for an annual adjustment under the GS system, less the amount of any across-the-board pay increase approved by the secretary; and (3) the amount historically spent for performance-based cash awards.[231] These sources of funds for pay raises and bonuses were consistent with the legislative requirement that the overall amount allocated for the compensation of NSPS employees be no less than the amount that would have been available under the GS system.[232] In 2005, Secretary England told SASC that the department took it as a "basic covenant issue with its employees" that budget pressures could not be allowed to reduce NSPS pay levels.[233]

The inclusion of annual pay adjustments in pay pool funding was particularly controversial because it meant that NSPS employees would not necessarily receive the across-the-board pay raises—often thought of as cost of living increases (COLAs)—that were approved by the president and Congress for other federal employees. One expert on pay-for-performance systems explained in Senate testimony: "Employees expect their salary to be held at least constant against market as long as they meet standards. When pay-for-performance is used in lieu of market adjustments, employees feel management is trying to put one over on them."[234]

The funds available in a pay pool were allocated largely on the basis of performance ratings. Employees with a rating of 3 ("valued performers") were eligible for one or two shares; employees with a rating of 4 ("exceeds expectations") were eligible for three or four shares; and employees with a rating of 5 ("role model") were eligible for five or six shares. Employees in the upper half of the evaluation range (e.g., "high 4s") usually received the higher number of shares than employees in the lower half of the range ("low 4s").[235] However, nonperformance factors—such as an employee's position in the rate range, attrition and retention rates for critical personnel, and private-sector salary levels—could also be considered in allocating shares.[236] For this reason, a lower-rated employee could receive a greater pay increase than a higher-rated employee, even within the same pay pool.[237]

After determining the number of shares to be awarded, the pay pool manager would determine the value of each share, as a percentage of employee pay, based on the amount of funding available in the pay pool.[238] Shares could be paid out either as pay increases or as one-time bonuses.[239] Pay pools self-corrected against grade inflation, because as the number of high ratings in a pool increased, the value of each share would decrease.[240] As a result, however, no consistent dollar value was associated with any job rating. Highly rated employees in a pay pool with many poor performers could expect larger pay raises than similar employees working in a strong pay pool.[241]

Employees could see inconsistencies in ratings and payout distributions, but lacked basic information about the way the pay pools worked, because pay pool members were prohibited from disclosing any information related to pay pool deliberations, recommended and final ratings, and salary decisions.[242] This lack of information created the impression that the NSPS was a "black box,"[243] instilling a "sense of mistrust and doubt among many employees." A focus group convened by the NSPS PEO complained: "It is unclear how the payout decisions are made—how do they decide what percentage goes to salary and what percentage go to bonuses? This is very important. There are long-term impacts for these decisions."[244]

Transparency concerns were heightened by the fact that pay pools could and often did overrule the rating recommendations of line supervisors and managers. Employees "wanted to know how their direct supervisors rated their work and were not satisfied by either the lack of explanation or the prohibition placed upon supervisors to not share their recommended ratings," while supervisors "felt they had lost their authority over their employees" as they had to sign their own names to ratings that were actually made by others.[245] One employee told an NSPS PEO evaluation team: "Our boss was not allowed to tell us why our rating was changed. They weren't told why. They weren't allowed to tell us. The word *transparency* has taken us in the opposite direction."[246]

Pay pools were intended to enhance confidence in the pay-for-performance system by providing fairness and consistency across the department, but they appear to have had the opposite effect. The unions asserted NSPS pay pool decisions were "made in the dark and kept secret," and that these decisions were made not by supervisors, but by "a group of pay pool managers who don't work with you and don't know your performance."[247] AFGE president John Gage testified that the pay pools "do whatever they want" on ratings and salary decisions without providing any information to the supervisor or the employee. He added: "Employees are not fools, Senator. They understand that the supervisor's rating, which should be the employee's performance matched to that performance plan, has nothing to do with the real rating he is going to get or the money he is going to receive."[248]

After NSPS fell apart, at least one advocate traced the failure back to the "fatal flaw" of an untested pay pool system. "The pay pools violated one of the primary tenets of salary management—employees need to know what they can expect," he concluded.[249]

Other Pay Mechanisms

The NSPS performance management, pay banding, and pay pool mechanisms were designed to link pay to performance, ensuring that those who made the greatest contribution to the department's mission would receive the greatest reward. The architects of the NSPS pay system also hoped to enhance the DOD's ability to respond to market pressures by paying more to recruit and retain workers whose services were in greater demand outside the department and paying less to workers whose skills were not in demand.[250] The implementing issuance establishing the NSPS pay system states that it is DOD policy not only to link pay to performance, but also to ensure "appropriate consideration of both national and local rates paid by employers in the private sector."[251]

The goals of pay-for-performance and pay-to-market are not mutually consistent. All career fields, whether they are in high demand or low demand, can be expected to include a mix of high and low performers. For this reason, a system that focuses on pay-for-performance may not be successful in responding to market pressures and vice versa.[252]

While the NSPS was largely designed around pay-for-performance, the system included several mechanisms intended to provide flexibility to respond to market pressures. For example, the secretary was authorized to provide unique "rate range adjustments" for career groups based on market conditions[253] and "targeted local market supplements" to address market issues unique to a particular occupation and a region.[254] In addition, managers were authorized to set the starting rate of pay for new hires "anywhere within the assigned pay band,"[255] to use flexible pay increases associated with promotions and reassignments, and to pay retention incentives of up to 25 percent of basic pay employee with "unusually high or unique qualifications" to recruit and retain employees with critical skills.[256]

Given enough time, these mechanisms might have given the DOD more market-based compensation structure. In practice, however, market-based flexibilities had a negligible impact, because they were rarely used. The department reduced its own market flexibility by providing all or most of the government-wide COLA to NSPS employees in the first NSPS performance cycle.[257] In the second cycle, Congress mandated that NSPS employees receive at least 60 percent of the COLA, and the DOD chose to allocate the remaining 40 percent to performance pay pools rather than to market-based rate adjustments for targeted career groups.[258] Congress also changed the law in 2007 to require that all NSPS employees receive the same locality pay raises as GS employees, eliminating the department's ability to use these funds for targeted local market supplements.[259]

The NSPS market mechanisms were perceived by many as being *less* effective than the old civil service system, which rewarded employees with critical skills primarily through promotions and changed assignments. By collapsing multiple pay grades and steps into a few broad pay bands, the NSPS left fewer promotion and career progression opportunities available to employees.[260] In fact, any change within an NSPS pay band was considered a "reassignment"—with a maximum 5 percent pay raise[261]—even if substantial new duties were involved, leading some to conclude that there was little incentive to assume a supervisory position.[262]

The market flexibilities offered by the NSPS may have made it easier for the department to attract skilled candidates as new hires by offering them salaries more commensurate with their experience.[263] Even here, however, there were problems: existing employees felt disadvantaged by the ability of outside hires to negotiate higher starting salaries.[264] One supervisor told an NSPS PEO evaluation team: "I personally think this is an outrage. These are key positions. Being able to attract leadership is critical. Not every position should be filled from outside; sometimes internal employees are in the best position to fill these positions."[265]

Assessment
The architects of the NSPS sought to develop a single system that was flexible enough to meet the full range of the department's civilian personnel needs in a manner that was efficient and equitable—a tall order for such a large and diverse workforce. Moreover, by trying to solve such a wide range of personnel problems with a single system, the NSPS

established multiple points of failure, ensuring that skeptics and opponents of the new system would always be able to focus on shortcomings while ignoring successes.

By several measures, the NSPS pay-for-performance system was a striking success. Over a period of just three years, the department managed to bring 211,000 employees into an entirely new personnel system without any pause or perceptible adverse effect on ongoing DOD programs and operations. The initial spiral of 11,000 employees faced technical issues with the performance management system and the supporting IT system that had been designed to support it; however, with the total commitment of the department's senior leadership, these problems were quickly overcome.[266]

Overall, the NSPS outperformed the old GS in several areas while falling short on others. A comprehensive study conducted on behalf of the NSPS PEO demonstrates the mixed nature of the record.

On the positive side of the ledger, most NSPS employees agreed that their performance appraisals were a fair reflection of their performance[267] and gave them the information they needed to understand what they had to do to improve their ratings.[268] Employees generally understood how their work related to their organization's goals and priorities[269] and had a sense of personal empowerment with regard to work processes.[270] Roughly half of NSPS employees expressed satisfaction with the recognition that they received for doing a good job[271] and that the system rewarded creativity and innovation,[272] while much smaller numbers disagreed.

The NSPS was a significant improvement over the GS system in the manner that it addressed employees at the extremes of the performance spectrum. With regard to high performers, one focus group employee explained: "If someone is a valued employee, you don't have to wait to give that person a raise. This is a positive for employees who really deserve more money."[273] With regard to poor performers, the NSPS performance management system rated 297 out of 10,000 employees (2.9 percent) less than fully successful, dramatically more than the 150 out of 250,000 non-NSPS employees (0.06 percent) who received unacceptable ratings.[274] While employees "expressed general ambivalence" as to the effectiveness of NSPS disciplinary mechanisms, senior leaders believed that the NSPS provided increased ability to address poor performers, creating optimism that they could be removed from the workforce over time.[275]

Other areas were more mixed. With regard to new talent, for example, some managers reported the NSPS allowed them to become more competitive in recruiting more highly skilled employees, but others complained of hiring delays due to pay negotiations, difficulties hiring for specific pay ranges and specialty positions, and challenges caused by internal business rules.[276] Overall, most NSPS employees and senior leaders did not believe that the system had improved the hiring of new employees or the quality of applicants.[277] Similarly, some supervisors expressed "appreciation for the increased flexibility in making assignments,"[278] but this flexibility was undermined by backlogs at personnel centers, which resulted in reported delays of up to eight months for reassignments at some locations.[279]

On the negative side of the ledger, a preponderance of employees believed that the NSPS failed in its primary purpose of "strengthening the link between pay and performance, improving pay levels, and recognizing and rewarding performance."[280] NSPS employees believed that the predominance of "3" ratings had hurt employee morale,[281] while the lack of transparency of business rules and the pay pool process undermined employee confidence that rewards were based on merit.[282] Far from feeling empowered, many supervisors felt that they were undercut by pay pools, which rejected their recommendations and undermined their credibility with employees.[283] Overall, "managers identified retaining supervisors, perceived pay inequities between current and new employees, top-of-pay-band pay caps, tailoring vacancy announcements within broad pay bands, and ratings inflation as challenges to retention."[284]

The NSPS, in the short time available to it, did not make civilian compensation responsive to market pressures. Tools such as market-based pay increases and targeted local market supplements were not used and were subsequently withdrawn in whole or in part by Congress. Market factors could be considered in setting salaries for new hire salaries, but the availability of this tool for new employees created a sense of unfairness for existing employees. The NSPS PEO study states: "Many employees believe that salaries are more market-sensitive for new hires, allowing organizations to recruit employees with high-level expertise more effectively. However, because salaries are not market-sensitive for existing employees, some perceive inequity."[285]

By far, the biggest problem faced by the NSPS pay system was growing employee resistance. The PEO survey found that employees exhibited "a reluctance to credit NSPS for any improvement" and believed that the NSPS was worse or much worse than the previous system.[286] The negative employee views extended to virtually every aspect of the NSPS. A plurality of NSPS employees thought that the system was worse on hiring, placement, and promotions; worse on pay levels; worse on performance management; worse on labor-management relations; worse on employee recognition and rewards; worse on workforce shaping; and worse on employee conduct and discipline than the previous system.[287] In September 2008, the GAO found that the longer employees served in the NSPS, the more they disliked it, and expressed concern that growing discontent could lead to the system's failure.[288]

Change is always difficult in an institution as big and bureaucratic as the DOD, and the comprehensive nature of the NSPS gave employees many potential targets for dissatisfaction. With time, the NSPS probably would have overcome these negative employee perceptions, as the Lab Demo and Acq Demo programs had in an earlier era.[289] Some of the problems experienced by the NSPS would have been worked out through minor changes and adjustments to the system. Employees would likely have come to accept other shortcomings. Federal employees have, after all, been living with the shortcomings of the GS system for the last four decades.

Unfortunately for the advocates of the NSPS and pay-for-performance in the federal government, the political problems caused by the department's insistence on radical changes to labor relations and employee appeals systems meant that the NSPS simply did not *have* the five to seven years needed to prove that the new pay-for-performance approach could work. By 2009, a change in control of Congress and the election of a new president had created a new political environment. The unions, whose views had been dismissed by the department, felt empowered. Negative employee views of the NSPS system made it vulnerable, and an inflamed political opposition ensured that it would not survive.

LABOR RELATIONS AND THE COLLAPSE OF THE NSPS

Some senior DOD officials hoped to use the second chance afforded to the department by Secretary England's intervention in NSPS implementation to reset the labor relations provisions and develop a more constructive relationship with the unions. England brought in Mary Lacey to head the implementation effort, in part, because of her experience working with the unions as she ran the Lab Demo program in one of the Navy research laboratories. He hoped she would be able to work through the labor relations provisions with the unions in a constructive manner.[290] However, she was not allowed to do so.

Instead, the White House insisted on a "union-busting" approach. The NSPS team got a call from the White House and was told "here is your labor relations system," Michael Dominguez remembers. The system was not designed or developed by the DOD, and the department was not authorized to change it.[291] "We were . . . basically prevented from moderation," OPM associate director Ron Sanders explained. "We ran up against some ideological objectives from the White House that precluded a more pragmatic approach."[292] Even in the final stages of the "meet-and-confer" process before the issuance of the NSPS rule, Sanders said, the attitude of senior officials at the OMB remained: "Why give? You don't have to give. If you don't have to give, why give?"[293]

During the strategic pause in NSPS implementation in early 2004, the department gave up on trying to redefine what a union was or who it could represent. When the draft rule implementing the NSPS was published in February 2005, however, the proposed language still undercut nearly every aspect of employees' collective bargaining rights.

First, the draft rule expanded the list of nonnegotiable "management rights" to issues that had previously been subject to collective bargaining, including the procedures used to hire, assign, and direct employees; to assign work and make decisions regarding outsourcing; to lay off, retain, or discipline employees; and "to take whatever other actions may be necessary to carry out the Department's mission."²⁹⁴ The preamble to the proposed rule stated: "The Department can take action in any of these areas without advance notice to the union."²⁹⁵

Second, the draft rule prohibited collective bargaining with regard to DOD "policies, regulations or similar issuances."²⁹⁶ "Issuances" were defined to include any "document . . . to carry out a policy or procedure of the Department," without regard to who approved it, as long as it was issued at the DOD or component level.²⁹⁷ Not only were these issuances exempt from collective bargaining, they would automatically override existing collective bargaining agreements.²⁹⁸ In short, a collective bargaining agreement would be binding only on the union and the employees it represented. It would not be binding on the department, which would have the power to change it at any time.

Employee representatives objected to these provisions at every opportunity,²⁹⁹ telling Congress that the proposal "effectively eliminates collective bargaining" by taking previously negotiable issues, including "procedures and arrangements for overtime, shift rotation, flexible and compressed work schedules, safety and health programs, and deployment away from regular worksite" off the table.³⁰⁰ The AFGE promised to initiate "the biggest grassroots mobilization of American workers ever seen" in opposition to the proposal.³⁰¹

The unions asserted that these provisions were unnecessary, because government-wide regulations already allowed the department to act without prior collective bargaining in case of an emergency. When the DOD argued that the existing definition of "emergency" was too narrow and constraining, the unions offered to extend it to cover any exigency "requiring action reasonably necessary to carry out the Department's national security mission before collective bargaining concerning the action can be completed."³⁰²

The DOD rejected this proposal on the basis that DOD managers and supervisors needed the freedom "to make split-second decisions to deal with operational realities free of procedural constraints" at all times.³⁰³ Even postimplementation bargaining would be too burdensome, the department contended, because "the reality of DOD's operational environment today is that change is constant, and as a consequence, so too would be post-implementation bargaining."³⁰⁴ The final rule implementing the NSPS preserved the limitations on collective bargaining without significant substantive change.³⁰⁵

The administration effort to maintain freedom of action also extended to the employee grievance and appeals processes. Congress authorized the department to establish new processes, as long as they provided NSPS employees fair treatment consistent with the merit principles. The processes could be established within the department, but would have to provide for appeal to the MSPB.³⁰⁶ To meet these requirements, the department proposed a Rube Goldberg–like approach that appeared to be designed not for efficiency or effectiveness, but to maximize the likelihood that management would prevail in as many appeals as possible.

Under the proposed system, employees would first take their cases to the administrative judges of the MSPB.³⁰⁷ After an administrative judge made a "decision," no relief could be ordered until the DOD had a chance to review the decision and decide what to do.³⁰⁸ If the department agreed with the administrative judge, the decision would become final, and the department would determine whether or not it would serve as a precedent.³⁰⁹ If the department disagreed with the decision, it could modify or reverse it.³¹⁰ A decision could be appealed to the full MSPB only after the department acted.³¹¹

Moreover, the standards of review were weighted against employees. Any penalty imposed on an employee was presumed to be valid, "unless such penalty is so disproportionate to the basis for the action as to be wholly without justification."³¹² If a penalty was found to be excessive, "the maximum justifiable penalty"—defined as "the severest penalty that is not so disproportionate to the basis for the action as to be wholly without justification"—would have to be imposed.³¹³

Equally important, Senator Levin pointed out at a 2005 hearing of SASC, was what the draft regulation did not say. "It does not require either DOD officials or reviewing authorities to take into account any of the many factors that might justify a reduced penalty, such as employees' past record, whether the offense is intentional or advertent, the extent to which the employee was on notice or warned about the conduct in question, and the consistency of the penalty with those imposed on other employees for the same or similar offenses." Even convicted murderers, Levin pointed out, "are not always subjected to the maximum permissible penalty."[314] The DOD rejected these concerns and retained the appeals process largely unchanged in the final rule implementing the NSPS.[315]

The NSPS labor relations and appeals rules preserved maximum flexibility and discretion for the department, but that flexibility came at a high cost: the rules were never implemented.

One week after the final NSPS rule was published in the *Federal Register*, ten unions filed a lawsuit in federal court challenging the labor relations and appeals provisions.[316] On February 27, 2006, Judge Emmet Sullivan ruled that the NSPS rules "entirely eviscerate collective bargaining," in violation of the statute. The judge's ruling prohibited the department from implementing any of the labor relations and appeals provisions of the final rule.[317] Over the next several months, Spiral 1 of the NSPS was rolled out *without* the labor relations and appeals provisions.

The Justice Department appealed the NSPS opinion to the DC Circuit Court of Appeals, but two events in the next few months made the implementation of the proposed labor relations and appeals systems appear less likely than ever.

First, on June 27, 2006, the DC Circuit Court overturned the labor relations provisions in the new DHS personnel system.[318] The DHS collective bargaining rule contained provisions (virtually identical to the NSPS rule) that expanded nonnegotiable management rights and provided for "Departmental issuances" to override collective bargaining agreements.[319] The court determined that these provisions violated a statutory requirement to safeguard the right to collective bargaining, because it gave the department "the right to unilaterally abrogate lawfully negotiated and executed agreements," rendering the scope of bargaining "virtually nil."[320] It was difficult for many to see how the court, having made this determination for DHS, would be able to uphold virtually identical provisions under the NSPS statute.

Second, in November 2006, Democrats gained six seats in the Senate and thirty-one seats in the House of Representatives, regaining control of both chambers. From the outset, the administration had taken a "Republican-only" approach to the NSPS, ignoring the concerns of

Democrats and foregoing the opportunity afforded by the Collins bill to enact bipartisan legislation. Secretary England had rebuilt relations with Democrats but had not been allowed to address their concerns about the NSPS labor relations and appeals provisions. Now, the future of the NSPS would be in the hands of leaders whom the department had slighted for the previous three years.

On March 6, 2007, the House Armed Services Committee (HASC) held a hearing on the subject "The National Security Personnel System— Is It Really Working?" One member of the committee—a Republican— referred to the NSPS as "another failed policy" of Secretary Rumsfeld.[321] At a second House hearing two days later, another Republican representative asked a panel of outside experts whether the new Congress should "just drop the whole idea" of the NSPS or take other steps to address perceived problems.[322] The witnesses responded by suggesting that the focus going forward should be on getting the performance management system right[323] and that the labor relations and appeals provisions should be repealed.[324]

On May 18, 2007, the DC Circuit Court surprised many observers by overturning the district court decision and upholding DOD's labor relations rules. The court recognized that provisions of the NSPS statute "that seem to bestow a right" to collective bargaining "appear to work at cross-purposes" with other provisions that "simultaneously appear to snatch it away."[325] However, the court determined that the right to collective bargaining was "subject to the provisions of this chapter" and could, therefore, be overridden by other parts of the statute.[326] On this basis, the court held that the statute afforded the DOD "broad authority to curtail collective bargaining" until the sunset date of the labor relations provision in 2009.[327]

There are three important points about the court's decision. First, it is a perfectly plausible interpretation of an unclear statute—after all, the labor relations provisions were negotiated by administration officials who wanted flexibility to establish a new labor relations system. Second, the decision was at odds with the promise made by Secretary Rumsfeld and other senior DOD officials that the NSPS would preserve employees' collective bargaining rights. Third, the decision came too late to save the labor relations and appeals provisions of the NSPS, because Congress was already well on its way to addressing the issue itself.

On May 8, 2007 (a week before the appeals court decision), HASC voted to repeal the authority for DOD-unique labor relations and appeals systems and reinstate full collective bargaining rights for NSPS employees.[328] The House even proposed to revoke the authority for the NSPS performance management system, require that NSPS employees receive the same annual pay adjustments (COLAs) as other federal employees, and eliminate the authority for flexible NSPS approaches to hiring, assignments, promotions, and reductions in force.[329]

Two weeks later, SASC voted to repeal the DOD labor relations authority, reinstate collective bargaining rights,[330] and exclude "wage-grade" employees—blue collar workers who were not part of the GS and whose salaries were already established on a market basis—from the NSPS.[331] The Senate bill was more modest than the House bill, proposing no change to the performance management and pay-for-performance systems and providing that rates of pay would continue to be exempt from collective bargaining.[332]

The final bill, signed into law six months later, brought a definitive end to the NSPS labor relations and appeals systems.[333] Unlike the House bill, however, the final law sought to preserve the core NSPS authority to establish a flexible new personnel system. The DOD's authority to deviate from government-wide requirements for RIFs was repealed, but the NSPS performance management system and the DOD's flexibility to address hiring, assignments, and promotions was untouched.[334] The *Washington Post* quoted a congressional aide who explained: "We want them to do collective bargaining, but we want to give the department a fair chance to show that pay for performance can work."[335]

For a time, it appeared that this compromise would save the NSPS. The bill passed Congress by overwhelming bipartisan votes of 370–49 in the House and 90–3 in the Senate. The federal employee unions hailed the legislation as a victory, calling it "an early Christmas present from this Congress," a "light at the end of the tunnel," and "a victory for Defense workers."[336] AFGE president John Gage announced, "There haven't been many wins in our history bigger than this one."[337] From the DOD perspective, the legislation allowed the NSPS to move forward, with an additional 100,000 DOD employees converted over the next year.[338] The department had reason to hope that it would have time to work out the bugs in the system and gain employee acceptance for the new performance management and pay-for-performance systems.

On May 22, 2008, the DOD published a proposed rule implementing the legislative changes to the NSPS. By far the most contentious aspect of the proposed rule was a provision defining "rates of pay" (which were exempt from collective bargaining) to include all of the internal business rules used to set pay.[339] The preamble to the rule explained that "a rate of pay cannot be understood as simply an amount. A rate amount only has meaning in the context of the required set of conditions that define what the rate is and when it applies."[340] This definition provoked outrage from the unions, who complained that the proposed rule was "dirty pool," designed to eliminate the right to collective bargaining just as Congress had restored it.[341]

The DOD had painted itself into a corner. The NSPS sought maximum flexibility for the department by leaving all of the detailed operational requirements to be established in implementing issuances and business rules. This approach would only work as long as the implementing issuances and business rules remained exempt from collective bargaining. It was not practical for the DOD to conduct lengthy negotiations with the unions every time a pay pool wanted to change the control points or revise the way it allocated available funds between pay raises and bonuses. Secretary England promised to narrow the definition of rates of pay in response to congressional concerns, but the real fix was to avoid the problem altogether by not extending the NSPS to any union employees.[342]

With the election of a new president in 2008, the process of reexamination began again. During the campaign, candidate Barack Obama had promised that if he were elected, he would "substantially revise these NSPS regulations, and strongly consider a complete repeal."[343] With his election, the unions sought to rid themselves of the NSPS entirely. One union leader called the NSPS "a system that is completely untenable and should never have been pursued."[344] A second called it "the biggest affront to the federal workforce in modern history," adding, "We want it gone this year.³⁴⁵ When the new Congress convened, the federal employee unions lobbied for a complete repeal of the NSPS, arguing that it should be possible to transition all employees back to the GS within a few months.

In the face of this determined opposition from important political allies, the incoming administration had only a narrow window for continued civilian personnel reform. On March 16, 2009, the new deputy secretary of defense, William Lynn III, announced that the DOD and the OPM would initiate a complete review of the NSPS and that the department would postpone any further conversions to the NSPS until the review was complete.³⁴⁶ Incoming OMB director Peter Orszag informed Congress that the Obama administration "strongly supports the concept of rewarding excellence with additional pay."³⁴⁷ However, this position had been weakened by years of fights over collective bargaining and employee appeals.

In June 2009, HASC approved a provision terminating the NSPS and requiring the return of all NSPS employees to prior personnel systems within a period of twelve months.³⁴⁸ SASC tried to save central elements of civilian personnel reform, providing that the NSPS could continue unless the secretary determined that termination was in the best interest of the department.³⁴⁹ Even in the event of repeal, the Senate bill provided that the DOD would retain the authority for national-level bargaining and the ability to waive civil service provisions as needed to establish effective hiring, assignment, and performance management systems.³⁵⁰

In July, the Defense Business Board (DBB) completed the NSPS review directed by Secretary Lynn. The DBB report supported the performance management and pay-for-performance approaches objectives of the NSPS, but found major problems with the pay pool system, the use of a single pay band that included almost 70 percent of the DOD workforce, the lack of transparency in the system, and the use of confusing and opaque business rules.³⁵¹ If the NSPS was going to be continued, the DBB concluded, it would have to be "reconstructed" from the ground up. A simple "fix" would not "address the depth of the systemic problems discovered."³⁵² One DBB member elaborated that any new system would need a different name because the name "NSPS" had become "radioactive."[353]

The DBB report was far less than the ringing endorsement that would have been needed to save the NSPS from its critics. The federal employee unions insisted that the report had gotten the diagnosis right but was "way off on the cure." The NSPS would need to be repealed.[354] When the two armed services committees met to resolve their differences, the House conferees insisted that anything less than total repeal of the NSPS provision would be unacceptable. The House would not agree to an amended statute, and no waivers of the repeal would be permitted.[355]

At the Senate's insistence, the final provision authorized the department to develop new hiring and performance management systems, along with a workforce incentive fund to help attract and retain skilled employees and a civilian leadership training program.[356] However, the House would not permit the NSPS to continue in any form. The department would have to start over from the beginning and build any modified systems from the ground up in close consultation with employees and their representatives. With the fiscal year 2010 NDAA, the NSPS was fully and finally repealed.

The reform provisions included in the 2010 NDAA proved to be of little consequence. The DOD established a Defense Civilian Emerging Leader Program but made minimal changes to hiring practices and decided not to establish the workforce incentive fund. The department worked with the unions for six years to develop a new performance management system. When the effort was finally completed in 2016, the new system provided for three grades: outstanding, fully successful, and unacceptable.[357] The unions praised the result,[358] but it appeared in some ways to be a step backward from the statutory objective of better linking pay to performance.

With the repeal of the NSPS, the department was no longer ready to invest the energy and leadership required for comprehensive civilian personnel reform. In the best of times, it has been difficult for Democrats in Congress and the executive branch to advocate civilian personnel reforms that do not have the full support of the federal employee unions (although some have done so). After the demise of the NSPS, it became nearly impossible. "Perception is reality, and if employees believe they are being fed another NSPS, the system will be doomed from the start," Patricia Niehaus, president of the Federal Managers Association, told the *Washington Post*.[359] "If the new way smells anything like NSPS," the *Post* concluded, "it will stink to federal workers."

In many ways, the NSPS implementation effort was a model for successful reform efforts in the department. The department showed committed senior leadership over an extended period of time, including not only a dedicated program office reporting directly to the deputy secretary of defense, but engaged leaders at all levels in the military departments and defense agencies. The department took a systematic approach to developing regulations, guidance, and training by working through teams that included experienced managers from throughout the department and developed comprehensive outreach and training programs.

The problem was that the "big bang" approach to reform—requiring that the entire personnel system be changed at the same time—proved to be too much for the department to achieve. The DBB was probably correct when it concluded, "In essence, NSPS attempted to accomplish 'too much, too fast.'"[360] This problem was compounded by the administration's rigid insistence on labor relations and appeals provisions that made enemies of the unions and much of Congress and undermined employee acceptance of the system. "If we had moderated our goals," one senior OPM official lamented in 2008, the unions "wouldn't have had nearly as much ammunition." In "20/20 hindsight," he concluded, "more moderation in adverse actions, more moderation in the collective bargaining rules" might have brought about a different result.[361]

The revolutionary approach to reform may be able to achieve spectacular success if the conditions are precisely right. As the NSPS case shows, however, it is difficult to get the conditions right, and, if they are not right, the result is likely to be spectacular failure. In this case, the Bush administration seriously underestimated the strength and staying power of the opposition to the NSPS from the federal employee unions and their congressional allies, leading to such a failure. Unfortunately, the consequence of the failure of the NSPS was the loss of the single greatest opportunity for comprehensive defense civilian personnel reform in more than a generation.

THE ROAD FORWARD

In August 2015, Acting Under Secretary of Defense for Personnel and Readiness Brad Carson, charged by Secretary Carter with developing a new initiative to shape the "Force of the Future," proposed dramatic changes to the civilian personnel system. In language reminiscent of the NSPS, Carson's draft labeled the civil service system "a 66-year-old relic" designed to meet the needs of the "largely homogenous administrative and clerical positions at the time of its creation."[362] The draft proposed the implementation of a pay-banding system providing "additional managerial flexibility" to allow employees "more room to grow within each band."[363]

The reaction from federal employee unions was swift and definitive. The AFGE labeled the proposal "a bad flashback" and a "retread of failed policies from the Bush administration."[364] The International Federation of Professional and Technical Engineers said that the proposal "slashes workers' rights and is reminiscent of the discredited National Security Personnel System,"[365] while the United DOD Workers' Coalition compared the effort to "the illegal overreach of the failed NSPS program."[366]

Subsequent Force of the Future drafts watered down the proposal to call for a study that would focus on demonstration projects and develop best practices that could form the basis for new pilots.[367] Eventually, even this proposal was abandoned. Six years after the demise of the NSPS, the department was far from ready to start down the same path again. The "big bang" approach to civilian personnel reform had been tried and failed and would not be revisited any time soon.

Neither the repeal of the NSPS nor the rejection of a "new NSPS" meant the end of pay-for-performance in the DOD, however. The Lab Demo program, which had been exempted from the NSPS, was not affected by the repeal. The Acq Demo program, which had been absorbed by the NSPS, was reinstated as a free-standing program. The Defense Civilian Intelligence Personnel System (DCIPS), which was established in parallel with the NSPS, was allowed to continue after a brief pause.

The SES pay-for-performance system, which was similar to the NSPS in many ways, continued to operate without change. Subsequent reviews of these programs show that they provide helpful flexibilities for hiring and retention but still struggle to gain employee support.

A 2010 review of DCIPS conducted by NAPA found that senior intelligence component managers liked the DCIPS performance management system, the link of pay to performance, and the flexibility in setting pay for new hires through pay banding.[368] Employees agreed that DCIPS provided an improved link between individual performance objectives and organizational goals and priorities,[369] but were deeply skeptical of the fairness and validity of DCIPS performance ratings.[370] The perception of unfairness, the report concluded, "affects morale and severely undermines the system."[371] The panel recommended that DCIPS be continued but that the department "act with urgency to address the implementation issues that have been identified."[372]

A 2016 RAND review of the Acq Demo program concluded "that higher levels of contribution were associated with higher salaries, more rapid salary growth, more promotions, and a greater likelihood of retention."[373] However, Acq Demo employees expressed the same concerns about lack of transparency and fairness caused by the use of pay caps, business rules, and pay pools that were expressed by NSPS employees—a problem that does not appear to have improved over time.[374] As with the NSPS, Acq Demo employees and supervisors also found the performance management process to be burdensome and time consuming.[375]

Despite this mixed record, Congress and the DOD continue to view pay-for-performance systems favorably. In 2015 and 2016, Congress made the Lab Demo program permanent, extended the Acq Demo program through December 31, 2020, and authorized a new personnel Demo program for the department's cyber workforce.[376]

In addition, the DOD and Congress initiated a number of targeted but significant civilian personnel reforms within the framework of the existing civil service system. For example, Secretary Carter's FoTF initiative expanded the use of highly qualified experts (HQEs); increased the use of Science, Mathematics And Research for Transformation (SMART) scholarships for science, technology, and mathematics students; and ramped up the use of career-broadening rotational programs for DOD civilians.[377] Congress enacted legislation providing increased pay caps for critical acquisition and technology positions, direct hire authority for technical experts and financial managers, noncompetitive temporary and term appointments to meet critical hiring needs, and on-the-spot hiring of college students and recent graduates.[378]

In addition, Congress gave the department limited authority to weigh performance and market considerations in making decisions on employee pay, promotion, and retention within the existing civil service system. The FY 2016 NDAA included provisions that required the DOD to base employee separations in future RIFs primarily on performance rather than on seniority,[379] extended the probationary period for new DOD employees from one year to two years,[380] and delayed periodic step increases for any employee whose performance is rated as "unacceptable."[381] In contrast to similar provisions included in the NSPS rules, these changes were enacted and appear likely to be implemented without major controversy, perhaps because they took place within the context of a stable and predictable civil service system in which employees retained their labor relations and appeals rights.

What these changes had in common was that they were targeted changes to specific problems rather than broad efforts to change the entire system at one time. Each of the legislative changes was directed by Congress with specificity, avoiding concerns about the potential for abuse arising out of the open-ended authority of the NSPS. Each change could be considered on its own merits, avoiding the multiple points of failure risked by the "big bang" approach to reform taken in the NSPS. Also, each change could be implemented without the need to modify established labor relations and employee appeals processes and without the conflict and controversy associated with such changes.

This approach is the one that is most likely to bring about significant improvements in the defense civilian personnel system. Future reformers should recognize not only the problems with the existing system but also the things that it does well. The GS establishes a stable, predictable, widely accepted hierarchical structure that provides predictable opportunities for advancement and an assurance of fairness and equity across an exceptionally diverse workforce. The appeals and labor relations processes of the civil service system, as frustrating as they can be for managers and supervisors, provide an assurance of transparency and regularity that has gained the confidence of employees and helped keep the system remarkably free of favoritism, nepotism, and corruption for more than fifty years.

Within this framework, many additional steps could be taken to address the objectives that the NSPS sought and failed to achieve. For example, the department could seek the authority to pay signing bonuses to attract new civilian employees with critical skills, to provide targeted market supplements for specific career groups and occupations, and to pay higher salaries for top performers and individuals with critical skill sets. It could institute routine reviews to determine before the expiration of a new employee's two-year probationary period whether the employee's performance merits retention. And it could establish dedicated performance improvement managers to take the lead in counseling unproductive employees, making it possible for supervisors to take action against poor performers without sacrificing countless hours of their own time.

An incremental approach would recognize that while improvement is always possible, there is no one "right" personnel system that will fix all problems. For this reason, change would be targeted to specific parts of the system that are not working well and provide needed flexibility without tearing down structures and rules that remain useful. It would recognize the diversity of the defense civilian workforce and accept that a solution that works for scientists and engineers in a defense laboratory may not be appropriate for welders and wrench turners in an arsenal or a depot.

Finally, it would make it possible to treat employees as allies, not as enemies. Gaining the support of all employees is not possible, but reform efforts are far more likely to succeed if reformers are conscious of the interests and needs of affected constituencies and do as much as possible to understand and address them. The federal employee unions are not likely allies for federal civilian personnel reform, but, as the NSPS experience shows, excessively broad changes that unnecessarily aggravate their opposition are unlikely to pave the road to success.

A large bureaucracy like the DOD is always in need of improvement, and the department's leadership should always be striving to make the system work better, but throwing everything out and starting over again from scratch is rarely the right answer. An incremental approach to reform should make it possible to achieve measurable improvements in the defense civilian personnel system without undermining the foundations of that system and repeating the failures of the NSPS.

CHAPTER 2

LESSONS FROM THE NEVER-ENDING SEARCH FOR ACQUISITION REFORM

ON June 3, 2008, the Senate Armed Services Committee (SASC) convened a hearing on the DOD's acquisition of major weapon systems. The committee chair, Senator Carl Levin, began the hearing by declaring that acquisition cost overruns resulting from fundamental flaws in the acquisition system had reached "crisis proportions." DOD acquisition programs fail, Levin explained, "because the department continues to rely on unreasonable cost and schedule estimates, establish unrealistic performance expectations, insist on the use of immature technologies, and direct costly changes to program requirements, production quantities, and funding levels in the middle of ongoing programs."[1]

At the beginning of the next Congress, Senator Levin introduced the Weapon Systems Acquisition Reform Act of 2009 (WSARA), with Senator John McCain as an original cosponsor. WSARA was designed to put weapons acquisition "on a sound footing from the outset by addressing program shortcomings in the early phases of the acquisition process."[2] Within three months, WSARA was unanimously approved in both houses of Congress and signed into law by President Obama. "I don't think that it would be unfair to say that had the evolutionary, knowledge-based approach underpinning this bill . . . been in place just a few years ago," Senator McCain stated, "we might not be seeing a lot of the out-of-control cost growth that we have seen in some of the department's most poorly executed programs."³

The results appear to have been positive. The Government Accountability Office (GAO) reported that weapon systems programs established after the enactment of WSARA started with "higher levels of knowledge" than earlier programs.⁴ In 2017, the GAO found that these newer programs had experienced a net cost reduction of $3.5 billion from their initial estimates, in contrast to almost $500 billion in cost growth experienced by programs initiated before 2010. Cost growth even appeared to come to a standstill on older programs. The GAO reported in 2017 that only $8.6 billion of $484 billion in cost growth for the DOD's ongoing weapon systems portfolio had occurred after 2011.⁵

Despite these signs of progress, in 2014, the chair of the House Armed Services Committee (HASC), Congressman Buck McKeon, decried the futility of a seventy-year "cycle of failed acquisition reform" and assigned Vice Chair Mac Thornberry to lead a long-term effort to address the problem.⁶ Senator McCain, while acknowledging that WSARA had made some improvements, complained that "a systemic misalignment of incentives" made the existing acquisition system "unsustainable."⁷ Early the next year, McCain and Thornberry, the incoming chairs of the Senate and House armed services committees, announced that they would be taking a fresh look at acquisition reform.

With this action, the two chairs kicked off a new round in the seemingly never-ending cycle of acquisition reform efforts. Some of these acquisition reform efforts attempted to centralize control over major defense acquisition programs (MDAPs), while others sought to devolve more responsibility to the military services. Some attempted to rid the department of excess regulations, while others sought to rein in acquisition abuses with additional guidance. Some attempted to address the problematic relationship between DOD and the producers of its largest and most expensive weapon systems, while others sought increased use of commercial processes and commercial sources of supply.

This chapter focuses on efforts to address deficiencies that lead to poor outcomes in the acquisition of the major weapon systems on which the department spends tens of billions of taxpayer dollars every year. Acquisition outcomes are generally judged in terms of cost, schedule, and performance, with cost receiving the most attention because of the extraordinary investment of taxpayer dollars necessary to acquire a major weapon system. These outcomes could be considered in comparison to other weapon systems, such as predecessor or competitor systems; however, cost, schedule, and performance are judged most commonly against program baselines—the predicted performance of a particular acquisition program. The department's failure to meet a program baseline is easily understood as a broken promise, and repeated broken promises undermine public confidence in defense acquisition.

A number of common threads run through the successes and failures of forty years of acquisition reform. First, the general public is unlikely to be aware of the details of acquisition policy, but public outrage about the acquisition system is a critical precursor to change—both positive or negative. In the 1980s, members of Congress took advantage of the public reaction against spare parts scandals and procurement fraud cases to enact dozens of reform measures. In the 1990s, Vice President Al Gore capitalized on the same public disgust with the acquisition system to promote his own Reinventing Government proposals. A decade later, WSARA was enacted during a period when stories of billion-dollar overruns and contracting abuses, such as the tanker lease, had become widespread.

Second, sustained leadership is needed to make the change effective. Acquisition reform efforts are most likely to achieve full implementation when the legislative and executive branches agree on the reform agenda, work together to implement it, and provide continued leadership and senior-level focus in both branches. Resistance to change can come from entrenched contractors, program officials, acquisition bureaucracies in the Office of the Secretary of Defense (OSD) and the military services, and their supporters in Congress. Strong and continued leadership from the congressional defense committees and senior executive branch leaders is needed to overcome such an alliance.

For example, in 1986, the Packard Commission recommended that the DOD reduce its reliance on rigid military specifications and make greater use of commercial and off-the-shelf components and technologies.[8] Congress codified this preference in the Fiscal Year (FY) 1987 NDAA.[9] However, it was not until seven years later, when Secretary of Defense William Perry lent his personal leadership and issued a memorandum prohibiting the use of military specifications and standards except as "a last resort,"[10] that the department began to move in earnest to update and replace detailed design specifications with commercial standards and commercial item descriptions.

Similarly, Congress enacted statutes that addressed the use of immature technologies in major weapon systems in 2001 and 2002, but these staff-driven provisions did little to change the conduct of DOD acquisition officials. Six years later, when WSARA placed the same issue at the top of the agenda of the two armed services committees and received the endorsement of DOD senior leadership, these already-existing requirements began to have greater influence on the acquisition of major weapon systems. The enactment of legislation is only the first step in the reform process. Executive branch leadership is essential to effective implementation.

Finally, lasting change often requires overcoming built-in incentives in the acquisition system. For example, the establishment of the director of operational test and evaluation (DOT&E) in September 1983 significantly improved the objectivity and usefulness of operational testing because the newly independent DOT&E did not share in the incentives of acquisition officials to "sell" a program at any cost. By contrast, the Carlucci reforms of the early 1980s depended on the military services to implement the reforms, and 1990s acquisition reform efforts relied on the creativity of contractors and acquisition officials and ignored the incentives for them to preserve their programs. As a result, the Carlucci reforms never fully got off the ground and the 1990s acquisition reform initiatives were not implemented in a manner that was in the best interest of the government or taxpayers.

The department achieved its best acquisition outcomes after the implementation of the Packard Commission recommendations in the early 1990s and during the WSARA era of the last decade. These reform initiatives shared a clear problem definition—overly optimistic cost estimates, gold-plated requirements, and immature technologies that lead to weapon systems that take too long to develop, cost too much to buy, and fail to perform as expected—and a focused set of solutions for those problems.

By contrast, the scattershot legislative response to the spare parts scandals of the 1980s and the multiple acquisition reform initiatives of the Clinton administration were far less effective, at least as regards their effect on MDAPs. The 1980s spare parts reforms resulted in more competition for contracts of small to moderate size, temporary improvements in spare parts pricing, and improved contractor ethics. The 1990s reforms produced streamlined processes, more flexible specifications and standards, and improved access to commercial items and processes. However, the effect of these reform efforts on the acquisition of major weapon systems ranged from negligible to disastrous.

Several factors explain why some acquisition reforms yielded better results than others:

- First, one-size-fits-all solutions are unlikely to work for an acquisition process that can purchase everything from laptops to nuclear submarines. For this reason, the episodic focus of members of Congress on fixed-price contracts as a remedy for cost overruns was unrealistic, and the 1990s effort to extend commercial-type contracting practices to the acquisition of major weapon systems was strikingly unsuccessful. Fixed-price contracts and commercial-type practices are important tools in government contracting but have limited applicability to the acquisition of major weapon systems.

- Second, resources are limited, so focusing on low-priority problems or on too many problems can be counterproductive. For example, the congressional focus on spare parts pricing issues in the 1980s diverted attention from the more important issues of major weapons acquisition, while the dozens of acquisition reform initiatives in the 1990s distracted the department from the fundamentals of sound up-front MDAP decision making. Similarly, recent NDAAs containing long laundry lists of acquisition reform measures without a coherent theme may be self-defeating.

- Finally, eliminating paperwork and reducing overhead are helpful only if these actions actually lower costs. In the 1990s, the DOD cut regulations and the workforce without sufficient regard to the consequences. As a result, the department divested half of its acquisition workforce—including vital expertise in areas such as program management, systems engineering, developmental testing, quality control, and contracting—and then provided dramatically reduced guidance to the undermanned workforce that remained. The cuts saved hundreds of millions of dollars in overhead costs, but the department lost tens of billions of dollars as a result of poorly considered acquisition decisions.

Thirty years after the Packard Commission completed its final report, weapon systems still "cost too much, take too long to develop, and, by the time they are fielded, incorporate obsolete technology."[11] It would be unrealistic to expect that any new set of reforms could "fix" these problems, but there are changes that have the potential to improve outcomes and changes that can make the situation worse. Past reform efforts show that strong standards can help start new programs on a sound footing, organizational mechanisms are needed to ensure that those standards are enforced, and streamlined processes and flexible guidance can contribute to successful program execution. In any legislative or regulatory framework, favorable acquisition results depend on strong DOD leadership, sound judgement, and a trusted and experienced workforce.

THE NEED FOR ACQUISITION REFORM

The defense acquisition system is an almost unimaginably large and complex mechanism. Every year, the department spends roughly $300 billion to purchase everything from guided missiles to truck tires and from accounting services to nuclear reactors. Tens of thousands of military, civilian, and contractor employees serving hundreds of DOD organizations in every part of the world make millions of decisions that contribute to the success or failure of these purchases. Because the DOD operates with public funds, these decisions must be fair, consistent, and defensible and are frequently subject to appeal.

The acquisition of a major weapon system, with a procurement cost of at least $3 billion and a total life-cycle cost of up to $1 trillion, is particularly difficult. A major weapon system is likely to include multiple subsystems with hundreds of thousands of parts, many of which incorporate advanced technology that has never been used in an operational environment. It will almost certainly include millions of lines of software code, much of which will not be fully written and tested until the system is about to be fielded, if then. These systems are designed to ensure the superiority of US forces over a wide range of adversaries, to operate reliably under extreme conditions, and to be sustained, repaired, and upgraded over a period of decades.

The department's acquisition of major weapon systems begins with a formal requirements process to transform a military need and a set of technological concepts into a complete design for a functional and producible system. It includes a programming, budgeting, and appropriations process that takes more than two years to complete and is repeated annually. It requires a contracting process to select vendors, negotiate prices, and manage performance. It also includes processes to assess life-cycle costs and tradeoffs that lie decades into the future to ensure that the new or upgraded system is integrated into military strategy and tactics and is fully manned and supported when it becomes available.

The difficulty of accomplishing these tasks is increased by a central reality of the defense acquisition system: there is no free, competitive market for major weapon systems. Cutting-edge military systems are unique products designed from the ground up over a period of years and built in relatively small quantities for a single buyer.[12] Even as commercial technologies are increasingly incorporated into DOD systems, they must be customized at great expense to meet military needs. As a result, the DOD cannot simply select the best available product and purchase it from the private sector. Rather, it must work with private sector firms to design, develop, and produce a new weapon system.

Along the way, the department faces a dizzying array of policy issues and choices. For example:

- How can the department budget for a system that has not even been designed yet?

- How can the department ensure that the best contractor is selected and that the selection is defensible?

- When competition is not possible, how can the department determine whether the amount it is paying for a product is fair and reasonable?
- When fixed-price contracting is not appropriate, how can the department determine which contractor costs should be reimbursed?
- How can the department incentivize creativity by assigning appropriate intellectual property rights to the contractor without precluding future competition or limiting future interoperability?
- How can the department provide an appropriate level of testing to ensure successful performance of a new system without unnecessarily complicating or delaying the development of the system?

The miracle of the defense acquisition system is that it provides a framework in which these and other questions can be answered in a relatively predictable, reliable, and defensible manner. The acquisition system remains flawed and makes mistakes; however, given the number of people involved and the complexity of the problems to be solved, we should perhaps be surprised that the results are not far worse. Major fraud cases like the "Ill Wind" scandal of the late 1980s and the more recent "Fat Leonard" case have been relatively infrequent, and the dollar amounts involved have been extremely low relative to the cost of MDAPs. Reviews conducted by the Defense Contract Audit Agency and others reveal larger dollar amounts of questioned or unsupported costs, but these amounts are still a small fraction of the hundreds of billions of dollars spent annually on defense procurement. Similarly, independent bid protest reviews identify mistakes on the part of procurement officials but rarely find significant misconduct.

The defense acquisition system as we know it today took shape in the first decades of the Cold War, as the United States struggled to come to grips with large peacetime defense budgets and massive expenditures for complex weapon systems that incorporated rapidly evolving technology. This system has consistently produced the most technologically advanced weapon systems in the world. Despite occasional failures, these weapons have proven their worth on the battlefield, and, at least as important, have enabled the United States to deter potential aggression by rivals with numerically superior forces.

In some ways, the 1950s and early 1960s were a golden age for defense acquisition. Defense spending in these years averaged about 10 percent of the gross domestic product of the United States, far more than the 3.5 percent the nation spends on defense today.[13] This level of spending provided headroom with which the department could initiate many acquisition programs in a relatively short period of time, allowing for greater experimentation than today's tight budgets permit. It enabled the department to take multiple approaches to a single problem, discarding unsuccessful solutions along the way. As Thomas McNaugher describes it, the "wasteful duplication"[14] of 1950s resulted in a period that was "exceptionally creative in the annals of American military research and development."[15]

From the point of view of acquisition policy, however, this period was hardly a model of success. The 1970 Fitzhugh Commission described major problems with the technological base, the formulation of requirements, acquisition philosophy, cost estimating, testing, contracting, and program management. For example, the acquisition process included an impractical "contract definition" phase during which bidders were required to develop detailed specifications and detail maintainability, reliability, and training requirements for a system that existed only on paper. Development work would come to a virtual halt while twelve to eighteen months were spent developing and reviewing proposals, a single copy of which could weigh as much as a ton.[16]

The commission found that this process resulted in cost overruns, schedule slippages, and performance failures that "surpass significantly those which can be attributable to unavoidable causes."[17] Major acquisition programs in the 1950s were regularly marred by cost growth of 200 to 300 percent.[18] Professor Ronald Fox of the Harvard Business School reports contemporaneous testimony that in the 1960s, new weapon systems rarely met performance expectations and that about 90 percent of these systems ended up costing at least twice as much as was originally estimated.[19]

The acquisition problems of the 1950s and 1960s led to the McNamara and Packard reforms of the 1960s and 1970s that shaped much of the defense acquisition system as we know it today. In the 1960s, Secretary of Defense Robert McNamara established a new planning and programming system and centralized responsibility for acquisition execution in a single program manager for each weapon system.[20] In the 1970s, Packard established the Defense Systems Acquisition Review Council (a predecessor of the Defense Acquisition Board [DAB]) and the milestone review process for MDAPs.[21]

Acquisition results improved in the 1960s and the 1970s, but cost growth remained unacceptably high. A 1979 RAND review found that the annual rate of program cost growth dropped only from 7–8 percent per year in the 1960s to 5–6 percent per year in the 1970s.[22] In 1983, the Grace Commission reviewed program cost estimates for twenty-five major weapon systems initiated between 1971 and 1978 and determined that the total cost of the programs had grown by 323 percent from program initiation. Some of this cost growth was attributable to unanticipated inflation, but, even after removing this factor, the commission found that program cost had grown by 183 percent—almost tripling from initial estimates.[23]

One potential source of DOD acquisition problems is a top-heavy organization that encumbers decision making rather than empowering it. Senior DOD officials have complained that program managers spend as much as 80 percent of their time responding to leadership and preparing for senior reviews ("managing up") rather than overseeing contractor activities.[24] The Defense Acquisition Performance Assessment of 2006 identified "overlapping layers of reviews and reviewers at the expense of quality and focus" as a source of "multiple revisions to program documentation" that contributed little to program success.[25] In 2015, the GAO reported that program offices took an average of more than two years and 5,600 staff days to document forty-nine information requirements (some of which provided little value added) in advance of milestone reviews.[26]

Another potential cause of acquisition problems is an understaffed and undertrained acquisition workforce manned by civilians who are paid significantly less than their private-sector counterparts and by military officers who rotate through assignments every two to three years[27] and are pushed into retirement just when they reach the top of their game. In 1986, the Packard Commission found that the defense acquisition workforce is "undertrained, underpaid, and inexperienced."[28] A report of the

Business Executives for National Security two decades later concluded that "gaps in acquisition workforce skills are the proximate cause of most of the system's ills."[29] These personnel shortcomings are further exacerbated by the near-constant turnover among political appointees serving in the most senior acquisition positions.

Others contend that acquisition problems arise from excessively rigid and burdensome statutory and regulatory requirements. In 1993, Vice President Al Gore's National Performance Review pointed to "1,600 pages of the Federal Acquisition Regulation and another 2,900 pages of agency-specific supplements" that buried procurement offices "under an avalanche of regulations and thousands of overseers watching closely for violations of these rigid rules."[30] Since that time, twenty-five years of acquisition reform have only exacerbated the problem by "adding more layers of sign off, mountains of paperwork, and hundreds of additional regulations."[31]

With regard to the acquisition of major weapon systems, however, program performance has been driven first and foremost by the front-end decisions that shape an acquisition program for better or for worse. David McNicol of the Institute for Defense Analyses (IDA) reported in 2004 that cost growth in the DOD's weapon systems portfolio has largely been driven by a handful of poor-performing programs that experienced extreme cost growth.[32] McNicol found much of this cost growth attributable to unrealistic cost estimates and requirements problems.[33] More targeted studies of poor-performing programs confirm that program failures consistently result from unrealistic requirements, low-ball cost estimates, and other bad decisions made at the front end of the acquisition process.[34] A well-calculated risk has an appropriate place in a balanced investment portfolio, but when risks are piled on top of risks without careful consideration, wasteful failure is an expected outcome.

The persistence of poor front-end decision making on MDAPs appears to be the product of a counterproductive incentive structure built into the acquisition culture. As Paul Francis of the GAO explained twenty-five years ago, the primary measure of success for an MDAP—for government officials and contractors alike—is the ability to obtain and maintain funding.³⁵ Acquisition officials who engage in "undue optimism, parochialism, and other compromises of good judgment," Francis concluded, are generally acting rationally to protect their programs from the disruption, delay and cancellation that might take place if an accurate cost and performance picture were revealed.³⁶ These behaviors exist "not because they are overlooked or under-regulated, but because they enable more programs to survive and thus more needs [of contractors and acquisition officials] to be met."³⁷

1981–1982: THE CARLUCCI INITIATIVES

The election of Ronald Reagan in November 1980 marked a sea change in American politics. After almost five decades of gradually expanding government under the leadership of centrist Democrats and Republicans alike, President Reagan declared in his inaugural address that "government is not the solution to our problems; government is the problem."³⁸ President Reagan's agenda called for simultaneously cutting domestic programs to reduce the reach of the federal government and undertaking a major defense buildup to counter the growing might of the Soviet Union. The president kept his promise of defense growth, doubling the defense budget from $142 billion in fiscal year 1980 to $276 billion just five years later.³⁹

The Reagan defense build-up heightened concerns about wasteful defense spending and placed the troubled acquisition process under intense scrutiny. In early 1981, HASC created a new special panel on defense procurement procedures, chaired by Congressman Dave McCurdy, which held eighteen days of hearings and received testimony from more than ninety witnesses.⁴⁰ A GAO witness noted that the forty-seven MDAPs then in progress had an estimated cost of $316 billion, of which $171 billion—or more than half—was the result of cost growth over initial estimates.⁴¹

SASC and the Senate Governmental Affairs Committee (SGAC) soon followed with hearings of their own.⁴² Senator John Tower kicked off the SASC hearings by noting that Secretary of Defense Caspar Weinberger "need not spurn the nickname of 'Cap the Knife' when it comes to streamlining management and acquisition policy. In fact, to keep his reputation, he may have to go the extra mile."[43] Senator William Cohen observed that the department's MDAPs had experienced more than $47 billion in cost growth in the last quarter alone. "It is painful to realize that this one quarter's cost overrun effectively swallows up the domestic budget cuts we worked so long and hard to pass earlier this year."[44]

The incoming DOD leadership sought to allay concerns about the acquisition system from the outset. On March 2, 1981, Deputy Secretary of Defense Frank Carlucci directed a thirty-day assessment of the defense acquisition system "with the priority objectives of reducing cost, making the acquisition process more efficient, increasing the stability of programs, and decreasing the acquisition time of military hardware."[45] The review identified a number of systemic problems leading to cost growth in acquisition programs:

> We try to do too much at one time by looking for quantum jumps in capability, which is excessively costly;
>
> Early cost, schedule, and performance estimates are overly optimistic; . . .
>
> Too many systems compete for scarce resources—we fail to fund the higher priority systems fully;
>
> Too much paperwork and too many regulations in the process;
>
> Too many reviews of technical issues by OSD and Congress (micromanagement); [and]
>
> Instability caused by starts, stops, stretchouts, redirections and inordinately long decision times.[46]

In response to these problems, the deputy secretary initiated an acquisition improvement plan (AIP), under which acquisition costs would be driven down by reducing program risk and increasing program stability. To reduce program risk, the AIP proposed the use of evolutionary preplanned product improvements (P^3I) and the use of appropriate contract types. To increase program stability, the AIP proposed budgeting to the most likely cost, a requirement for full funding, and the increased use of multiyear contracts and economic order quantities.[47] Secretary Carlucci argued that "major emphasis must be placed on the front end of the program if we are to avoid some of the common pitfalls that have often characterized program performance in the past."[48]

Skepticism about the plan's potential was widespread. Comptroller General Charles Bowsher told the SGAC that although the GAO supported Secretary Carlucci's initiatives in principle, "it will take some time to see how they work out."[49] As the comptroller general explained, "we have all been somewhat disappointed" that previous reforms had not achieved more positive results.[50] Similarly, Representative McCurdy indicated that the Carlucci initiatives "look great on paper, but I am somewhat doubtful whether or not they will actually ... even be implemented once they get from that secretarial level down through the system."[51] DSB Chair Norman Augustine stated that "making the suggestions is the easy part. Implementing them, I would submit, is a very challenging undertaking."[52]

In fact, there was ample reason to worry about follow through, because the AIP had a major implementation problem built into its structure. At the same time that Secretary Carlucci sought to impose new policies on the department's acquisition programs, he also proposed to "move toward controlled decentralization of the acquisition process to the Services," "reduce the data and briefings required by the Services and other DOD staffs," substantially increase dollar thresholds for OSD review of major programs, and delegate acquisition responsibility "to the lowest levels of the organization."[53] This hands-off approach reflected Secretary Weinberger's preference for allowing the services to manage defense acquisition programs, with minimal direction from the OSD.[54]

Without centralized OSD control, Carlucci had few levers to ensure compliance with his new policies. Carlucci himself recognized the downside of this approach, acknowledging that delegation of additional authority to the services was likely to result in "further reduction in SecDef control over acquisition of major programs at [the] front-end" and to "restrict SecDef ability to redirect" programs initiated by the services.[55] As Fox explained, the "central problem in weapons acquisition reform during the first half of the 1980s" became a "disjunction between policy formulation in the Office of the Secretary of Defense and policy execution in the military Services."[56]

The gap between recommendation and implementation was particularly dramatic with regard to fixed-price contracts. The Carlucci memorandum recognized that the inappropriate use of fixed-price contracts could lead to "a high risk situation for the contractors and to cost overruns for DOD" and proposed to address the problem by giving program managers "the responsibility to tailor contract types to balance program needs and cost savings with realistic assessment of an acceptable balance of contractor and government risk."[57] Program managers, however, reported to the service secretaries, not the deputy secretary. Contrary to the Carlucci recommendation, the Navy dramatically *increased* the use of fixed-price development contracts in the 1980s, with predictably disastrous results. Cost overruns reached billions of dollars, and senior acquisition officials spent years trying to dig out of the resulting problems.[58]

The one area in which Carlucci was able to make progress was in the use of independent cost estimates (ICE) to improve the realism of MDAP funding decisions. DOD acquisition rules had long called for the development and consideration of ICE to ensure full funding of acquisition programs, but it was widely understood that these estimates carried little weight with the military services.[59] As the presidentially appointed Grace Commission explained, the military services were all "inclined to underestimate proposed weapons systems costs, either to make its system appear more cost-effective than proposed systems of competing services, or to be allowed to start even more weapons."[60]

Tellingly, Carlucci was able to make progress on this issue mainly because he had a lever *outside* the acquisition system that he could to use to advantage: the deputy secretary personally ran the program review process, which served as the basis for DOD funding decisions. Carlucci required an additional briefing book in the program review process, expressly addressing a range of management issues, including "Budgeting to Likely Cost."[61] The consideration of cost estimates in the funding process enabled Carlucci to revisit decisions that he had been unable to control in the acquisition process. While the military services rarely budged from their own cost estimates in the acquisition review process, Carlucci achieved more favorable results when the issue was revisited in his own program reviews.[62]

Even this achievement was turned into a black eye for the acquisition system by the department's ham-handed approach to Congress. In early 1983, Chuck Spinney, a previously obscure Pentagon analyst, prepared a briefing showing that the department had systematically underestimated the cost of major weapon systems over a period of thirty years. While this finding should not have come as a surprise to anybody who closely followed defense acquisition issues, the department initially tried to keep the report away from Congress and the public, dismissed Spinney as "a lousy systems analyst,"[63] and allowed him to brief members of Congress only after being threatened with a subpoena.[64]

The result was to inflate the importance of Spinney's work. Spinney was invited to present his entire two-hour briefing virtually without interruption in an extraordinary joint hearing before the members of the Senate Armed Services and Budget Committees.[65] This process helped turn a highly technical and largely unsurprising briefing into a flashpoint for critics of the defense acquisition system and create the impression that the department's cost estimates were getting worse, when in fact they were improving. Within a month, Spinney's picture appeared on the cover of *Time* magazine, with the caption: "U.S. Defense Spending: Are Billions Being Wasted?"[66]

Carlucci was unable to make a lasting effect with his other initiatives. The final report of Secretary Carlucci's implementation task force hammered home the near impossibility of trying to implement new policies without strong organizational mechanisms to enforce them. With regard to program stability, the report found, acquisition personnel remained skeptical that the OSD could provide "the long-term commitment of funding at levels required to achieve stability."[67] With regard to long-range planning, "lack of priority by management" resulted in major programs that continued to lack well-defined and consistent reliability, readiness and support objectives, or the resources to achieve them.[68] And with regard to P³I, the task force could not identify a single program that had considered a P³I alternative or a reduction in scope through a P³I approach.[69] The task force report concluded that "the *single largest barrier* to implementation at this juncture is the assumption that complete implementation can occur without extraordinary management action on a systematic, or systems, approach."[70]

Major defense contractors complained that the Carlucci initiatives were "still mostly top-level talk and grass-roots inaction."[71] Carlucci's staff held regular meetings to track the implementation of the AIP initiations, but the tracking effort suffered from the absence of metrics by which to measure progress, and, when Carlucci left the department at the end of 1982, the implementation meetings stopped altogether.[72] By early 1983, an influential HASC member expressed concern that the Carlucci initiatives were "gathering cobwebs and dust,"[73] and a senior DOD acquisition official was quoted as saying that "there are few demonstrable results so far. Unfortunately, the mills of the Gods grind slowly and people are doing business here the way that they are used to doing business. Rome was not built in a day."[74]

A series of three GAO reports in 1986 confirmed that the AIP had largely been abandoned without implementation. The first report found that despite the commitments made in 1981, the "DOD has not carried through with its action plans on most of the program's initiatives, and is not monitoring actions to ensure that results are being achieved."[75] The second report found that of the eight action items that formed the heart of the AIP, only the multiyear funding recommendation had been fully implemented, and concluded that DOD "no longer monitors actions taken under this initiative."[76] The final report concluded that 66 percent of industry program managers and 57 percent of government program managers believed that the AIP had made "little or no difference."[77]

The failure of the Carlucci initiatives showed that good intentions and sound policies are not enough to improve the defense acquisition system. Strong organization and management are needed to ensure that those policies are actually implemented. In July 1983, the Grace Commission noted that "one omission from the Acquisition Improvement Program is any consideration of organizational change."[78] The commission suggested that a stronger OSD hand was needed in the management of the acquisition process because "OSD's objectivity would allow the elimination of marginal programs from the DOD budget, something the services are generally not able to do because of their vested interest in their own programs."[79] The department rejected this recommendation, leaving organizational problems in the acquisition system to be addressed by future rounds of reform.

1983–1985: THE ERA OF WASTE, FRAUD, AND ABUSE
With the failure of the Carlucci initiatives, Pentagon leadership lost control of the acquisition reform narrative for almost a decade. Members of Congress, driven by stories of waste, fraud, and abuse, increasingly came to believe that the department could not reform itself and that real improvements would require legislative action. The department was left in a protective crouch, trying to at fend off unneeded, unwanted, and—in many cases—counterproductive reform proposals.

The department's public relations problems began with a drumbeat of stories detailing cost overruns and performance shortfalls on the Bradley Fighting Vehicle,[80] the Trident submarine,[81] the C-5A aircraft,[82] the Airborne Warning and Control System (AWACS) aircraft,[83] the M-1 tank,[84] the Viper anti-tank rocket,[85] the Divad air-defense system,[86] and other programs. As one article put it, "If the Edsel had been built to military specifications, it probably would be with us today; generals would be photographed with it, contractors would be promising third-generation, rocket-assisted, amphibious Edsels, and congressmen from the contractors' districts would be warning of an Edsel gap."[87]

Some critics suggested that the United States would be better off purchasing larger numbers of more rudimentary weapons because "complex technology is usually relatively ineffective" and "results in massive sacrifices in the quantity of arms to achieve what seems on the surface to be improvements in quality."[88] One article quoted Pentagon sources as saying that stealth technology would never work: "Stealth is a joke, and we all know it's a joke."[89] Dina Rasor of the Project on Military Procurement even asserted that "the more money spent, . . . the worse the equipment seems to get. . . . The only way to get procurement under control is to cut the Pentagon's money."[90]

The negative press had little immediate effect on continued funding for specific weapon systems, but it established a public perception that the acquisition system was out of control. David Stockman, the director of the Office of Management and Budget (OMB) under President Reagan, reinforced this impression when he told a journalist that the Pentagon was full of "blatant inefficiency, poor deployment of manpower, [and] contracting idiocy," and that there was "a kind of swamp of $10 to $20 to $30 billion worth of waste that can be ferreted out if you really push hard."[91]

Then, as 1982 turned into 1983, reformers struck gold with the leak of a memo identifying thirty-four spare parts at Tinker Air Force Base in Oklahoma for which prices had increased by 300 percent or more in the previous year.[92] Within a month, two House committees convened hearings on spare parts pricing.[93] Tinker Air Force Base officials insisted that the apparent price spike was the result of earlier, unrealistic cost estimates for parts that had not been procured for several years.[94] However, a number of questionable practices emerged, including the use of "price-redeterminable" contracts, which allowed contractors to raise prices after an order had been placed;[95] the fragmentation of large requirements into separate orders, which eliminated quantity discounts;[96] improper proprietary markings;[97] the failure of contractors to provide technical data as required in their contracts;[98] efforts by prime contractors to prevent their subcontractors from selling directly to the government;[99] the arbitrary assignment of overhead charges to individual parts;[100] and high "pass-through" charges for subcontractor parts on which prime contractors provided little or no value added.[101]

Additional examples of overpriced spare parts soon began to surface. Representative John Kasich reported that spare parts prices at Wright-Patterson Air Force Base had unexpectedly jumped by 40 percent in a single year. A machine screw for the Minuteman II missile, which had previously cost $1.08, now cost $36.77—an increase of 3,400 percent.[102] A review by the DOD inspector general found that the department was paying a contractor at Lemoore Naval Air Station $112 for a microcircuit that was available in the federal supply system for $2.37, $44 for a lightbulb that was available for 17 cents, and $110 for a diode that was available for 4 cents.[103] One congressman worried that these reports were "just the very tippy-tippy top of the iceberg."[104]

On July 25, 1983, Secretary Weinberger responded with a ten-point program to reform spare parts procurement. The proposed steps were vague and generic: offer incentives to employees who "pursue cost savings," take "stern disciplinary action" against employees who allow abuses to continue, "alert defense contractors to the seriousness of the problem," "refuse to pay unjustified price increases," and "take steps to obtain refunds in instances where we have been overcharged."[105] On August 29, the secretary issued a supplemental memorandum requiring more specific actions, including added resources for the review of technical data packages and the breakout of spare parts procurements, accelerated plans for computer programs to assist in spare parts pricing, employment of value engineering and contract incentives to encourage contractor cost reduction efforts, new contract evaluation factors, and expanded training for the acquisition workforce.[106]

These measures would require the investment of time, resources, and management attention. "'Reform the Pentagon' will always be a popular slogan," Deputy Secretary of Defense Paul Thayer testified, but progress would be impossible without hiring additional personnel and making up-front investments to automate antiquated business systems.[107] Within a period of a few months, the Army required each of its major procuring activities to appoint a program manager and supporting team dedicated to the spare parts breakout program,[108] the Navy established teams to reexamine contract provisions and provisioning clauses,[109] and the Air Force established a new spare parts pricing group to review prices for "the entire spectrum of spare parts pricing."[110] At the peak of the effort, the department requested and Congress approved an additional 5,800 personnel to handle the increased workload for spare parts procurement.[111]

Nonetheless, the drumbeat of negative press continued with reports of cases in which contractors billed the department $436 for a hammer,[112] $1,118 for a plastic stool cap,[113] $9,609 for a hexagonal wrench (available in hardware stores for 12 cents),[114] $7,417 for a simple three-inch steel pin,[115] $387 for a plain flat washer (available for $3.00),[116] and $221 for a pair of pliers.[117] In 1984, when the Project on Military Procurement released information showing that the Air Force was paying $7,622 for a coffee maker ("capable of making fresh coffee after everyone is dead"), the story made it not only to the *New York Times*, the *Wall Street Journal*, and the *Today Show*, but also to Johnny Carson's *Tonight Show*.[118] A year later, the cartoonist Herblock responded to reports that the department had paid $640 for a toilet seat by beginning to portray Secretary Weinberger with a toilet seat for a collar.[119]

A layman might not have any point of reference for how much a nuclear submarine or an antiaircraft system should cost, but anybody could understand that something was wrong with a $436 hammer and a $9,609 Allen wrench. It did not matter that the department could explain the pricing in many cases. The image was at least as important as the reality. As Congressman Charles Schumer explained, "What welfare mothers did for social spending in the 1970s, $6,000 coffee pots are doing for defense spending in the 1980s."[120] By early 1984, Under Secretary of Defense for Research and Engineering Richard DeLauer complained that critics of the acquisition process were "slicing us up into little bitty pieces, creating motherhood issues around all the pieces and then getting legislation passed."[121]

The credibility of the defense acquisition system was further undermined by allegations of fraud, beginning with the Trident submarine program managed by General Dynamics (GD). As the fraud investigations proceeded, Secretary Weinberger criticized GD for its "extraordinary poor performance" and said that the Trident program "has been extremely disappointing to me," while Admiral Hyman Rickover criticized the company for its "ruthless money-making schemes."[122] The image of GD—and the Pentagon—took a major hit when the general manager of the company's Electric Boat Division, Panagiotis Takis Veliotis, fled to Greece while under investigation for taking kickbacks and was sued by GD for "conspiracy to defraud the company."[123]

A few months later, it was disclosed that GD had billed the government $22 million for flights by its executives on corporate jets, including more than seventy trips by the company's chief executive officer to his farm in Georgia. Deeper investigation revealed questionable billings for meals, entertainment, and country club and resort fees.[124] GD was forced to publicly "withdraw" costs billed to the department for boarding a company executive's dog at a kennel, acknowledging at a Senate hearing that "we have a good deal of work to do . . . to make sure that things that are not allowable are not submitted."[125]

By early 1984, a GAO witness testified that "all major defense contractors routinely billed the Pentagon for entertainment, personal travel, promotional giveaways, and other questionable items," and the DOD inspector general (DOD IG) reported that 45 of the nation's 100 largest defense contractors were under criminal investigation.[126] A Pentagon spokesman told the press that the department found the contractors' conduct "nauseating," and Secretary Weinberger announced that all defense contractors would be required to certify, under penalty of perjury, that their overhead charges did not include inappropriate expenses.[127]

In this environment, the public could easily conclude that the Pentagon had lost control over the acquisition system and that aggressive legislative action was required to address the problem. At first, members of Congress struggled to overcome Pentagon objections to even minor legislative proposals. After it took two years for Congress to enact a provision extending the notification period for sole-source contracts, Senator Levin exclaimed, "My God, you would have thought we were trying to turn the Pentagon into a four-cornered building."[128]

The early 1980s saw a handful of landmark legislative proposals enacted into law after years of effort to overcome the department's objections: the Nunn-McCurdy law, which targeted weapon systems that experienced more than 25 percent cost growth;[129] the requirement for an independent inspector general;[130] the establishment an independent director of operational test and evaluation;[131] and the landmark Competition in Contracting Act.[132] These reforms continue to serve as a foundation of the department's acquisition processes to the present day.

Soon, however, DOD opposition became a badge of honor for many members of Congress. Senator David Pryor asserted that if his competition amendment was not opposed by the Pentagon, "I might worry that our proposal was not strong enough," and Senator Gary Hart announced that "anything the Pentagon can live with will not bring real reform."[133] The armed services committees hired dedicated staff to address procurement policy issues, but still found that "with everyone's limited time, attention, and understanding, we were not successful in structuring a process to allow us ... to rise above piecemeal, uncoordinated, and reactive legislating."[134]

By the mid-1980s, the floodgates opened and Congress began to enact massive packages of procurement legislation. Some of this legislation focused on contractor ethics and criminal fraud allegations, establishing new prohibitions, penalties, and enforcement mechanisms.[135] Whether because of the legislation or because of changes in contractor behavior driven by public and shareholder concerns, criminal fraud allegations against large defense contractors virtually disappeared after the Ill Wind Scandal of 1988–1989 and remain a relatively minor concern in the defense acquisition system today.

The bulk of the reform legislation, however, focused on spare parts purchases. Key provisions required the department to issue regulations to control spare parts prices, establish competition advocates, identify the actual manufacturer of spare parts, prohibit limitations on direct subcontractor sales to the government, limit prime contractor charges on "pass-through" parts, ensure purchases in economic order quantities, obtain "best customer pricing" for commercial items, limit the use of prequalification requirements, and ensure that a minimum percentage of contracts were competed.[136]

This legislation appeared to be relatively successful as long as it had the attention of members of Congress and the senior DOD leadership. Significant resources were devoted to spare parts breakout and price reasonableness reviews, competition rates increased rapidly, and abusive spare parts prices disappeared from the headlines. A 1987 GAO review of Defense Logistics Agency (DLA) spare parts purchases showed a significant increase in the level of competition; an increase in the percentage of larger, more economic purchases; an increased use of price analysis; and a trend toward lower or more stable prices.[137]

Whether the spare parts initiatives actually saved money or were an "optical illusion," with money shifted from one pocket to another, is difficult to know.[138] A 1987 GAO report dodged the issue, concluding that "we could not quantify how much the initiatives, as opposed to other factors, helped achieve these results. However, we found substantial evidence that the initiatives are being implemented, and it is likely that they have had an effect."[139] Three years later, the DOD IG reported that the department had identified hundreds of thousands of spare parts for purchase from the actual manufacturer rather than the prime contractor and expected savings in the hundreds of millions of dollars, but questioned whether the savings would actually be achieved.[140]

In any case, the changes lasted only as long as spare parts remained a top priority for Congress and the department. Without sustained management attention, the acquisition workforce reductions of the 1990s deprived the department of the resources needed to ensure spare parts breakout and competition, conduct price analysis, and otherwise challenge contractor prices.[141] By 1998, the DOD IG was again raising concerns about spare parts pricing—in one case, noting price increases of as much as 13,163 percent.[142] From 2000 to 2002, a series of GAO reports showed significant increases in spare parts prices for DLA,[143] the Navy,[144] and the Marine Corps.[145] Subsequent reports indicate that the problem of overpriced spare parts continues to this day.[146]

Perhaps more important than the limited success of legislative spare parts initiatives was the extent to which these initiatives distracted Congress and the department from the larger problems posed by MDAPs. Altogether, the massive procurement reform packages of 1984 and 1985 included only three measures that directly addressed the acquisition of major weapon systems: a weapon systems "warranty" requirement,[147] a requirement to establish competitive alternative sources on MDAPs,[148] and a requirement to track contractor costs through "work measurement programs."[149] Not one of these provisions was even modestly successful, and all were repealed within a few years.

The warranty provision suffered from conceptual and practical problems. The conceptual problem was that warranties are a risk allocation method developed in the context of arms-length consumer relationships. In a negotiated contract between the department and a sole-source contractor, the contractor is likely to insist that the department pay for any warranty, and the government will benefit only if it is better at pricing risk than the contractor. Not surprisingly, the department failed to conduct cost-effectiveness analyses before agreeing to warranty provisions and paid substantially increased contract prices without any assurance of payback.[150]

The practical problem was that the effective use of warranties required administrative systems—which the DOD did not have and seemed unable to develop—to track defects and claim remedies under warranty provisions.[151] After the GAO reported that the $270 million a year that the DOD spent on weapon systems warranties "resulted in a financial return of approximately 5 cents for every dollar spent,"[152] Congress accepted failure and repealed the provision.[153] Far from improving weapon systems acquisition, the warranty requirement cost the department more than a billion dollars over a decade, with no discernible effect on product quality.

The problem with the requirement for competitive alternative sources was that as much as Congress might have wanted to maintain multiple sources throughout the development and production of major weapon systems, the costs of doing so were often prohibitive.[154] The provision was changed from a requirement to a preference in 1992,[155] but with the end of the Cold War, even a preference was no longer realistic. In light of declining defense budgets, the Section 800 Panel explained, second-sourcing was simply "no longer a viable or affordable program,"[156] and the provision was repealed.[157]

Finally, the requirement for the department to track contractor expenditures on labor, materials, and overhead in a specific format was "a very high-cost, ineffective way to do this business."[158] Seeking to avoid expensive paperwork requirements, Congress amended the provision to ensure that the information had to be provided only "in the form and manner maintained by the contractor."[159] At this point, the Defense Contract Audit Agency pointed out that it already had a statutory right of access to contractor cost information,[160] and the provision was repealed.[161] With these repeals, the procurement reforms of 1984 and 1985 came up completely empty with regard to the acquisition of major weapon systems.[162]

If the reformers who shone a spotlight on spare parts abuses in the early 1980s thought that they would be able to mobilize support to achieve broader reform of the acquisition system, they were misguided. Not only did the spare parts reforms have a minimal effect on the statutory and regulatory framework for MDAPs, but these reforms also required the department to devote considerable energy and resources to comparatively small spare parts purchases, which distracted attention from much larger expenditures for weapon systems acquisition. The failure of the spare parts reforms of the 1980s showed that even when senior leaders in Congress and the department devote significant time and attention to acquisition reform, they have limited bandwidth. For this reason, it is not enough for an acquisition reform effort to correctly identify a set of problems and address them. To be truly successful, acquisition reform must identify and address the *most important* problems.

1986–1992: THE PACKARD COMMISSION

The flurry of legislative reform proposals enacted in 1984 and 1985 concerned many in the acquisition community who believed that congressional "micromanagement" was counterproductive and sought to regain the initiative for the executive branch. John Douglass, who then served on the National Security Council staff, summed up the executive branch view: "If we don't do something, the Hill is going to do it for us. . . . For God's sake, don't let that crowd, who are inclined to pork and special interest and are advised by a bunch of staff guys that don't understand the acquisition system at all, handle this."[163]

In March and April 1985, two senior members of Congress threw the executive branch a lifeline by proposing a presidential commission on acquisition reform to help ward off more unwanted acquisition legislation.[164] Secretary Weinberger tried to show that the department was on top of the situation and avoid an independent review by establishing a new assistant secretary of defense for acquisition and logistics,[165] but the change resulted in a battle for control between competing assistant secretaries.[166] "You have anarchy—call it something else, but it's really anarchy," Donald Hicks, the under secretary of defense for research and engineering, told the press.[167] President Reagan finally persuaded Secretary Weinberger to accept a commission by telling him that the independent review was likely to "vindicate the department's policies and management."[168]

The president's Blue Ribbon Commission on Defense Management, established on July 15, 1985, quickly became known as the Packard

Commission after former deputy secretary David Packard was brought back to Washington to lead the review. "I intend to take a pretty tough attitude on this," he told the press. "We're not going to accept all the answers we hear."[169] While Packard avoided public criticism of Secretary Weinberger, he concluded that "fundamental" change was needed to put the system on sound footing.[170]

The final report of the Packard Commission, when it came out in June 1986, had much to offer both those who believed that the acquisition system was broken and those who were concerned that Congress was making the problem worse. The headline conclusion of the report—that "deeply entrenched" problems with the defense acquisition system resulted in weapon systems that "cost too much, take too long to develop, and by the time they are fielded, incorporate obsolete technology"[171]—confirmed years of criticism from Congress and the public. At the same time, the commission complained that the proliferation of statutory directives led to an acquisition system that "has become ever more bureaucratic and encumbered by unproductive layers of management and overstaffing."[172]

The commission found that the fundamental cause of cost and performance problems on weapons programs was the flawed front end of the acquisition process, which incentivized overly optimistic cost estimates and unrealistic performance expectations by program officials who spent more time "selling" their programs than managing them.[173] As Dr. William Perry, who led the commission's Acquisition Task Force, explained to SASC, "there is a great tendency to overstate requirements," due to "a huckster environment where people are trying to sell their program[s]. It is not putting too fine a point on it to say that this does not encourage cost realism, and as a result we end up with understated costs."[174]

"More money and better engineering invested at the front end," the commission concluded, "will get more reliable and better performing weapons into the field more quickly and cheaply."[175] The department should reduce cost and risk through the extensive use of prototypes and early operational testing,[176] make early tradeoffs between quantity and quality,"[177] and promote stability through program baselining and the use of multiyear contracts.[178] This "Formula for Action" was not dissimilar to

Packard's reform package in the early 1970s or Carlucci's AIP in the early 1980s. Indeed, Packard himself told SASC that he had tried to put some of these ideas into effect himself over sixteen years before, but "bureaucracy caught up with it" and the proposed changes were abandoned.[179]

The primary difference between the Packard Commission and previous reform efforts was that the commission also recommended organizational and management changes to ensure that policy changes would actually be implemented. First and foremost, the Packard Commission recommended the establishment of a single, senior DOD official—an under secretary of defense (acquisition) (USD[A])—who would be responsible for the entire acquisition system.[180] The commission recommended giving the new USD(A) broad authority "to determine that new programs are thoroughly researched, that military requirements are verified, and that realistic cost estimates are made before the start of full-scale development,"[181] and making the USD(A) a cochair of the Joint Requirements and Management Board to ensure against gold plating in the military requirements process.[182]

The USD(A) would be reinforced by a "comparable senior position" in each of the military departments.[183] Finally, each service acquisition executive (SAE) would appoint a number of program executive officers (PEOs) to whom program managers would report, and the "Defense Acquisition Executive should insure [sic] that no additional layers are inserted into this program chain of command."[184] By implementing these recommendations, the commission believed, the department would establish a "short, unambiguous chain of command" to ensure the implementation of policy improvements.[185]

David McNicol notes that the "attitude prevalent in the DOD acquisition communities toward the policy that all major defense acquisition programs (MDAPs) should be 'realistically costed' seems to be much like those of most American drivers to speed limits."[186] McNicol said that the Packard Commission model for ensuring realistic cost estimates bears a resemblance to the system for enforcing speed limits:

- Propensity to speed—the services generally prefer at least somewhat optimistic costing of weapon system acquisition programs;

- Speed limit—DoD policy is that MDAP budgets be based on realistic estimates of cost;
- Police—the independent weapon system cost-estimating groups—detect and ticket speeders;
- Court—the DAB—tries alleged violations of the speed limit (among many other matters); and
- Judge—the Under Secretary of Defense (Acquisition, Technology, and Logistics)—resolves disputed cases.[187]

This same analogy of cops on the beat supported by courts and judges applies equally to the implementation of long-standing policies that favor better engineering at the front end of system development; the use of mature technologies; early tradeoffs between cost, schedule, and performance; and extensive use of prototypes and developmental testing. Without enforcement, these policies—because they often run counter to the interests of program advocates—had a minimal effect. The innovation of the Packard Commission was to provide a mechanism for the enforcement of acquisition policy without the takeover and centralization of the entire acquisition system.

As soon as the commission released its report, President Reagan promised to implement its recommendations—"even if they run counter to the will of the entrenched bureaucracies and special interests"[188]—and signed National Security Decision Directive (NSDD) 219, directing the development of charters for the USD(A) and the SAEs in anticipation of the enactment of legislation establishing those positions.[189] Congress also acted with record speed, slipping a provision creating the new position of USD(A) into the conference report on an unrelated bill just days after the publication of the commission's final report.[190] More complete implementing legislation followed in the next defense authorization act.[191]

The reaction from the Pentagon was less enthusiastic. Secretary Weinberger told the press that he had "no quarrel with" the commission, but did not "agree with every jot or tittle of the report."[192] Secretary of the Navy John Lehman promised to implement the Packard Commission recommendations but may have revealed his actual views when he told Congress that the "remarkable progress achieved in five years in the naval recovery program" had been possible only because of Secretary Weinberger's decision to delegate management authority for the acquisition system to the service secretaries.[193]

The first USD(A), Richard Godwin, came straight out of industry and had little understanding of the way the department functioned, which left him constantly vulnerable to being undercut.[194] Soon after Godwin had been confirmed, Secretary Weinberger decided to remain as the milestone decision authority (MDA), effectively making the USD(A) an advisor to the secretary—rather than a decision maker—on MDAPs.[195] Then, Godwin's authority was further diluted as key DOD directives were rewritten to codify the department's new organization. For example:

- The charter for the USD(A) was rewritten—over Godwin's objection—to provide that where agreement could not be reached between the USD(A) and the military services, "the matter shall be presented jointly to the Secretary/Deputy Secretary of Defense for resolution."[196]
- DOD's basic acquisition directive was rewritten—over Godwin's objection—to provide that the USD(A) was to "develop," rather than "establish" acquisition policies and practices for MDAPs.[197]
- DOD's acquisition procedures were rewritten—over Godwin's objection—to provide that the DAB, rather than advising the USD(A), would make recommendations to the secretary of defense.[198]
- The Joint Requirements Oversight Council (JROC) was created by the Joint Chiefs of Staff to defang Godwin's effort to assert control over the Joint Requirements and Management Board, as recommended by the Packard Commission.[199]

Godwin ran into a similar brick wall when he endeavored to exercise his statutory authority to "direct" the service secretaries on acquisition matters. When Godwin directed the cancellation of the Deadeye program over Secretary Lehman's objection, Lehman appealed to Deputy Secretary Taft, who sided with the secretary of the Navy.[200] Godwin complained that although the secretary often supported his recommendations, the need to get his decisions individually ratified undermined his position in the department to the extent that his job was no longer "doable."[201] He told SASC, "Yes, I have the authority to direct, or a better way to put it is, I have the authority to write a letter."[202]

Even when Godwin sought information about acquisition programs, he found the services unwilling to comply. When Godwin asked for the Navy's air plan to assist in DAB deliberations on aircraft issues, he was advised that the Navy "had looked into the matter and they did not think this was an acquisition matter, and, accordingly, it was refused."[203] When he requested that the services provide "baseline plans" for MDAPs to address the program stability recommendations of the Packard Commission, he received none.[204] When the services did give Godwin status reports on major weapon systems, he found that the reports gave no clues about to the real problems that the systems were facing.[205]

The services also resisted the Packard Commission's recommendations to modify their own internal organization. For example, the Packard Commission recommended that the service acquisition executives should be appointed in consultation with the USD(A) and should devote full time to their acquisition responsibilities.[206] Godwin was not consulted on the appointment of the SAEs, and each of the military departments initially appointed either the secretary or the deputy secretary (both of whom had substantial other responsibilities) as SAE.[207]

Similarly, the services complied with the letter but not the spirit of the commission's recommendation to establish a three-tier acquisition structure, layering the new structure on top of existing organizations and reporting requirements.[208] David Graham of IDA reported in 1988 that none of the military departments had eliminated layers of oversight, and that "existing chains of command continue to be responsible for the control of program resources, the assignment of program office staff resources, and the interpretation of instructions, directives, and regulations."[209] Packard Commissioners William Perry and James Woolsey told HASC that the commission's recommendations had been followed "in form but not in substance." As a result, "the situation may be worse today than it was two years ago when the Packard Commission was formed."[210]

In September 1987, Godwin resigned after only a year in office, telling the press that he had been thwarted by the military services.[211] Some outside observers attributed Godwin's failure to his inexperience with the Pentagon and with Washington political infighting.[212] Others recognized that the Packard reforms just did not have the support that they needed from DOD leadership.[213] The "ultimate determinant of the Acquisition Executive's influence over the Service Secretaries," HASC concluded, "is not his official precedence in the DOD hierarchy, but the support accorded him by the person who runs the entire department, the Secretary of Defense. If he has the Secretary's obvious support, his executive level is largely a formality; if he does not, his executive level is largely irrelevant."[214]

By the time that Robert Costello was confirmed to succeed Godwin as USD(A) on December 18, 1987, there was barely a year left in the administration. Costello sought no major changes in the department's acquisition directives and appears to have been content to work with the organization as it was, supporting acquisition decisions made by the military services.[215] The issues that he chose to emphasize—the defense industrial base, the acquisition workforce, and the institution of total quality management[216]—were unlikely to antagonize the powerful service secretaries, but these issues also did little to accomplish the Packard Commission's goal of ensuring a sound foundation for major weapon programs. Perhaps as a result, David Graham's 1988 review found that little progress had been made on ensuring cost-performance tradeoffs for major weapon systems, baselining had contributed little to program stability, and decisions based on overoptimistic projections continued to "bias decisions toward starting new programs rather than upgrading existing systems."[217]

In 1989, President George H. W. Bush took office and promised "to improve the defense procurement process and management of the Pentagon" in a manner "which will fully implement the Packard commission report."[218] A month later, incoming Secretary of Defense Dick Cheney promised SASC that he would "move as rapidly as possible to carry out that instruction," understanding "that we have to do a lot more than we have in the past."[219] David Berteau, then the acting assistant secretary of defense for force management, reports that Secretary Cheney made acceptance of the Packard Commission recommendations a litmus test for political appointees in the department, dismissing holdover secretaries of the military departments when they failed to show sufficient support for the new acquisition chain of command.[220]

A defense management review completed by Secretary Cheney in June 1989 concluded that the USD(A) should be responsible for "policy, administration, oversight and supervision regarding acquisition matters DOD-wide"; his authority should "extend to directing the Secretaries of the Military departments" where necessary; and he should "have the full confidence and active support of the Secretary and Deputy Secretary."[221] This message was echoed by key members of the incoming team. Donald Atwood, the nominee to be deputy secretary, told Congress that the USD(A) would be "held accountable for supervising the entire acquisition system" and "empowered to enforce compliance with Defense-wide policies."[222] John Betti, the USD(A) nominee, said that he had been personally assured by Secretary Cheney that "I have the right to direct the service Secretaries and any of the other elements of DOD in matters of acquisition," and he planned to excise that authority.[223]

When Betti followed his predecessors out the door after little more than a year in office, some commentators took it as a sign that the Pentagon was still resisting change and that the job was not doable.[224] The circumstances under which Betti departed told a different story, however. While Godwin had resigned because he could not get the authority that he thought he needed, Betti lost his job because he failed to exercise the authority that he had been given. Tasked to conduct a major aircraft review for the secretary of defense,[225] Betti had embarrassed the secretary by giving the Navy's A-12 program a clean bill of health[226] just weeks before the contractor announced that the program would miss schedule milestones, incur massive cost overruns, and fail to meet performance requirements.[227] Far from undercutting the USD(A) as Godwin's resignation had, Betti's departure sent the message that the under secretary would be responsible and accountable for managing the acquisition system.

Within months after Betti's resignation, a new version of DOD's primary acquisition directive delegated MDA authority to the USD(A) for the first time, giving the under secretary direct control over key acquisition decisions.[228] In April 1991, the new under secretary, Donald Yockey, issued a memorandum to the military services that required his approval "before taking significant steps on any of the Pentagon's 200 top weapons programs." At about the same time, he overruled a Navy decision to maintain two contractors for the Seawolf submarine program despite the reduction of purchase quantities after the end of the Cold War.[229] From the beginning of 1991 forward, the USD(A) was firmly established as the central figure in DOD acquisition.[230]

The results appear to have been positive. McNicol, in the most definitive study on MDAP costs growth to date, finds that cost growth for programs initiated from 1987 to 1993 averaged about 35 percent, considerably higher than the average 12 percent cost growth for programs initiated in the previous six-year period.[231] McNicol concluded that change in the funding climate—from the "relatively accommodating" period of the early 1980s to the "relatively constrained" period beginning in the late 1980s—had a far greater effect on cost growth in the 1980s than did any changes in acquisition policy or processes.[232]

However, the period of full Packard Commission implementation coincided with the extreme budgetary dislocation caused by the end of the Cold War, with the Berlin Wall coming down at the end of the 1989 and the Soviet Union falling apart in 1991. Although McNicol characterizes 1987–1989 and 1990–1993 as identical periods of "constrained funding," the defense budget fell by less than 4 percent in constant dollars between 1988 and 1991, compared to a precipitous 22 percent drop from 1991 to 1994.[233] Despite these cataclysmic budget changes, McNicol finds no change in the department's acquisition performance. The programs initiated before effective implementation of the Packard recommendations—in the relatively stable Cold War period from 1987 to 1989—showed an average cost growth of 34 percent, and programs initiated postimplementation—in the period of drastic post–Cold War budget reductions from 1990 to 1993—showed an average cost growth of 36 percent.[234]

Moreover, the period of full Packard Commission implementation from 1990 to 1993 resulted in significantly better acquisition outcomes than the period that followed. After 1994, the defense budget stabilized, dipping an additional 5 percent from 1995 to 1997, and then more than recovered this loss in the next three years. Yet, McNicol's data show that cost growth on acquisition programs initiated during this period of relatively stable budgets averaged 66 percent—roughly double the cost growth on programs initiated in the far more volatile post–Packard Commission period.[235] In short, while acquisition performance in the post–Packard Commission period was undoubtedly affected by the downturn in defense spending, the implementation of the Packard Commission reforms resulted in better outcomes than either the measures that preceded them or the measures that followed them.

1993–2004 REINVENTING GOVERNMENT

The Packard Commission's push for acquisition reform was not limited to recommendations for organizational change. The commission also found that although a preference for commercial item acquisition had long been embedded in federal procurement laws and regulations,[236] the defense acquisition system remained biased in favor of more costly military specifications and military-unique products.[237] In addition, the commission concluded that it would be possible to substantially reduce the number of personnel in the defense acquisition system by "reducing reporting chains, eliminating duplicative functions and excessive regulations, and establishing an environment in which program managers and their staffs can operate as centers of excellence."[238]

Congress responded by enacting a statutory preference for the use of commercial items, but little more was done to implement these Packard recommendations.[239] Through the last half of the 1980s, DOD officials complained about burdens imposed by statutory requirements, while members of Congress lambasted DOD officials for their continued reliance on detailed military specifications and expressed frustration with the department's inability or unwillingness to identify specific laws that were in need of amendment or repeal.[240]

Finally, in late 1990, Congress established the so-called Section 800 Panel, an independent advisory commission charged with making specific recommendations for streamlining and codifying the acquisition laws.[241] In January 1993, the panel submitted an eight-volume report that ran to more than 1,800 pages and included recommendations to amend or repeal nearly three hundred laws.[242] Key members of Congress directed their staffs to review the report and put together appropriate legislation, and over the next nine months, the staffs of SASC, the SGAC, and the Senate Small Business Committee met on a bipartisan basis to comb through the recommendations and decide on a course of action for each.[243] The resulting bill was introduced as the Federal Acquisition Streamlining Act (FASA) on October 16, 1993, by Senator John Glenn, then the chair of the SGAC.[244]

At the same time, newly elected president Bill Clinton assigned Vice President Al Gore to conduct a six-month National Performance Review.[245] The vice president soon identified the federal purchasing system as a focus of his effort, even appearing on the David Letterman show to ridicule procurement requirements by putting on safety goggles and smashing a glass ash tray with a hammer "on a U.S.-mandated maple plank."[246] The vice president's review put the weight of the administration behind the Section 800 Panel and FASA,[247] aligning the executive and legislative branches on a bipartisan basis behind a single approach to acquisition reform: the elimination of unnecessary bureaucracy and paperwork to enable the government to take advantage of rapidly developing commercial technologies.

FASA authorized the use of simplified procedures for purchases of less than $100,000 (the new "simplified acquisition threshold") and exempted these purchases from a raft of legal requirements, substantially reducing the manpower required to make small contract actions.[248] It established expedited contracting procedures for "micro-purchases" of $2,500 or less, enabling federal officials to make routine credit card purchases without having to go through the contracting process at all.[249] Most importantly, FASA exempted commercial item purchases from a broad array of statutory requirements that had left many commercial companies either unwilling to sell their products to the government or willing to sell only through third-party vendors, which added time and cost to the process.[250]

Government-unique laws and regulations imposed a high premium on sales to the government, Secretary of Defense William Perry explained. While many companies had been willing to accept these additional costs in the past, "as DOD's share of many contractors' sales continues to shrink, the companies are often no longer willing to accept the additional costs and production inefficiencies associated with complying with Government administrative requirements. The cost is too high in today's competitive environment."[251] FASA's commercial item exemptions swept these laws and regulations aside, giving the government new access to a broad array of commercial products and services, including cutting-edge commercial electronics technologies that have become an essential component of virtually every DOD system over the last two decades.

Secretary Perry drove the commercial items revolution into the defense acquisition system by issuing a memorandum that reversed the DOD's decades-old bias against performance specifications and nongovernment standards and authorized the use of military specifications and standards only "as a last resort, with an appropriate waiver."[252] The Perry memorandum explained that the greater use of performance and commercial specifications and standards would facilitate access to commercial state-of-the-art technology.[253] Members of Congress had made the same point for years,[254] but DOD officials resisted, expressing concern that without military specifications, "airplanes would fall out of the sky."[255] Only with the secretary's full-throated endorsement did specification reform become a practical reality.

By the late 1990s, thousands of military specifications and standards had been cancelled and replaced with commercial item descriptions or with simplified performance specifications.[256] According to one report, DOD "executed 476 contracts under the simplified commercial item procedures" in 1996. By 2011, "commercial acquisition procedures were used for almost one-fifth of all the contracting dollars DOD obligated—nearly 13 million contracts worth almost $75 billion."[257] Empirical data on savings are lacking, but it seems reasonable to conclude that the new commercial items policies "likely saved the federal government billions of dollars" by avoiding "unnecessary research and development, . . . the development of detailed design specifications, and extended acquisition lead times associated government-unique products," while achieving better access to technology than the DOD development process could ever have provided.[258]

At the same time, administration officials sought to reduce program costs on MDAPs and other traditional acquisition programs by eliminating inefficient, rule-bound procedures. In June 1993, then deputy secretary of defense Perry told HASC that he expected to achieve acquisition cost reductions of as much as 30 to 40 percent, saving "tens of billions of dollars" by streamlining the management and control of the acquisition system.[259] A study conducted by Coopers & Lybrand at Secretary Perry's request a year later concluded that the regulatory "cost premium" for ten large companies doing business with the DOD was 18 percent of the cost of work performed.[260] Coopers & Lybrand reported that half of this cost premium was the result of ten "key cost drivers."[261]

On February 9, 1994, just six days after his confirmation as secretary of defense, Perry presented a white paper that outlined his acquisition agenda. The paper called not only for the department to increase its use of commercial and dual-use technologies but also for the department to reduce acquisition costs by adopting more commercial-like processes for the acquisition of military unique systems.[262] "While each rule individually has (or had) a purpose for its adoption," Perry stated, "it often adds no value to the product itself, and when combined, contributes to an overloaded system that is often paralyzed and ineffectual, and at best cumbersome and complex."[263] He concluded that the department "must reduce the cost of the acquisition process by the elimination of activities that, although being performed by many dedicated and hardworking personnel, are not necessary or cost effective in today's environment."[264]

The *New York Times* endorsed this position and pushed it to an almost nonsensical extreme in a 1993 editorial: "Instead of designing tank parts to its own specifications, the Pentagon could purchase them just like any private company."[265] This statement raised the obvious question: which private companies were buying tank parts?

The department established teams to address key initiatives, including automated acquisition information, contract administration reform, procurement process reform, acquisition oversight and review, military specifications and standards, and electronic commerce.[266] More and more objectives were added, with the result that a later RAND review identified no fewer than sixty-three acquisition reform initiatives launched under the banner of acquisition reform in the 1990s.[267] In addition, the military services put forward their own proposals, including nineteen "lightning bolt" initiatives undertaken under the leadership of Air Force procurement official Darleen Druyun.[268]

As Eleanor Spector, the director of defense procurement in the 1990s, explained, however, "Change—even good change—when there is that much of it, is hard to absorb."[269] A study conducted by the Defense Systems Management College found that the plethora of initiatives left the workforce feeling "directionless." In the words of one program manager, "[The] top thinks they have a consolidated acquisition reform, but they don't."[270] A senior acquisition official told RAND that acquisition reform "has been good at cranking out policies, but hasn't made anything faster, better, or cheaper."[271] The RAND review concluded that fewer than half of the initiatives had resulted in changes to the DOD's directive on the acquisition of major weapon systems.[272]

There were two more serious problems with the department's approach:

- First, advocates of regulatory streamlining failed to recognize the value provided by the existing system. The GAO later noted that "Coopers and Lybrand did not attempt to assess the benefits resulting from the cost drivers it identified,"[273] and a RAND review pointed out that it made no sense to assume "that the factors affecting cost elements such as materials costs and contractor profits would remain unchanged if government regulations were eliminated."[274]

- Second, the savings available from the streamlining turned out to be far smaller than anticipated. In 1996, the GAO reported that ten contractors included in the DOD's "Reinvention Laboratory" for reducing oversight costs had achieved savings of only about $119 million, or barely 1 percent of costs.[275] A year later, the GAO found the situation essentially unchanged. The laboratory participants reported "little success in addressing 9 of the top 10 cost drivers."[276]

In 2001, RAND revisited government and industry studies that had predicted huge savings from applying commercial processes to weapons acquisition and found them to have been based largely on "expert opinion, anecdotal information, or projections derived from commercial analogies that may or may not be appropriate."[277] The RAND study concluded that savings of the magnitude predicted by Secretary Perry could only be achieved on less complex systems "characterized by low technological risk, commercial derivative items, and large production runs."[278] Regulatory cost savings on more advanced weapon systems were unlikely to be more than 3.5 percent and would achieve this level only if "virtually all burdensome regulations and oversight"[279] were removed "from all programs and by all government customers for each major government contractor or contractor facility"—an unlikely prospect that would likely have resulted in other acquisition problems.[280]

Unfortunately, Congress and the White House cut the budget without waiting for the savings to materialize. The result was a dramatic downsizing of the acquisition workforce. One of the first directives implementing the National Performance Review was a presidential memorandum that directed a reduction of 252,000 positions, or not less than 12 percent, in the federal civilian employee workforce.[281] By 2000, the administration had far exceeded this goal, reducing the workforce by 426,000, or close to 20 percent. Many of these cuts fell on the acquisition workforce. By one count, the DOD acquisition workforce alone was reduced by roughly 50 percent—from 460,000 to 230,000—during the 1990s.[282]

The bulk of the workforce reductions fell on engineers, logisticians, developmental testers, and other acquisition professionals whose work was barely affected by the streamlined procurement procedures authorized in FASA.[283] To meet goals for the reduction of this workforce, the department was required to shed entire organizations and capabilities.[284] By the end of the decade, the DOD IG found that the cuts had increased the backlog in closing out completed contracts, increased program costs from contracting out for technical support, resulted in insufficient staff to manage requirements, reduced scrutiny and timeliness in reviewing acquisition actions, and decreased opportunities to develop cost savings initiatives.[285] Later reviews found that, as a result of the cuts, contracting professionals were "understaffed, overworked, under-trained, under-supported and, most important, *under-valued*,"[286] and characterized the department's failure to adequately fund the acquisition workforce as "penny wise and pound foolish."[287]

As the department's acquisition expertise declined in the 1990s, the department fell back on the hope that new, commercial-style acquisition procedures would render rigorous government analysis of contractor cost, schedule, and performance superfluous. The department's new hands-off approach to major weapon systems found its most extreme expression in two new acquisition approaches: price-based acquisition (PBA) and total system performance responsibility (TSPR).

PBA sought to minimize paperwork by establishing contract prices on the basis of "market prices, competitive alternatives, and parametric analysis based on price, rather than cost."[288] In its most extreme form, PBA called for the use of "fixed-price, variable performance, multiphase contracts," under which the contractor would be paid a fixed price (not requiring audit), while performance requirements remained "flexible."[289] A RAND review found "little compelling quantifiable evidence" to back up claims that PBA had resulted in overhead and contract management savings,[290] that the use of PBA had encouraged greater numbers of civilian commercial firms to compete for DOD contracts,[291] or that PBA had played a major role in inducing contractors to reduce costs.[292] The report concluded that PBA "assumes a market structure and market dynamics that do not exist in the defense marketplace for truly non-civilian commercial items, particularly for sole-source defense-unique items."[293]

TSPR was an effort to reduce oversight costs by delegating system responsibility to contractors, providing them broad discretion as to how to meet program objectives with minimal oversight. Under a typical TSPR contract, the contractor was "held responsible for configuration control, materiel management, depot level maintenance, support engineering, modifications, and . . . spares management."[294] While PBA was only experimentally used for large military-unique, sole-source acquisitions,[295] TSPR spread like a weed through the department. By March 2000, the GAO reported that the Air Force alone had entered or was planning to enter into TSPR contracts for sixty-four new or modified systems.[296]

No comprehensive review of the TSPR program appears to exist, but examples of extreme program failures attributed to TSPR included the Air Force's Space-Based Infrared System[297] and Global Positioning System[298] programs, and the Army's Terminal High-Altitude Area Defense program.[299] A DSB report found that TSPR had "marginalized" DOD program managers and undermined analysis to the point that "today's government systems engineering capabilities are not adequate to support the assessment of requirements, conduct trade studies, develop architectures, define programs, oversee contractor engineering, and assess risk."[300]

A RAND review concluded that TSPR "contributed significantly to the high cost growth, particularly when combined with optimistic assessments of cost savings" from the planned use of commercial management approaches.[301] As one chastened Air Force acquisition official made clear, "If you don't do the work right upfront—for the detail and the rigor and the engineering design—and you only discover the problems at the back end of the program, that's the absolute worst time."[302]

As a result of the department's deregulatory focus, DOD contracting officials complained about not having access to "the technical details (hours to be expended, materials consumed, etc.) they needed to properly determine whether a contractor fully understood a program's scope and objectives and had estimated the appropriate effort (and therefore the appropriate cost) for achieving those objectives."[303] Others believed that contractors drove up costs through changes and sole-source sustainment contracts. One acquisition official told RAND that "the contract wanted to have everything quick, so it was vague, and we are now spending dearly for that vagueness."[304]

In 2001, the George W. Bush administration took office. Far from questioning the previous administration's assumptions, the new team insisted that the deregulation of the acquisition system had not gone far enough. On September 10, 2001, Secretary of Defense Donald Rumsfeld declared, "Our business processes and regulations seem to be engineered to prevent any mistake," and, as a result, "have become so burdensome that many businesses have simply chosen not to do business with the Department of Defense."[305] Disregarding a decade-long focus on reducing regulatory burdens and enhancing market access, the secretary established the new Senior Executive Council to "streamline the acquisition process and spur innovation in our traditional supplier base."[306]

In 2002, Deputy Secretary Paul Wolfowitz canceled an acquisition governance directive that reflected the reform initiatives of the 1990s, complaining that it was "overly prescriptive and [did] not constitute an acquisition policy environment that fosters efficiency, creativity, and innovation."[307] The department even proposed to eliminate a policy that required independent technological assessments of critical technologies before the acquisition of major weapon systems (although this decision was reversed when the armed services committees complained).[308]

The acquisition team's major innovation was an emphasis on evolutionary acquisition as a means to rapidly field new weapons systems without relying on immature technologies.[309] Unfortunately, the department proposed an evolutionary acquisition approach under which the requirements for a system would not be known at the outset of a program and would instead evolve as the system was developed. Under this construct, evolutionary acquisition apparently meant that the department would no longer seek to hold its contractors to a firm performance baseline. Any acquisition plan was "at best, speculative," Assistant Secretary of the Air Force Marv Sambur explained, so "we must be willing to accept and fund programs that are not fully defined 10 years down the road."[310]

The mantra of the new administration was "Acquisition Excellence" rather than "Acquisition Reform," but otherwise the new reform looked very much like the old reform.[311] For the first four years of the Bush administration, the department's most important acquisition decisions continued to be plagued by the same lack of discipline that characterized the late 1990s. A 2004 assessment of the decade of acquisition reform concluded that DOD and industry had "suffered from a contagious trend of unmerited optimism in defining and supporting both cost and schedule program risks, especially across the most complex programs."[312] As McNicol observed, the policy of budgeting to a realistic cost estimate "was not abandoned" during the acquisition reform period beginning in the 1990s, but it was "less rigorously enforced" than it had been in the past.[313]

In 2009, Gene Porter and his colleagues at IDA reviewed eleven programs initiated between 1995 and 2006 and found that these programs experienced "exceptionally high cost growth" because they had relied on "unproven management theories" that had little relevance to large and complex military weapon systems.[314] Several common threads ran through the programs, including a "general weakness in initial program definition and costing," "unstable and defective 'requirements' processes," overreliance on immature technologies, a "lack of robust early systems engineering," and unrealistic hopes for schedule compression and concurrency.[315] As the report demonstrated, "It is simply not possible to reliably cost a poorly defined program, and a lack of definition usually results in cost estimates on the low side, leading inevitably to cost growth when the true complexity of the program is realized."[316]

Similarly, RAND reviewed six Air Force MDAPs initiated between 1996 and 2001, that were the "'worst of the worst' in terms of high cost growth and schedule slippage,"[317] and found that they "were characterized by immature designs and technology or failure to recognize the complexity of system integration," "unstable requirements that were incomplete, unclear, or disputed," and "serious cost-estimation issues."[318] These Air Force programs, like the programs reviewed by IDA, failed because they relied on "unproven acquisition strategies" and overly optimistic cost savings estimates emerging from acquisition reform initiatives that "failed to encourage adequate Air Force oversight."[319]

Four MDAPs that cast a shadow over the acquisition system for the next decade demonstrated the excessive optimism and lack of discipline that characterized acquisition decisions reached in this period:

- **Joint Strike Fighter (JSF).** In October 2001, the department awarded a major development contract for the JSF, despite warnings about low levels of technical maturity for key technologies.[320] Development costs quickly grew by over 80 percent, and the program fell two years behind schedule.[321] Rather than reconsidering its strategy, the DOD pushed forward with a strategy of concurrent development, testing, and manufacturing activities[322] that Under Secretary of Defense Kendall later characterized as "acquisition malpractice."[323] Fifteen years later, Senator McCain characterized the JSF acquisition as "a textbook example of why this committee has placed such a high priority on reforming the broken defense acquisition system."[324]

- **Tanker lease.** In January 2002, the Air Force agreed to lease one hundred Boeing 767 tanker aircraft for six years each for an estimated $30 billion,[325] despite the fact that the Air Force's own analysis showed a lease to be more expensive than a purchase.[326] The Air Force ultimately abandoned the lease approach and saved billions of dollars by purchasing the aircraft on a competitive basis. However, this change in direction did not happen until after the secretary and his SAE resigned under a cloud;[327] the department's senior civilian acquisition official, Darleen Druyun, was convicted of a criminal conflict of interest;[328] and the DOD suspended the Air Force's decision authority for major contracts.[329]

- **Future Combat Systems (FCS).** In May 2003, the Army decided to proceed with the highly accelerated acquisition of a family of manned and unmanned ground vehicles, air vehicles, sensors, and munitions incorporating dozens of new technologies, none of which were mature, even though the "lack of system definition precluded realistic initial costing and sound systems engineering."[330] The Army's decision to use an unregulated "other transaction agreement" with a lead systems integrator assuming much of the government's oversight responsibility gave the department limited visibility into the cost and technical development of the program.[331] In 2009, when the projected costs of the FCS program had ballooned to more than $200 billion,[332] Secretary Gates cancelled the program—but only after the Army had spent $20 billion, missing out on an entire cycle of ground force modernization with virtually nothing to show for the investment.[333]

- **Littoral Combat Ship (LCS).** In May 2004, the Navy decided to start building the LCS on an extremely aggressive schedule that called for concurrent design and construction, despite the lack of program definition.[334] Just months after the contractors started work, the department updated its Naval Vessel Rules, imposing new requirements that the commercial designs could not meet.[335] As a result, the cost per vessel quadrupled[336]—a disaster that in the words of a later Navy acquisition executive, almost "broke the Navy."[337] Ten years later, Senator McCain described the LCS as "a program chosen for affordability that doubled in cost since inception and is subject to the risk of further cost growth as testing continues" and "a system designed for flexibility that cannot successfully demonstrate its most important warfighting functions."[338]

In the same period, numerous other programs received acquisition approval despite immature designs and technologies, unjustifiably low cost estimates, poorly defined requirements, and highly concurrent acquisition schedules. These included the Global Hawk program,[339] the Advanced Extremely High Frequency (AEHF) Satellite System,[340] the National Polar-Orbiting Operational Environmental Satellite System (NPOESS),[341] and the Warfighter Information Network-Tactical (WIN-T) program.[342] Over the next decade, these programs experienced unit cost growth ranging from a low of 88 percent for the WIN-T program[343] (which was subsequently cancelled without achieving its promised terrestrial networking capability) to a high of more than 150 percent for NPOESS and Global Hawk.[344]

An independent review of Air Force acquisition during this period found a "seriously flawed" requirements development process in which "technical feasibility is often overestimated, [p]erformance trades are not emphasized, . . . [technology readiness levels (TRLs) are] waived for milestone review, and milestone exit and entrance criteria are not enforced,"[345] resulting in "frequent cost-schedule performance issues" and "numerous Nunn-McCurdy breaches."[346] Another review found that Navy shipbuilding programs "often proceed to contract award with significant technical risk, unclear expectations between buyer and builder, and cost uncertainty,"[347] with the result that "the Navy has not been able to execute programs within cost and schedule estimates." A third review found that overly optimistic funding forecasts, weak baselines and analyses of alternatives (AoAs), and underestimating of risk, particularly technology risk levels, resulted in the termination of twenty-two Army MDAPs prior to completion.[348]

In June 2005, Deputy Secretary of Defense Gordon England directed a comprehensive acquisition review to address "a growing and deep concern within the Congress and within the [DOD] Leadership Team about DOD acquisition processes."[349] The report, completed early the next year, attributed the department's acquisition problems to a "Conspiracy of Hope," in which "industry is encouraged to propose unrealistic cost, optimistic performance and understate technical risk estimates during the acquisition solicitation process and the department is encouraged to accept these proposals as the foundation for program baselines." The results included "poorly defined requirements," an "absence of systems engineering thinking," "too much concurrency," TRLs that were too low, and excessive cost, schedule, and performance risk.[350]

This "Conspiracy of Hope" has been a defining feature of the defense acquisition system for decades. Unlike the Carlucci initiatives, the Packard Commission report and other previous acquisition reform initiatives, which at least attempted to control the system's tendency toward overoptimism, however, the acquisition reform initiatives of the 1990s and early 2000s embraced the hope. McNicol reports that average cost growth on MDAPs almost doubled in the Acquisition Reform period, growing from an average 36 percent from 1990 to 1993 to 66 percent from 1994 to 2000.[351] Davis and Anton, applying a different methodology, show a slightly smaller but still significant growth in contract costs, with the five-year rolling average increasing from below 6 percent per year in 1995 to more than 8.5 percent ten years later.[352]

The Acquisition Reform era brought about a dramatic and essential revolution in the acquisition of commercial items and commercial technologies. With regard to acquisition of major weapon systems, however, the experimentation can only be characterized as a failure. The department sought to empower program managers and contractors by pruning excessive layers of oversight and regulation, but this approach was unlikely to produce favorable results if the programs were unexecutable. The track record of MDAPs initiated in the Acquisition Reform period shows that faith in the creativity and good intentions of program managers and contractors was no substitute for informed analysis and sound decision making at the front end of the acquisition process.

2007–2014: THE WSARA ERA

By 2005, key members of Congress were raising concerns about systemic issues with the defense acquisition system. The new era of reform began with a series of SASC subcommittee hearings convened by Senator McCain to address troubled acquisition programs in the Army and the Air Force.[353] These hearings focused on questionable contracting approaches, such as the use of commercial processes and "other transactions" for the purchase of major weapon systems. As Senator McCain explained, "with hundreds of millions of dollars or even billions of dollars at stake, the taxpayer needs the protections built into the traditional procurement system."[354] As a result of the McCain hearings, the FCS program and the C-130J aircraft program were converted to traditional acquisition contracts.[355]

At about the same time, the GAO began to provide Congress with an annual assessment of major weapon programs collected in a single volume. The first two reports, in 2003 and 2004, caught the attention of congressional staff because these reports demonstrated that most MDAPs were experiencing significant cost overruns and schedule delays, and that few of these programs lived up to the department's own standards for technological and design maturity at program initiation.[356] The third report, in 2005, got members' attention by adding a summary showing that the acquisition unit cost of the department's largest acquisition programs had increased by an average of roughly 50 percent since the first full estimate.[357] In the previous year alone, costs had increased by almost $70 billion (14 percent), while program schedules had slipped by nine months.[358]

When Gordon England came before SASC in April 2005 for confirmation as deputy secretary of defense, the top concern of the committee was the apparent breakdown in the acquisition system. Senator Levin began by saying, "We have problems, Mr. Secretary. We need you to use your particular talent to address those problems."[359] Senator John Warner asked the nominee to make acquisition his top priority, suggesting that he go back and read the report of the Packard Commission.[360] Secretary

England promised to do so, telling members of the committee that, if confirmed, acquisition problems "will be my primary emphasis."[361] He did not wait even that long. On June 7, 2005, less than a month after assuming the role of acting deputy secretary, England directed a comprehensive review of "every aspect of acquisition, including requirements, organization, legal foundations (like Goldwater-Nichols), decision methodology, oversight, checks and balances—every aspect."[362]

Three months later, SASC convened its first full committee hearing on the acquisition process since the beginning of the Acquisition Reform era in the early 1990s. Senator Warner kicked off the hearing by noting that "despite 20 years of acquisition reform, many of the same acquisition problems identified by David Packard still exist today."[363] Senator Levin attributed the problem to "unstable budgets, immature technologies, and fluctuating requirements" and a general failure by the department to exercise discipline at the front end of the acquisition process. "The department has policies in place that are designed to address those risks," he said. "Unfortunately, the department does not appear to have complied with its own policies."[364]

Senator McCain convened an acquisition reform hearing in his own subcommittee in November 2005. Asked by Senator McCain to identify "the single most important cause of cost growth" in defense acquisition programs, each of the five expert witnesses focused on poor decision making at the front end of programs. "The consensus view," Gene Porter of IDA stated, is that the single most important cause of cost growth on MDAPs "is the premature initiation of programs before their technical risks and associated costs are adequately understood."[365] In 2006, the GAO reported that DOD programs that started with mature technologies experienced an average research and development cost growth of 4.8 percent, while programs with immature technologies grew by 34.9 percent.[366]

In response, Congress enacted a series of legislative provisions that were directed at the acquisition of major weapon systems. By far the most important of these provisions established the requirement for a "Milestone B certification," a determination that an MDAP meets technological maturity requirements and is based on reasonable cost and schedule estimates, before proceeding to full-scale development.[367] The certification would be made by the MDA—in the case of the largest and most important programs, by the under secretary of defense for acquisition, technology, and logistics (USD[AT&L]).[368] Members of Congress had expressed concern that the department was not complying with its own policies for program initiation. Now, the USD(AT&L) would be personally responsible and accountable for ensuring such compliance.

The singular focus of the Milestone B certification requirement was diluted by a flood of other acquisition provisions enacted over the next three years. A handful of key provisions limited the use of commercial procedures, "other transaction" authority, and "Lead System Integrators" on MDAPs.[369] Others addressed fixed-price contracts, multiyear contracts, interagency purchases, contracting for services, contracting for information technology, wartime contracting, the use of task and delivery orders, acquisition ethics and conflicts of interest, and domestic content requirements. In enacting this legislation, Congress apparently failed to appreciate the adage that a focus on everything can often be the same thing as a focus on nothing.

In late 2007, former assistant secretary of the navy John Young was confirmed as USD(AT&L). Young acknowledged at his nomination hearing that the department's major acquisition programs had been plagued by optimistic estimates and unrealistic requirements[370] and pointed to the new thresholds for technology readiness determinations at key milestones as a "fundamental step" to improve the acquisition process.[371] The under secretary also promised "to do a much better job of structuring programs to realistic requirements, realistic schedules, and as realistic as possible an estimate of the budget."[372]

Young's efforts appear to have made a difference: data in the DOD's 2016 annual report on defense acquisition performance revealed that the number of MDAPs experiencing extreme cost growth after Milestone B dropped precipitously beginning in 2007.[373] Nonetheless, key members of Congress remained unsatisfied, in large part because they were still seeing the results of programs that had been initiated under a less disciplined regime. In 2007, the GAO reported unit cost growth of 33 percent for the JSF program, 54 percent for the FCS program, 170 percent for the

V-22 Osprey, 134 percent for the Evolved Expendable Launch Vehicle program, and 311 percent for the SBIRS program.[374] In 2008, the GAO reported that cost overruns on the department's portfolio of MDAPs totaled $295 billion, with development costs increasing by 40 percent and production costs increasing by 26 percent.[375]

In June 2008, Senator Levin convened another SASC hearing on the defense acquisition system. Young testified that he had established new policies requiring that programs be funded to the level of an independent cost estimate and instituting "quick-look technology readiness assessments" to inform decisions about technology maturity levels.[376] Young added that he had used milestone decisions to promote risk reduction on MDAP programs and had specifically refused to grant milestone approval for programs that failed to meet technology readiness standards.[377] A GAO witness testified approvingly about these changes but indicated that it was still too early to determine what effect they would have on acquisition programs.[378]

The SASC hearing was followed by two additional highly critical reports on the DOD acquisition system. A joint Air Force–National Academy of Sciences task force found that the DOD had allowed its capacity of "domain-knowledgeable and experienced systems engineers" to deteriorate to the extent that it no longer had the capacity to perform these tasks on many programs,[379] while a DSB Task Force on Developmental Test and Evaluation found that a similar loss of expertise in service developmental test and oversight organizations.[380] These losses in technical experience and intellect, the two reports indicated, fed a lack of rigor in up-front decisions that resulted in poor program outcomes.

WSARA, introduced by Senators Levin and McCain on February 29, 2009, differed from earlier acquisition reform efforts in that it focused almost completely on a single issue: the need for the department to start major weapons programs on a sound footing.[381] As Senator Levin said in introducing the bill, "The key to successful acquisition programs is getting things right from the start."[382] Senator McCain agreed, stating that the "key to managing defense procurement programs effectively is starting them right by requiring key program reviews up front to catch costly design flaws and technology risks before we actually buy them."[383]

On March 26, 2009, the incoming nominee for the position of USD(AT&L), Ashton Carter, offered his endorsement, agreeing that "many of our acquisition problems arise out of programs that are built on unreasonable cost and schedule estimates, unrealistic performance expectations, and immature technologies" and saying that "the bill's provisions get at the heart of the matter as regards programs in their early phases."[384] Within weeks, both houses approved the bill by unanimous votes and President Obama signed it into law.[385]

WSARA, in its final form, largely retained its focus on sound decision making at the front end of the acquisition process. Section 101 of the legislation established a new, Senate-confirmed director of cost assessment and program evaluation (D/CAPE) and required D/CAPE concurrence on cost and schedule estimates before the initiation of major acquisition programs.[386] Section 102 established within USD(AT&L) two new positions (director of developmental test and evaluation and director of systems engineering) that were charged with reinvigorating the department's systems engineering and developmental testing capabilities.[387] Section 104 required independent assessments of technological maturity and integration risk before key acquisition decisions are made.[388] Section 201 required consideration of trade-offs between cost, schedule, and performance objectives at the front end of programs, in the requirements process, and in the analysis of alternatives (AoA) process.[389]

The congressional effort to ensure sound acquisition decision making was necessarily limited by the legislative toolbox itself. Congress can legislate organization and process, but it cannot ensure sound practice.[390] For example, legislation can be written to require the preparation of ICE and assessments of TRLs, but Congress cannot ensure that these estimates and assessments are sound. Similarly, legislation can be written to provide focus on systems engineering or developmental testing, but Congress cannot hire engineers or make technical decisions. As former under secretaries Jack Gansler and Paul Kaminski pointed out at the SASC hearing, "simply writing a memo, passing a law, doesn't change the system,"[391] because "people ... make the system work. I don't care how good a process you put in place, if you don't have people who are experienced and know what they're doing ... you're going to end up with problems."[392]

Carter and his deputy and successor, Frank Kendall, supported the drive for sound decisions at the front end of the process, at least in principle. "Do not kid yourself at the beginning of a program," Carter told SASC. "Do not buy in cheap. Do an independent cost estimate. Be sure you know what you are getting into."[393] Kendall endorsed David Packard's acquisition "rule" that "the initial decision to go ahead with full-scale development of a particular program is the most important decision of the program."[394] "This decision is too important to get wrong," Kendall stated.[395]

Once in office, Carter and Kendall focused their energy on their own "better buying power" (BBP) initiatives. While BBP included measures to address affordability at program initiation, it included initiatives such as prioritization of requirements through the use of "affordability caps," "should-cost" reviews to improve program performance, proper use of contract types to incentivize industry, open system architectures and other strategies to promote real competition, and the elimination of unproductive processes and bureaucracy.[396] As Carter pointed out, he was responsible not only for starting new programs out right, but also for managing the department's billions of dollars of investment in existing programs in the middle or end of their life cycles.[397]

Kendall, like his predecessors, tried to avoid any outright veto of acquisition decisions by the military services; instead, he says, he applied pressure to tailor acquisition strategies to ensure full funding and reduce program risk.[398] Perhaps as a result, acquisition officials in the military services complained that his reviews were too intrusive and burdensome.[399] From an outside perspective, this reaction is exactly what would be expected if a defense acquisition executive were to exercise the responsibility of policing new program starts and insisting on the information needed to cut through expected salesmanship from the military services and their contractors.

In 2011, the GAO's annual reports on MDAPs began to take note of changes in the department's acquisition practices. That year, the GAO found "continued improvement in the knowledge DOD officials had about programs' technologies, designs, and manufacturing processes for programs that recently progressed through key points in the acquisition process."[400]

A year later, the GAO noted that "the 16 future MDAPs we assessed intend to invest significantly more funds prior to entering system development or production than current programs,"[401] which "should reduce their technical risk."[402] In 2013, the GAO reported that "many of the programs that began in the last 5 years had mature technologies and held a preliminary design review (PDR) prior to the start of system development ... providing a better foundation to avoid future cost and schedule problems."[403] The GAO explained: "Fourteen of the 19 programs with critical technologies either mature or nearing maturity started development in the last 5 years. In contrast, all 13 programs that reported having at least one immature technology at development start began more than 5 years ago."[404]

In 2014, the GAO identified a surprising new trend. For the first time in memory, acquisition costs on many major weapons programs were going down, not up. According to the GAO, "50 of 80 programs in the portfolio decreased their total acquisition costs and the majority of the cost increases can be traced to either the effects of additional procurement quantities or inefficiencies experienced in a few programs."[405] The new trend was especially strong for programs initiated after the enactment of WSARA and the implementation of the BBP initiatives. The GAO, in its 2016 report, noted that these programs had "collectively *reduced* their total estimated acquisition costs by over $580 million since their first full estimates" (emphasis added).[406]

Three years later, the GAO's analysis showed that cost growth remained at a standstill. The GAO reported that the DOD's overall portfolio of major weapon systems had experienced cost growth totaling over $484 billion since the programs established their first full estimates, but this increase was now old news. "Notably, $476 billion of this cost growth occurred in programs 5 or more years ago. Since 2011, the portfolio's cost has only grown by $8.6 billion."[407] Moreover, average costs on newer programs continued to trend downward: while the 59 MDAPs initiated *before* 2010 had experienced a $486 billion cost increase since their original estimate, the 19 MDAPs initiated in or *after* 2010 had experienced a $3.5 billion cost *decrease*.[408]

The DOD's own data confirmed these trends. First, with regard to the overall acquisition portfolio, the department's five-year moving average of earned value data for MDAPs showed that average annual cost growth had dropped from 9 percent in 2011 to just 3 percent in 2015.[409] Second, the department reported in 2016 that no program initiated since 2007 had experienced more than marginal growth in quantity-adjusted unit procurement costs.[410] Third, with regard to programs initiated after WSARA and BBP, the DOD calculated, pursuant to a requirement in the FY 2016 NDAA establishing a penalty for cost overruns on programs initiated after the enactment of WSARA,[411] that "because of the savings we have achieved, we have built up a 'credit' of more than $25 billion in underruns across the DoD."[412]

The acquisition programs initiated after WSARA still have many years to run, however, and the full results of these programs will not be known for as much as a decade. There is always the risk that measures taken to hold down costs early in the program cycle will cause long-term costs to grow. Studies of weapon systems show that many programs continue to experience significant cost escalations well into production.[413] The department made the mistake of believing early returns in judging that the acquisition reforms of the 1990s had successfully controlled MDAP costs,[414] only to see those costs skyrocket as the effect of undisciplined program decisions came home to roost.

In addition, the more recent GAO reports indicate that the DOD may have started backsliding on the enforcement of program initiation standards. The GAO reported in 2015 that the "six programs that started system development in 2014 are at risk for adverse cost and schedule outcomes due to early knowledge deficits."[415] The GAO expressed similar concerns in 2016 and 2017, indicating that "new programs started each year fulfill only some of the best practices intended to achieve a level of knowledge that would demonstrate they are capable of meeting their performance requirements while meeting cost and schedule commitments"[416] and that "new programs continue to implement only some of the knowledge-based best practices that are necessary at program start to provide sufficient knowledge as to whether a program is capable of meeting its performance requirements while also meeting its cost and schedule commitments."[417]

Nonetheless, based on the track record to date, it is difficult to judge the track record of the WSARA and BBP reforms to have been anything less than an unparalleled success.

ASSESSMENT

Political Success

Almost every senior official in Washington supports acquisition reform, if only because nobody wants to endorse multi-billion-dollar cost overruns for weapon systems that do not work as advertised. While a change in control of the White House or Congress inevitably resets the agenda, acquisition reform has rarely been a *partisan* issue. Nonetheless, it has been a *political* issue. Recurring debates over the law, regulation, policy, and practice that govern the acquisition system have determined which reform initiatives are enacted and implemented and which ones are not. For example:

- ***The Carlucci Initiatives*** of the early 1980s increased the use of ICE on MDAPs, but only because Carlucci was able to enforce consideration of the issue in the department's program review process—a tool outside the acquisition system. The department's determination to devolve acquisition management to the military services meant that the balance of the Carlucci initiatives lacked an organizational structure to ensure their implementation. As a result, the new policies had little effect on programmatic decisions. When Carlucci left the department, the reforms essentially vanished without a trace.

- ***The Spare Parts Reforms*** of the mid-1980s were launched entirely by Congress in the face of DOD opposition. The proliferation of legislative reforms overwhelmed the department's ability to implement them. Early measures, such as CICA and the creation of the DOT&E, made a significant mark on the acquisition system, but later reforms were implemented only for as long as they remained a congressional priority. The spare parts initiatives and the few mid-1980s efforts to address the acquisition of major weapon systems were largely repealed or faded away within a few years of their enactment.

- ***The Packard Commission*** in the late 1980s came at a time when the department and the acquisition community were looking for relief from the churn of congressionally driven reforms, and Congress was receptive to a new approach. The recommendations included an organizational mechanism—the new USD(A)—to ensure that substantive reforms were actually implemented. Change was initially stymied by the resistance of the military services, but the arrival of a new secretary of defense who was committed to the reforms enabled effective implementation of the new organizational structure.

- ***The Era of Acquisition Reform*** in the 1990s was launched with the convergence of an independent review, bipartisan legislation, and an incoming administration, which sought to "reinvent government" by eliminating unneeded regulations and bureaucratic processes. This alignment led to a revolution in the acquisition of commercial items and to dramatic (but largely unsuccessful) changes in MDAP acquisition, but eventually resulted in a proliferation of initiatives that exceeded the department's capacity to implement.

- ***The WSARA-Era Reforms*** of the late 2000s were also brought about by a convergence between bipartisan legislation and the acquisition reform agenda of a new administration. They also benefited from the steady tenure of the longest-serving senior acquisition team of the last forty years. Like the Packard Commission recommendations, WSARA included organizational tools—in particular, milestone certifications—that empowered the USD(AT&L), making it possible for the department to overcome institutional resistance to new acquisition policies.

Several common strands run through this history. First, the support of the public and the acquisition community is an important catalyst for change. The general public is unlikely to be aware of the details of acquisition policy, but public outrage about acquisition abuses can be an effective catalyst for change. In the 1980s, members of Congress took advantage of the public reaction against spare parts scandals and procurement fraud cases to enact dozens of reform measures. In the 1990s, Al Gore capitalized on the same public disgust with the acquisition system to promote his own Reinventing Government proposals. A decade later, WSARA was enacted during a period when stories of billion-dollar overruns and abuses became widespread.

Second, acquisition reform efforts are most likely to achieve full implementation when the legislative and executive branches agree on the reform agenda and work together to provide continued leadership and senior-level focus in both branches. The Carlucci initiatives, which were exclusively an executive branch effort, faded away when the deputy secretary left the department. By contrast, the Packard Commission recommendations, FASA, and WSARA enjoyed the bipartisan support of Congress and a new administration that was fully committed to the reform measures. Each was fully implemented and resulted in a major change in the acquisition system, thanks to the determined leadership of several successive under secretaries.

Finally, incentives matter. No matter how sound a policy might be (e.g., the early system engineering and developmental testing, reasonable cost estimates, and mature technologies), it does not do any good if it is never implemented. As the GAO and others have pointed out, contractors, acquisition officials, and service leaders have well-established incentives to "sell" their programs with overly optimistic cost estimates and promises of revolutionary performance and to preserve those programs by withholding bad news. In the absence of a plausible approach to alter these incentives, acquisition reform initiatives can only succeed by counterbalancing and overcoming them.

A number of reform efforts have taken this approach. The independent DOT&E successfully established an independent source of performance information to counterbalance the views of service officials and others who had the incentive to sell their own programs. The Cost Analysis Improvement Group (CAIG) and later the Cost Assessment and Program Evaluation (CAPE) did the same thing with regard to cost estimates and cost information. The Packard Commission recommended the establishment of an acquisition executive who would have the power to "direct" the services to ensure that key decisions on major weapon systems were made by an official who was independent of the "selling" process. The WSARA-era reforms required milestone certifications for the same reason.

By contrast, the Carlucci reforms depended on the military services to implement them, while 1990s acquisition reform efforts relied largely on the creativity of contractors and acquisition officials instead of oversight and regulations. As a result, the Carlucci reforms never fully got off the ground, and the 1990s acquisition reform initiatives for major weapon systems were led astray by incentives that did not align with the best interest of the government and taxpayers.

Substantive Success

While there has been near unanimous agreement over the years on the need for acquisition reform, there has been much less agreement on what the content of that reform should be. Four of the five cycles of acquisition reform discussed in this chapter achieved a significant degree of implementation, but that does not mean that they all achieved positive results. On the contrary, each round of acquisition reform took a different substantive approach, which had a different effect on acquisition outcomes.

- ***The Spare Parts Reforms*** brought about increased competition that resulted in substantial savings for the taxpayer and independent testing that had a favorable effect on the performance of weapon systems. However, the large packages of mid-1980s acquisition reform legislation focused excessively on spare parts, driving a huge implementation effort with little or no enduring gain. The handful of legislative provisions that addressed MDAPs generated regulatory churn but had no discernible effect on acquisition outcomes. Each of these provisions was repealed within a few years of its enactment.

- ***The Packard Commission*** recommendations focused on the implementation of an organizational structure to enable sound acquisition decision making. These reforms resulted in more disciplined decisions on major weapon systems and better acquisition outcomes than either the measures that preceded them or those that followed. Unfortunately, the Packard-era reforms remained effective only as long as the department remained committed to them. The establishment of a defense acquisition executive with the authority to veto unwise acquisition decisions only worked for as long as the position was occupied by a leader who had the strength to say "no" and the wisdom to know when to say it.

- *The Era of Acquisition Reform* gave the department vastly improved access to technology developed in the private sector and likely saved the taxpayers billions of dollars in development costs. With regard to major weapon systems, however, the department's faith in commercial processes and the empowerment of contractors resulted in undisciplined decision making and a damaging loss of capability in the acquisition workforce. Program after program was approved with overly optimistic cost estimates, unrealistic performance expectations, and immature technologies, with predictable results in the form of multibillion-dollar cost overruns and lengthy schedule delays.

- *The WSARA-Era Reforms* improved decision making at the front end of the acquisition process by requiring higher degrees of technological maturity and more reliance on ICE than in earlier periods. These initiatives may have enhanced the reach of an already bureaucratic OSD acquisition organization, but they also brought about a reversal in the cost growth that has plagued major weapons programs for the past four decades. It is still too early to reach a final verdict on post-WSARA programs because most of these programs are still under way, and there is always the risk that latent problems or changes in leadership may cause long-term costs to grow.

Again, several lessons emerge from this history. First, one-size-fits-all solutions do not work well in the acquisition system. The 1990s reforms brought about streamlined processes for acquiring commercial items and dual-use technologies that revolutionized the defense acquisition system, but efforts to apply similar processes to the acquisition of major weapon systems proved to be a disaster. Similarly, 1980s-era provisions that mandated the use of competitive alternative sources did not work for many programs because the DOD simply could not afford the necessary investment. A department that buys everything from laptops to nuclear submarines must recognize that the same processes and the same reforms are unlikely to apply to both.

Second, the objectives of reform are not always consistent with each other. For example, reduced regulation and streamlined processes can be worthwhile to the extent that they enable sound business judgement and expedite desirable programs, but these measures become counterproductive when they undermine discipline in the acquisition process and result in poor program performance. Similarly, a reduction in the size of the acquisition workforce can lower overhead costs but may hurt more than it helps, such as in the late 1990s when it deprived the department of the capacity to perform essential acquisition functions. Successful acquisition reform initiatives must balance multiple, competing objectives rather than focusing on just one objective.

Third, the bandwidth of the acquisition community is limited, so prioritization is vital. In the 1980s, dozens of disparate legislative provisions pointed the acquisition system in many different directions, which required added resources to implement and produced limited results. In the 1990s, a plethora of acquisition reform initiatives from within the department overwhelmed the absorption capacity of the acquisition system. Recently enacted NDAAs risk the same problem, with too many initiatives chasing too few implementation resources—particularly in light of congressionally imposed requirements for headquarters reductions.

The most successful reforms have been those that identified a critical subset of the problems facing the acquisition system and developed a focused set of solutions for those problems. The Packard Commission reforms and the WSARA-era reforms identified poor front-end decision making—which resulted from the incentives of participants in the acquisition process to "sell" their programs—as the source of the most significant (and most costly) problems in the acquisition of major weapon systems.

Each of these efforts developed a focused solution to the problem. For the Packard Commission, the solution was the establishment of the USD(A) as an independent reviewing authority. For WSARA, the solution was the institution of milestone certification requirements to provide concrete standards for the USD(AT&L)'s review. Other parts of the

Packard and WSARA packages complemented these changes rather than competing with them. It is probably not a coincidence that the two most focused and coherent sets of reforms implemented in the past forty years were also the most successful.

THE ROAD FORWARD

In 2015, new chairs—Senator John McCain and Representative Mac Thornberry—ascended to the leadership of SASC and HASC. They set out to make their mark on the defense agenda, including acquisition reform, in ways that reflected their very different personalities.

HASC Chair Mac Thornberry was deliberative almost to a fault. He had been designated by his predecessor to lead an acquisition reform effort in the House in late 2013, more than a year before he became chair.[418] Over the next three years, he led at least six full committee acquisition reform hearings, consulting with a broad range of DOD officials and outside experts and examining specific case studies to highlight the strengths and the weaknesses of the acquisition process.[419] Thornberry generally deferred his own questions until all other members had a chance to complete theirs,[420] and published his proposals early in the year to ensure an opportunity for others to express concerns.[421]

HASC took more than a year to put together the Acquisition Agility Act, which addressed requirements for a modular, open system approach; rules for technology development and prototyping; consideration of program cost, schedule, and performance goals; transparency of data and metrics; and rights in technical data on MDAPs.[422] These provisions were consistent with best practices developed over a period of years, had largely been worked out in advance with the department, and were adopted with minimal change in the final conference report on the bill.[423] The major question that the HASC provisions raised was the same question faced by previous legislative pronouncements on acquisition policy: To what extent would they be implemented in practice?

By contrast, Senator McCain was known for the restless energy that had long made him an engine of reform in the Senate. A *Washington Post* columnist described the new SASC chair as a "man in a hurry":

McCain agrees that he is a man in a hurry. "Big hurry, a big hurry—really big," he told me in his office Tuesday afternoon. "I'm not only making up for lost time," he said, but "I feel in a way this could be a two-year sprint because we know what the numbers are the next time around in the Senate and I also am up for reelection, and don't think the tea party doesn't view me as their number-one target." . . . "Every day that goes by," he said, "you're never going to be able to do over again."[424]

Senator McCain pushed hard for previous rounds of acquisition reform, including not only WSARA but also the preference for fixed-price contracts, restrictions on the use of multiyear contracts, and prohibitions on the use of lead system integrators and other transactions authority for the acquisition of major weapon systems. Despite the enactment of this legislation, he remained convinced that the acquisition system remained broken and that dramatic action was needed to fix it.

In 2014, Senators Levin and McCain sent out letters to thirty-one acquisition experts seeking their views on deficiencies and needed reforms in the acquisition process.[425] A few of the experts asserted that the defense acquisition system "does not work and cannot be repaired."[426] Others asserted that significant progress was being made as a result of WSARA and BBP and maintained that the existing system was "successful by many measures."[427] Some called for more audits and testing,[428] while others wanted less.[429] Some called for increased competition,[430] while others warned of cases in which competition would not work.[431] Some wanted the military chiefs in the acquisition chain of command,[432] while others opposed the idea.[433] Some called for greater reliance on commercial processes in the acquisition of major systems,[434] while others warned against it.[435]

Despite the lack of consensus, and without even holding hearings, Senator McCain moved forward and pushed his committee to produce what he called "the most sweeping acquisition reforms in a generation."[436] The McCain legislation centered on three provisions that threatened to uproot the defense acquisition organization and, with it, the established acquisition process. The first provision codified a statutory role for the service chiefs in milestone decisions on MDAPs;[437] the second provision provided that the SAEs, not USD(AT&L), would serve as the MDA for MDAPs;[438] and the third provision divided USD(AT&L) into two separate offices, one responsible for research and engineering and the other responsible for acquisition and support.[439]

The delegation of authority to the military departments, and to the chiefs, was driven by a real concern about the bureaucracy and sluggishness of the defense acquisition system. Army Acquisition Executive Heidi Shyu reflected a widely held view in the acquisition community when she told SASC in 2015 that "defense acquisition is a highly risk-averse, compliance-based process with a checklist mentality that has become unduly cumbersome."[440] Ms. Shyu testified that everybody on "the acquisition bus"—including "all of the stakeholders within the Army, as well as OSD and CAPE and Comptroller and Congress"—"has a separate steering wheel and a brake." When a program gets in trouble, instead of trying to help, "they will shoot out the windows, the tires, and the kneecap of the bus driver."[441]

An independent review by the GAO found that MDAPs required an average of over two years and 5,600 staff days to complete the steps necessary to document up to forty-nine information requirements for the milestone decision process.[442] The GAO identified eight different levels and fifty-six different organizations that can review the information and documentation necessary to support a milestone decision.[443] "Empower the PEOs, empower the Heidi Shyus of the world, empower the service chiefs," Army Chief of Staff Mark Milley was quoted as saying in 2015. "Cut us loose and see what happens. If we fail, fire us."[444]

However, the change comes with a huge risk. The delegation of power effectively cuts the heart out of the Packard Commission reforms by removing from the acquisition decision-making process the independent authority established as a check on the incentive of the services to "sell" their programs with unrealistic promises of cost, schedule, and performance estimates. The periods in which OSD oversight has been the most lax have also been the periods in which poor program decisions have led to the most dramatic growth in costs. The department's experience with 1990s acquisition reform demonstrates that savings achieved by streamlining processes, while desirable, can rapidly be overwhelmed by the added cost of even a handful of poorly considered programs that are initiated without proper review and oversight.

The tradeoff of reduced oversight in exchange for reduced overhead might be worthwhile if, as Senator McCain believed, the existing system were producing unacceptable results, with huge cost overruns "par for the course."[445] However, the programs that Senator McCain cited to make his case—FCS, the Expeditionary Combat Support System, the Expeditionary Fighting Vehicle, and the presidential helicopter[446]—were initiated before the enactment of WSARA and the BBP initiative. Programs initiated since that time have been established on a sounder footing and have had a far better track record.

The decision to split the USD(AT&L) in two was driven by Senator McCain's concern that the department was not responding fast enough to investments by potential adversaries in potentially disruptive technologies. McCain told the Chamber of Commerce in 2015 that "in the face of these trends, . . . our Defense department has grown larger but less capable, more complex but less innovative, more proficient at defeating low-tech adversaries but more vulnerable to high-tech ones."[447] In the view of Bill Greenwalt, the acquisition policy expert on McCain's committee staff, the existing acquisition structure was built to optimize cost, schedule, and performance over a fifteen- to twenty-year acquisition cycle but stifles innovative efforts to field new technologies on a more rapid, iterative basis.[448]

The risk in this legislation is that the creation of two under secretaries will increase bureaucracy rather than reducing it and that both under secretaries will be impotent rather than empowered. It has been difficult enough for a single acquisition executive with directive authority to lead change in the acquisition system. Two under secretaries with divided authority may find it impossible to do so. Moreover, the shortfall in defense innovation is not a problem of organization and process, it is a problem of resource allocation. If the department is spending too much money on legacy weapon systems and too-big-to-fail successors to those systems, the answer is not to buy the same things with different organizations and processes—it is to buy different things.

Past reform efforts show that successful acquisition outcomes are most likely within an organizational framework that includes mechanisms to overcome (or at least counterbalance) incentives to "sell" acquisition programs with unrealistic cost, schedule, and performance expectations. Well-intended policies will not ensure that programs are started on a sound footing unless these policies are actually implemented, and implementation requires empowered leadership. Streamlined processes and reduced bureaucracy are desirable, but only if these approaches can be achieved without sacrificing program performance. Similarly, an appropriately sized, trained, and qualified acquisition workforce can help achieve desirable program outcomes only if the programs are properly designed and executable.

The most effective step to reduce the risk of returning to the dramatic cost growth experienced by MDAPs initiated in the 1990s and early 2000s would be to reinstitute an OSD gate-keeping process, while ensuring that it focuses exclusively on the key front-end affordability and risk decisions that drive program cost and performance, rather than second-guessing program details. Over a longer period of time, it may also be possible to build an alternative buttress against poor front-end program decisions by building a set of longer-tenured and more professional PEOs and program managers who can stand up to the pressure to promise more than they can perform.

In the absence of such dramatic measures, DOD leaders could take a number of steps to reduce the risk of poor program decisions that lead to extreme cost growth arising from the lack of a "cop on the beat" by providing levers for independent judgment and sound decision making within the new organizational framework. For example, the DOD could authorize the under secretary to participate in the MDAP milestone briefings and integrated product team meetings of the military services, and to field best practices teams to provide substantive expertise and support to program offices during the development of acquisition strategies and risk reduction plans. Similarly, the department could give the new under secretary of defense for research and engineering authority to co-chair the JROC and lead AoAs for MDAPs.

Such steps could help establish a framework that makes sound decisions more likely and reduce, but not eliminate, the risks created by reversing the Packard Commission reforms and undermining the independent authority established as a check on the incentive of the services to "sell" their programs. We should probably not expect more than that until Congress and the department, inevitably, launch yet another new round of reform.

CHAPTER 3

AUDITING THE PENTAGON

ON February 18, 1987, Comptroller General Charles Bowsher appeared before the Senate Governmental Affairs Committee (SGAC) to testify about waste, fraud, and abuse in the federal government. The heart of the problem, he testified, was the dysfunctional state of federal financial systems, which rendered them incapable of accounting for the expenditure of funds. While there had been "some computerization," Bowsher testified, the government still lacked "a modern system" to process budgets and show how the money is actually spent.[1] The comptroller general proposed a solution for the problem: "You have to have audited financial statements to achieve discipline and accountability."[2]

In a lengthy two-volume report entitled *Managing the Cost of Government, Building an Effective Financial Management Structure*, the General Accounting Office (GAO) laid out the comptroller general's case.[3] The GAO argued that improved accounting systems, capped by audited financial statements, would enable the government to compare planned and actual costs, provide reliable project status reports to senior officials, establish user fees covering the full cost of services, compare the costs of similar operations across the government, provide more accurate budget estimates, measure the input of cost and the output of performance, and increase accountability for the management of federal funds.[4]

Three years later, Congress enacted the Chief Financial Officers Act of 1990 (CFO Act),[5] requiring the preparation of financial statements for all agency programs that were substantially commercial in nature and establishing a pilot program for the preparation of full financial statements by a number of federal agencies, including the Department of the Army and the Department of the Air Force. The Government Management Reform Act of 1994 imposed a more comprehensive goal, requiring that all federal agencies prepare and submit audited financial statements to the Office of Management and Budget (OMB) not later than March 1, 1997, and every year thereafter.[6]

Over the following decades, the DOD invested hundreds of millions of dollars in planning activities, billions of dollars in efforts to compile and reconcile financial data, and tens of billions of dollars in new financial systems. Legislation was enacted, plans developed, organizations created, training conducted, systems built, management consultants hired, and audits conducted. The DOD tried a piecemeal approach of working to address material weaknesses one at a time. It tried a grand design approach of envisioning a perfect system and trying to build it. It tried an architectural approach of mapping existing business processes into future systems. It tried an investment-oriented approach, with review boards and approval processes. It tried creating new offices, agencies, cross-functional teams, councils, and committees. It tried auditing its way to auditability by using financial statement audits to identify deficiencies to be remedied. None of these approaches worked.

By 2015, twenty-one out of twenty-four federal agencies were regularly receiving clean audit opinions on their financial statements, but the DOD was not one of them. In fact, the DOD inspector general (IG) identified "pervasive and long-standing material weaknesses, which caused those financial statements to be unauditable."[7] When the department nonetheless deployed a force of 1,200 auditors and spent almost a billion dollars in an effort to complete a full financial audit in 2018, the results were predictable.[8] The Army, Navy, Air Force, and almost all defense agencies received disclaimers, meaning that the accountants could not find sufficient accurate information to express an audit opinion. Deputy

Secretary of Defense Patrick Shanahan dismissed the failure, telling the press, "We never thought we were going to pass an audit, right? Everyone was betting against us, that we wouldn't even do the audit."[9]

This chapter will trace two cycles of the department's failed effort to achieve auditability: the first in the 1990s and the second in the 2000s. In each cycle, the department tried three separate approaches: a grand strategy, a set of partial solutions, and an effort to audit its way to auditability. In each case, the grand strategies proved too ambitious and produced few positive results, while the effort to audit for auditability identified major problems but too few solutions. Most of the department's limited successes have been the result of the partial solutions approach, accomplished by leaving the responsibility in the hands of the components and functional owners and accepting improved systems and processes that were less than perfect for financial management purposes.

A number of substantive lessons can be learned from this record of failure:

- First, successful DOD reform efforts generally focus on a clearly defined problem and a targeted set of solutions for that problem. The department's lack of an auditable financial statement is not a single problem. It is the product of a series of linked problems with deficient systems, poor controls, dysfunctional processes, misaligned objectives, and stovepiped organizations, each of which must be addressed individually. Together, this accumulation of thousands of small problems is so pervasive in the department that these problems are not susceptible to being solved by management fiat or indeed by any set of steps that could be taken by a single administration.

- Second, trying to solve all these linked problems at the same time is a recipe for failure. The Corporate Information Management (CIM) program of the 1990s began with the ambition of designing new business systems from the ground up to implement a comprehensive vision of the information needed to run the department. The Business Enterprise Architecture (BEA) of the 2000s envisioned a comprehensive financial management blueprint that would map existing business processes into an ideal "to be" system. Both initiatives proved beyond the capacity of the department, producing few concrete results despite the expenditure of hundreds of millions of dollars.

- Third, because so many problems need to be addressed, a failure to prioritize can be fatal. In the 1980s, the department sought to identify and address hundreds of weaknesses in its internal accounting and administrative controls, but its efforts were spread so thin that they resulted in no discernible progress toward an effective, modern financial system. More recently, the department has used financial statement audits in an effort to identify deficiencies that need to be corrected, but the audits found such pervasive problems that they provided little help for prioritization.

Important political lessons can also be learned from the department's audit experience:

- First, the problem has not been lack of effort, so proposals to make the department "try harder" by imposing legislative penalties for failure to reach audit goals or establishing incentives for success are unlikely to make much of a difference. Across the last four decades, the department has assigned a series of capable, intelligent civilian and military leaders who have worked hard to achieve auditability goals. Still, the effort to achieve an auditable financial statement has dragged on for decades, with no successful ending in sight. The department's financial systems and processes have taken decades to build and will take decades to fix.

- Second, top-down approaches that fail to address the needs of the department's components and functional communities have not worked. Senior leaders who have the scope of authority to lead change across the organizational and functional divides of the department have lacked the bandwidth and expertise to address complex issues of business processes, system design, and data alignment. As a result, they have been unable to overcome the fragmentation of authority, direction, and control over DOD business processes among multiple functional communities and organizational layers with their own unique data and performance needs.

- Third, new organizational structures have proven largely ineffective because, regardless of any legal authority that may have been delegated, they have not actually owned the systems and processes that they wanted to change. The Defense Business Operations Fund (DBOF) and Senior Financial Management Oversight Council (SFMOC) of the 1990s and the Business Transformation Agency (BTA), Deputy Chief Management Officer (DCMO), and Defense Business Systems Management Committee (DBSMC) of the 2000s all fell short of expectations because the services retained control over their own business processes and insisted on retaining unique data requirements.

Not only does the department's objective of an auditable financial statement require addressing an impossibly broad array of systems, process, and data problems, it may also be the wrong objective. The purpose of audited financial statements in the private sector is to demonstrate the value of a business to outside investors and creditors—an objective that is largely irrelevant for a government agency.[10] Financial statement accounting is inherently "backward-looking, based on historical accounting data and designed to provide a broad assessment of organizational performance" rather than a forward-looking approach to provide decision support.[11] The DOD does not have investors, and its objective is not to maximize the value of its assets but rather to defend the United States and protect its interests around the world. It may be possible to assign an accrual-based cost to trained military units and the equipment that they use, but no sale price exists to which this cost can be readily compared.[12]

Perhaps for these reasons, DOD managers generally see little value in financial statements. The department's senior leaders, budgeters, and program managers use data from the budget systems that control their available resources. However, it appears that nobody at the DOD uses data from financial statements for management purposes.[13] As Harvard Business School professor and former DOD comptroller Robert Anthony explained in a 1996 article, "In some 40 years of service as a government official and a consultant on government accounting matters, I have never used financial information prepared in accordance with

[GAO accounting standards], nor can I recall discussions with government managers that referred to such information."[14]

The GAO has responded to concerns about the utility of financial statements by arguing that these statements are a critical measure of the health of an agency's financial systems.[15] This assertion is true to a point. Auditable financial statements are an objective that is readily understood by members of Congress and senior DOD leaders, who know that such statements are regularly produced by private sector companies, by state and local governments, and now by most federal agencies. The pressure to produce auditable financial statements in accordance with the CFO Act has been an important catalyst for financial reform and has helped to drive investments in upgraded finance and accounting systems during the last five administrations.

Even so, a misaligned objective risks wasting resources by prioritizing the wrong tasks. Efforts to assess the depreciated value of military assets, predict future environmental liabilities, follow audit trails of years-old financial transactions, and track down inventories of contractor-held property serve little practical purpose. The time and effort that the DOD has spent on shortsighted efforts to audit unsupportable financial statements and reconcile documentation for individual transactions would almost certainly have been better spent to fix the department's underlying systems and processes. As a former director of the Army Office of Business Transformation has pointed out, "the Pentagon could buy literally thousands of $1,280 coffee cups and millions of gallons of $26 fuel, and—as long as these transactions were faithfully reported on the financial statements—it would 'pass' [an audit] . . . with flying colors."[16]

In some cases, single-minded pursuit of the auditability objective may even risk compromising program performance. The auditability objective requires simple, streamlined systems with as few data elements as possible to produce the audit trails needed to support financial statements. By contrast, DOD business managers often seek to maintain uniquely tailored data sets with complex measures and categories that enable them to monitor their programs and organizations more effectively. While the functional communities' resistance to streamlined business systems and processes has often been characterized as irrational, an accounting-driven business process reengineering is not helpful if it undermines the organization's ability to meet its business needs.

Despite this litany of obstacles, the department's financial systems and processes are better today than they were when the CFO Act was enacted in 1990. The DOD has consolidated its finance and accounting operations in the Defense Finance and Accounting Service (DFAS) and saved billions of dollars by eliminating unneeded finance and accounting centers. The military services and defense agencies have implemented modern enterprise resource planning (ERP) systems, which have improved the flow of financial data and enabled the department to eliminate hundreds of obsolete and redundant systems. The department has fielded new logistics systems that provide near-complete asset visibility, new contracting systems that enable electronic data interchange, and new personnel and pay systems that have dramatically reduced the problem of soldiers getting the wrong paychecks.

The department does not just have an accounting and auditing problem. It also has a data problem. It still lacks consistent data elements and data definitions that would enable it to accurately compile data across the department and compare costs across different programs and organizations. It still lacks consistent accounting approaches that would enable it to assign full costs to these programs and organizations and to set accurate prices for reimbursable activities. Critical information on program performance is still hoarded in one-off local systems that do not feed into the department's official records. As a result, time-consuming data calls and independent studies are still required to produce basic information that should be readily available to senior decision makers faced with important management decisions.

DOD systems, processes, and controls remain deeply flawed, and, until this problem is addressed, the department will have difficulty producing timely, relevant, and accurate information to support management decisions. Former deputy secretary of defense John Hamre once compared addressing the department's financial management problems to changing the tires on a car while going sixty miles an hour because funds need to continue to flow even as the system is changed.[17] However, given the breadth and depth of the DOD's problems, the effort may be more akin to rebuilding the vehicle's engine without slowing down. The key to success is to break down the financial management puzzle into manageable pieces with clear objectives, rather than trying to solve the whole puzzle at once.

THE ROAD TO THE CFO ACT AND THE GOAL OF A CLEAN AUDIT

No organization as large and complex as the DOD has ever been successfully audited. The DOD has an annual budget of roughly $600 billion a year, accounting for about half of all federal discretionary spending.[18] Its assets have an estimated value of $2 trillion[19]—an amount roughly equal to the combined value of Apple, AT&T, ExxonMobil, General Electric, Walmart, Verizon, and Microsoft.[20] Every year, the department processes roughly 12 million commercial invoices and 200 million pay transactions for military and civilian employees.[21]

These simple statistics, however, do not begin to convey the complexity of the department's operations. The DOD not only runs the most powerful military and the largest acquisition system in the world but it also owns and operates extensive systems of depots, arsenals, and warehouses; worldwide transportation and communication networks; multiple hospital and school systems; and several chains of grocery stores, department stores, and restaurants. The department even runs its own law enforcement system and judiciary systems. In many ways, the DOD is more comparable to an economy than to a company.

The DOD's early computer systems were not intended to produce coherent financial records; rather, they were developed to serve the business needs of users in stovepiped functional communities.[22] Over a period of decades, hundreds of individual projects were undertaken in DOD components "without consistent, central guidance or scrutiny"[23] and without any effort to comply with established reporting standards and requirements. One long-time DOD financial manager described the "shirt-pocket" automated information systems developed by early managers, noting that what was rolled up into accounting reports "was not accurate information from the manager of the funds, but selected values manually transcribed from the many listings."[24] Not surprisingly, he reported, "The differences in update timing and multiple sources of input assured full employment for hordes of accountants trying to reconcile multiple reports of allotments, commitments, obligations, receipts and disbursements all independently reported and processed through separate systems."[25]

The department's financial operations are complicated by the intricate business relationships between its component pieces, in which money flows vertically and horizontally from organization to organization. In some cases, one component makes purchases under the contracts of another component (e.g., when an Army command places an order under a Navy contract). In some cases, funds are transferred from one component to another (e.g., when DOD components are "taxed" to support the Defense Acquisition Workforce Development Fund, which is then used to support transfers back to the military services and defense agencies to hire and train personnel). In yet other cases, funds appropriated to one component are "suballocated" or "suballotted" to another component (e.g., when funds appropriated to the COCOM Exercise Engagement and Training Transformation account are transferred to the combatant commands to fund training exercises).

In addition, DOD organizations engage in commercial transactions with each other, with one component selling a product or service to another, making the department both the buyer and the seller. For example, the Defense Logistics Agency (DLA) purchases spare parts in anticipation of future aircraft repair needs. Over a period of months or years, the DLA sells these parts to the military services for use in maintenance facilities or to be shipped to forward units. In the latter case, the military service might also pay the United States Transportation Command (TRANSCOM) for shipping. TRANSCOM, in turn, might use Air Force pilots and planes to expedite some of the shipments. Each of these entities would also purchase finance and accounting services from DFAS and communication services from the Defense Information Systems Agency to support its operations.

As a result of these complex transactions, the financial results from individual DOD components cannot be simply aggregated to generate a grand financial picture of the organization as a whole, as would typically be done by a major corporation with multiple business units. Rather, intra-agency transactions must first be documented on both sides (matching purchases and sales) and reconciled to avoid double counting and ensure the traceability of funds from cradle to grave. This reconciliation process requires matching transactions recorded by different organizations in separate sets of books, using different systems, with different data elements, and at different times. It is made nearly impossible by the fact that few existing financial systems are designed to record to whom a product was transferred or from whom it was purchased.

The problem of documenting intergovernmental transactions (IGTs) has not been solved anywhere in the federal government and continues to be identified by the GAO as a major impediment to a favorable audit opinion on the federal government's financial statements.[26] However, the volume of business activity conducted between DOD components dwarfs the IGT volume of the rest of the federal government. Overall, the Department of the Treasury records unmatched transactions between federal agencies of about $20 billion per year, with transactions between the DOD and civilian agencies accounting for about half of that amount.[27] By contrast, the department recorded over $80 billion in unmatched transactions between internal DOD buyers and sellers in Fiscal Year (FY) 2015.[28]

The federal funding system adds an additional layer of complexity to the DOD's accounts. All DOD discretionary funds are appropriated by Congress for specific organizations and purposes and must be spent in accordance with the congressional appropriations. As DOD IG Eleanor Hill explained in 1998, the complex task of tracing the "color of money"—the assigned purpose of funds—in tens of thousands of appropriation accounts and line items from receipt to expenditure "is a root cause of the formidable DOD problems with the accuracy of accounting data, the complexity of our contracts, the difficulty of properly managing disbursements and progress payments, the high overhead costs of DOD budget and accounting operations, and the considerable restrictions on the flexibility of mangers to shift funds quickly to meet contingencies."[29]

A typical DOD accounting code is at least fifty to sixty digits long and may include codes identifying the military service, command, budget activity, accounting station, transaction type, appropriation and suballotment, beginning and ending fiscal year, weapon system and project unit, contractor code, contract, and line item.[30] At a House hearing in 2000, the GAO provided an example of an actual line of code from the Army's Operations and Maintenance appropriation: 2162020573106325796BD26 FBQSUPCA200GRE12340109003AB22WORNAAS34030.[31] Because the DOD's finance, accounting, and supporting systems are not fully linked, the GAO reported, "the line of accounting must be manually entered multiple times, which compounds the likelihood of errors. An error in any one character in such a line of code can delay payment processing or affect the reliability of data used to support management and budget decisions."[32]

In the late 1970s, the GAO found the finance and accounting systems and operations of the DOD and other federal agencies to be in a state of complete disarray.[33] Comptroller General Elmer Staats told an annual gathering of government financial management professionals in 1980 that finance and accounting weaknesses led to managers buying parts that they did not need, agencies allowing ineffective programs to continue, and "cost overruns, missed deadlines, the poor quality of government services, and fraud involving Federal funds."[34] The problems were so bad that the Army lost track of how much money it had and needed special legislation to cover $225 million of excess spending, while the Air Force was caught changing year-end financial reports to avoid disclosing the expenditure of millions of dollars before the funds were appropriated.[35]

In the early 1980s, the president's Private Sector Survey on Cost Control (the "Grace Commission") reported that senior federal officials did not have "ready access to management information as would be normal in private sector operations."[36] Even the most basic information was missing: the federal government did not know "the full extent of how much it spends for consulting services, what kinds of contracts are awarded, what the average mark-up is, the difference between quality performance and non-quality performance, or whether the service has been previously procured elsewhere in the Government."[37]

OMB Deputy Director Joseph Wright Jr. reported that OMB had identified 332 accounting systems and 600 other major management and administrative systems in the federal government and that "most of them are incompatible, even within individual agencies."[38] Wright announced a new management agenda, labeled "Reform '88," which promised institutional improvements in "four broad areas: the budget process, financial management systems, resource management, and a management information system that ties them all together."[39] The reform effort took two tracks: (1) implementation of the Federal Managers' Financial Integrity Act of 1982 (FMFIA), which required each federal agency to conduct an annual review of its internal controls, develop a plan for addressing any deficiencies, and report to Congress on the results;[40] and (2) the establishment of consistent accounting standards for all federal agencies.

The FMFIA effort identified thousands of material weaknesses in internal controls and accounting systems, sending agencies off in endless directions with little prioritization. Despite this massive effort, many systems were not evaluated, many weaknesses remained uncorrected, many corrections were not tested to see if they were working, and more deficiencies were identified every year.[41] As a result, the FMFIA reporting system accomplished little beyond adding to the paperwork burden on federal agencies. "Agencies have devoted considerable resources to making vulnerability assessments, and the vulnerability of thousands of operations and functions have been assessed," GAO concluded. "However, these efforts have often not resulted in reliable and useful information to agency managers, and the vulnerability assessment process has been widely criticized as a paper exercise."[42]

The administration's broader effort to improve accounting systems and processes was not any more successful. In the course of the 1980s, the OMB published common accounting data elements, standards for agency financial management systems, and a uniform chart of accounts, claiming that with these actions, the government's financial management problems were "well on the way to resolution."[43] In practice, however, finance and accounting systems continued to be developed without regard to the new standards.[44] Moreover, many of these development efforts were unsuccessful, leaving agencies to rely on the same antiquated systems that had been in place a decade or more earlier. For example, the Army's effort to develop a consolidated pay and personnel system was canceled when the Army determined that the software "was useless,"[45] and a new Navy financial system was terminated after its price tag grew from $33 million to $479 million and users began to doubt that the system would ever be successfully deployed.[46]

By 1985, Comptroller General Charles Bowsher concluded that federal financial processes and systems were "obsolete . . . unreliable, inconsistent, and all too often irrelevant,"[47] suffering from poor quality of financial information, poor linkages between the phases of the financial management process, excessive focus on funds control, and inadequate attention to monitoring actual program results.[48] In a lengthy two-volume report, the GAO recommended a fundamental restructuring and rebuilding of the federal financial management structure that would include: (1) strengthened accounting, auditing, and reporting; (2) improved planning and programming; (3) a streamlined budget process; and (4) systematic measures of performance.[49]

The key measure of success for the new system would be consolidated financial reports, which would be prepared by federal agencies and audited on an annual basis.[50] Building this new financial structure would require extensive system development efforts, organizational changes, and investments in people.[51] It would also require federal agencies to adopt an accrual-based accounting system like those commonly used in the private sector. The accrual system would have to be applied to both budgeting and accounting, the GAO asserted, because "it is difficult to compare the [budget] authority granted by the Congress with actual program costs incurred when data are not on the same basis."[52]

Accrual-based accounting would require a fundamental change in federal finance and accounting systems. The federal budget and appropriations system have historically worked on an "obligation" basis: Congress controls expenditures by establishing in appropriations acts the amount of money that federal agencies and agency components may commit for specific purposes—for example, by placing orders, entering contracts, or hiring employees. In an accrual-based system, by contrast, costs are recognized not when a commitment is made, but when work is actually performed and resources are consumed. Only by recording the cost of a product or service in the same period when it is used, accountants point out, can an organization understand the relationship between what is delivered and what it actually costs.⁵³

Accrual-based accounting tracks costs through a chart of accounts that is designed to address program objectives rather than appropriations accounts, requiring the use of a completely different set of data elements. It requires data on asset valuation and depreciation—data that comes from multiple appropriations but has never been systematically collected by the department because it was not perceived to serve any useful purpose. To account for such costs with existing accounting systems, DOD comptroller Bob Hale explained in 2011, "You would have to get a team of experienced analysts to go in, look at the budgetary data in those categories, in some cases estimate what portion were attributable to [a particular asset] and come up with that data."⁵⁴ For a department that works on the basis of obligation and expenditure accounting, Hale concluded, accrual-based standard general ledger accounts "might as well be in Greek."⁵⁵

The comptroller general's proposals found a friendly audience in the SGAC, and bills requiring federal agencies to prepare financial statements for annual audits were introduced both by outgoing Republican chair William Roth in 1986 and by incoming Democratic chair John Glenn in 1987.⁵⁶ Bowsher testified in support of both bills,⁵⁷ but his testimony changed over time to reflect the reality that Congress was unlikely to change its own budget process. In 1986, the comptroller general testified that a single system was needed for both budgeting and accounting,⁵⁸ but by 1987, he was calling only for accrual-based accounting⁵⁹—conspicuously omitting any mention of a linkage to the federal budget system.⁶⁰ Instead, his statement held out the vague hope that "if the accounting system being developed meets expectations," Congress might "envision shifts in the budget in future years to more accurately reflect where the funds are actually being spent."⁶¹

Frank Hodsoll, the OMB deputy director for management, endorsed the push for auditable agency financial statements in 1990, labeling it "the cornerstone of the administration's financial management improvement strategy."⁶² Outside groups took up the cause, and a legislative mandate for auditable financial statements was endorsed by the American Institute of Certified Public Accountants; the Association of Government

Accountants; the National Association of State Auditors, Controllers, and Treasurers; and the Financial Executives Institute.[63] A series of task forces, studies, talk-show appearances, and infomercials followed, with editorials and letters to the editor in newspapers around the country building pressure on Congress to act.[64]

The Chief Financial Officers' Act of 1990 (CFO Act) was approved by both houses of Congress in the final days of the 101st Congress and signed into law by President George H. W. Bush on November 15, 1990.[65] The CFO Act was passed so quickly that the chair of the House Appropriations Committee, who had opposed the legislation, reportedly did not learn of its enactment until after the fact.[66] The new statute required the preparation and audit of financial statements by all revolving funds and other agency components performing substantial business functions and full audits of several larger federal agencies, including the Department of the Army and the Department of the Air Force, on a pilot basis.[67] Four years later, Congress enacted the Government Management Reform Act of 1994, which extended the requirement for auditable financial statements to all federal agencies.[68]

The comptroller general had achieved his objective of a legislative mandate for auditable financial statements, but at a cost: the important principle of conformity between budget and accounting was jettisoned along the way. The DOD and other federal agencies were left in the untenable position of running "two 'separate, uncoordinated systems' for budgeting and accounting."[69] For example, one system tracks the organizations to which appropriations are allocated, while the other tracks the organizations that actually spend the money. As a result, the two systems cannot agree on the amount of money that is available to a DOD component for a given purpose, rendering management decisions difficult to make and even more difficult to enforce.

Former DOD comptroller Robert Anthony, considered by many to be the father of accrual-based accounting in the department, concluded in 1996 that the trade-off had not been worth it. The CFO Act appeared to be based on the hope that "managers will focus their attention on the accrual accounting components," he wrote. "Unfortunately, this hope is unrealistic. Regardless of the conceptual merit of the accrual accounting statements, managers will continue to focus on the budgetary amounts since this is where the money comes from."[70] Any business trying to run two separate sets of books in this way, he concluded, "would soon be bankrupt."[71]

Former deputy DOD comptroller Don Shycoff made the same point a few years later, writing that "the Department has enough trouble keeping one set of books. Two are impossible."[72] "Portraying costs one way and managing another did not work in the past and will not work in the future," he explained. "Allocating costs to programs whose managers have no say over the requirements generating those costs will merely produce another set of numbers. This will not result in better decisions."[73]

THE 1990s: THE BUSH I AND CLINTON ADMINISTRATIONS

The administration of President George H. W. Bush faced a difficult budget situation when it came into office in January 1989. The Gramm-Rudman-Hollings Deficit Reduction Act of 1985[74] required the achievement of a balanced budget by 1991 through a series of decreasing deficit targets enforced by a sequestration requirement. The new president had promised in no uncertain terms that he would not raise taxes, and the Democratic Congress was undisposed to restrain domestic spending in the absence of significant concessions from the administration. As a result, the defense budget, which had been dropping in real terms since 1987, was under extreme pressure. This pressure increased rapidly, as the accelerating collapse of the Soviet bloc fed public expectations of a "peace dividend."[75]

The new administration promised management reforms that would make the Pentagon more efficient.[76] The initial work of the Defense Management Review program focused on the implementation of the Packard Commission recommendations for reforming the defense acquisition system,[77] but the Pentagon soon announced a more ambitious management agenda, which was projected to save $39 billion and eliminate 42,000 DOD jobs over a five-year period by eliminating unnecessary paperwork, consolidating logistics functions, and transitioning to DOD-wide, uniform data systems.[78]

Over the next three years, Deputy Secretary Donald Atwood issued several hundred defense management review decisions (DMRDs) intended to reform DOD business processes, with anticipated savings ranging from a few million dollars to more than $10 billion.[79] Three major initiatives, in particular, became the heart of the administration's financial management agenda: the CIM program to overhaul the department's business information systems, DBOF to modernize its business operations, and DFAS to consolidate and update its finance and accounting operations.[80]

Grand Design I: The Corporate Information Management (CIM) Program
In November 1989, Deputy Secretary Atwood issued DMRD 925, announcing the CIM initiative to develop integrated business information systems for the department.[81] The Executive Level Group (ELG) of senior DOD and industry officials established by the deputy secretary recommended that rather than trying to improve existing business systems and processes or even develop new information technology (IT) systems to automate existing or improved business processes, the department should start from scratch with a set of "guiding principles and operating fundamentals"[82] to identify the goals of its business operations and the types of information that would be needed to achieve those goals. Information system solutions would be developed only after new business policies, procedures, and measurements had been built from the ground up.[83]

The department established functional groups of experts to review its information requirements in eight initial business areas: Civilian Payroll, Civilian Personnel, Contract Payment, Distribution Centers, Financial Operations, Government Furnished Material, Materiel Management, and Medical.[84] Each of the working groups was directed to develop a "functional vision," including proposed policy and guiding principles, before considering new business systems or processes.[85] The department established a director of defense information to assist in the development of business plans, a Center for Information Management to support data standardization, and an Information Policy Council, a CIM Council, and an Information Technology Policy Board to facilitate the adoption of new policies, standards, and requirements.[86]

The basic principle underlying CIM—that new or upgraded business systems should be acquired only after the department's data needs are fully understood and its business processes have been fully engineered—was consistent with the widely accepted "best practices" of the time.[87] Unfortunately, the CIM requirement to understand all aspects of an organization's business process before beginning any improvements was completely impractical as applied to an entity as large and complex as the DOD. As early as 1991, DOD functional groups reported that simply identifying and cataloging existing information systems had been a difficult undertaking, and they did "not have enough expertise" to take the next step and prepare a detailed strategy for moving to standard systems.[88] If the DOD had fully carried out the sequential approach as envisioned by the ELG, a pause of several years would have been required before initiating any improvements. Indeed, the ELG itself estimated that "about a decade" would be required to implement its plan.[89]

Neither the department nor the Congress was willing to wait that long. Senator Glenn told DOD witnesses, "We need controls now. We can't just wait for something 8 or 10 years down the road."[90] The budgets of the military services for new and upgraded IT systems had already been reduced by $3.5 billion on the assumption that the department would field standardized DOD-wide systems at a much lower cost of $1.3 billion.[91] As a result, funds for new finance and accounting programs were dropped,[92] funds for routine upgrades to existing systems were jeopardized,[93] and the military services were faced with the prospect of "living with technology and systems from the 70s and 80s that are ill-suited to the demands of the current environment"[94] until CIM produced results.

Not surprisingly, the service secretaries, "concerned about the slow progress of the CIM effort and the amount of funding stripped from their . . . budgets . . . asked the DOD Comptroller to come up with a technique for getting more immediate cost savings."[95] DOD comptroller Sean O'Keefe responded by refocusing the CIM program on short-term improvements in business processes and information systems. Instead of waiting for the development of improved business processes and new data standards, CIM would begin to identify interim or "migratory" solutions from among existing systems to serve as a basis for short-term improvements pending the completion of the review.[96]

O'Keefe was able to make progress on finance and accounting systems, approving migratory system projects to standardize civilian payroll, military pay, retiree and annuitant pay, travel payments, transportation payments, contractor debt management, and nonappropriated fund payroll.[97] The GAO complained that the department had short-circuited the CIM process and failed to achieve significant savings by fielding interim systems solutions without first reengineering business processes,[98] but at least the department had a plan to eliminate some of its most obsolete and redundant finance and accounting systems.

Other working groups ran into a brick wall. While authority for finance and accounting systems had been centralized through the creation of DFAS, the military services retained control over other business processes and were unwilling to accept information solutions—interim or otherwise—that failed to meet their unique needs.[99] In the logistics area, for example, the Joint Logistics System Center (JLSC), staffed with 250 personnel from the military services and the DLA,[100] made little progress, because each of the components continued to insist on its "'unique' ways of doing business."[101] The JLSC ignored the OSD's requirement to field interim systems within three years, developing an alternative strategy to field migratory systems over a seven- to eight-year period,[102] while the individual components continued to spend huge sums of money on their own separate IT systems.[103] Not surprisingly, the GAO found that "the CIM initiative has had little effect on materiel management and depot maintenance business practices."[104]

Former deputy comptroller Don Shycoff, an early proponent of CIM, concluded in 1995 that the department's efforts to manage the CIM program were "troublesome at best" and demonstrated that the OSD "has proven that it cannot manage" business operations.[105] Shycoff reported that "each Military Service continues to find ways to pursue its unique developments"[106] and, as a result, the functional teams had "not shown any measurable results except in the medical area."[107] Even in the medical area, the GAO found that "CIM's impact and usefulness have been limited by its organizational placement, underutilized analyses, and the lack of a strategic plan to guide decision making."[108]

In early 1994, the new DOD comptroller, John Hamre, gave the program a new, narrower mandate. Instead of trying to address all the business systems and processes of the department, CIM would focus on finance and accounting systems, addressing the one area in which his predecessor had left a workable plan of action. In the period of a year, Hamre told the SGAC, the department would eliminate 75 percent of its existing finance systems while, at the same time, developing a comprehensive plan for streamlining its accounting systems.[109] "I am responsible," he testified. "In two years . . . I will come back, and if we haven't fixed these problems, then you can ask the President to relieve me. But I am responsible."[110]

Hamre also argued that data standardization was needed to enable electronic data interchange and the fielding of new, modern finance and accounting systems.[111] Unfortunately, much of the data needed to support the finance and accounting requirements was not controlled by the comptroller but was the responsibility of other functional communities. "The way we have set up the CIM process," Hamre explained, "I cannot standardize my items DOD-wide on personnel issue items. That community has to be the one to take the lead."[112] When the department tried to establish a corporate data dictionary, the GAO found that functional managers flooded the system with tens of thousands of nonstandard data elements from existing management information systems.[113] The DOD responded to the criticism by telling the GAO that "data standardization is not something that happens all at once, and it does not happen quickly when it is done correctly."[114]

The last remnants of the CIM effort to institute common business and financial systems across the department suffered a similar fate, unable to overcome the continuing resistance of the military services. In case after case, the mismatch between conceptual design and user demands resulted in ballooning costs, development and deployment delays, failure of systems to meet performance expectations, and program terminations. In 1998, for example, the Air Force was allowed to withdraw from the Defense Joint Accounting System (DJAS) and work on a service-specific system instead. In 2000, the DOD IG reported that DFAS had started the program without an adequate feasibility study, analysis of alternatives, economic analysis, or acquisition program baseline and had not reengineered business processes.[115] In 2003, after the expenditure of approximately $120 million, the DOD comptroller canceled further development of DJAS.[116]

The Defense Procurement Payment System, the Defense Standard Disbursing System, and the Joint Computer Aided Acquisition and Logistics System suffered similar fates at about the same time.[117] In virtually every case, these CIM programs were unable to overcome a continuing tension between the desire of the CFO community for simple, streamlined systems that could produce the audit trails to support financial statements and the resistance of functional communities in the DOD components to changes in their business processes and the uniquely tailored data sets that supported these processes. While the functional communities' resistance to business process reengineering (BPR) has often been characterized as irrational, it is important to keep in mind that an organization's finance and accounting systems should generally be designed to support its business needs, not the other way around.

By the end of the Clinton administration, the department was no longer talking about the CIM program. As Comptroller General David Walker later testified, CIM had been expected to save billions of dollars by replacing two thousand duplicative systems and reforming "all DOD's functional areas, including finance, procurement, material management, and human resources through consolidating, standardizing, and integrating information systems."[118] He reported that "8 years after beginning CIM, and spending about $20 billion on the initiative, expected savings had yet to materialize. The initiative was eventually abandoned."[119]

CIM was not without its accomplishments. DOD comptroller Bill Lynn testified in 2000 that the department had eliminated 228 finance and accounting systems over the previous decade and expected to eliminate another 60 in the next three years.[120] While Lynn was overly optimistic in predicting that the remaining finance and accounting systems would be compliant with accounting standards, it would undoubtedly be easier to address the shortcomings in 30 best-in-breed finance and accounting systems than to try to fix hundreds of overlapping and redundant legacy systems, none of which met applicable requirements. Had the department followed GAO recommendations and insisted on the original CIM concept of fielding only perfectly studied systems with fully reengineered processes, it would likely not have made even this much progress.

On the other hand, the department's larger data problems—the initial target of the CIM program—had been deferred for so long that they were now identified as a newly discovered problem. In 1999, Lynn announced that the department had just initiated a "third phase" of financial reform, in which it would seek to "upgrade the interfaces with functional systems that feed data into finance and accounting reports." This effort Lynn stated, would "take several years and substantial new resources."[121] Ten years after Deputy Secretary Atwood kicked off the CIM program, not only did the program no longer exist, but the bulk of the effort had yet to begin.

The CIM program suffered from the overambitious objective of reinventing all DOD business processes and systems at the same time. In light of the multiplicity and complexity of those processes, it should not have been surprising that the functional groups tasked with identifying data needs from basic principles soon reported that they lacked the expertise to do so. Even if the department had been able to find the expertise, a slow-burning reform effort taking eight to ten years to produce results was never going to be an easy sell in the DOD political and budget environment. The department achieved limited success in fielding "migratory" finance and accounting systems by not insisting on perfect solutions before moving forward. In other functional areas, it appears that CIM may have *slowed* progress on needed improvements in business processes and systems by freezing ongoing improvement programs in the components without ever developing adequate DOD-wide replacements.

Partial Solutions I: DBOF and DFAS
Before the CIM program was a year old, Deputy Secretary of Defense Atwood took two additional actions designed to improve the department's financial performance and accountability. First, in the summer of 1990, Atwood directed that the six finance and accounting centers then

managed by the military departments be merged into a new Defense Finance and Accounting Service (DFAS).[122] A month later, the deputy secretary directed that the nine industrial and stock funds operated by the military services and defense agencies be consolidated into a new Defense Business Operations Fund (DBOF).[123]

The establishment of DFAS and the creation of DBOF were intended to serve similar purposes. By consolidating the business and financial activities of the department, the two initiatives were intended to streamline and rationalize the department's support functions, placing them on a sound business footing. Both initiatives were intended to facilitate the development of new business and accounting systems and processes in the department, and both initiatives would need those new systems and processes to succeed. As Atwood told the Senate Armed Services Committee (SASC), "without these two tools, responsive financial and ADP [Automatic Data Processing] systems, no management can operate successfully."[124]

As similar as the two initiatives may have appeared on the surface, they differed in one crucial aspect: their relationship to the military services. DFAS absorbed finance and accounting functions, organizations, and manpower from the military services, bringing together policy, resources, and operations in a new entity. By contrast, DBOF was a purely administrative construct, creating a single accounting entity without changing the underlying organizational structure. The military services continued to manage their own largely independent commercial and industrial activities, with their own employees and their own business processes.

The DFAS merger enabled the department to unify policies and practices and to standardize information requirements and formats.[125] The effort was successful enough that the department barely paused before directing that DFAS absorb additional finance and accounting services from the military services, bringing in thousands of additional employees.[126] In all, DFAS took charge of 6 service finance and accounting centers, 330 installation-level offices, 300 finance and accounting systems, and roughly 28,000 of the 46,000 DOD employees then working in finance and accounting.[127] By 1999, DFAS had closed all of the installation-level offices and was working out of 5 finance and accounting centers and 20 regional operating locations.[128] It had eliminated 200 obsolete and redundant finance and accounting systems and 8,000 unneeded positions[129] and was on its way to a steady employment level of just 11,000 by 2017.[130]

The downside was the exacerbation of the department's problem with "unmatched disbursements," as contractors were overpaid, receipts could not be located, and service members received the wrong paychecks. Under the old system, the service financial offices understood the linkages between finance and accounting systems and functional feeder systems. When data were missing, they knew where to find it. When the finance and accounting systems were taken away and given to DFAS, however, the institutional knowledge of linkages between systems was broken, and the reconciliation of accounts became far more difficult.[131] The department was eventually able to bring the problem under control by developing "responsibility matrices" and spending thousands of person-years tracking unmatched disbursements and improper payments.[132] Despite these difficulties, Hamre concluded, the department's financial problems would have been dramatically worse, absent the "path-breaking decision" by Cheney and Atwood to consolidate the department's finance and accounting operations in DFAS.[133]

The creation of DBOF was far less successful. DBOF was intended to make the business operations of the department more efficient by making the costs of those operations more visible to their users.[134] The department already had forty years of experience running so-called revolving funds—known as "stock funds" and "industrial funds"—to purchase supplies and conduct repair work on behalf of operational customers, who reimbursed them for the work out of appropriated funds.[135] Because the revolving funds were paid by customer fees rather than direct congressional appropriations, they were not bound to appropriations accounts and funding structures, freeing them to use accrual accounting and match costs against work performed.[136] However, each fund had its own accounting system and its own unique mix of direct appropriations and customer reimbursements, making it impossible to determine their relative efficiency.[137]

DOD Deputy Comptroller Don Shycoff, known as the "father of DBOF," believed that creating a single fund would enable the department to institute a unified "business-type cost accounting system to focus on the cost of the output rather than on 'what does it cost to run my activity.'"[138] In Shycoff's vision, DBOF would "provide the operating forces better visibility of the true costs of their operations" and enable business managers "greater flexibility to make tradeoffs between elements of expenses."[139] The GAO agreed that the successful institution of cost-based business practices in DBOF would "mark a fundamental improvement in the manner in which Defense conducts business."[140]

The problem was an insurmountable gap between DBOF objectives and the available tools. The DOD did not have "the policies, procedures, and systems in place to implement and operate the Fund in a 'business-like' manner,"[141] the GAO reported. Because the military services' organizational structures, financial systems, and terminology were not uniform and their existing systems produced unreliable data, the information used to determine costs would be unreliable.[142] If DOD systems were not upgraded to address these problems, the GAO warned, "the business concepts of the Fund may be discredited and the opportunity to make this fundamental change in the management of Defense will be jeopardized."[143]

The DOD plowed ahead, as Shycoff sought to take advantage of what he saw as a rare window for reform. He told the GAO that "every 25 years, an administration is willing to spend some of its capital on management improvements. We needed to take advantage of that situation. Another 25 years would be too long."[144] Shycoff acknowledged that when DBOF was first established, it would be little more than a paper entity. In the fund's first year, he told the Senate, DBOF would be "just a name change."[145]

Building common finance and accounting systems to support DBOF proved to be far more difficult than anticipated. Finance and accounting systems can only record transactions in accordance with business processes that actually exist, so common finance and accounting systems require common business processes. Because DBOF was a paper creation, however, it had no direct authority over the business processes that would have to be reengineered to create a common system. Rather, operational management and control of the department's business activities, such as shipyards and aviation depots, remained in the military services.[146] As a consequence, the effort to establish common finance and accounting systems became a process of endless negotiation.

In early 1991, the GAO reported that "although DFAS developed an inventory of [finance and accounting systems used by then-existing stock and industrial funds], no other tasks were completed and work was suspended in late 1991."[147] In late 1992, Shycoff announced the designation of the Defense Business Management System (DBMS) as the primary system to support the fund's implementation.[148] Because the DBMS did not perform all the functions found in DBOF's existing systems, however, those systems would continue to operate.[149] Moreover, the GAO pointed out, "DOD has yet to determine the priority of the changes that must be made to DBMS in order to assimilate functions now performed by the 82 systems or the cost and complexity of implementing these changes."[150]

In April 1994, the DOD tried announcing that it would select interim migratory systems for DBOF by the end of the fiscal year and start implementing them shortly thereafter.[151] Once again, progress was limited: by mid-1995—four years after DBOF was established—the department was still relying on the same eighty "disparate," "unlinked," and "antiquated" systems that it had inherited from the old stock and industrial funds to produce DBOF data.[152] The GAO found that the department still had not begun to address critical issues, including "improvements needed to meet minimum technical requirements, data conversion from the existing systems to the interim migratory systems, development of interfaces with nonfinancial systems, . . . and training of personnel who will operate and enter data into the interim migratory systems."[153]

The department's progress in developing common accounting policies was not much better. In February 1993, the department claimed to have substantially completed the policies to govern the fund's operations.[154] The GAO summarily rejected the department's conclusion, finding that none of the required policies for capital asset accounting, intrafund transactions, common costs, cash management, revenue recognition, and major real property maintenance and repair had yet been developed.[155] A year later, the GAO reported little progress: only eighteen of forty-four scheduled tasks covering DBOF policies, procedures, and systems, had been completed.[156]

The absence of coherent policies and uniform systems resulted in "a serious problem with the accuracy, consistency, completeness, timeliness and usefulness of the [DBOF] financial reports."[157] In 1993, 1994, 1995, and again in 1996, the GAO found multi-billion-dollar discrepancies between DBOF's financial and budget reports and between the operating results as reported by the military services and by DBOF.[158] As a result, the GAO reported, the department was "not in a position to know if the prices being charged DBOF's customers are reasonable, since the net operating results is [sic] a key factor in setting prices. Given the current environment, it is conceivable that some prices might be too high, while others might be too low to recover the costs of providing goods and services."[159]

Congressional investigators claimed that DBOF was subject to "rampant overcharging and undercharging for goods and services, resulting in wild fluctuations in monthly cash balances."[160] DBOF was alleged to have "manipulate[d] prices, maximizing the value of their sales," generating so much extra cash that the chair of the House defense appropriations subcommittee tried to use $1.9 billion out of DBOF surpluses to build two new destroyers.[161] Senator Grassley, a strong DBOF critic, told the press that "we may have reached a point in our history where the time has come to call in the FBI, to lock the doors, seal the safes and filing cabinets and begin a top-to-bottom audit of the government's books."[162]

Initially, the department claimed that the finance and accounting problems had been there all along, and DBOF had simply brought them out into the open so that they could be addressed.[163] The military services were less forgiving. As Shycoff explained, the services never wanted to give up authority to DBOF in the first place and blamed the fund "for almost every action affecting any activity in the fund: consolidation of supply depots came about because of the DBOF; funding below what the military Services want is a result of the fund; bases close because of the fund."[164] Indeed, Shycoff believed that the services were fundamentally opposed to the business-oriented approach of the working capital funds and wanted to kill the concept.[165]

DBOF problems were soon compounded by dramatic prices increases that made some DBOF services unaffordable. DBOF was only partially to blame for the price increases, which the GAO attributed to the failure of fund activities to achieve planned productivity increases, the inclusion in DBOF rates of costs (e.g., headquarters costs) for which customers did not previously have to pay, and the allocation of fixed overhead costs across a steadily declining workload.[166] As post–Cold War budgets declined and prices went up, commanders began to cut back on work in the depots, resulting in even more price increases because there was less and less work to which overhead costs could be charged. The result was a "death spiral":

> Commanders began telling their logisticians to repair tanks without sending them to expensive depots. "All of a sudden," [Pentagon comptroller John] Hamre says, "depot and supply managers are seeing a dropoff in demand. They can't react in time; they can't just fire federal civilians overnight. So the suppliers in the DBOF system, the depots, the supply centers, the shipyards, started losing money." Prior-year losses are made up by raising next year's prices. As the increases hit the field commanders, Hamre says, they thought: "This isn't working at all. I'm cutting back on what I'm putting into the system, and the prices go up. I'm going into a death spiral."[167]

In July 1993, Senator Ted Stevens—the highest ranking Republican on the influential the Defense Appropriations Subcommittee—complained at a Senate hearing that DBOF appeared to be "breaking apart" because of unaffordable costs.[168] A few months later, Deputy Comptroller Alice Maroni reported that "Congress reminds us almost daily of the problems we've had implementing DBOF."[169]

In 1993, the DSB Task Force convened by the incoming Clinton administration recommended that the department "defer further DBOF expansion until adequate financial and management systems are in place to allocate costs properly and provide visibility to the effects on force readiness."[170] A second task force, composed of finance and management experts, proposed a "Defense Business Operations Fund Improvement

Plan" to address shortcomings in policies, procedures, systems, and data.[171] Improvements did not come fast enough to save the fund, however. In 1996, the department announced that DBOF would be terminated and broken back up into separate working capital funds to be managed by the military services and defense agencies.[172]

The military services initially resisted the establishment of both DFAS and DBOF. The two initiatives experienced significant transition problems—some the result of inherited systems and processes and others caused by dislocation and disruption of the workforce. DFAS was able to overcome these problems in large part because the new agency brought finance and accounting operations, locations, and personnel and funding under direct management that enabled the comptroller to direct the implementation of new finance and accounting systems and processes on an ongoing basis. DBOF, by contrast, left control of business operations and personnel in the hand of the military services and lacked a comparable ability to control systems and processes. As a result, it proved unable to institute common systems and policies, and collapsed of its own weight.

Auditing for Audit I
During the 1990s, while the DOD attempted with limited success to address its financial problems through management reforms, the GAO and Congress pursued a separate course—seeking to audit the department into auditability. The effort began in early 1989, when the GAO sought a test case to conduct a comprehensive audit of an agency financial statement. The Air Force, which was believed to have the best financial management system in the DOD, if not the federal government, was selected for the audit.[173] Air Force officials spent thousands of hours in "extensive, manual, time-consuming efforts" to assemble data from across the service and compile a financial statement for GAO review.[174]

The results were devastating: Air Force accounting systems did not include any information on several major categories of items, including weapon systems and accounts payable; Air Force inventory systems could not provide reliable data on quantities or values of inventories; and the Air Force was unable to reconcile intra-agency transactions.[175] Warner Robins Air Logistics Center could not explain an account with a negative balance of $2.1 billion;[176] Air Force Systems Command could not explain a $7 billion discrepancy between its disbursement and obligation records;[177] and the Air Force had to make billions of dollars of other "unsupported and arbitrary adjustments"[178] to make its accounts balance. The GAO concluded that the Air Force financial statements were "unauditable" and stopped the audit without offering an opinion.[179]

Air Force Secretary Donald Rice pushed back, asserting that the GAO findings were "fundamentally misdirected."[180] Rice stated that the concept that government agencies should have the same auditable balance sheets as for-profit companies "offers a narrow CPA's [certified public accountant] view of the information needed for defense decision making that has a limited relationship to the real problems of defense management" and "has not been accepted by the Congress or the Executive Branch."[181] "No cost savings are identified," Rice stated, and "implementation costs, likely to be in the billions for the DOD, are ignored."[182] Rice asserted that existing Air Force financial systems were adequate to ensure the proper stewardship of federal funds and suggested that the GAO should go "back to the drawing board" and prepare a report "recognizing that Air Force systems comply effectively with existing requirements."[183]

Members of Congress, who were receptive to claims of waste, fraud, and abuse at the DOD in the wake of the 1980s-era procurement scandals, sided with the GAO. Senator Glenn said that the GAO findings "go to the heart of Congress' ability to rely on the information provided to it by the Department of Defense."[184] "When financial accountability is lost and inaccurate cost information exists," he stated, "our ability to make sound choices with the taxpayers' money is lost."[185] Senator Joseph Lieberman added that "every small businessman or woman that I deal with in Connecticut" has to produce reliable accounting records and that sloppy bookkeeping "is certainly a luxury the Government cannot afford with the taxpayers' money."[186]

Within a year, Congress enacted the CFO Act, effectively ending the debate. Although some DOD officials continued to express doubts about the utility of financial statements,[187] Congress endorsed the GAO view by enshrining the objective of auditable balance sheets in law. In February 1992, when the SGAC revisited the issue of Air Force financial management, the GAO reported that although the Air Force had not yet tried to put together another full financial statement, its annual account balance with the Treasury alone had required $62 billion worth of adjustments. "That is a staggering amount of adjustments," the comptroller general testified, "and I think it is an indication of the [Air Force financial management] problems."[188]

Asked by Senator Glenn why the Air Force had dropped its plans to continue to prepare consolidated financial statements on an annual basis, Air Force comptroller Michael Donley responded that the department had continuing questions about "the utility of the product" and "didn't feel like we needed to go over the same ground fiscal year after fiscal year."[189] "We felt that we had been through the wringer on the production of the fiscal year 1988 statements," he said, "and we didn't feel like we were anxious to do that again in 1989."[190] Glenn objected, saying that "everybody thought, including GAO" that a consolidated financial statement was needed, and "I don't understand why you just decided on your own not to do it."[191]

Donley promised that the Air Force would take short-term, "manpower-intensive" measures to make immediate progress toward auditable financial statements and would comply with the CFO Act by preparing an agency-wide financial statement for fiscal year 1993. The Air Force would revise its policies and procedures "to place greater emphasis on our general funds general ledger."[192] It would update directives and internal procedures to ensure the proper classification of transactions before posting and strengthen the reconciliation process for erroneous entries. It would "train and educate field personnel" on the new accounting policies and procedures.[193] In effect, Donley relented and agreed to adopt the GAO approach of auditing its way to auditability.

Next, it was the Army's turn. In August 1992, Senator Glenn convened a hearing to consider the "first ever outside audit of the U.S. Army."[194] The Army audit had no better results than the Air Force audit. The GAO declined to express an audit opinion on the Army statements, reporting that the Army's accounting for inventory was incomplete and unreliable, the value of military equipment was not properly reported, real property accounts could not be substantiated, significant liabilities were not reported, and controls over contractor-held property were not in place.[195] In the preparation of its financial statement, the Army had made roughly 12,000 changes, totaling $250 billion, without a documented explanation.[196] As Senator Glenn pointed out, the dollar value of these unsupported audit adjustments approached the value of the entire defense budget.[197]

A second audit a year later found that equipment was not properly reported, real property accounts were inaccurate, liabilities were not all reported, and controls over contractor-held property were not in place.[198] The Army made $93 billion of adjustments to bring general ledger balances into agreement with operational systems, a $196 billion correction "for computer errors," and an additional $7 billion of adjustments "to make general ledger balances agree with the budget execution system."[199] In addition, the GAO found that serious weaknesses in the Army disbursement process put the service at risk of making improper payments and allowed unauthorized persons to be paid.[200]

Attention-grabbing horror stories proliferated: 2,200 individuals who should not have been paid received paychecks;[201] an Air Force base accountant was able to divert $2 million of Air Force funds to his personal bank accounts over a three-year period; an Army finance clerk was able to falsify documents to create a "fictitious or 'ghost'" soldier on the payroll system" and divert the monthly paychecks to his own accounts; and a sergeant major in the Army continued to receive full pay for two years after she was separated from duty.[202] "Better attention to internal controls," Senator Glenn reported, "might have stopped the Army from paying deserters, and even a dead deserter, soldiers on AWOL [absent without leave], and in at least one case a ghost employee who never existed at all."[203]

At a 1993 hearing, Senator Glenn expressed frustration at the lack of visible progress toward auditability. "We are flopping around $50 billion here, $20 billion there," he said.[204] "Why is it taking so long?" he asked. "Do you need more money? Do you need more people?"[205] The comptroller general noted the change in administrations, telling Glenn that "right now we are somewhat halfway in the river" and that new leadership was needed to get the rest of the way.[206]

Other witnesses suggested that system and process improvements were needed before the audit approach would have a chance of succeeding. Alvin Tucker, the acting DOD CFO, told the SGAC that the multiyear effort to produce auditable financial statements had "proven what all parties knew at the outset: that DOD's accounting systems cannot yet produce financial statements that meet the standards required for audit."[207] "It is clear that this is a task that cannot be accomplished in one gigantic leap," he testified. "It must be broken down in parts, and we need to approach it in doable steps."[208] The Army comptroller agreed, testifying that "we are years away from financial statements that can meet the requirements of the CFO Act. Therefore, auditing to determine what we already know seems an inefficient use of these resources."[209]

Vice President Al Gore's National Performance Review took note of the burden imposed by the layering of reports on top of reports in financial management legislation and regulations, suggesting that these reports "need to be reviewed and consolidated, and the amount and type of information requested needs to be changed or eliminated."[210] Nonetheless, the review endorsed the audit approach.[211] A year later, the administration endorsed the extension of the requirement for auditable financial statements to all federal agencies.[212]

By the end of the decade, eighteen of twenty-four federal agencies covered by the CFO Act received unqualified audit opinions.[213] As the GAO pointed out, however, most of these agencies achieved clean financial statements only through "heroic efforts,"[214] such as having "consultants create the financial records at year-end, applying statistical sampling to establish values as of a point in time, and worst of all, neglecting processing of transactions to produce the financial statements."[215] Fifteen federal agencies receiving favorable audit opinions lacked integrated financial management systems, fifteen had inadequate procedures for reconciling discrepancies in their financial records, fourteen failed to comply with the requirements of the Standard General Ledger system, fifteen were noncompliant with the federal accounting standards, and twenty-one had weak information security systems.[216] While these agencies were able to produce clean financial statements, they were not able to produce timely, accurate financial information to support business decisions.

At the DOD, which was too big to achieve auditability through heroic measures, the audit strategy was a flat-out failure. In the absence of effective business processes and systems, the department had begun a laborious process of trying to reconcile expenditures to supporting documentation through what John Hamre called "dirty old pick-and-shovel work."[217] At great expense, contractors hired by DFAS managed to reconcile payments on 4,300 out of 10,900 suspected "problem contracts," only to see the universe grow by another 20,000 contracts.[218] The department's backlog of $19 billion of "unmatched disbursements" was reduced to $12 billion, but an additional $2.5 billion of new problems continued to appear every month.[219]

The coda for Glenn's eight-year effort to foster financial improvements at the Pentagon came in the form of a front page article in the *Washington Post* entitled "Losing Control: Defense Department Billions Go Astray, Often Without a Trace."[220] Over the last eight years, the department had created $7 billion worth of "negative unliquidated obligations," the *Post* reported, by paying bills twice or mistakenly charging them to the wrong accounts.[221] The Pentagon paid private contractors $500 million to $750 million that it did not owe them every year because of "errors made in a paper-based system in which harried clerks are judged by how quickly they make payments."[222] John Hamre sent a letter assuring the chair of the House Appropriations Committee that Congress could rely on materials provided in support of the defense budget, but even he could not deny the serious problems in the department's finance and accounting operations.[223]

The 1995 elections brought a Republican Congress, and Congressman Stephen Horn, the new chair of the key House subcommittee, assumed the mantle of congressional leadership on government-wide financial management issues. Over the next six years, Horn chaired at least sixteen subcommittee hearings on government-wide financial management issues, including three hearings focused exclusively on DOD audit issues. From the outset, Horn made it clear that he was as committed to the audit approach as Glenn had been, asserting that "Agency financial statements will help our Government come clean by confronting weak controls and possible fraud or waste."[224]

For the rest of the decade, the DOD continued to plow resources into short-term fixes intended to address symptoms such as unmatched disbursements and improper payments. In 1995, the department announced fifteen "interim initiatives" to "show the Congress that we do mean business and to show our financial management community and the rest of the department that we really do intend to make improvements."[225] The objectives included an immediate reduction in the department's $18 billion of unmatched disbursements, strengthened efforts to prevent expenditures from accounts that were already in deficit, renewed attention to the elimination of Anti-Deficiency Act violations, and an "attack on fraudulent actions."[226] The Senior Financial Management Oversight Council, chaired by the deputy secretary, was established to oversee the effort.[227]

In the absence of modern business systems with effective internal controls that could address unmatched disbursements, validate intragovernmental and intra-agency transactions, and value existing assets, the department established an array of integrated process teams, tiger teams, and working groups to undertake a costly manual reviews of records.[228] Senior leaders decided not "to try to reconstruct all of the old records that are incomplete and in some cases no longer exist" and focused instead on "getting more recent records straight"[229] and establishing "prevalidation" requirements to reduce future problems.[230] Because the existing systems were not designed to prevalidate disbursements, however, even this work had to be done manually.[231] "It takes time," DOD Comptroller Bill Lynn explained. "We are working our way through it."[232]

While the numbers of unmatched transactions, improper payments, and Anti-Deficiency Act violations were driven down, the sheer number of DOD transactions made the effort to "audit fidelity back into the system"[233] impractical. "I'm already concerned how long it will take" with these interim approaches, Air Force Comptroller Bob Hale told Congressman Horn in 1995, worrying that his son would be "sitting here someday telling you that 'Gee . . . it will be 5 years before we have . . . auditable statements.'" "That will be the hearing in 2025," Representative Horn replied, indicating that it had already been scheduled.[234]

In 1996, the Navy underwent its first audit, with results that were every bit as dismal as those achieved by the Army and the Air Force. The GAO reported over $225 billion of errors in the Navy's consolidated financial reports, including $66 billion of material omissions, $43 billion of misrecorded or double-counted items, and $116 billion in misclassifications.[235] The control practices used in the Navy's financial operations were "fundamentally deficient," unusual trends and large variances in account balances were "not investigated, explained, or resolved," and adjustments totaling billions of dollars were "routinely made to accounting records and account balances . . . without adequate documentation."[236] Needless to say, neither the Naval Audit Service nor the GAO was able to express an audit opinion on the Navy statements.

Two years later, in 1998, the entire department went into audit as a part of the first comprehensive audit of the consolidated financial statements of the US government. Because of pervasive problems in finance and accounting systems across federal agencies, the GAO was unable to determine the reliability of significant portions of consolidated financial statements and declined to express an audit opinion.[237] The GAO found material deficiencies in every area of the department's accounting, including inventories of property, plant, and equipment; military equipment; inventory (including in-transit inventory); environmental liabilities; postretirement health care costs; cost of operations; intra-agency transactions; cash activity; disbursements; checks issued; and amounts in suspense accounts.[238]

Despite ten years of effort and the acceptance of hundreds of audit recommendations, DOD IG Eleanor Hill testified, "The financial statement data for most DOD funds remains unreliable and essentially not in condition for audit."[239] Two subsequent audits of consolidated federal financial statements, in 1999 and 2000, produced similar results. In each case, the GAO was unable to express an opinion on the government's books,[240] and, in each case, DOD accounting deficiencies were a primary cause of the problem.[241] The results of the 1999 audit, the acting DOD IG testified, "were identical to the previous poor results." Improved financial statements would be possible only with "sustained and probably even intensified commitment" that "will certainly take several more years."[242]

In 2000, the GAO reported that "almost one of every three dollars in contract payment transactions was made to adjust a previously recorded transaction."[243] In one case, efforts to reconcile a single contract that involved 162 payments resulted in an estimated 15,000 adjustments.[244] Overall, the department made an eye-popping $7.6 trillion of adjustments in the preparation of its financial statements, of which at least $2.3 trillion were unsupported. The assistant DOD IG testified that "the notion of accounting [adjustments] being made on a mass scale to compensate for incomplete and inaccurate financial reporting input is completely foreign to corporate America, as is the prospect of such adjustments being unsupported by clear audit trails."[245]

As the decade progressed, a rising chorus of auditors and financial managers expressed the view that the audit path was unproductive and unsustainable. "In my opinion," Deputy DOD IG Derek Vander Schaaf testified in 1994, "using more audit resources to attempt to gain full compliance with the act would suboptimize our audit efforts."[246] In 1998, IG Eleanor Hill told a House hearing that the department's commitment to financial statement audits was reducing the audit community's coverage of other financial and management issues to dangerously low levels and that these audits "are not necessarily the most efficient audit approach to identifying the scope and causes of such problems."[247] When Acting DOD IG Don Mancuso made a similar point a year later, he found support from both DOD Comptroller Bill Lynn and the GAO's Gene Dodaro.[248]

By 2001, SASC concluded that the resources used by the department in a fruitless effort to audit itself into auditability would be better spent addressing the underlying problems in the DOD's finance and accounting systems.[249] Section 1008 of the FY 2002 National Defense Authorization Act (NDAA) effectively terminated the DOD's first effort to audit for auditability, prohibiting the department from expending more than minimal resources to develop, compile, report on, and audit annual financial statements until such time as the secretary concluded that "the systems used within the Department of Defense for the preparation of financial statements allow the achievement of reliability in those financial statements."[250]

The DOD IG endorsed the provision on the ground that "labor intensive efforts to audit the convoluted workarounds and poorly documented transactions that currently characterize most major DOD financial statements" were a waste of resources.²⁵¹ What the legislation did, the IG explained, was to avoid expensive audits for the purpose of "telling everybody what they already know—that these statements are unauditable."²⁵² The department had spent hundreds of millions of dollars on short-term fixes designed to address the symptoms of weak financial systems and show progress toward auditability, and had nothing tangible to show for the effort.

THE 2000s: THE BUSH II AND OBAMA ADMINISTRATIONS

Grand Design II: The Business Enterprise Architecture (BEA)
As the 1990s wound down and it became increasingly evident that the audit strategy was not producing results, the GAO began to develop a new approach. To be effective, the GAO asserted, future financial reforms would have to be based on a comprehensive systems architecture containing "detailed information . . . necessary to determine whether implementation of the department's future financial management environment is 'workable'—that is, whether the planned environment is practical, cost-effective, and feasible."²⁵³ In 2000 and 2001, the GAO elaborated on this prescription, arguing that an integrated system architecture would have to define the department's business processes; describe information needs and flows, work locations, and system applications; identify hardware, software, data, communications, and security requirements; and explain how the hundreds of improvement initiatives planned by the department would fit into the plan.²⁵⁴

Without such an architecture, the GAO argued, the DOD would run "the serious risk that its components will spend billions of dollars modifying and modernizing financial management systems independently from one another, resulting in DOD perpetuating an existing systems environment that suffers from duplication of systems, limited interoperablity, and unnecessarily costly operations and maintenance."²⁵⁵ Consequently, until a fully developed architecture was in place, the department should limit business systems investments to expenditures for fully proven systems that "involve no additional development or acquisition cost," "stay-in-business maintenance needed to keep existing systems operational," and other "relatively small, cost effective, and low risk" system improvements.[256]

In early 2001, Donald Rumsfeld, the president's nominee for secretary of defense, was greeted at his SASC hearing by a lecture from Senator Robert Byrd on the "utter disarray"[257] in the Pentagon's books. How could the department expect Congress to consider a $50 billion increase in the defense budget, Byrd asked, "when DOD's own auditors say the Department cannot account for $2.3 trillion in [unmatched] transactions in 1 year alone?"[258] Rumsfeld responded by describing the task of bringing order to the department's finances as "terrifying" and pledging to make the issue one of his top priorities.[259] Upon his confirmation, Rumsfeld commissioned an independent study group to review the issue and report back to him.[260]

The study group reinforced the GAO's push for a new architecture, confirming that the DOD had "hundreds and hundreds of feeder systems" that "grew up over the decades" and "can't speak to each other."[261] While financial management improvements were under way at the department, the study group reported, "they are narrowly focused, do not have sufficient senior leadership and urgency behind them, and are not part of an integrated DoD-wide strategy."[262] To address this deficiency, the study group concluded that the department should "develop and implement [a] DOD-wide integrated systems architecture,"[263] establish "a centralized oversight process,"[264] and "stop the practice of investing in systems that do not incorporate standardization."[265]

Lacking other persuasive alternatives, Rumsfeld directed the development of "a DOD-wide blueprint—an Enterprise Architecture ...—that prescribes how the Department's financial and nonfinancial feeder systems and business processes will interact."[266] To support the effort, the secretary approved a $100 million fund to develop an enterprise architecture, define and implement standard data requirements, document the flow of financial data, and develop a compliance process.[267] By the beginning of 2002, the department had established a program office and brought a contractor on board to assist in the development of the required BEA.[268] The DOD schedule called for documenting the "as-is" environment by May 2002, assessing compliance with federal financial requirements by July 2002, developing Defense-wide standards by August 2002, reengineering business processes by September 2002, and developing a "to-be" architecture and implementation plan by January 2003.[269]

In March 2002, DOD Comptroller Dov Zakheim told SASC that the new plan would be "the most comprehensive and integrated management reform ever attempted within DOD"[270] and "really different from anything we have had before."[271] He asserted that the DOD would have a "finished blueprint" ready for implementation within a year: "Just as an architect uses a blueprint to construct a building, the Department will use a systems blueprint to construct its future financial management infrastructure."[272] As suggested by the GAO, Zakheim promised not to fund any business system improvements until he was "convinced that they would all fit in with one another."[273] He predicted that the new plan would result in a clean audit opinion within seven years.[274] "I think it is important to set the bar high," Zakheim told SASC. "I think we can clear the bar, and we owe that to the taxpayer."[275]

A few members of Congress compared the new BEA approach to the failed CIM program. The BEA plan was "not the first ambitious reform plan launched by a new administration," Congressman Chris Shays noted, pointing out that previous plans had "floundered in the shallowest of changing priorities and management neglect."[276] Representative John Tierney observed that CIM had been abandoned after eight years and $20 billion.[277] Zakheim's deputy, Larry Lanzillotta, insisted that the new BEA would be different because of the support of the secretary and other senior officials throughout the department. He told Representative Tierney that "I believe now that the moons are all aligned. We have the highest support for fixing financial management [that] I think the Department has ever had. I think that there's no daylight between the Secretary of Defense's position and each of the service secretaries."[278]

Congress also endorsed the plan, codifying the requirement for the DOD to develop a comprehensive BEA and transition plan and prohibiting the expenditure of more than a million dollars for the improvement of a defense financial system before the completion of the BEA, absent a determination of urgent need.[279] On this basis, Congress cut the department's IT budget by $400 million. The conference report on the bill explained that "the conferees expect the Department to achieve these reductions by ... restricting the development of ... business systems until the Department has completed its proposed architecture and transition plan and is in a position to ensure that business system expenditures will be consistent with that architecture and plan."[280]

Over the following months, the comptroller's team documented the department's complex structure of existing, "as-is" business systems in a "museum-like exhibit" that took up an entire wall inside the Pentagon.[281] In early 2002, Zakheim showed SASC a chart displaying a complex web of connections among 673 accounting, finance, personnel and pay, property, budget, inventory, and other management information systems, which he said represented an "85 percent complete" representation of the department's existing processes.[282] Unfortunately, this impressive display turned out to be woefully underinclusive. Within two weeks, the department had identified an additional 200 systems.[283] In June the total reached 1,127,[284] and, in October, it was 1,731.[285] By 2003, when the entire BEA was supposed to be complete, the department's count had quadrupled to 2,300 existing systems.[286] Zakheim told SASC that "the real number is much higher, probably at least twice as high as the number we [count] now."[287]

Like the CIM program, the Business Management Modernization Program (BMMP), which was established by the department to oversee the development and implementation of the BEA,[288] developed an extensive governance structure, including its Executive Committee, Steering Committee, Domain Owner's Integration Team, and Directorate for Business Management and Systems Integration.[289] Like the CIM program, the BMMP was built around the department's existing stovepipes, with seven business lines, known as "domains": logistics, acquisition/procurement, installations and environment, human resources, accounting and financial management, strategic planning and budgeting, and technical infrastructure.[290] Also, like the CIM program, the BMMP promised to use industry best practices[291] and incorporate all applicable federal accounting, financial management, and reporting requirements.[292]

Unfortunately, the BMMP proved to be just as overwhelmed by the magnitude of the task as the CIM program had been. The DOD required a one-time data call to compile its list of the thousands of business systems in use, but the GAO expected much more. For the BEA to be effective, it would have to specify what data were in the systems, where these data came from, and who was using these data and for what purposes. This kind of detailed information could not be assembled through data calls. A smaller entity might have been able to unleash a team of auditors to piece together a map of its "as-is" business structure, but, as former DOD comptroller Robert Hale later concluded, the Pentagon was just "too big."[293]

The DOD's first effort, published in the spring of 2003, fell far short. The proposed "as-is" architecture lacked descriptions of current business operations, data used by those business operations, technology standards being employed, and performance metrics being used. The proposed "to-be" architecture lacked information about the functions, processes, and activities to be performed, the systems or applications to be developed or acquired, the physical infrastructure needed, and the organizations that would be accountable. The proposed transition plan did not include a gap analysis, an identification of systems to be phased out and a strategy for replacing those systems, or an estimate of the resources needed to accomplish the effort.[294] The department's own verification and validation contractor concluded that the BEA had limited utility, was not easily understandable, and "lacked the depth and detail needed to begin building and implementing modernized systems and making operational changes."[295]

Senior DOD officials promised to address these issues.[296] Unfortunately, the next version of the BEA, delivered a year later, showed little improvement. The department had made "no significant changes . . . to the architecture since the initial version was released," the comptroller general told SASC, and, as a result, "the program has yielded very little, if any, tangible improvements in DOD's business operations."[297] The department's verification and validation contractor, he pointed out, had also concluded "that this latest version of the architecture retained most of the critical problems of the initial version."[298]

In early 2004, Senator Daniel Akaka complained that the department still did not have a working blueprint, still had not started to field new systems, and still did not have an effective investment control system. "In short," he concluded, "we are pretty much where we started."²⁹⁹ Senator Levin was equally critical, noting that "despite spending $200 million on the project . . . the Department of Defense has yet to develop even such basic elements of an enterprise architecture as DOD-wide standards and data elements." "This is a major failure," he concluded.³⁰⁰

Zakheim acknowledged that the task was more difficult than the department had anticipated. Echoing the lessons of the CIM program a decade earlier, he told SASC that "we cannot shut down the Department of Defense for nearly a decade, throw out all old business processes and systems, and start from scratch."³⁰¹ "When we look[ed] at the finance and accounting domain," his deputy, Larry Lanzillotta, explained, the department found 180,000 business rules, processes and regulations that would have to be reviewed to make sure that they were valid. "The problem," Lanzillotta concluded, "is one of workload."³⁰² Like the initial CIM vision, the BEA standard established by the GAO turned out to be an unscalable mountain for the department.

By the middle of 2004, Zakheim and Lanzillotta had left the department and the BEA effort was reassigned to USD(AT&L) Michael Wynne and the new comptroller, Tina Jonas. At Wynne's first financial management hearing, he told SASC that he experienced an "epiphany," in which he saw a "blinding flash of the obvious": the architectures and business systems of the different military departments "do not have to be the same."³⁰³ For this reason, the department would now adopt a "tiered approach" to governance, under which the comprehensive, enterprise-wide BEA would be limited to a "visionary" statement, establishing policy, goals, and standards that would be applicable across the department.³⁰⁴ Everything else, he announced, "we are delegating to the services."³⁰⁵ Under the new, "federated" architecture, individual DOD components would be allowed to pursue their own separate business modernization plans, with only top-level issues and basic business rules addressed on a DOD-wide basis.³⁰⁶

Wynne and Jonas designated two of their deputies—Tom Modly and Paul Brinkley—to spearhead the development of the new, more narrowly focused BEA effort. The old "idealistic" approach had not produced a whole lot of value, Brinkley acknowledged, although the department was trying to figure out if any of its pieces might be salvageable.[307] By contrast, a new, more realistic architecture would establish a "powerful and deliverable objective" by "focusing on data standards that, regardless of whether we have 2,000 logistic systems or one logistics system ... enable us to interoperate and communicate and act as a single enterprise to support joint warfighting."[308] By establishing more realistic standards, the department would also be able to put in place a more effective investment management process.[309]

The new version of the BEA and transition plan, published on September 30, 2005, identified six business enterprise priorities of the department—personnel visibility, acquisition visibility, common supplier engagement, materiel visibility, real property visibility, and financial visibility—and sought to establish common capabilities, data standards, and business rules for each.[310] The BEA specifically incorporated a common financial language, which took the form of a standard financial infrastructure system (SFIS) and a standard accounting classification structure (SACS).[311] As a BMMP official explained, "SFIS allows people and systems throughout the department to communicate with each other using a common business vocabulary," which enables the department to link together disparate business systems rather than trying to impose a single, department-wide solution.[312]

The comptroller general testified that the department's revised BEA approach had "great conceptual merit" and was "clearly superior to where they were headed before,"[313] and his architecture expert asserted that the new approach was likely to meet standards mandated by the Treasury, OMB, the Federal Accounting Standards Advisory Board, and the Joint Financial Management Improvement Program.[314] As a result, BEA-compliant systems held the promise of sharing "timely, accurate, and reliable, financial information" and providing "a good start and a reasonable foundation upon which to build."[315] After years without progress, the GAO told Congress, "today the glass could be described as half full."[316]

However, the new BEA and transition plan were far from complete. For example, the department's architecture did not include "a top-down capability gap analysis between the 'as-is' and 'to-be' architectures that describes capability and performance shortfall and clearly identifies which system investments" are to address these shortfalls.³¹⁷ The transition plan did not include a comprehensive list of legacy systems or identify which systems were to be phased out as new systems were built. Most importantly, the new BEA and transition plan did not link to the twenty separate architectures and transition plans maintained by the DOD components.³¹⁸ "While DOD has developed plans that address aspects of business transformation at different organizational levels," the comptroller general pointed out, "these plans have not been clearly aligned into a comprehensive, integrated, and enterprise-wide approach to business transformation."³¹⁹

Ken Krieg, Wynne's successor as USD(AT&L) and the third person to head the BEA effort in less than two years, readily acknowledged the shortfall. The new BEA was "not a finally finished product," Krieg told SASC. "I full-well admit that there is a lot of work left to be done in the architecture."³²⁰ On the other hand, Krieg questioned the value of collecting more extensive information on the department's existing systems, suggesting that after years of wasted effort, the department now knew that this approach was a dead end that had soaked up resources without providing anything useful.³²¹

In fact, neither the DOD nor the components ever filled in the details of the architecture. In a 2006 review, the GAO found that the Air Force had not yet established a configuration management system, the Navy had not yet addressed performance requirements for its architectural environment, and the Army had fully addressed only one of thirty-one core elements of the architectural framework.³²² In 2007, the GAO reported that the latest version of the BEA had yet to be augmented by mature subsidiary architectures in the components.³²³ In 2008, the GAO reported that the BEA "continues to represent the thin layer of DOD-wide corporate architectural policies, capabilities, rules, and standards"³²⁴ and was not supplemented by well-defined service architectures that were sufficient to "effectively and efficiently guide and constrain business system investments across all levels of the department."³²⁵

None of these problems were ever addressed. More than a decade after the DOD promised to develop a comprehensive system architecture, the GAO found that the BEA had "yet to be federated through the development of aligned subordinate architectures for each of the military departments" and the department's transition plan still "lacked important content, such as time-phased milestones, performance measures, and finance resource needs for all business systems."[326] Despite a ten-year effort that cost at least $379 million, the GAO concluded that "DOD has not yet demonstrated that the BEA has produced business value for the Department."[327]

An Institute for Defense Analyses (IDA) team led by Paul Ketrick concluded that the federated architecture was essentially no architecture at all. The BEA identified business process flows and processes that were critical to business operations, the IDA reported, but it contained "no data that describe the real structure of the enterprise," had no "set of blueprints and architecture detail for each capability," and "does not map people, processes and systems." Most devastatingly, the report concluded that "there is more organizational information about the Department in Wikipedia than one can find in the BEA."[328]

The DOD continued to give lip service to the BEA, but the attention of senior officials moved elsewhere. The BEA, like the CIM program, suffered from the overambitious objective of trying to comprehend all the details and all the defects of the department's business systems before trying to address any of them. The department made a "noble attempt" to develop a workable BEA, but it never had the discipline to build strong standards and stick to them. In the end, the BEA process became a way to "pay contractors a lot of money" to map processes (sometimes more than once) without achieving definable results.[329] Once again, the DOD had tried the comprehensive, top-down model of business reform, and, once again, it had failed.

Partial Solutions II: ERPs, BTA, and DCMOs
While senior DOD leaders endeavored first to implement and then to circumvent the GAO's BEA recommendations, the department looked for an approach to link stovepiped legacy systems into a working finance and accounting system. In 1998, DFAS initiated a project to establish the DFAS Corporate Database (DCD) to "crosswalk detailed transaction data from nonstandard finance and feeder systems into a standard

format. . . . ."³³⁰ While the objective of the DCD was to develop usable finance and accounting data with minimal changes to existing financial management and feeder systems, the department soon found that the cost of cross-walking data from a maze of inconsistent feeder systems was prohibitive. DFAS responded by determining that the DCD would receive only summary data from feeder systems. This approach addressed the cost problem but limited the utility of the system.³³¹

DOD officials sought a solution in the private sector. In the 1990s, many companies had turned to commercial ERPs that linked finance and accounting, inventory management, personnel management, and other data requirements in an integrated approach. ERPs were off-the-shelf systems that were intended to replace company-specific, in-house-designed business systems.³³² They were designed to be tailored to the needs of complex business organizations and to be fielded on a modular, phased basis. By 2001, corporate spending on ERPs was estimated at about $20 billion a year, and more than 60 percent of the Fortune 1000 companies had ERP systems installed or were in the process of implementing these systems.³³³

In the late 1990s, however, private sector companies began to report significant difficulties in implementing ERPs. In 1999, the failed implementation of an ERP at Hershey Foods prevented the company from delivering $100 million worth of candy in time for Halloween, leading to an 8 percent drop in the company's stock price.³³⁴ A year later, similar problems led to a 20 percent drop in Nike's stock price, prompting company chairman Phil Knight to comment, "This is what you get for $400 million, huh?"³³⁵ Problems with the implementation of ERPs reportedly led some companies to go out of business altogether.³³⁶ As a result, articles began to appear in the trade press proclaiming melodramatically that "ERP is dead."³³⁷

Even when ERPs were successfully implemented, the process rarely took place without significant pain and disruption. ERPs required companies either to reengineer their business processes to accommodate the logic of the software modules or undertake the expensive process of rewriting off-the-shelf software to meet their business needs.³³⁸ As a result, *CIO Digital Magazine* reported that private sector ERP projects "have only a 7 percent chance of coming in on time, most certainly will cost more than estimated, and very likely will deliver very unsatisfying results." Moreover, "today's enterprise has a little better than a 50 percent chance that users will want to and will actually use the application."[339] One IT executive later summed up the feelings of many: "To the finance directors of the world, ERP stands for Expense, Regret, Pain. Sadly, our industry has a long history of invasive, disruptive initiatives that have been carried out at the expense of their customers."[340]

Just as these warning flags were going up, the DOD decided that ERPs were the way to go. The department took a few cautious steps in 1998 and 1999, with investments in the Navy's ERP pilot projects and the first phases of the Army's Logistics Modernization Program (LMP) and the DLA's Business Systems Modernization (BSM) program.[341] Then the floodgates opened. In 2003, the Navy began its "converged ERP" program, the Air Force initiated the Defense Enterprise Accounting and Management System (DEAMS) program, and the Army and the Marine Corps initiated Global Combat Support Systems-Army (GCSS-A) and Global Combat Support Systems-Marine Corps (GCSS-MC) to integrate the logistical and financial data of their tactical units. A year later, the Army began its General Fund Enterprise Business System (GFEBS) program and the Air Force initiated its Expeditionary Combat Support System (ECSS) program.[342] Within a period of just two years, the department initiated six major programs, betting billions of dollars on ERPs as the wave of the future.

DOD components, like private sector companies, found it difficult to accept the business process changes required for successful ERP implementation. At the DOD, the problem was exacerbated by efforts to implement ERPs across an entire military service or defense agency—a scale not seen in the commercial world—in a single increment, rather than by delivering small amounts of capability in a learning process.[343] Moreover, as the DOD IG pointed out, the department's ERP development programs were not coordinated, the systems were not designed as part of an integrated financial management structure, and they did not share common data elements with each other or with the thousands of feeder systems in the department.[344]

The problems showed up first in the early pilot projects. In 2004, the GAO reported that the Army's LMP program and the DLA's BSM program were behind schedule, hundreds of millions of dollars over budget, and would not meet performance expectations.[345] Neither system would remedy long-standing asset visibility problems because each was designed to address only a small part of the problem and would continue to rely on legacy systems to provide key data.[346] The two systems required dozens of interfaces with legacy systems and many of them did not work, requiring costly and error-prone manual reentry of transactions.[347] The LMP and BSM programs, the GAO concluded, were "prime examples of DOD business system modernization projects costing billions of dollars" without delivering the intended capabilities.[348] The Navy's ERP pilot programs employed more disciplined processes, but they were not interoperable with each other, resulting in stovepiped systems that did not markedly improve the service's business operations.[349]

In October 2005, Deputy Secretary of Defense Gordon England sought to address shortcomings in the acquisition of new business systems by establishing "an accountable, top-level organization"—the BTA—to "serve as the corporate headquarters function for implementing and driving business change that is DOD-wide in scope."[350] As BTA codirector Paul Brinkley explained, the BTA was established to cut across stovepipes and "consolidate and centralize transformation efforts across the department, establishing "single-point accountability for the delivery of enterprise-wide services and capabilities within the Department."[351]

However, the military services had already made major commitments to ERPs and did not welcome second-guessing from the OSD. Instead of bringing single-point accountability, the BTA soon found itself limited to running a handful of defense-wide programs—the Defense Integrated Military Human Resources System (DIMHRS), the Defense Travel System (DTS), and the Defense Agencies Initiative (DAI)—while the components continued to go their own ways. Within two years, the BTA was telling the GAO that it had "neither the authority nor the responsibility" to direct the actions of the military departments.[352] Moreover, BTA officials asserted, "under DOD's tiered approach to investment accountability," the military departments had sole responsibility for validating their own compliance with DOD and government-wide requirements.³⁵³

The BTA's flagship project—the DIMHRS program—ran into the same problems as the earlier CIM efforts to force common business solutions across the department. Once again, the department discovered that the "traditionally separate communities and organizations" in the military services were "reluctant to adopt the uniform processes and business rules within the commercial-off-the-shelf product."³⁵⁴ The Navy and Marine Corps sought to withdraw from DIMHRS in 2006, having decided that their needs could be met better by an existing Marine Corps system. The Army and the Air Force continued to participate but insisted on a need "to evaluate their respective requirements," reporting that DIMHRS software could meet their needs only "under certain conditions."³⁵⁵

In 2009, three years after the system was supposed to have been deployed and with hundreds of software issues still to be resolved, the DIMHRS program was put on indefinite hold.³⁵⁶ A year later, it was terminated. "After 10 years of effort, poor performance and difficulties with that program, I would say that what we've gotten for half a billion dollars is an unpronounceable acronym," Secretary of Defense Robert Gates told SASC. "Many of the programs that I have made decisions to cut have been controversial within DOD. I will tell you this one was not."³⁵⁷ A year later, Gates also shut down the BTA, transferring its remaining programs to other offices.³⁵⁸

The service ERP programs initially fared little better. In 2007 and 2008, the GAO reported that the three Army ERPs were at risk because the Army had chosen to "simply to adapt the processes used by the legacy systems" without reengineering its business processes;³⁵⁹ the two Air Force ERPs were at risk because of a failure to identify and address multiple interfaces with legacy systems and to prepare users for anticipated changes to systems and processes;³⁶⁰ and the Navy ERP program had failed to mitigate risks associated with converting data from existing systems to the new system and preparing users for the operational changes associated with the new system.³⁶¹ As a result, these programs were plagued by "trouble tickets," interface problems, accounting noncompliances, and other deficiencies.³⁶²

By 2010, the department's six largest ERPs had experienced schedule delays ranging from two to twelve years and incurred cost increases ranging from $530 million to $2.4 billion, for a total of $6.9 billion in cost overruns—and were still far from completion.[363] The programs could not be effectively implemented, the GAO reported, "because the program office does not have the authority to compel the user organizations to execute their part of the mitigation strategy."[364]

Once again, Comptroller General David Walker had a ready answer, telling Congress that the DOD needed "a top-level management official" at the level of the deputy secretary of defense, who could address the department's financial management problems by cutting across stovepipes and addressing cross-cutting issues on a sustained basis.[365] He later elaborated: "If the Department of Defense does not develop a Chief Management Officer at [the deputy secretary level] who is responsible and accountable for this, who can take a more strategic and integrated approach on a sustained basis over a period of time, and if we do not link resources with responsibility, this effort will not succeed."[366]

In 2005, Senators John Ensign and Daniel Akaka, the chair and ranking Democrat of the SASC subcommittee with jurisdiction over financial management issues, introduced a bill to implement the GAO recommendation.[367] Senator Robert Byrd backed the proposal, offering it as an amendment to the FY 2006 NDAA when it came to the Senate floor.[368] Fundamental change was needed, Byrd told the Senate, because years of reform plans were "just are not getting the job done. They do not amount to a hill of beans. They are not doing the work."[369]

The DOD rejected the idea of a second deputy, arguing that the change "would be just adding layers and players to an already burdened organization." The department had tried to establish a deputy secretary for management once before, USD(AT&L) Michael Wynne noted. "It was in 1972, and the job went unfilled for several years. Congress finally repealed the statute after some organizational dysfunction."[370] At the suggestion of SASC Chair John Warner, the Byrd amendment was modified to direct the department to provide for a pair of independent studies, so that the concept could be "studied step by step before the Congress is called upon to render its judgement."[371]

After both reports endorsed the concept of a chief management officer (CMO),[372] the DOD tried to finesse the issue by designating Deputy Secretary of Defense Gordon England to serve concurrently as the agency CMO.[373] Congress codified the deputy secretary's new responsibilities, but also provided him with a new deputy chief management officer (DCMO) "to ensure that a senior official of the Department has formal responsibility, on a full-time basis, for assisting the CMO in accomplishing his or her duties in the development, approval, integration and oversight of policies, procedures, processes, and systems for the management of the Department."[374] For good measure, the provision designated the service under secretaries as the CMOs of the military departments.[375]

The new organizational requirements took effect at the beginning of the Obama administration in 2009, with William Lynn, the new deputy secretary, becoming the department's first statutory CMO. At his nomination hearing before SASC, Lynn promised to "empower the DCMO to resolve cross-functional issues that the Department faces in fielding business transformation programs."[376] The GAO soon reported, however, that the DCMO position, "although full-time, does not have decision-making authority."[377] Tellingly, the office remained vacant for more than a year and a half before a nominee could be identified, nominated, and confirmed.

By the time SASC held a hearing on Beth McGrath's nomination in March 2010, the moment for empowerment had long passed. Ms. McGrath identified problems with the department's absence of cross-functional governance, lack of BPR, weak performance measures, and rigid funding process. When it came to addressing these issues, however, she could only promise to "work with key stakeholders in the Department" to find better approaches.[378] Ms. McGrath testified, "The Department will rely heavily on the military department CMOs to help ensure proper governance is in place within each military department to successfully field these systems."[379] When Ms. McGrath was asked whether she would play a role in the planning, development, and implementation of specific business systems by the military departments, she testified that she would "set policy" for such actions.[380]

Congress tried to strengthen the DCMO by designating her as the vice chair of a new committee, the DBSMC, with approval authority for all business systems investments in excess of $1 million and responsibility for ensuring compliance with the BEA, cross-domain integration, and BPR.[381] Unfortunately, the DBSMC investment review process turned out to be toothless, routinely approving virtually all funding requests. An IDA review explained, "Few are willing or incentivized to stop poorly performing programs. In many cases there are disincentives for stopping, including the political costs associated with recognizing that sunk costs have realized little or no value."[382] The DBSMC meetings became mired in trivia, and before long senior DOD officials stopped attending the meetings, sending representatives instead. "They just skipped the meetings," former under secretary of the army Joe Westphal recalls. "There was no consequence. Nobody was called on the carpet."[383]

In 2013, the GAO found that the DCMO had routinely approved business system investments without ensuring compliance with even minimal requirements. For example, the DCMO made no effort to validate service assertions that they had performed BPR and were in compliance with the BEA, and no business system investment was denied approval for either reason.[384] The DCMO explained that "a large increase in the number of systems to be reviewed" and the short time for implementing the investment review process forced the office to rely on service representations that BPR had taken place and that business system investments were BEA compliant, even in the absence of documentation or plans.[385]

The advent of new service CMOs in 2009 had a more favorable impact, perhaps because the deputy secretaries of the military services actually owned the business systems and processes that they were charged with modernizing. As a result, two of the three military departments were able to plow through institutional resistance and field less-than-perfect solutions that were nonetheless a significant improvement over the legacy systems that they replaced.

In the Navy, Under Secretary Bob Work pushed forward with the planned ERP deployment while seeking to standardize and streamline business processes in parallel. Alone among the services, the Navy took an incremental approach to the deployment of its ERP program, accepting the delivery of small amounts of capability to "gather necessary data, be in line with software refresh rates, and to minimize the risks inherent in ERP acquisition."[386] Moreover, the Navy adopted several key "best practices" for managing the ERP program, implementing a program-level Earned Value Management System, ensuring the traceability of requirements, and proactively managing risks.[387] As a result, the Navy ERP was deployed to more than 70,000 users, enabling the department to shut down almost a hundred legacy systems by 2016.[388] While the system was far from ideal, it was a significant improvement over the systems that it replaced.

In the Army, Under Secretary Joe Westphal recruited a three-star general to head his Office of Business Transformation and formed a "cabinet council" of assistant secretaries and key military officials to drive business process changes across stovepipes.[389] The GFEBS and GCSS programs were re-scoped to make them more manageable, and the Integrated Personnel and Pay System-Army (IPPS-A) was initiated on a sounder footing, after consideration of user requirements.[390] As a result, GFEBS was fully deployed to 35,000 users in in July 2012, and the Army was able to phase out forty-eight legacy systems, with another sixty-two systems scheduled for sunset in the future. The deployment of LMP, GCSS-A, and IPPS-A enabled the Army to phase out an additional eleven systems, with forty-nine more systems scheduled for future sunset.[391] Like the Navy ERP, the new Army systems were far from being able to produce auditable financial statements but were vastly superior to the legacy systems that they replaced.

The Air Force CMO structure was not nearly as successful, as Air Force ERPs continued to suffer from the absence of a clear champion within Air Force senior leadership and a "confusing" and "ineffectual" governance structure that constantly changed through the life of the program.[392] Over a period of eight years, the ECSS program had ten different organizational constructs, five program executive officers, and six program managers.[393] Program officials complained that they had to spend "crucial time 'feeding the governance monster' by completing nonessential tasks that 'just didn't matter to the success of the program,'" rather than addressing issues critical to program success.[394]

As a result, the Air Force ERPs succumbed to the efforts of functional communities to hold on to old systems and processes. For example, the Air Force required DEAMS "to operate in such a way as to allow the legacy systems to remain the systems of record until the ERP was proven to be effective."[395] As IDA pointed out, this approach violated "two of the fundamental leading practices of ERP implementation, namely to severely limit the number of customizations, such as RICE objects, and to re-engineer business processes rather than modifying the ERP to reflect existing business processes."[396] Only one existing Air Force system was sunset as DEAMS was stood up, while the new system was expected to interface with more than 100 legacy systems.[397] Moreover, DEAMS was "intolerant of bad data," requiring manual workarounds when it was flooded by large quantities of bad information produced by flawed feeder systems.[398]

Similarly, the Air Force initiated the ECSS acquisition without conducting any BPR.[399] Instead, it purchased three off-the-shelf ERP software products and left the task of requirements development and program planning almost completely in the hands of the contractor.[400] Rather than drawing a hard line against customization of the commercial, off-the-shelf (COTS) software, the program office developed a pattern of giving in to the demands of Air Force functional communities to retain existing processes and reports.[401] Like DEAMS, ECSS had to be designed to interface with hundreds of legacy systems that functional users refused to relinquish. As a result, ECSS was estimated to be twenty-eight times more complex than any previous ERP system, as measured by the number of interfaces to be developed.[402] At a 2011 hearing, Senator Claire McCaskill pointed to the unprecedented number of interfaces, telling the Air Force: "It is trouble to have that many interfaces. It is not going to happen."[403]

In the face of these problems, the Air Force had to delay full-scale deployment of DEAMS, forcing it to rely on legacy systems to meet congressional auditability requirements.[404] As of June 2016 (thirteen years after program initiation), DEAMS was deployed to major Air Force commands on only a limited basis and remained unable to meet three of the nine goals for the program's first increment.[405] The ECSS program was restructured twice—in 2009 and again in 2010—before being terminated in 2012.[406] By that time, the Air Force had spent more than a billion dollars on the program and estimated that even with the expenditure of another billion dollars, ECSS was unlikely to yield more than a quarter of the capacity that the Air Force originally sought.[407] "I am personally appalled at the limited capabilities that program has produced relative to that amount of investment," the Air Force comptroller testified, adding that "the rest of the senior Air Force leadership feels that way as well."[408]

With remarkable consistency, the DOD set out to purchase COTS business systems, only to run into resistance from functional users accustomed to old ways of doing business. All too often, the department responded by tailoring the COTS systems to fit existing processes and creating multiple interfaces with outdated and unreliable legacy systems. As a result, the cost of the projects ballooned and deployment was delayed. Even so, the Army and Navy ERPs—much like the DFAS finance and accounting systems developed twenty years earlier—were superior to the obsolete and error-prone systems that preceded them.

If the point of the ERP systems was to produce auditable financial statements, the investment in ERPs would have to be judged a failure. If, however, the objective was to meet the information needs of the department's functional communities and provide more timely and accurate data for them to use in business decisions, the record is more mixed. The Army and Navy success stories, coupled with the Air Force failures, demonstrate that effective governance at the service level—by officials who actually "own" the systems and processes to be replaced—can make a significant difference, and incremental progress is far better than no progress at all.

Auditing for Audit II
After the failure of the DOD's first attempt to audit its way to auditability in the 1990s, the department got the message that there was no quick and easy path to an auditable financial statement. The independent study group convened by Secretary Rumsfeld to review DOD financial

management issues reported that getting to a "clean" audit opinion would be "a long-term process" that could take as long as eight to ten years.[409] The new comptroller, Dov Zakheim, likewise acknowledged that the department was unlikely to be auditable for seven years or more. "We are not looking for Band-Aids," Zakheim told SASC, explaining that the department would not be able to produce an auditable financial statement until "we have cleaned up our business operations and we can monitor and track those."[410]

In June 2003, Zakheim's deputy explained that it would cost the department an estimated $1.8 billion to prepare a financial statement for audit in 2004, with an additional $500 million needed for the IG to perform the audit. Even in the unlikely event that this approach resulted in a clean audit opinion, it would still not provide timely information to support the department's business decisions. "Then you have to do that again in 2005 and do it again in 2006 and have to continue to do that," he continued. "That doesn't make economic sense."[411] The IG's office confirmed that it would need 2,000 to 3,000 more auditors to review a full DOD financial statement, the equivalent to hiring "every accounting student that is graduating this year."[412]

Nonetheless, the CFO Act was still the law, and the *Blueprint for New Beginnings* that accompanied President Bush's first budget called for "holding agency heads accountable for obtaining and maintaining unqualified or 'clean' opinions on their agencies' annual financial statement audits."[413] As the document explained, "The President believes that Government must ensure a basic level of financial accountability that is expected of any company in the private sector."[414] The President's Management Agenda and OMB's management scorecard for federal agencies likewise called for the achievement of auditable financial statements.[415]

By the end of the year, the DOD comptroller bent to the pressure and called on the services to develop comprehensive "midrange financial improvement plans [FIPs]" to support the goal of achieving an unqualified audit opinion by FY 2007.[416] When Senator Levin reminded Zakheim of previous statements on the futility of trying to achieve a successful audit through heroic end-of-the-year efforts and asked whether the department would be better off spending a billion dollars on improved business systems, Zakheim conceded that 2007 was "definitely a reach." Nonetheless, he insisted that "2007 is a goal that the DOD components have signed up to. They gave us a list of milestones and achievements, literally line by line in the financial statements, when they are going to get things done."[417]

Zakheim retired several weeks later, leaving the acting comptroller, Larry Lanzillotta, to acknowledge the impossibility of the task. "I can't get a system in place in 2007, it just isn't going to happen," Lanzillotta told a House hearing. "I think we need the heroic effort and the reason I am pushing that is because if I don't have a milestone out there, if I don't say 2007, say climb tall mountains, leap tall buildings, we won't make the progress we need to get this done."[418] The department's first audit attempt, Lanzillotta later added, was "going to be ugly."[419]

In September 2004, the GAO reviewed the department's plans for meeting the new auditability objective and reported that the 2007 goal "was set without direct input from all major DOD components," and that "the milestone dates identified in the component plans were based on assertion dates prescribed by the DOD Comptroller and not on actual estimates of effort required."[420] While 2007 "is a goal," the comptroller general told SASC, "there is not a plan to reach that goal and it is not a realistic goal."[421] A few months later, he added that "they don't have a plan to meet that date, and they don't have a prayer to meet that date."[422]

The armed services committees responded by prohibiting the services from spending more money on the audit effort until the department could provide detailed information on the projected costs of implementation.[423] A year later, Congress prohibited expenditures for "any financial management improvement activity relating to the preparation, processing, or auditing of financial statements" until a comprehensive plan was in place.[424] The most effective way to fix the department's financial management problems, SASC concluded, was not to conduct more audits, but "to attack the problems at the root, by fixing the Department's business systems and processes so that they provide timely, reliable, and complete data for management purposes."[425]

The 2007 audit goal was abandoned, but the department's push for an early audit had at least one lasting result: the FIPs submitted by the services became building blocks for annual DOD-wide Financial Improvement and Audit Readiness (FIAR) plans required by Deputy Secretary England in December 2005 to serve as a consolidated roadmap for the department's efforts to "fix internal controls, correct processes, and obtain an unqualified audit opinion."[426] The FIAR Plan, Deputy Comptroller David Patterson told the Senate in 2006, "unites DOD's functional and financial operations and comprehensively guides the effort to incrementally eliminate material weaknesses to achieve an independently verified and clean audit opinion."[427]

The initial FIAR plan was a loosely connected set of twenty-plus "initiatives," such as a Military Equipment Initiative, a Fund Balance with Treasury (FBWT) Initiative, and a Statement of Budgetary Resources (SBR) Initiative. For each initiative, the plan provided a description of challenges, deficiencies, risks, and limitations, as well as projected dates for achieving favorable audit results—but no actual description of the actions that would be taken to address the identified problems.[428] Gantt charts included in the report's appendices created the illusion of a time-phased plan, but the milestones were so generic as to provide no guidance at all. In November 2006, the GAO reported that it could not comment on the specific focus areas and milestones in the FIAR plan in the absence of detailed subordinate plans that explained how the milestones would be met.[429]

Over the next three years, the FIAR plan became vastly more complex, spiraling out to include more than 120 pages of "Key Milestones" in ever more finely defined categories.[430] As the GAO pointed out, however, the plan still failed to provide clear guidance on such basic issues as the needed improvements in policies, processes and controls, and systems and data; actions needed to address make those improvements; and realistically attainable dates for components to achieve financial statement auditability.[431] Rather than providing a blueprint for attaining financial accountability, former DFAS director Zack Gaddy says, the expanded FIAR plan provided a "soda straw view of the world," allowing the components to pick and choose milestones to address without ever making real progress.[432]

Over the next few years, the Bush administration pointed to favorable audit opinions achieved by a handful of defense agencies and favorable reviews of selected line items in the department's financial statements as an indication of progress.[433] "In fiscal year 2001, only $879 billion in combined DoD assets and liabilities received unqualified audit opinions," DOD comptroller Tina Jonas wrote. "By FY 2007, DoD had cleanly audited $1.3 trillion, or 36 percent of its assets and liabilities."[434] However, the progress was mostly an illusion since the balance-sheet emphasis of the early FIAR plans incentivized the services to prioritize the valuation of large items—such as real estate, facilities, and military equipment—without developing the business systems and processes needed to document transactions and produce the timely, reliable data that would be useful for management purposes.[435]

As a result, the vast majority of the department—including the three military departments—remained unaudited and unauditable. Beginning in 2002, the DOD comptroller determined annually that the DOD's financial statements were not reliable for audit due to material weaknesses in thirteen areas covering every aspect of the statements. At the end of the Bush administration six years later, the department's financial statements remained unreliable due to material weaknesses in the same thirteen areas.[436] At a Senate hearing in 2007, Senator Tom Coburn noted that "I think we are kind of like we are on a paddleboat and we are going against the current. We haven't lost any, but I am not sure we have made any headway. As we continue to change things and change techniques and change strategies, I am not sure we are any closer to the goal."[437]

The year 2009 brought a new administration and a new comptroller. Bob Hale was greeted at his nomination hearing by a startling question from Senator Ben Nelson: "Do you honestly think that it's possible to get an audit of DOD?" "That is the law," Hale responded, "and we are trying to pursue it." Wouldn't it be more plausible, Nelson asked, to achieve results in a more rational way by "stair-stepping" through partial audits in certain areas? "I think the answer is yes," Hale responded. "There may be some priorities we can impose on the audit, that lead most quickly to getting verification that we have good data." "I'm mindful of the challenge," Hale concluded. "It's Herculean," Nelson replied.[438]

True to his word, Hale issued a DOD-wide memorandum making the achievement of an auditable SBR—tracking funds received, obligated, and expended through end-to-end processes like procure-to-pay, hire-to-retire, and order-to-cash—the highest priority of the FIAR plan. The audit plan would be restructured into five "waves": (1) auditability of appropriations received; (2) the SBR audit; (3) auditability of the existence and completeness of DOD assets; (4) a full audit, except for valuation of legacy assets; and (5) a full financial statement audit.[439] "If we try for everything," Hale explained, "I am afraid we will again get nothing. I believe firmly we have to pick some priorities and go after them, and we have done that."[440]

Hale did not see the investment required to achieve an auditable balance sheet as anything other than a waste of money. Achieving a full audit, he told a Senate hearing, "would likely require the expenditure of large sums to acquire and improve information, especially the historical costs of existing assets that, frankly, are just not used to manage the Department."[441] His strategy was to get the data that the department could actually use first and then fight over further requirements, if possible, at a later date.[442]

Despite Hale's effort to refocus the debate, the full auditability goal would not go away.[443] The House-reported version of the FY 2010 NDAA directed the DOD to develop "a plan to achieve a full, unqualified audit of the Department of Defense by September 30, 2013."[444] At the Senate's insistence, the provision was revised to prioritize the SBR audit and emphasize systemic fixes, and to extend the auditability goal until September 30, 2017, when the DOD had predicted that its financial statements would be "validated as ready for audit."[445] Even so, the bottom line was that the effort to achieve auditability would again be calendar-driven rather than event-driven.

When Leon Panetta was nominated to replace Robert Gates as secretary of defense a year later, he sought to accelerate the goal. "If I am confirmed," Panetta told SASC, "one of the first things I am going to do is to try to see if we can't take steps to try to improve on that timetable."[446] Upon taking office, Panetta pushed his staff to move the goal for a full financial audit up to 2014.[447] When he was told that this objective was unachievable, Panetta substituted the goal of achieving audit readiness of the department's SBR by 2014, while remaining on track for full auditability by 2017.[448]

Even as Panetta was raising the audit bar, the department was missing existing milestones, reporting delays in readiness validation for Army, Navy, Air Force, and DLA statements of appropriations received and in the deployment of the GCSS-Army, GCSS-Marine Corps, and Air Force ECSS programs, and the DLA's Enterprise Business System (EBS).[449] The Navy and Marine Corps believed that they would be able to meet the 2014 deadline, but the Army had not planned to have an auditable SBR until 2015,[450] and the Air Force reported that the new goal would mean reliance on financial systems dating to the Vietnam War era, requiring "labor-intensive" manual workarounds.[451] Nonetheless, Congress quickly codified the requirement for a 2014 SBR audit.[452]

Over the next few years, the DOD's schedule continued to slip. In September 2011, the GAO reported that the Navy had failed to properly execute its civilian pay plan and that the Air Force had failed to properly execute its military equipment plan. In each case, the failures were pervasive, including insufficient control and substantive testing, inadequate identification of the universe of transactions, absence of effective information systems controls, and ineffective corrective action plans.[453] The GAO also found that the Navy and Marine Corps had failed to implement effective training, controls, processes, and documentation to support their statements of FBWT.[454] "As we go through these processes," Navy comptroller Gladys Commons explained to SASC in April 2012, "we are finding that we need to take more corrective actions than originally planned." As a result, "we are moving some of the dates out."[455]

The biggest test—and ultimately, the biggest failure—came with the Marine Corps' effort to undergo an early audit of its SBR. The Marine Corps believed that it was far ahead of the other services in addressing its financial management problems and sought to undergo an audit of its financial statements as early as 2006.[456] Finally, in September 2009, with Bob Hale's new incremental strategy in place, the Marine Corps got the green light to go ahead with an SBR audit. It would be a test case for the department's new effort to audit its way to auditability. "You can't learn to swim on the beach," Hale explained.[457]

The initial results were not encouraging. The Marine Corps received a disclaimer of opinion on its FY 2010 SBR "because it could not provide supporting documentation in a timely manner," "support for transactions was missing or incomplete," and the service "did not have adequate processes, systems controls, and controls for accounting and reporting on the use of budgetary resources."[458] For example, the Marine Corps recorded payments before recording expenses, resulting in "abnormal balances," and it could not identify documentation for "bulk obligations" bundling multiple transactions.[459] Overall, the auditors communicated 70 notices of findings and recommendations and 139 recommendations for corrective action.[460]

The Marine Corps tried to explain away the results, arguing that "time ran out" due to an arbitrary reporting deadline established by the OMB.[461] An audit is "a process, not an event," a senior Navy financial official wrote. "So despite an indecisive first battle, the war is far from over." In fact, there was still "a good probability that a positive opinion would be rendered in 2011, or other value realized" from the audit.[462] Unfortunately, the Marine Corps remediation plan focused on "short-term corrective actions based on extensive manual effort and adjustments" rather than systemic fixes,[463] and took no action at all on a number of recommendations.[464] When the Marine Corps tried again the next year, the DOD IG issued another disclaimer of opinion—"basically for the same reasons as the fiscal year 2010 disclaimer."[465]

A few months after the second failed Marine Corps audit, Senator Tom Coburn introduced the Audit the Pentagon Act of 2012, seeking to establish incentives for the department to meet auditability requirements and penalties for a failure to do so. The proposed penalties included a prohibition on the expenditure of funds for new weapon systems, new qualification requirements for DOD CFOs, the establishment of a second deputy secretary to serve as CMO, and the transfer of DFAS from the DOD to the Department of the Treasury.[466] "DOD's inability to pass an audit has potentially wasted billions and undermined our readiness and morale," Senator Coburn explained. "Forcing DOD to pass an audit is the kind of common-sense reform the American people expect us to embrace."[467]

The armed services committees were not convinced that the penalties would be effective, agreeing only to require the DOD to produce a list of statutory and regulatory requirements that could be reduced or eliminated when the department achieved an unqualified audit opinion.[468] The accompanying conference report made it clear, however, that other senators shared Coburn's frustration with missed audit deadlines. "If DOD shows a lack of progress," the report announced, "further legislation—which could include . . . penalties for failure to achieve meaningful progress—is likely to be required."[469]

Having seen the Marine Corps fail twice to produce an auditable SBR, the DOD comptroller decided to lower the bar, pursuing audits of a narrower schedule of budgetary activity (SBA). While an SBR must account for all active appropriations, including older appropriations for which accurate data were not available, an SBA would cover only current-year appropriations. The theory was that if the department could produce clean SBA audits for several years running, the older appropriations would expire, enabling the department to move on to an SBR audit.[470] Senator Coburn excoriated the department, stating that an SBA audit "is meaningless to me as an accountant." Hale responded by saying that he did not want to waste money and time doing audits that were going to fail, and that the SBA was an important step on the way to auditability.[471] "It was sort of a bait and switch," Hale later acknowledged, "but we had to get something."[472]

Once again, the Marine Corps led the way, submitting an SBA for audit in FY 2012. The GAO warned that the Marine Corps had yet to remedy material deficiencies identified in the FY 2010 and FY 2011 SBR audits, with 130 of 177 recommendations remaining open.[473] Nonetheless, the department pushed forward and appeared—initially, at least—to produce a signal accomplishment on which the department could build. On December 20, 2013, the DOD IG issued an unqualified opinion on the Marine Corps SBA.[474] Two months later, Secretary of Defense Chuck Hagel held a ceremony to congratulate the Marine Corps on its achievement. "I know that it might seem a bit unusual to be in the Hall of Heroes to honor a bookkeeping accomplishment," Hagel said, "but, damn, this is an accomplishment."[475]

Before long, however, the department's signal audit accomplishment became a black eye. As the GAO later reported, the audit team did not believe that the clean opinion was justified but was "instructed" by senior IG officials that "the Marine Corps had 'earned' an unqualified opinion and that the audit documentation needed to be updated to support the clean opinion."[476] On March 23, 2015, the IG withdrew the audit opinion, acknowledging that in light of recently obtained evidence, "our original unmodified opinion is not reliable."[477] After the GAO reported that the IG had failed to conduct "sufficient audit procedures . . . under professional auditing standards,"[478] Senator Grassley weighed in, demanding that the deputy IG for audit be fired on the grounds that he had "rigged" the result by overruling his staff.[479]

The rest of the department followed a similar trajectory from initial optimism to a cold dose of reality. In 2012 and 2013, the Army asserted audit readiness "for 9 processes at 10 different installations,"[480] the Navy received a favorable audit opinion for its military equipment,[481] and the Air Force received unqualified audit opinions for its Treasury reconciliation and budget authority distribution processes.[482] A series of articles by DOD financial officials proclaimed success: "Takeaways from a Successful Audit," "FIAR IN SEVEN EASY STEPS," and "Audit Ready Every Day!"[483] A senior Army financial manager declared, "I am optimistic that we will meet the challenge to be audit ready by the 2014 and 2017 dates. We understand the challenges, have a sound plan in place, and have the resources to accomplish the mission."[484]

As the FY 2014 SBR audit deadline approached, the GAO and the DOD IG continued to report "pervasive material weaknesses" in "nearly every key aspect of DoD's financial management operations."[485] The department continued "to make billions of dollars of unsupported, forced adjustments, or 'plugs,' to reconcile its Fund Balance with Treasury (FBWT)."[486] It continued to record "billions of dollars of disbursement and collection transactions in suspense accounts because the proper appropriation accounts could not be identified and charged, generally because of coding errors."[487] Management seemed more focused on "meeting scheduled milestone dates and asserting audit readiness" than on actually "completing actions to resolve extensive control deficiencies."[488] Given the large volume of transactions, the complexity of DOD operations, and "the inability of the current systems to produce data that comply with accounting standards," the IG concluded, it appeared unlikely that the department would be able to meet its audit deadlines.[489]

Congress declined to back off the goals. "Congress best helps DOD fulfill its obligations," Senator Coburn told DOD Comptroller Robert Hale at a May 2014 hearing of the Homeland Security and Government Affairs Committee, "by holding DOD accountable for its failure to comply with the law."[490] Senator Ron Johnson added that the department should "just start conducting audits." "A couple of years ago, we knew we were not ready and we would have simply wasted time," Hale responded. "The auditor probably would have come in and said you are not even close, and so we would end up paying them to do nothing." "I totally disagree with that assessment," Johnson interrupted. "I do not see how spending money on an audit to determine how bad you really are is a waste of money."[491]

After some resistance, the DOD witnesses closed the gap by asserting that regardless of what went before, they were ready for audit now. Army Comptroller Bob Speer agreed that the department needed to "get in the game and start playing. . . . You cannot win it if you do not play."[492] Speer understood that the DOD was still years away from a successful audit, but he believed that the department had achieved enough and that it was at least ready to start the process.[493] Regardless of his intentions, the DOD would now press forward toward audit at full tilt.

The results were as predicted: the services were unable to provide sufficient appropriate evidence to support their financial statements and received audit disclaimers,[494] with the Army, Navy, and Air Force audits identifying 305, 220, and 225 material deficiencies, respectively.[495] The DOD's November FY 2016 FIAR Plan Update acknowledged systemic problems with IT systems, journal vouchers and manual adjustments, universe of transactions, service provider integration, intragovernmental transactions, and accruals that went to the heart of the department's financial management systems and processes. For example, shortcomings in IT systems caused the services to rely on manual work-arounds that "cost too much money and do nothing to address root causes of audit deficiencies," and the department's inability to reconcile intragovernmental transactions resulted in an inability to account for roughly $100 billion of imbalances every year.[496] As bad as these problems were, the DOD comptroller told HASC, many of the defense agencies lagged even behind the military services in their efforts to achieve auditability.[497]

Press accounts cherry-picked a single devastating number from a DOD IG report: the Army had been unable to adequately support $2.8 trillion in journal voucher adjustments for the third quarter of FY 2015, and $6.5 trillion for the full year.[498] "U.S. Army Fudged Its Accounts by Trillions of Dollars, Auditor Finds," screamed one headline.[499] "Audit Reveals Army's Trillion-Dollar Accounting Gaffes," shouted another.[500] The DOD comptroller "thinks the whole Department is poised for a major breakthrough; that the looming congressionally mandated September 2017 deadline is within reach," Senator Grassley stated on the Senate floor, but "the probability of earning a department-wide clean opinion is slim to none."[501] The Pentagon should reconsider undertaking a full audit, he concluded, because "this job is just too big for the pick-and-shovel routine and the cost could be astronomical."[502]

The year 2017 brought another new administration, and with it, a new comptroller who was well aware that a financial audit was not a useful end in itself. "No one is going to buy or sell the Department of Defense on the open market; we don't sell stock shares," David Norquist told the press.[503] Far from backing off on a full financial audit, however, Norquist announced his commitment to the goal even before taking office. "It is time to audit the Pentagon," Norquist told SASC at his nomination hearing in May 2017. "President Trump has called for 'conducting a full audit of the Pentagon.' If confirmed, I would implement the President's vision."[504]

Norquist was well qualified to take on the audit effort, having guided the Department of Homeland Security to a clean audit a decade earlier.[505] To his credit, he focused his efforts on the basic building blocks for a successful audit, including the establishment of a verifiable universe of transactions. Nonetheless, the task remained Herculean.

The audit would require about 1,200 auditors and cost about $870 million, and was not likely to be successful in the first year, Norquist told a reporter in October. "The scale of our audit is enormous. It is significantly larger, I think, than any financial statement [audit] undertaken."[506] In March 2018 testimony before the Senate Budget Committee, Norquist upped his cost estimate to $918 million in the first year and $4.2 billion over the Future Years Defense Program (FYDP).[507] These numbers were almost certainly understated because the department's estimates have never included the time expended by regular DOD employees to prepare for the audit, improve the documentation of transactions, and meet the information requests of auditors with supporting documentation.[508] Moreover, the effort was unlikely to produce a clean audit even in the five-year period of the FYDP. In all likelihood, Norquist told the Senate, it would take more than ten years to get to a clean audit.[509]

On November 15, 2018, the audit was completed. The department tried to paint a happy face on the auditors' disclaimer of opinion, with Deputy Secretary Shanahan telling the press, "We never thought we were going to pass an audit, right? Everyone was betting against us, that we wouldn't even do the audit."[510] However, the twenty material weaknesses identified by the auditors covered every area of the department's finance and accounting operations: financial management systems and information technology; universe of transactions; financial statement compilation; fund balance with Treasury; accounts receivable; operating material and supplies; inventory and related property; general property, plant, and equipment; government property in possession of contractors; accounts payable; environmental and disposal liabilities; legal contingencies; beginning balances; journal vouchers; intragovernmental eliminations; statement of net cost; reconciliation of net cost of operations to budget; budgetary resources; entity level controls; and oversight and monitoring.[511]

Moreover, these same weaknesses had been identified in partial audits two years earlier, and bore a striking similarity to deficiencies identified by similar DOD-wide audits in 1998, 1999, and 2000. After decades of trying to improve its financial systems and processes, the DOD was not measurably closer to the auditability goal than it had been at the outset. A clean audit remains at least a decade and $10 billion away—if, in fact, it can be achieved at all.[512]

ASSESSMENT

The effort to achieve a clean financial statement for the DOD remains an imposingly difficult task. The DOD is not only significantly larger than any public or private organization that has ever been audited, it is also dramatically different. The department is essentially an entire economy, with internal supply systems, transportation and communications networks, law enforcement and judiciary systems, hospital and school systems, dormitories, stores, and restaurants. DOD components conduct hundreds of billions of dollars of transactions with each other every year, so the same federal dollar may be "spent" multiple times before it ever leaves the department. As a result, the financial results from individual DOD components cannot be simply aggregated to generate a financial picture of the organization as a whole, as is typically be done by other federal agencies and corporations with multiple business units.

Nonetheless, each of the last five administrations has made a major effort to improve the department's systems and processes and achieve an auditable financial statement. Legislation has been enacted, plans developed, organizations created, training conducted, systems built, management consultants hired, and audits conducted. Over this period, the department has twice tried to solve its financial management problems with "grand design" approaches and twice tried to audit its way to auditability. Throughout the period, the DOD and its components have also tried partial solutions to improve business systems and processes and provide better information to support management decisions.

Some of these efforts have yielded worthwhile business improvements. The service ERPs and other new finance and accounting systems may not be able to produce auditable financial data, but they are far more reliable than the patchwork of legacy systems that they replaced. The new systems may still have far too many interfaces with "feeder systems" that support unique business processes, but hundreds of interfaces have been eliminated and virtually all interfaces are now automated. Data definitions may still be inconsistent throughout the department, but the partial implementation of the Standard Financial Information Structure (SFIS) has at least brought a common language closer than ever before.

As a result of these and other improvements, the DOD is much less likely than it was in the 1990s to lose track of valuable assets, overspend accounts, overpay contractors, or send soldiers the wrong paychecks. Electronic data interchange is the norm, and hundreds of obsolete and error-prone business and financial systems have been eliminated. The DOD can almost always accurately account for the expenditure of appropriated funds, making Anti-Deficiency Act[513] violations exceedingly rare.

Other efforts have been less successful, leaving behind a trail of abandoned organizations and uncompleted initiatives. Grand designs intended to solve all of the DOD's financial management problems at once proved to be beyond the capacity and patience of the department. Audit programs created useful pressure to make improvements, but calendar-driven goals and a focus on symptoms rather than causes led to billions of dollars of wasted effort. Top-down approaches were unsuccessful because senior leaders lacked the bandwidth to remain focused on complex issues of business processes, system design, and data alignment. Efforts to delegate the problem to new offices and organizations failed because the new structures did not own the systems and processes that they were charged with reforming.

Billions of dollars have been spent on the development of incomplete and unhelpful blueprints and designs. Tens of thousands of hours have been spent on transitory, workforce-intensive efforts to reduce unmatched disbursements, undocumented transactions, and unsupported journal voucher entries. The department has too often placed the cart before the horse by focusing its financial improvement efforts on audits for which it is not ready rather than addressing the underlying problems that make it unauditable. The result has been years of wasted effort trying to follow undocumented and untraceable audit trails.

Moreover, shortcomings in the DOD's business systems and processes have real-world consequences: the department has major data problems. The DOD still lacks consistent data definitions and accounting approaches that would enable it to accurately compile data across the department, compare costs across different programs and organizations, and establish appropriate prices for reimbursable activities. Critical information on program performance is still hoarded in one-off local systems that do not feed into the department's official records. Time-consuming data calls and independent studies are still required to produce basic information that should be readily available to senior decision makers faced with important management decisions.

A number of common lessons emerge from this checkered history. First, the department's lack of an auditable financial statement is the product of a series of linked problems with deficient systems, poor controls, dysfunctional processes, misaligned objectives, and stovepiped organizations. Trying to solve all these problems at once has been a recipe for failure, as grand-design approaches intended to solve all the DOD's financial management problems at the same time proved to be beyond the capacity and patience of the department. In particular, the Pentagon lacked the time and the expertise to implement the ambitious CIM program of the 1990s, which was eventually abandoned after the expenditure of billions of dollars. Similarly, the comprehensive BEA strategy of the 2000s foundered on the department's inability to produce even a comprehensive list of its existing business systems.

Because there were so many problems to address, a failure to prioritize has been fatal. In the 1990s, the DOD rushed into full audits with minimal preparation, in an effort to audit itself into auditability. The audits identified hundreds of billions of dollars of unsupported adjustments, undocumented journal vouchers, unreconciled intra-agency transactions, material omissions, misrecorded or double-counted items, and missing audit trails. Lacking a prioritized plan for addressing these issues, the department wasted hundreds of millions of dollars on short-term efforts to reconstruct undocumented transactions and manually "prevalidate" disbursements without addressing the underlying problems. Similarly, legislative audit deadlines enacted in the 2000s resulted in a headlong rush to audit that was more calendar driven than event driven, undermining more thoughtful prioritization of the department's financial improvement expenditures.

The more successful DOD reform efforts have defined a subset of the department's business problems and developed a targeted set of solutions for those problems. The DOD's "partial solutions" efforts often struggled, taking far longer and costing far more than anticipated, but many ultimately produced favorable results. In the 1990s, DFAS was able to achieve substantial workforce efficiencies and field a handful of interim, or "transitional" finance and accounting systems. Although the new systems were far from perfect and continued to depend on unreliable data from legacy feeder systems, they were a substantial improvement over the patchwork of obsolete and error-prone systems that they replaced. Similarly, the ERPs fielded by the Army, Navy, and DLA in the 2000s took longer and were more expensive than anticipated, but were a significant improvement over the legacy systems that preceded them.

Second, because financial systems and processes cross all organizational lines in the department, a top-down approach that fails to fully address the needs of the department's components and functional communities has not worked. Efforts to circumnavigate the top-down problem by creating new organizational structures have also run into trouble because the new structures lacked history and clout within the department. For example, DBOF's efforts to implement modern business systems were unsuccessful in the 1990s because the key business processes remained under the ownership and control of functional stovepipes within the services, who proved consistently unwilling make the changes necessary to field common systems. In the 2000s, efforts to empower the DBSMC, BTA and DCMO to solve defense-wide systems problems were unsuccessful because these organizations could not overcome resistance from the components and functional stovepipes that owned the underlying business processes.

The more successful DOD reform efforts have placed responsibility for business system improvements in the hands of officials who owned the business processes to be supported. The consolidation of responsibility for business systems and business processes in a single owner made it possible for the department to overcome opposition from functional silos and undertake more effective business process reengineering. For example, DFAS—unlike DBOF—brought together both policy and resources in a new entity that had full responsibility for carrying out its assigned functions. As a result, DFAS was far more successful in its efforts to standardize information requirements and field improved business systems. Similarly, the service ERP programs of the 2000s were far more successful than defense-wide efforts like the DIHMRS program.

Third, and most important, the DOD still does not have a good rationale for why it is trying to achieve a clean audit opinion on its financial statement at all. In the private sector, a balance sheet that reflects accurate values of assets and liabilities—the ultimate goal of a financial audit—is used to demonstrate the value of a business to outside investors and creditors. Federal agencies, on the other hand, do not have investors and are not judged on the value of their assets. Rather, they are judged by the benefit that they provide to the country as a whole. Changes in the dollar value of DOD assets hardly matter to the taxpayers. What does matter is the military effectiveness of the armed forces and their ability to protect and defend the nation's interests.

Current and former DOD officials report that they have not been able to identify any management purpose that would be served by financial statements. Comptrollers and functional managers rely on systems already in place to track weapon system acquisition programs, service contract expenditures, inventory availability, personnel costs, travel expenditures, and a thousand other key data elements. They might want faster or more accurate data, but it is not clear how financial statements would meet that need. Members of Congress also remain far more interested in program funding and execution levels than in the value of agency assets and liabilities—even for federal agencies that have achieved favorable audit opinions.

Even the GAO has yet to identify a management decision that would be better supported by an auditable financial statement. The GAO has argued that a financial statement audit provides a critical measure of the health of an agency's financial systems. However, the GAO has reported that most federal agencies have achieved clean financial statements only through "heroic efforts," which have failed to resolve underlying problems with business systems and processes. Not only are the financial statements of little use, but these agencies remain unable to produce timely, accurate financial information to support business decisions.

The DOD comptroller has made the case that financial audits can be used to identify shortcomings in the department's business systems and processes that can then be prioritized for action. However, the recent audit did not identify any significant deficiencies that were not already known to the department from decades of partial audits. DOD officials already knew that the department's existing business systems and processes lacked audit-ready controls, were unable to establish a definitive universe of transactions for audit, lacked effective mechanisms to account for intragovernmental and intra-agency transactions, were unable to estimate accruals, and could not consistently account for suballocations, suballotments, and transfers of funds from one organization to another.

Until these known problems have been effectively addressed, the department's efforts to achieve a full financial audit will continue to require workforce-intensive workarounds to develop audit trails—without producing a favorable opinion. Even an audit optimist would be hard pressed to explain how the department could be expected to pass a full audit when it continues to receive disclaimers on partial audits. What is needed under these circumstances is not the expenditure of another $10 billion for audits over the next ten years, but a comprehensive effort to prioritize the problems most worth addressing and to assign these problems to managers who are empowered to address them.

The financial statement and the audit are required by law, but the extraordinary commitment of resources that the department continues to expend in trying to achieve a clean audit are not. Congress and the public have come to see auditable financial statements as a sign of healthy agency financial systems and would certainly complain if the DOD were to abandon the audit effort altogether, but the department could take many steps short of a multi-billion-dollar audit effort to improve its business systems and processes and ensure that more accurate and timely data are available to support management decisions. In the long run, these steps would do more to improve the quality of the department's financial statements than a reckless rush to audit.

The key to future success is to learn from the past by defining what the DOD expects to achieve through financial management changes and then breaking the problem into solvable pieces, accepting partial solutions, prioritizing efforts that address causes rather than symptoms, and placing responsibility for action in the hands of leaders who own and control the processes and systems that they seek to reform. To this end, the DOD should focus on improving financial information that is useful in making business decisions and avoid manual workarounds and heroic efforts to develop audit trails that the department's systems and processes fail to produce.

For example, DOD leaders could focus their IT efforts on fielding key business systems (like new acquisition and readiness data systems) that are needed to enhance functional business processes, rather than producing auditable financial statements. They could develop new processes for tracking intragovernmental transfers of funds and work to take more complete advantage of the capabilities of the existing service ERPs. They could focus their accounting efforts on working capital–funded agencies and other business-like entities in the department, and focus their audit efforts on tracking funds from appropriation through expenditure to assure Congress and the taxpayers that public money is spent as intended.

The DOD's current inability to produce auditable financial statements has not helped the department's public image. However, a series of failed audits that cost billions of taxpayer dollars will help even less. An ordered, stair-step approach to DOD financial management would attack the underlying causes of financial management problems rather wasting time and effort trying to treat the symptoms. Unlike the grand strategies of the CIM and BEA programs, this approach would break the problem into achievable pieces that would demonstrate real progress.

There is no guarantee that the department will achieve an unqualified audit opinion with a stairstep approach. Such an audit may not be achievable at all. Incremental steps will also be costly and time consuming, but would have the advantage of bringing about measurable improvement to the DOD's business systems and processes and to the quality of data available to support the department's business decisions.

AFTERWORD

ON February 1, 2018, John Gibson was sworn in as the DOD's first full-time chief management officer (CMO)—the newly established, third-highest-ranking civilian position in the Pentagon. Within a month, Gibson established nine process improvement teams and predicted that he would be able to generate $25 billion a year in savings to be redirected to higher priority military needs.[1] In April, Gibson published his National Defense Business Operations Plan, promising reform initiatives on IT infrastructure, service contracting, commodity purchasing, inventory management, warehouse optimization, shared services, real property management, medical care, vendor invoicing, travel reform, civilian personnel data, and military pay processes.[2]

By November, the reform initiatives were showing no sign of progress, and Gibson was out of office, fired by Secretary of Defense Jim Mattis for "lack of performance." The *Wall Street Journal* quoted an unnamed official who asserted that senior DOD officials did not understand how difficult it was to achieve savings in the Pentagon. A second official reported that the whole effort was "foundering."[3]

The DOD should be a target-rich environment for cost reduction initiatives. Billions of dollars are spent on weapons programs that are later abandoned. Hundreds of millions more are invested in spare parts that turn out to not be needed. State-of-the-art data centers are underutilized and overstaffed. The department leases expensive commercial real estate while complaining that existing bases have excess capacity. Experienced pilots sit at desk jobs while the Air Force increases bonuses to address pilot shortages. Military health care facilities cost far more to operate than their civilian counterparts, but even so, service members complain about poor service.

The department is filled with hard-working, dedicated public servants, but they serve in a complex and often inefficient organization. Each military department and defense agency has its own bureaucracy, as does every base, installation, command, office, program, and activity. Actions are governed by hundreds of thousands of pages of charters, regulations, instructions, directives, and other guidance documents—many of which are inevitably out-of-date because the process for updating them is so cumbersome and time consuming. It can take the department months to respond to a letter, years to make a policy decision, and decades to solve a problem.

Multiple DOD systems and processes—including the security clearance process, the civilian hiring process, the military talent management process, the military disability evaluation process, the defense travel system, the contract writing system, and the readiness reporting system—are widely known to be in need of overhaul. So why haven't these problems been addressed? What is the next secretary of defense, deputy secretary of defense, or chief management officer to do?

As the case studies in this book have shown, defense management reform efforts are underway all of the time. Success is not easy, but it is possible. Successful reform requires identifying and understanding management problems, prioritizing the right ones to address, breaking down the tasks into manageable pieces, avoiding one-size-fits-all approaches, and developing tailored solutions. It requires working across the defense establishment to build and maintain support, developing effective mechanisms to overcome cultural and institutional resistance, and providing dedicated attention to implementation over an extended period of time.

Above all, successful reform requires sustained leadership from the top. Leadership from the secretary is powerful, but a secretary of defense has limited bandwidth and cannot be expected to devote time to any but the most urgent and vital of reforms. Deputy secretaries have often taken the lead on defense management issues, but are also challenged to provide the needed level of attention. One recent deputy reported that his inbox regularly grew by about a foot an hour.[4] The secretary and deputy secretary must assign responsibility and show support for any major initiative, but are rarely good candidates to lead day-to-day reform efforts.

The new CMO may be able to play a leadership role in some areas and assist in others, but should not expect to issue orders and have them followed. The CMO does not own the major business systems and processes of the department, and must have the engaged support of the functional owners to succeed in any reform effort. These functional owners remain accountable for the performance of their systems and processes, and will not blindly accept changes imposed by outside officials. For this reason, the CMO cannot solve defense management problems alone—and may even make matters worse if other leaders take the view that the establishment of the new position absolves them of responsibility for reform.

Leadership and accountability are widely distributed in the department, so a distributed approach to defense reform problems is almost always needed. A secretary and deputy who are serious about reform should identify the strongest leaders among their senior advisors and charge each with undertaking one or more major domain-specific reform efforts in the course of his or her tenure. Service secretaries and service chiefs should do the same. Because of the bandwidth limitations of senior officials, a small number of reform targets should be carefully selected.

The secretaries and chiefs should be regularly briefed on the status of reform efforts and should use the briefings as occasions to make necessary course corrections and demonstrate their continued support. Even with the endorsement of the secretaries and chiefs, major management reform efforts are unlikely to succeed unless reform leaders reach out and engage with other key stakeholders. Senior leaders need to be willing to make decisions, but those decisions are most likely to hold up if they are based on broad input and awareness of potential impacts. There is no substitute for communication and inclusion in the battle for defense reform.

Leaders who communicate, build consensus, and make tough decisions should be able to drive reform forward, saving money and making the department more efficient. Legislation can help by setting goals, providing tools and authorities and removing impediments. No matter how strong the effort, however, there are no magic solutions. Progress is possible, but the department's management problems will never be "solved." Leaders still have to lead and managers still have to manage.

NOTES

INTRODUCTION

1. Defense Business Board, *Transforming the Department of Defense's Core Business Processes for Revolutionary Change*, Report FY 15-01 (Washington, DC: Defense Business Board, February 9, 2015), 18, http://www.dtic.mil/dtic/tr/fulltext/u2/a618526.pdf.
2. Defense Business Board, 21.
3. Defense Business Board, 65.
4. Defense Business Board, 27.
5. Defense Business Board, 25, 26, 30–33.
6. Craig Whitlock and Bob Woodward, "Pentagon Buries Evidence of $125 Billion in Bureaucratic Waste," *Washington Post*, December 5, 2016, https://www.washingtonpost.com/investigations/pentagon-buries-evidence-of-125-billion-in-bureaucratic-waste/2016/12/05/e0668c76-9af6-11e6-a0ed-ab0774c1eaa5_story.html?utm_term=.34bd161a41a3.
7. Whitlock and Woodward.
8. *The Future of Defense Reform: Hearing Before the Committee on Armed Services, United States Senate*, S. Hrg. 114-315, 114th Cong. (October 21, 2015) (statement of Robert M. Gates, former Secretary of Defense), 16–17, https://www.gpo.gov/fdsys/pkg/CHRG-114shrg20923/pdf/CHRG-114shrg20923.pdf.
9. *Future of Defense Reform*, 21.
10. National Defense Authorization Act for Fiscal Year 2002: Report to Accompany S. 1416, S. Rep. No. 107-62, 107th Cong. (2001), 326, https://www.congress.gov/107/crpt/srpt62/CRPT-107srpt62.pdf.
11. Report to Accompany S. 508, S. Rept. 100-413, 100th Cong. (July 6, 1988), http://whistle20.tripod.com/sr100-413excerpts.htm#100-413-p5.
12. Whistleblower Protection Act of 1989, Pub. L. 101-12, 103 Stat. 16, 101st Cong, (1989), https://www.gpo.gov/fdsys/pkg/STATUTE-103/pdf/STATUTE-103-Pg16.pdf.
13. Weapon Systems Acquisition Reform Act of 2009, Pub. L. 111-23, 123 Stat. 1704, 111th Cong. (2009), https://www.gpo.gov/fdsys/pkg/PLAW-111publ23/pdf/PLAW-111publ23.pdf.
14. Goldwater Nichols Department of Defense Reorganization Act of 1986, Pub. L. 99-433, 100 Stat. 992, 99th Cong. (1986), https://www.gpo.gov/fdsys/pkg/STATUTE-100/pdf/STATUTE-100-Pg992.pdf.
15. *30 Years of Goldwater-Nichols Reform: Hearing Before the Committee on Armed Services, United States Senate*, S. Hrg. 114-316, 114th Cong. (November 10, 2015) (statement of Jim Thomas, Vice President and Director of Studies, Center for Strategic and Budgetary Assessments), 38.

16. *30 Years of Goldwater-Nichols Reform* (statement of Senator Jack Reed), 5.

17. James R. Locher, III, *Victory on the Potomac: The Goldwater-Nichols Act Unifies the Pentagon*, ed. Joseph G. Dawson, Texas A&M University Military History Series (College Station: Texas A&M University Press, 2002), 10.

18. Combatant Commands: Assigned Forces; Chain of Command, 10 U.S.C. § 162 (2010), https://www.gpo.gov/fdsys/pkg/USCODE-2010-title10/pdf/USCODE-2010-title10-subtitleA-partI-chap6-sec162.pdf.

19. *Future of Defense Reform*, (statement of Senator John McCain), 3.

20. Senate Committee on Armed Services, "Hearings," 114th Cong. (2016), https://www.armed-services.senate.gov/hearings?c=114.

21. National Defense Authorization Act for Fiscal Year 2017: Conference Report to Accompany S. 2943, H. Rep. No. 114-840, 114th Cong. (November 30, 2016), https://www.congress.gov/114/crpt/hrpt840/CRPT-114hrpt840.pdf.

22. National Defense Authorization Act for Fiscal Year 2017, Pub. L. 114-328, 130 Stat. 2000, 114th Cong. (2016), SEC. 911(c)(2), https://www.gpo.gov/fdsys/pkg/PLAW-114publ328/pdf/PLAW-114publ328.pdf.

23. National Defense Authorization Act for Fiscal Year 2017: Report to Accompany S. 2943, S. Rpt. No. 114-255, 114th Cong. (2016), 248–49, https://www.congress.gov/114/crpt/srpt255/CRPT-114srpt255.pdf.

24. National Defense Authorization Act for Fiscal Year 2017: Report, 253.

25. National Defense Authorization Act for Fiscal Year 2017, S. 2943, 114th Cong. (2016), SEC. 941(c)(1), https://www.congress.gov/bill/114th-congress/senate-bill/2943.

26. National Defense Authorization Act for Fiscal Year 2017: Report, 245–46.

27. Department of Defense (DOD), *Report to Congress: Restructuring the Department of Defense Acquisition, Technology and Logistics Organization and Chief Management Officer Organization—In Response to Section 901 of the National Defense Authorization Act for Fiscal Year 2017 (Public Law 114–328)* (Washington, DC: Office of the Under Secretary of Defense for Acquisition, Technology, and Logistics, August 1, 2017), 16–21, https://www.acq.osd.mil/fo/docs/Section-901-FY-2017-NDAA-Report.pdf.

28. US Government Accountability Office (GAO), *Defense Management: DOD Needs to Implement Statutory Requirements and Identify Resources for Its Cross-Functional Reform Teams*, GAO-19-165 (Washington, DC: GAO, January 2019, https://www.gao.gov/assets/700/696470.pdf; GAO, *Defense Management: DOD Senior Leadership Has Not Fully Implemented Statutory Requirements to Promote Department-Wide Collaboration*, GAO-18-513 (Washington, DC: GAO, June 2018), https://www.gao.gov/assets/700/692749.pdf.

29. Senate, *Wedtech: A Review of Federal Procurement Decisions* (Washington, DC: Subcommittee on Oversight of Government Management of the Committee on Governmental Affairs, May 1988), 145–57.

30. Lobbying Disclosure Act of 1995, Pub. L. 104-65, 109 Stat. 961, 104th Cong. (1995), https://www.gpo.gov/fdsys/pkg/PLAW-104publ65/pdf/PLAW-104publ65.pdf.

31. DOD Acquisition Law Advisory Panel, *Streamlining Defense Acquisition Laws* (Washington, DC: DOD, Defense Systems Management College, January 1993).

32. Federal Acquisition Streamlining Act, "On Agreeing to the Conference Report: Final Vote Results for Roll Call 425," September 20, 1994, http://clerk.house.gov/evs/1994/roll425.xml.

33. Federal Acquisition Streamlining Act of 1994, Pub. L. 103-355, 108 Stat. 3243, 103rd Cong. (1994), https://www.gpo.gov/fdsys/pkg/STATUTE-108/pdf/STATUTE-108-Pg3243.pdf.

34. "Military Commissions Act of 2006," *Congressional Record* 152, no. 123 (September 27, 2006): S10243 (Sen. Levin), https://www.congress.gov/crec/2006/09/27/CREC-2006-09-27-senate.pdf.

35. Military Commissions Act of 2006, Pub. L 109-366, 120 Stat. 2600, 109th Cong. (2006), https://www.gpo.gov/fdsys/pkg/PLAW-109publ366/pdf/PLAW-109publ366.pdf.

36. National Defense Authorization Act for Fiscal Year 2010, Pub. L. 111-84, 123 Stat. 2190, 111th Cong. (2009), Title XVIII, Military Commissions Act of 2009, https://www.gpo.gov/fdsys/pkg/PLAW-111publ84/pdf/PLAW-111publ84.pdf.

37. The SLC includes the secretaries of the military departments, the service chiefs, the under secretaries of defense, and the combatant commanders.

38. The DMAG includes the under secretaries of the military departments, the vice chiefs of the services, the under secretaries of defense, and other senior Office of the Secretary of Defense leaders.

39. DOD, "Remarks by Secretary Carter on the Force of the Future" (Washington, DC: DOD Press Office, March 30, 2015), https://dod.defense.gov/News/Speeches/Speech-View/Article/606658/remarks-by-secretary-carter-on-the-force-of-the-future/.

40. DOD, *Force of the Future* (Washington, DC: DOD), posted online by Government Executive, September 16, 2015, https://www.govexec.com/media/gbc/docs/pdfs_edit/091515cc1.pdf.

41. National Defense Authorization Act for Fiscal Year 1997, Pub. L. 99-661, 100 Stat. 3816, 99th Cong. (1986), SEC. 907, https://www.gpo.gov/fdsys/pkg/STATUTE-100/pdf/STATUTE-100-Pg3816.pdf.

42. DOD's Inadequate Use of Off-the-Shelf Items, Committee Print S. Prt. 101-62, 101st Cong. (October 30, 1989) (Washington, DC: GPO, 1989), 16–17.

43. SAE International, "A New Way of Doing Business: A Memorandum by William J. Perry, 29 June 1994" (Washington, DC: SAE International, 2018), https://www.sae.org/standardsdev/military/milperry.htm.

44. Chief Financial Officers Act of 1990, Pub. L. 101-576, 104 Stat. 2838, 101st Cong. (1990), https://www.gpo.gov/fdsys/pkg/STATUTE-104/pdf/STATUTE-104-Pg2838.pdf.

45. Deficit Reduction Act of 1984, Pub. L. 98369, 98 Stat. 494, 98th Cong. (1984), Division B: Spending Reduction Act of 1984—Title VII: Competition in Contracting, https://www.gpo.gov/fdsys/granule/STATUTE-98/STATUTE-98-Pg494/content-detail.html.

46. Bob Stump National Defense Authorization Act for Fiscal Year 2003, Pub. L. 107-314, 116 Stat. 2458, 107th Cong. (2002), SECs. 802 and 803, https://www.gpo.gov/fdsys/pkg/PLAW-107publ314/pdf/PLAW-107publ314.pdf.

47. National Defense Authorization Act for Fiscal Year 2008, Conference Report to Accompany H.R. 1585, H. Rep. No. 110–477, 110th Cong. (2007), https://www.congress.gov/110/crpt/hrpt477/CRPT-110hrpt477.pdf.

48. Authorization of Appropriations for Aircraft, Missiles, and Naval Vessels for the Armed Forces, and for Other Purposes, Pub. L. 87-53, 75 Stat. 94, 87th Cong (1961), https://www.gpo.gov/fdsys/pkg/STATUTE-75/pdf/STATUTE-75-Pg94-3.pdf.

49. *Select Acquisition Reform Provisions in the House and Senate Versions of the FY2018 National Defense Authorization Act*, R44920 (Washington, DC: Congressional Research Service, August 21, 2017), 1, https://www.everycrsreport.com/files/20170821_R44920_520834201ff5d2716bcef8dd54da5aa4d353d7db.pdf.

50. Christopher Hanks et al., "Reexamining Military Acquisition Reform: Are We There Yet?" RAND Monograph MG-291-A (Santa Monica, CA: RAND Corporation, 2005), 48, 108, https://www.rand.org/content/dam/rand/pubs/monographs/2005/RAND_MG291.pdf.

51. National Defense Authorization Act for Fiscal Year 2016, S. 1376, 114th Cong. (2015), SEC. 351, https://www.congress.gov/bill/114th-congress/senate-bill/1376.

52. National Defense Authorization Act for Fiscal Year 2016, Pub. L. 114-92, 129 Stat. 726, 114th Cong. (2015), SEC. 346, https://www.gpo.gov/fdsys/pkg/PLAW-114publ92/pdf/PLAW-114publ92.pdf.

53. House of Representatives, "Comprehensive Pentagon Bureaucracy Reform and Reduction Act," discussion draft (Washington, DC: United States Congress (115th), April 16, 2018), https://armedservices.house.gov/sites/republicans.armedservices.house.gov/files/wysiwyg_uploaded/4TH_ESTATE_001_xml.pdf.

54. *Financial Problems: Are the Agencies Getting Better: Hearing Before the Committee on Governmental Affairs, United States Senate*, S. Hrg. 103-932, 103rd Cong. (July 28, 1994) (statement of Senator John Glenn), 1.

CHAPTER 1

1. *Transforming the Department of Defense Personnel System: Finding the Right Approach: Hearing Before the Committee on Governmental Affairs*, S. Hrg. 108-185, 108th Cong. (June 4, 2003) (statement of Donald H. Rumsfeld, Secretary of Defense), 17, 21–22, https://www.gpo.gov/fdsys/pkg/CHRG-108shrg88252/content-detail.html.

2. "Policy Debate Slows Defense Bill" (Washington, DC: Congressional Quarterly, 2004), http://library.cqpress.com/cqalmanac/cqal03-835-24342-1084261.

3. Defense Science Board (DSB), *Report of the Defense Science Board Task Force on Human Resources Strategy* (Washington, DC: Defense Science Board, February 2000), 25, http://www.dtic.mil/docs/citations/ADA374767.

4. *High Risk: Human Capital in the Federal Government: Hearing Before the Oversight of Government Management, Restructuring and the District of Columbia Subcommittee of the Committee on Governmental Affairs*, S. Hrg. 107-65, 107th Cong. (February 1, 2001) (statement of Comptroller General David Walker), 14, https://www.gpo.gov/fdsys/pkg/CHRG-107shrg70977/content-detail.html.

5. "HRM02: Reform the General Schedule Classification and Basic Pay System," in *Reinventing Human Resource Management*, accompanying Report of the National Performance Review (Washington, DC: Office of the Vice President, September 1993), https://govinfo.library.unt.edu/npr/library/reports/hrm02.html.

6. National Commission on Public Service, *Urgent Business for America: Revitalizing the Federal Government for the 21st Century: Report of the National Commission on Public Service* (Washington, DC: National Commission on Public Service, January 2003), 10, https://www.brookings.edu/wp-content/uploads/2016/06/01governance.pdf.

7. Civil Service Reform Act of 1978, Pub. L. 95-454, 92 Stat. 1184 (October 1978) (codified in Definitions, 5 U.S.C. § 4701; Research Programs, 5 U.S.C. § 4702; Demonstration Projects, 5 U.S.C. § 4703).

8. President's Blue Ribbon Commission on Defense Management, *A Quest for Excellence: Final Report by the President's Blue Ribbon Commission on Defense Management, Appendix* (Washington, DC: The Commission, June 1986, 158 (Appendix J), https://assets.documentcloud.org/documents/2695411/Packard-Commission.pdf (main body), https://babel.hathitrust.org/cgi/pt?id=mdp.39015018611981;view=1up;seq=1 (appendices).

9. In this book, GAO refers to the General Accounting Office and the Government Accountability Office. The General Accounting Office was renamed the Government Accountability Office on July 7, 2004.

10. U.S. General Accounting Office (GAO), *Federal Personnel: Observations on the Navy's Personnel Management Demonstration Project*, GAO/GGD-88-79 (Washington, DC: GAO, May 1988), 17–18, http://www.gao.gov/assets/220/210118.pdf.

11. Merit Systems Protection Board, *Federal Personnel Research Programs and Demonstration Projects: Catalysts for Change* (Washington, DC: Office of Policy and Evaluation, December 1992), 36, http://www.dtic.mil/dtic/tr/fulltext/u2/a259037.pdf.

12. James R. Thompson, *Designing and Implementing Performance-Oriented Payband Systems* (Washington, DC: IBM Center for the Business of Government, 2007), 21, http://www.businessofgovernment.org/sites/default/files/ThompsonPaybandReport.pdf.

13. GAO, *Federal Personnel: Observations on the Navy's Personnel Management Demonstration Project*, 19.

14. GAO, 2.

15. GAO, 13, 16; Michael Gibbs, *Pay Competitiveness and Quality of Department of Defense Scientists and Engineers* (Santa Monica, CA: RAND, 2001), xii, https://www.rand.org/content/dam/rand/pubs/monograph_reports/2007/MR1312.pdf.

16. GAO, *Federal Workforce: Pay, Recruitment, and Retention of Federal Employees*, GGD-87-37 (Washington, DC: GAO, February 1987), 7–8, http://www.gao.gov/assets/210/209058.pdf.

17. Defense Science Board, *Report of the Defense Science Board 1987 Summer Study on Technology Base Management* (Washington, DC: Defense Science Board, December 1987), 9, http://www.dtic.mil/get-tr-doc/pdf?AD=ADA196469.

18. GAO, *Federal Personnel: Status of Personnel Research and Demonstration Projects*, GAO/GGD-87-116BR (Washington, DC: GAO, September 1987), http://www.gao.gov/assets/80/76718.pdf.

19. Naval Research Advisory Committee, *Science & Technology: Community in Crisis*, NRAC 02-03 (Arlington, VA: Naval Research Advisory Committee, May 2002), 19, http://www.dtic.mil/docs/citations/ADA423395.

20. Merit Systems Protection Board, *Federal Personnel Research Programs and Demonstration Projects: Catalysts for Change*, x.

21. National Defense Authorization Act for Fiscal Year 1995, S. 2182, 103rd Cong. (1994), SEC. 342, https://www.congress.gov/bill/103rd-congress/senate-bill/2182/text.

22. *Expanding Flexible Personnel Systems Governmentwide*, S. Hrg. 107-151 (statement of Assistant Secretary of Defense Charles S. Abell), 97.

23. GAO, *Human Capital: Implementing Pay for Performance at Selected Personnel Demonstration Projects*, GAO-04-83 (Washington, DC: GAO, January 2004), http://www.gao.gov/new.items/d0483.pdf; Silvia Montoya and John D. Graham, *Modernizing the Federal Government: Paying for Performance*. Occasional Paper (Santa Monica, CA: RAND Corporation, 2007), 22, https://www.rand.org/pubs/occasional_papers/OP213.readonline.html), 26–27.

24. National Academy of Public Administration, *Broadband Pay Experience in the Public Sector, A Report by the Human Resources Management Panel* (Washington, DC: Center for Human Resources Management, August 2003), 15, 17, http://www.napawash.org/images/reports/2003/03_07BroadbandPay%20ExperiencePublicSector.pdf.

25. Office of Personnel Management, *Alternative Personnel Systems in the Federal Government: A Status Report on Demonstration Projects and Other Performance-Based Pay Systems* (Washington, DC: Office of Personnel Management, December 2007), 14–15, http://www.dtic.mil/dtic/tr/fulltext/u2/a476623.pdf.

26. Office of Personnel Management, 38. See also James Thompson and Beth Asch, "Compensating the Civilian Workforce," in Institute for Defense Analyses, *2010 Defense Economics Conference: Managing the DoD Civilian Workforce*, NS D-4315 (Alexandria, VA: Institute for Defense Analyses, 2010), 42–44 (comments of James Thompson, associate professor of public administration, University of Illinois at Chicago), http://ensa.us.com/conferences/IDA%20NS%20D-4315_FINAL%202010.pdf.

27. Defense Science Board, *Report of the DSB Task Force on Defense Science and Technology Base for the 21st Century* (Washington, DC: Defense Science Board, 30 June 1998), 39, http://www.acq.osd.mil/dsb/reports/1990s/DefenseScienceandTechnologyBaseforthe21stCentury.pdf.

28. Defense Science Board, 39.

29. Defense Science Board, 39.

30. Defense Science Board, 39–40. See also *"Leap Ahead" Technologies and Transformation Initiatives within the Defense Science and Technology Program: Hearing Before the Subcommittee on Emerging Threats and Capabilities*, S. Hrg. 107-340, 107th Cong. (June 2001), 131–32.

31. National Defense Authorization Act for Fiscal Year 1996, Pub. L. 104-106, 110 Stat. 186 (1996), SEC. 4308, https://www.congress.gov/bill/104th-congress/senate-bill/1124/text?overview=closed. See President's Blue Ribbon Commission on Defense Management, *A Quest for Excellence*, 167 (Appendix K).

32. Office of Personnel Management, "Civilian Acquisition Workforce Personnel Demonstration Project; Department of Defense (DoD)," *Federal Register* 64, no. 5 (January 8, 1999): 1453–54, https://www.gpo.gov/fdsys/pkg/FR-1999-01-08/pdf/FR-1999-01-08.pdf.

33. Tim Kauffman, "Union-Busting, DoD Style," *Federal Times,* February 16, 2004, 1.

34. Cubic Applications, Inc., *DOD Civilian Acquisition Workforce Personnel Demonstration Project*, vol. I, *Management Report*, Interim Evaluation Report (Alexandria, VA: Cubic Applications, Inc., July 2003), http://acqdemo.hci.mil/docs/Interim_Report_Vol1_FINAL.pdf; SRA International, Inc., *Department of Defense (DoD) Civilian Acquisition Workforce Personnel Demonstration Project (AcqDemo)*, Summative Evaluation Report (Fairfax, VA: SRA International, Inc., June 2006), 19, http://acqdemo.hci.mil/docs/Summative_Evaluation.pdf.

35. Cubic Applications, *DOD Civilian Acquisition Workforce Personnel Demonstration Project:*, vol. II, *Technical Report*, II-11–II-12 (responses to questions 20, 27, 34, 35, and 36), http://acqdemo.hci.mil/docs/Interim%20Report%20Vol2_FINAL.pdf.

36. Cubic Applications, II-12 (responses to questions 52 and 52).

37. Cubic Applications, II-11–II-13 (responses to questions 17, 19, 38, 39, and 64).

38. SRA International, *Department of Defense (DoD) Civilian Acquisition Workforce Personnel Demonstration Project (AcqDemo)*, 20.

39. GAO, *Human Capital*; National Academy of Public Administration, *Recommending Performance-Based Federal Pay* (Washington, DC: Human Resources Management Panel, May 2004), http://www.napawash.org/images/reports/2004/04_08RecommendingPerformanceBasedFederalPay.pdf.

40. Defense Science Board, *Report of the Defense Science Board Task Force on Human Resources Strategy*, 40.

41. *Transforming the Department of Defense Personnel System* (statement of Paul Light, professor of public service, New York University), 47.

42. *An Overlooked Asset: The Defense Civilian Workforce: Hearing Before the Oversight of Government Management, the Federal Workforce and the District of Columbia Subcommittee*, S. Hrg. 108-100, 108th Cong. (May 12, 2003) (statement of Comptroller General David M. Walker), 76.

43. *Expanding Flexible Personnel Systems Governmentwide* (statement of Bobby L. Harnage Sr., national president, American Federation of Government Employees, AFL-CIO), 116–19 and (Colleen Kelley, national president, National Treasury Employees Union), 131–32.

44. *Expanding Flexible Personnel Systems Governmentwide*, (statement of Bobby L. Harnage Sr.), 116.

45. *Expanding Flexible Personnel Systems Governmentwide*, (statement of Bobby L. Harnage Sr.), 112–14, 118; (statement of Colleen Kelley), 135–36.

46. *The Human Capital Challenge: Offering Solutions and Delivering Results: Joint Hearing, Before the Oversight of Government Management, The Federal Workforce and the District of Columbia Subcommittee and Subcommittee on Civil Service and Agency Organization*, S. Hrg. 108-91, 108th Cong. (April 2003) (statement of Representative Tom Davis), 10;

Notes to Chapter 1

(statement of Del. Eleanor Holmes Norton), 15; (statement of Representative Chris Van Hollen), 18; (statement of Senator Lautenberg), 20; (statement of Senator Voinovich), 23; and (statement of Representative Jo Ann Davis), 24, https://www.gpo.gov/fdsys/pkg/CHRG-108jhrg87717/html/CHRG-108jhrg87717.htm.

47. Establishment of Human Resources Management System, 5 U.S.C. § 9701 (2002) (as codified by the Homeland Security Act of 2002, Pub. L. 107-926, 116 Stat. 2135 [2002]).

48. Dr. David S. Chu (former under secretary of defense for personnel and readiness), interview by the author, April 12, 2017; Dr. Chu, interview by Diane T. Putney and Alfred Beck, 5–6, 24.

49. Anthony R. Crain, "The Brief, Eventful History of the National Security Personnel System," Occasional Papers, Number 1 (Washington, DC: Historical Office of the Secretary of Defense, February 2017), 12, http://history.defense.gov/Portals/70/Documents/occasional_papers/NSPSBOOK-FEB9WEB.PDF?ver=2017-04-17-134923-437; Douglas A. Brook and Cynthia L. King, "Enactment and Implementation of the National Security Personnel System: Policy Made and Policy Unmade," *Public Administration Review* 71, no. 6 (November/December 2011): 900; Shane Prater and Eric Timmerman, "National Security Personnel System (NSPS): A History of Creation and Enactment of the Legislation Authorizing Its Establishment" (master's thesis, Naval Postgraduate School, March 2008), 38, http://www.dtic.mil/dtic/tr/fulltext/u2/a479920.pdf.

50. Charles Abell (former principal deputy under secretary of defense for personnel and readiness), interview by author, August 9, 2017.

51. Dr. Ronald P. Sanders (associate director of national intelligence for human capital), interview by Diane T. Putney, July 14, 2008, http://history.defense.gov/Portals/70/Documents/oral_history/OH_Trans_SANDERSRonald7-14-2008.pdf; Dr. Chu, interview by Putney and Beck, 7–9; Crain, "The Brief, Eventful History of the National Security Personnel System," 15, 16–17; Brook and King, "Enactment and Implementation of the National Security Personnel System," 901; Prater and Timmerman, "National Security Personnel System (NSPS)," 41–53.

52. Dr. Chu, interview by Putney and Beck, 12.

53. Crain, "The Brief, Eventful History of the National Security Personnel System," 15; Prater and Timmerman, "National Security Personnel System (NSPS)," 53–54.

54. *Transforming the Department of Defense Personnel System* (statement of Comptroller General David M. Walker), 39.

55. Prater and Timmerman, "National Security Personnel System (NSPS)," 54–55.

56. William J. Haynes III, general counsel, DOD, letter to Speaker of the House Hastert for DOD's Proposal (April 10, 2003).

57. 5 U.S.C. § 9902b (2003) (as proposed to be codified by the Defense Transformation for the 21st Century, S. 927 § 101, 108th Cong. [2003]). See also Robert L. Goldich et al., *Defense Department Original Transformation Proposal: Compared to Existing Law*, RL31916 (Washington, DC: Congressional Research Service, updated May 19, 2003), http://www.au.af.mil/au/awc/awcgate/crs/rl31916.pdf.

58. 5 U.S.C. § 9902c (2003) (proposed).

59. 5 U.S.C. § 9902(b), §9902(f), and §9902(g) (2003) (proposed).

60. 5 U.S.C. § 9902(b) (2003) (proposed); Goldich et al., *Defense Department Original Transformation Proposal.*

61. 5 U.S.C. § 9902(a) (2003) (proposed); Goldich et al., *Defense Department Original Transformation Proposal.*

62. 5 U.S.C. § 9903(d) (2003) (proposed).

63. 5 U.S.C. § 9903 (2003) (proposed).

64. Defense Transformation for the 21st Century, S. 927 § 112, 108th Cong. (2003) (proposed).

65. 5 U.S.C. § 116 (proposed).

66. 5 U.S.C. § 201 (proposed).

67. 5 U.S.C. § 202 (proposed).

68. 5 U.S.C. Title III (proposed).

69. 5 U.S.C. § 401 (proposed).

70. 5 U.S.C. § 411 (proposed).

71. Dr. Chu, interview by author, April 12, 2017; Dr. Chu, interview by Putney and Beck, 10–12.

72. Civil Service and National Security Personnel Improvement Act, H.R. 1836, 108th Cong. (2003), https://www.congress.gov/congressional-report/108th-congress/house-report/116/1.

73. Defense Transformation for the 21st Century, S. 927, 108th Cong. (2003).

74. "Policy Debate Slows Defense Bill," https://library.cqpress.com/cqalmanac/document.php?id=cqal03-835-24342-1084261; Civil Service and National Security Personnel Improvement Act, H. Rep. 108-116, 108th Cong. (2003), 106.

75. Dr. Chu, interview by the author, April 12, 2017; Dr. Chu, interview by Putney and Beck, 15, 17–18. See also Prater and Timmerman, "National Security Personnel System (NSPS)," 79.

76. 5 U.S.C. § 9902 (2003) (as proposed to be codified by the Civil Service and National Security Personnel Improvement Act, H.R. 1836 § 102, 108th Cong. [2003]).

77. Civil Service and National Security Personnel Improvement Act, H. Rep. 108-116, 108th Cong. (2003) (Minority Views).

78. "Policy Debate Slows Defense Bill," https://library.cqpress.com/cqalmanac/document.php?id=cqal03-835-24342-1084261.

79. "Policy Debate Slows Defense Bill."

80. National Security Personnel System Act, S. 1166, 108th Cong. (2003).

81. 5 U.S.C. § 9903(e) (as proposed to be codified by the National Security Personnel System Act, S. 1166 § 2, 108th Cong.). (2003). See also *Transforming the Department of Defense Personnel System* (statement of Senator Collins), 2.

82. 5 U.S.C., §9902(j) (proposed).

83. 5 U.S.C., § 9902(f)(3), (4), and (5) (proposed).

84. 5 U.S.C., § 9902(i) (proposed).

85. 5 U.S.C., § 9902(c)(2) (proposed).

86. 5 U.S.C., § 9902(h) (proposed).

87. Charles Abell, interview by author, August 9, 2017.

88. *Transforming the Department of Defense Personnel System* (statement of Donald H. Rumsfeld, secretary of defense), 21.

89. Michael Dominguez (former principal deputy under secretary of defense), interview by Randy Richardson, August 1, 2008, http://history.defense.gov/Portals/70/Documents/oral_history/OH_Trans_DOMINGUEZMichae%208-1-2008.pdf.

90. One union official later commented: "Had NSPS been implemented as first proposed, federal employee unions probably would not even exist today. . . . DoD would have stripped our right to collectively bargain and we would have disappeared" (see Alyssa Rosenberg, "Senate Sends Bill Ending Pentagon Pay System to President's Desk," *Government Executive*, October 22, 2009, http://www.govexec.com/defense/2009/10/senate-sends-bill-ending-pentagon-pay-system-to-presidents-desk/30185/).

91. Dr. Chu, interview by Putney and Beck, 19–20.

92. 5 U.S.C. § 9902(l) (as codified National Defense Authorization Act for Fiscal Year 2004, SEC. 1102).

93. 5 U.S.C. § 9902(e) (as codified National Defense Authorization Act for Fiscal Year 2004, SEC. 1102).

94. 5 U.S.C. § 9902(h)(3) (as codified National Defense Authorization Act for Fiscal Year 2004, SEC. 1102).

95. 5 U.S.C., § 9902(h)(4) and § 9902(h)(5) (as codified National Defense Authorization Act for Fiscal Year 2004, SEC. 1102).

96. 5 U.S.C., § 9902(h)(8) (as codified National Defense Authorization Act for Fiscal Year 2004, SEC. 1102).

97. 5 U.S.C., § 9902(d)(2) (as codified National Defense Authorization Act for Fiscal Year 2004, SEC. 1102).

98. 5 U.S.C., § 9902(m) (as codified National Defense Authorization Act for Fiscal Year 2004, SEC. 1102).

99. Dr. Chu, interview by author, April 12, 2017.

100. *Transforming the Department of Defense Personnel System* (statement of Comptroller General David M. Walker), 5.

101. *Transforming the Department of Defense Personnel System* (statement of Comptroller General David M. Walker), 5.

102. *Transforming the Department of Defense Personnel System* (statement of Comptroller General David M. Walker), 5.

103. "DoD Welcomes Union Input, Chu Says," *Federal Times*, February 16, 2004, 6.

104. Dr. Chu, interview by the author, April 12, 2017; Dr. Chu, interview by Putney and Beck, 37–38.

105. Dr. Chu, interview by Putney and Beck, 37.

106. Michael Dominguez, interview by author, April 19, 2017.

107. Douglas A. Brook, Nicholas M. Schroeder, and Cynthia L. King, *National Security Personnel System: The Period of Implementation (November 24, 2003–January 16, 2009)* (Monterey, CA: Center for Defense Management Research, January 23, 2010), 13–14, http://edocs.nps.edu/npspubs/institutional/newsletters/CDMR/NSPS_Implementation_Report.pdf;

Crain, "The Brief, Eventful History of the National Security Personnel System," 23; Rebecca Davies, "Department of Defense National Security Personnel System: The Transition to Pay for Performance" (master's thesis, Massachusetts Institute of Technology, 2004), 53, https://dspace.mit.edu/bitstream/handle/1721.1/17849/56606018-MIT.pdf?sequence=2.

108. Crain, "The Brief, Eventful History of the National Security Personnel System," 20 (citing interview of Sharon Seymour, former associate director, personnel plans and programs for NSPS).

109. Crain, 20.

110. Dr. Chu, interview by the author, April 12, 2017; Dr. Chu, interview by Putney and Beck, 4–5; Brad Bunn (former NSPS PEO), interview by Diane T. Putney, August 14, 2008, http://history.defense.gov/Portals/70/Documents/oral_history/OH_Trans_BUNNBradley8-14-2008.pdf.

111. DOD, "Science and Technology (S&T) Reinvention Laboratory Personnel Management Demonstration Program," *Federal Register* 68, no. 63 (April 2, 2003): 16121, https://www.gpo.gov/fdsys/pkg/FR-2003-04-02/pdf/FR-2003-04-02.pdf; Prater and Timmerman, "National Security Personnel System (NSPS)," 26–29.

112. Brad Bunn, interview by Putney, 3, 13, 14.

113. Brook, Schroeder, and King, *National Security Personnel System*.

114. Brad Bunn, interview by Putney, 17–19.

115. Brook, Schroeder, and King, *National Security Personnel System*, 35.

116. DOD, "National Security Personnel System: Pre-Collaboration Labor Relations System Options" (Arlington, VA: NSPS Program Office, February 6, 2004).

117. DoD did not have anybody working on the labor relations issue until December 2003. Brook, Schroeder, and King, *National Security Personnel System*, 7. See Brad Bunn, interview by Putney, 11, 15.

118. American Federation of Government Employees, AFL-CIO, "Statement of AFGE President John Gage Before the Defense Business Board Task Group on the National Security Personnel System" (Washington, DC: American Federation of Government Employees, AFL-CIO June 25, 2009), 3–4, http://studylib.net/doc/7337436/final-version-of-doc-264815-np-gage-statement-on-nsps.

119. *Esprit de Corps: Recruiting and Retaining America's Best for the Federal Civil Service H.R. 1601, S. 129, and H.R. 3737: Hearing Before the Subcommittee on Civil Service and Agency Organization of the Committee on Government Reform*, Serial No. 108-163, 108th Cong. (2004) (statement of John Gage, national president, American Federation of Government Employees), 129–30, https://www.gpo.gov/fdsys/pkg/CHRG-108hhrg94772/content-detail.html.

120. American Federation of Government Employees, "DoD NSPS Meeting," memorandum (February 26, 2004), http://www.afge171.org/DEFCON/Docs/NSPS/20040226DoDNSPSMeeting.htm.

121. Brad Bunn, interview by Putney, 37–38; Brook, Schroeder, and King, *National Security Personnel System*, 10; Crain, "The Brief, Eventful History of the National Security Personnel System," 21.

122. Letter from Senators Lieberman, Levin, Durbin, and Akaka, and Representatives Waxman, Skelton, and Davis to Secretary Rumsfeld (February 25, 2004) (see Brook, Schroeder, and King, *National Security Personnel System*, 80–82).

123. Letter from Representatives Van Hollen, Wolf, et al. to Secretary Rumsfeld (March 29, 2004) (see Brook, Schroeder, and King, *National Security Personnel System*, 83–93).

124. Letter from Senators Lautenberg, Biden, et al. to Secretary Rumsfeld (April 20, 2004) (see Brook, Schroeder, and King, *National Security Personnel System*, 94–96).

125. *Department of Defense Authorization for Appropriations for Fiscal Year 2005: Hearing Before the Committee on Armed Services*, S. Hrg. 108-440, Pt. 6, 108th Cong. (March 2004) (statement of Senator Levin), 55, https://www.govinfo.gov/content/pkg/CHRG-108shrg93576/html/CHRG-108shrg93576.htm.

126. *Department of Defense Authorization for Appropriations for Fiscal Year 2005* (statement of Senator Levin), 55.

127. *Department of Defense Authorization for Appropriations for Fiscal Year 2005* (statement of Senator Warner), 955.

128. Letter from Senators Collins, Levin, Stevens, Voinovich, and Sununu to Secretary of the Navy Gordon England (March 3, 2004) (see Barbara L. Schwemle, *DOD's National Security Personnel System: Provisions of Law and Implementation Plans*, RL31954 (Washington, DC: Congressional Research Service, updated March 11, 2005), CRS-6, https://fas.org/sgp/crs/natsec/RL31954.pdf). See also David McGlinchey, "Senators Urge Pentagon to Increase Dialogue on Personnel Reform," *Government Executive*, March 3, 2004, http://www.govexec.com/pay-benefits/2004/03/senators-urge-pentagon-to-increase-dialogue-on-personnel-reform/16154/; Stephen Barr, "Pentagon Scales Down, Pushes Back Introduction of Performance-Based Pay System," *Washington Post*, January 18, 2006, http://www.washingtonpost.com/wp-dyn/content/article/2006/01/17/AR2006011701580.html; Stephen Barr, "Senators Prod Navy Secretary on Creation of Pay Systems for Civil Defense Workers," *Washington Post*, March 15, 2004.

129. *Critical Mission: Ensuring the Success of the National Security Personnel System: Hearing Before the Oversight of Government Management, the Federal Workforce and the District of Columbia Subcommittee of the Committee on Homeland Security and Governmental Affairs*, S. Hrg. 109-85, 109th Cong. (March 2005) (statement of Senator Voinovich), 3, http://frwebgate.access.gpo.gov/cgi-bin/getdoc.cgi?dbname=109_senate_hearings&docid=f:30599.pdf.

130. Brad Bunn, interview by Putney, 39.

131. David S. Chu, "Closing Remarks," in Institute for Defense Analyses, *2010 Defense Economics Conference: Managing the DoD Civilian Workforce*, NS D-4315 (Alexandria, VA: Institute for Defense Analyses, 2010), 129, http://ensa.us.com/conferences/IDA%20NS%20D-4315_FINAL%202010.pdf.).

132. *Esprit de Corps: Recruiting and Retaining America's Best for the Federal Civil Service* (colloquy between Representative Eleanor Holmes Norton and Ronald Sanders, associate director of OPM for strategic human resources policy), 112–13.

133. Letter from OPM Director Kay Cole James to Secretary Rumsfeld (March 9, 2004) (see Brook, Schroeder, and King, *National Security Personnel System*, 53–56).

134. Letter from OPM Director Kay Cole James to Secretary Rumsfeld (March 9, 2004) in Brook, Schroeder, and King, 12. See also Christopher Lee, "OPM Chief Faults Rumsfeld Plan: Defense Reconsiders Approach to Revamping Work Rules," *Washington Post*, May 17, 2004, http://www.washingtonpost.com/wp-dyn/articles/A31615-2004May16.html.

135. Michael Dominguez, "Keynote Address," in Institute for Defense Analyses, *2010 Defense Economics Conference: Managing the DoD Civilian Workforce*, NS D-4315 (Alexandria, VA: Institute for Defense Analyses, 2010), 16, http://ensa.us.com/conferences/IDA%20NS%20D-4315_FINAL%202010.pdf; Dr. Chu, interview by Putney and Beck, 42.

136. Michael Dominguez, interview by Richardson, 19–20.

137. Pete Brown (former executive director, Naval Sea Systems Command), interview by John Darrell Sherwood, August 12, 2008, http://history.defense.gov/Portals/70/Documents/oral_history/OH_Trans_BROWNPeter8-12-2008.pdf.

138. Brook, Schroeder, and King, *National Security Personnel System*, 13.

139. *Esprit de Corps: Recruiting and Retaining America's Best for the Federal Civil Service* (statement of Representative Davis), 116–17.

140. David Chu and Gordon England, "An Open Letter to DoD's Civilian Employees" (Washington, DC: DOD, April 6, 2004), http://www.afge171.org/news/2004/20040406DoDLetter.pdf.

141. Brook, Schroeder, and King, *National Security Personnel System*, 15; Brook and King, "Enactment and Implementation of the National Security Personnel System," 904; Crain, "The Brief, Eventful History of the National Security Personnel System," 22–23.

142. Gordon England (former secretary of the navy and deputy secretary of defense), interview by Putney and Beck, 16.

143. An April 2, 2004, AFGE press release stated: "Let us not forget, downplay, or even take for granted the fact that DoD's recent turn of direction is the result of the continuous and thunderous outpouring of outrage by federal employees ... since DoD announced its concepts paper on February 6th" (see Crain, "The Brief, Eventful History of the National Security Personnel System," 27).

144. Brook, Schroeder, and King, *National Security Personnel System*, 16 (quoting Timothy Curry, DoD executive director for labor-management relations).

145. American Federation of Government Employees, AFL-CIO, "Statement of AFGE President John Gage," 4.

146. Brad Bunn, interview by Putney, 32–33.

147. Stephen Barr, "Career Federal Worker Tapped to Oversee Pay, Personnel Overhaul at Defense," *Washington Post*, May 25, 2004, http://www.washingtonpost.com/wp-dyn/articles/A53189-2004May24.html; *Implementation by the Department of Defense of the National Security System: Hearing Before the Committee on Armed Services*, S. Hrg. 109-415, 109th Cong. (April 2005) (statement of Gordon R. England, secretary of the navy), 14, https://www.gpo.gov/fdsys/pkg/CHRG-109shrg28031/content-detail.html.

148. Gordon England, interview by Putney and Beck, 29; Michael Dominguez, "Keynote Address," 16.

149. *Critical Mission: Assessing Spiral 1.1 of the National Security Personnel System: Hearing Before the Committee on Homeland Security and Governmental Affairs*, S. Hrg. 109-927, (statement of Secretary England), 16–17; Brad Bunn, interview by Putney and Beck, August 14, 2008, 55–56.

150. *Implementation by the Department of Defense of the National Security System* (statement of Secretary England), 98.

151. Pete Brown, interview by Sherwood, 33, 36.

152. *Implementation by the Department of Defense of the National Security System* (statement of Secretary England), 18 and (statement of Dan G. Blair, acting director, Office of Personnel Management), 21; *Critical Mission: Assessing Spiral 1.1 of the National Security Personnel System* (statement of Linda M. Springer, director, Office of Personnel Management), 7, 28–30; DOD, "Department of Defense Human Resources Management and Labor Relations Systems; Final Rule," *Federal Register* 70, no. 210 (November 1, 2005): 66121, https://www.gpo.gov/fdsys/pkg/FR-2005-11-01/pdf/FR-2005-11-01.pdf (more than 120 representatives of the military departments, DOD components, and OPM were included in working groups).

153. DOD, "Department of Defense Human Resources Management and Labor Relations Systems; Final Rule," 66121; *Implementation by the Department of Defense of the National Security System* (statement of Secretary England), 14, and (statement of Dan G. Blair, acting director, Office of Personnel Management), 20; Brad Bunn, interview by Putney, 61–62.

154. *Improving Performance: A Review of Pay-for-Performance Systems in the Federal Government: Hearing Before the Oversight of Government Management, the Federal Workforce, and the District of Columbia Subcommittee of the Committee on Homeland Security and Governmental Affairs*. S. Hrg. 110-814. 110th Cong. (July 2008) (statement of Bradley Bunn, program executive officer, National Security Personnel System), 86.

155. *Improving Performance: A Review of Pay-for-Performance Systems in the Federal Government* (statement of Michael Dominguez), 4.

156. Gordon England, interview by Putney and Beck, 19.

157. The department held ten meetings to discuss system design with union representatives over a six-month period in 2004 (see DOD, "Department of Defense Human Resources Management and Labor Relations Systems; Final Rule," 66120; *Implementation by the Department of Defense of the National Security System* (statement of Secretary England), 14). An additional nineteen days of meetings took place during the formal "meet and confer" process established by the NSPS statute (see DOD, "Department of Defense Human Resources Management and Labor Relations Systems; Final Rule," 66122).

158. Brook, Schroeder, and King, *National Security Personnel System*, 21 (quoting Timothy Curry, DOD executive director for labor-management relations); Crain, "The Brief, Eventful History of the National Security Personnel System," 27.

159. Barr, "Pentagon Scales Down."

160. Karen Rutzick, "Pentagon to Finish Personnel System Tweaks Friday," *Government Executive*, February 9, 2006.

161. *The National Security Personnel System—Is It Really Working?: Hearing Before the Readiness Subcommittee of the Committee on Armed Services*, H.A.S.C. No. 110-26 (statement of Michael Dominguez, principal deputy under secretary of defense for personnel and readiness), 4, 13.

162. Crain, "The Brief, Eventful History of the National Security Personnel System," 26 (quoting Secretary England). See also Michael Dominguez, interview by Richardson, 5, 13.

163. Rose Marie Orens and Vicki J. Elliot, "Variable Pay Programs: Pay for Results," in *Paying for Performance: A Guide to Compensation Management*, 2nd ed., ed. Peter Chingos (New York: John Wiley & Sons, 2002), 20.

164. *Improving Performance: A Review of Pay-for-Performance Systems in the Federal Government* (statement of Charles H. Fay, professor, School of Management and Labor Relations, Rutgers University), 36.

165. *The National Security Personnel System—Is It Really Working?* (statement of Dr. Marick Masters, University of Pittsburgh Business School), 68.

166. *National Security Personnel System—Is It Really Working?* (statement of Dr. Marick Masters, University of Pittsburgh Business School), 10.

167. Howard Risher, *Pay for Performance: A Guide for Federal Managers* (Washington, DC: IBM Center for the Business of Government, November 2004), 4, 18, http://www.businessofgovernment.org/sites/default/files/Pay%20for%20Performance.pdf. See also Thompson and Asch, "Compensating the Civilian Workforce," 40; National Research Council (NRC), *Pay for Performance: Evaluating Performance Appraisal and Merit Pay* (Washington, DC: National Academy Press, 1991), 80–81, https://www.nap.edu/read/1751/chapter/1#v.

168. Jeffrey Pfeffer and Robert I. Sutton, "What's Wrong with Pay-for-Performance," *Industrial Management* 48, no. 2 (March/April 2006): 13.

169. Iris Bohnet and Susan Eaton, "Does Performance Pay Perform? Conditions for Success in the Public Sector," in *For the People: Can We Fix Public Service?* ed. John Donahue and Joseph Nye, (Washington, DC: Brookings Institution Press, May 2004), 241–50. See also Janet Wiscombe, "Can Pay for Performance Really Work?" *Workforce*, August 2001, 28, http://www.workforce.com/2001/07/29/can-pay-for-performance-really-work-live-copy/.

170. Bohnet and Eaton, "Does Performance Pay Perform?" 241. See also James S. Bowman, "The Success of Failure: The Paradox of Performance Pay," *Review of Public Personnel Administration* 30, no. 1 (2010): 70–88, http://journals.sagepub.com/doi/pdf/10.1177/0734371X09351824.

171. Bohnet and Eaton, "Does Performance Pay Perform?" 246. See also Steven Kelman, "The Right Pay," *Government Executive*, May 2003, http://www.govexec.com/advice-and-comment/viewpoint/2003/05/the-right-pay/14070/; Sungjoo Choi and Andrew B. Whitford, "Merit-Based Pay and Employee Motivation in Federal Agencies," *Issues in Governance Studies* 63 (November 2013): 3–4, https://www.brookings.edu/wp-content/uploads/2016/06/Choi-and-Whitford_Merit-based-pay_VII.pdf.

172. *The Status of Federal Personnel Reform: Hearing Before the Subcommittee on Federal Workforce, Postal Service, and the District of Columbia of the Committee on Oversight and*

Government Reforms, Serial No. 110-12, 110th Cong. (March 2007) (statement of Robert M. Tobias, director, Public Sector Executive Education, American University), 46–47, https://archive.org/details/gov.gpo.fdsys.CHRG-110hhrg36547. See also Robert Lavigna, "Why Government Workers Are Harder to Motivate," *Harvard Business Review*, November 28, 2014, https://hbr.org/2014/11/why-government-workers-are-harder-to-motivate; *Expanding Flexible Personnel Systems Governmentwide* (statement of Comptroller General David Walker), 20; *High Risk: Human Capital in the Federal Governments* (statement of Mr. Walker), 13.

173. Merit Systems Protection Board, *The Power of Federal Employee Engagement* (Washington, DC: Office of Policy and Evaluation, September 2008), https://www.mspb.gov/MSPBSEARCH/viewdocs.aspx?docnumber=379024&version=379721&application=ACROBAT. See also Merit Systems Protection Board, *Federal Employee Engagement: The Motivating Potential of Job Characteristics and Rewards* (Washington, DC: Office of Policy Evaluation, December 2012), https://www.mspb.gov/mspbsearch/viewdocs.aspx?docnumber=780015&version=782964&application=ACROBAT.

174. DOD, "Department of Defense Human Resources Management and Labor Relations Systems; Final Rule," 66124.

175. DOD, 66120. See also SRA International, *Program Executive Office (PEO), National Security Personnel System (NSPS)—2008 Evaluation Report* (Arlington, VA: SRA International, Inc., May 15, 2009), ES-1, http://www.dtic.mil/dtic/tr/fulltext/u2/a503182.pdf.

176. *Critical Mission: Assessing Spiral 1.1 of the National Security Personnel System* (statement of Linda M. Springer, director, Office Of Personnel Management), 7. See also Thompson, *Designing and Implementing Performance-Oriented Payband Systems*, 21.

177. DOD, "Department of Defense Human Resources Management and Labor Relations Systems; Final Rule," 66119.

178. Gordon England, interview by Putney and Beck, 22–23; *Implementation by the Department of Defense of the National Security System* (statement of Secretary England), 15; DOD, "Department of Defense Human Resources Management and Labor Relations Systems; Final Rule," 66124.

179. *Implementation by the Department of Defense of the National Security System* (statement of Secretary England), 15.

180. DOD, "Department of Defense Human Resources Management and Labor Relations Systems; Final Rule," 66119, 66124, 66125.

181. DOD, "Department of Defense Human Resources Management and Labor Relations Systems; Final Rule," 66119.

182. SRA International, *Program Executive Office (PEO)*, ES-2.

183. DOD, "Department of Defense Human Resources Management and Labor Relations Systems; Final Rule," 66119.

184. GAO, *Defense Transformation: DoD's Proposed Civilian Personnel System and Governmentwide Human Capital Reform*, GAO-03-741T (Washington, DC: GAO, May 1, 2003), 4, http://www.gao.gov/assets/110/109912.pdf. See also *Improving Performance: A Review of Pay-for-Performance Systems in the Federal Government* (statement of Charles H. Fay, Rutgers School of Management and Labor Relations), 170–71.

185. Crain, "The Brief, Eventful History of the National Security Personnel System," 24 (quoting Principal Deputy Under Secretary of Defense Charles Abell).

186. Establishment of Performance Appraisal Systems, 5 U.S.C. § 4302.

187. "HRM03: Authorize Agencies to Develop Programs for Improvement of Individual and Organizational Performance," in *Reinventing Human Resource Management*, Accompanying Report of the National Performance Review (Washington, DC: Office of the Vice President, September 1993), https://govinfo.library.unt.edu/npr/library/reports/hrm03.html.

188. See Merit Systems Protection Board, *The Federal Workforce for the 21st Century: Results of the Merit Principles Survey 2000* (Washington, DC: Office of Policy Evaluation, September 2003), https://www.mspb.gov/MSPBSEARCH/viewdocs.aspx?docnumber=253631&version=253918&application=ACROBAT; GAO, *Federal Workforce: Distribution of Performance Ratings Across the Federal Government, 2013*, GAO-16-520R (Washington, DC: GAO, May 9, 2016), https://www.gao.gov/assets/680/676998.pdf.

189. GAO, *Federal Performance Management: Agencies Need Greater Flexibility in Designing Their Systems*, GAO/GGD-93-57 (Washington, DC: General Government Division, February 1993), 6, http://www.gao.gov/assets/220/217619.pdf.

190. U. S Merit Systems Protection Board, *The Federal Workforce for the 21st Century: Results of the Merit Principles Survey 2000*, 26.

191. DOD, *Department of Defense Civilian Personnel Manual*, DoD 1400.25-M, SC1940. Subchapter 1940, "Performance Management," paragraph SC1940.5.5 (Washington, DC: Office of the Under Secretary of Defense for Personnel and Readiness, December 1, 2008), http://cpol.army.mil/library/general/nsps-archives/docs-regs/1940DEPSEC.pdf.

192. DOD, "Department of Defense Human Resources Management and Labor Relations Systems; Final Rule," 66200; Gordon England, interview by Putney and Beck, 28; Michael Dominguez, interview by Richardson, 8–9.

193. National Security Personnel System (NSPS), *Employee and Supervisor Guide for Performance Plans*, http://www.armycounselingonline.com/download/NSPS%20Supervisor%20Guide%20to%20Performance%20Plans.pdf.

194. DOD, *Department of Defense Civilian Personnel Manual*, DoD 1400.25-M, SC1940. Subchapter 1940, "Performance Management," paragraph SC1940.5.6.

195. Congressional Budget Office, "A Review of the Department of Defense's National Security Personnel System" (Washington, DC: Congressional Budget Office, November 2008), 22, https://www.cbo.gov/sites/default/files/110th-congress-2007-2008/reports/11-26-nsps.pdf.

196. Gordon England, interview by Putney and Beck, 55–56, 61–62.

197. DOD, *Department of Defense Civilian Personnel Manual*, DoD 1400.25-M, SC1940. Subchapter 1940, "Performance Management," paragraph SC1940.5.3.

198. DOD, paragraph SC1940.6.3.

199. DOD, paragraph SC1940.9.2.

200. DOD, paragraph SC1940.9.3.

201. DOD, paragraph SC1940.11.3.3.

202. DOD, paragraph SC1940.13.

203. *The National Security Personnel System—Is It Really Working?* (statement of Mr. Dominguez), 21. See *Improving Performance: A Review of Pay-for-Performance Systems in the Federal Government* (statement of Bradley Bunn, program executive officer, National Security Personnel System), 10.

204. SRA International, *Program Executive Office (PEO)*, 3-31–3-32. See also Brittany Ballenstedt, "Freedom to Manage: Under New Defense Personnel System, the Cost of Liberty Is High," *Government Executive*, January 1, 2008, http://www.govexec.com/magazine/features/2008/01/freedom-to-manage/26021/. See also Wendy Ginsburg, *Pay-for-Performance: The National Security Personnel System*, RL34673 (Washington, DC: Congressional Research Service, September 17, 2008), CRS-13, https://fas.org/sgp/crs/natsec/RL34673.pdf13; *Improving Performance: A Review of Pay-for-Performance Systems in the Federal Government* (statement of Federal Managers Association), 193–94.

205. SRA International, *Program Executive Office (PEO)*, 4-34.

206. SRA International, 2-5.

207. SRA International, 3-9.

208. SRA International, 3-9.

209. National Academy of Public Administration, *Broadband Pay Experience in the Public Sector*, ii, 1.

210. National Academy of Public Administration, *Broadband Pay Experience*. Private sector alternatives include pay ranges for specific positions, pay ranges for groups of jobs (i.e., grades), and a mixture of grades and ranges-by-position. See also PayScale, *2017 Compensation Best Practices Report* (Seattle: Payscale, 2017), https://www.payscale.com/content/report/2017-compensation-best-practices-report.pdf?_ga=2.191818090.1702190470.1506608328-1789973257.1506608328.

211. Risher, *Pay for Performance*, 21. See also James E. Colvard et al., *Civilian Workforce 2020: Strategies for Modernizing Human Resources Management in the Department of the Navy* (Washington, DC: National Academy of Public Administration, August 18, 2000), 41, http://www.dtic.mil/get-tr-doc/pdf?AD=AD100955540. See also National Academy of Public Administration, *Broadband Pay Experience in the Private Sector* (Washington, DC: Center for Human Resources Management, July 2003), 2, http://www.napawash.org/images/reports/2003/03_06BroadbandPayExperiencePrivateSector.pdf.

212. National Academy of Public Administration, *Broadband Pay Experience*. See also Montoya and Graham, *Modernizing the Federal Government*, 26.

213. PayScale, *2017 Compensation Best Practices Report*, 26. See also Mykkah Herner, "Which Compensation Structure Is Right for Your Company?" *PayScale*, May 8, 2017, http://www.payscale.com/compensation-today/2017/05/compensation-structure-right-company.

214. Thompson, *Designing and Implementing Performance-Oriented Payband Systems*, 7.

215. Risher and Fay, *Managing for Better Performance: Enhancing Federal Performance Management Practices*, IBM Center for the Business of Government, 7, http://www.businessofgovernment.org/sites/default/files/RisherFayReport.pdf.

216. *An Overlooked Asset: The Defense Civilian Workforce* (statement of Senator Voinovich), 2. See also *An Overlooked Asset: The Defense Civilian Workforce* (statement of

Comptroller General David M. Walker), 23; *Transforming the Department of Defense Personnel System* (statement of Paul C. Light, professor of public service, New York University), 47.

217. National Academy of Public Administration, *Broadband Pay Experience in the Private Sector*, 23–26.

218. National Academy of Public Administration, 17.

219. SRA International, *Program Executive Office (PEO)*, 1-6; Brook, Schroeder, and King, *National Security Personnel System*, 17.

220. SRA International, 2-2.

221. SRA International, 2-2. See also Defense Business Board, *Review of National Security Personnel System*, Report to the Secretary of Defense (Washington, DC: DOD, July 2009), http://dbb.defense.gov/Portals/35/Documents/Reports/2009/FY09-6_Review_Of _The_National_Security_Personnel_System_2009-7.pdf.

222. Howard Risher, "Learning from NSPS Failure: Pay Pools Doomed DoD's Personnel System," *Federal Times*, May 24, 2010, 23.

223. National Security Personnel System, *Managing Compensation under NSPS: A Guide for Managers and Supervisors* (Washington, DC: DOD, March 2007), 11, http:// cpol.army.mil/library/general/nsps-archives/docdir/Final-Comp-Guide-for-Production .pdf.

224. National Security Personnel System, 11–15.

225. National Security Personnel System, Appendix G (Compensation Rules and Business Rules Template). See also Appendices C (Determining Salaries), D (Salary Setting Approval Matrix), E (Recruitment and Relocation Incentives Checklist), and F (Promotions and Reassignments).

226. DOD, "Department of Defense Human Resources Management and Labor Relations Systems; Final Rule," 66147.

227. Dr. Chu, interview by Putney and Beck, 47.

228. SRA International, *Program Executive Office (PEO)*, 2-1.

229. DOD, *Department of Defense Civilian Personnel Manual*, DoD 1400.25-M, SC1940, subchapter 1940, "Performance Management," paragraphs SC1940.4.2 and SC1940.4.3.

230. DOD, paragraph SC1940.4.1.

231. DOD, subchapter 1930, "Compensation Architecture Pay Policy," paragraphs SC1930.9.2.1, SC1930.9.2.1.1, SC1930.9.2.2, and SC1930.9.2.1.3, http://cpol.army.mil/ library/general/nsps-archives/docs-regs/1930DEPSEC.pdf.

232. 5 U.S.C. § 9902(e)(4), as codified by the National Defense Authorization Act for Fiscal Year 2004, SEC. 1102.

233. *Implementation by the Department of Defense of the National Security System* (statement of Secretary England), 87. See also DOD, "Department of Defense Human Resources Management and Labor Relations Systems; Final Rule," 66125.

234. *Improving Performance: A Review of Pay-for-Performance Systems in the Federal Government* (statement of Charles H. Fay, Rutgers School of Management and Labor Relations), 171.

235. SRA International, *Program Executive Office (PEO)*, 2-5–2-6.

236. DOD, *Department of Defense Civilian Personnel Manual*, DoD 1400.25-M, SC1940. Subchapter 1940, "Performance Management," SC1940AP1. Appendix 1 to Subchapter 1940, 25.

237. See National Security Personnel System, *Managing Compensation under NSPS: A Guide for Managers and Supervisors*, 29.

238. DOD, "Department of Defense Human Resources Management and Labor Relations Systems; Final Rule," 66145 (section 9901.342).

239. DOD, section 9901.342(b)(2).

240. National Security Personnel System, *Managing Compensation under NSPS: A Guide for Managers and Supervisors*, 28. See also DOD, "Department of Defense Human Resources Management and Labor Relations Systems; Final Rule," 66146.

241. Congressional Budget Office, "A Review of the Department of Defense's National Security Personnel System," 22.

242. National Security Personnel System, "Pay Pool Management Products and Tools: Pay Pool Nondisclosure Statement," http://cpol.army.mil/library/general/nsps-archives/paypool.html.

243. SRA International, *Program Executive Office (PEO)*, 3-17.

244. SRA International, 3-16.

245. SRA International, 3-16, 3-20.

246. SRA International, 3-18.

247. American Federation of Government Employees, *AFGE News for DoD Employees*, September 19, 2008, 2, http://www.afge171.org/DEFCON/Docs/NSPS/200809019-NSPS_fall08_tabloid.pdf.

248. *Improving Performance: A Review of Pay-for-Performance Systems in the Federal Government* (statement of Mr. Gage), 39.

249. Risher, "Learning from NSPS Failure," 23.

250. Dr. Chu, interview by the author, April 12, 2017; Dr. Chu, interview by Putney and Beck, 44–45.

251. DOD, *Department of Defense Civilian Personnel Manual*, DoD 1400.25-M, SC1930. Subchapter 1930, "Compensation Architecture Pay Policy," paragraph SC1930.3.1.

252. See Thompson, *Designing and Implementing Performance-Oriented Payband Systems*, 15.

253. DOD, "Department of Defense Human Resources Management and Labor Relations Systems; Final Rule," 66141 (section 9901.322).

254. DOD, "Department of Defense Human Resources Management and Labor Relations Systems; Final Rule," 66140 (section 9901.304) and 66144 (section 9901.333).

255. DOD, "Department of Defense Human Resources Management and Labor Relations Systems; Final Rule," 66149 (section 9901.351);

256. National Security Personnel System, *Managing Compensation under NSPS: A Guide for Managers and Supervisors*, 16, 21.

257. *Critical Mission: Assessing Spiral 1.1 of the National Security Personnel System* (statement of NSPS PEO Mary Lacey), 14.

258. 5 U.S.C. § 9902(e)(7) (as codified by the National Defense Authorization Act for Fiscal Year 2008, Pub. L. 110-181. 122 Stat. 3 [2008], SEC. 1106). See National Security Personnel System, "January 2008 NSPS Payout Fact Sheet," http://www.dodfire.com/pay/FactSheet_2008.pdf; National Security Personnel System, "January 2009 NSPS Payout Fact Sheet," http://cpol.army.mil/library/general/nsps-archives/docs-comp/NSPS_Fact_Sheet_2009_Payouts_2008-12-22.pdf; Stephen Barr, "Defense Begins Transition to Merit-Based Pay," *Washington Post,* September 17, 2007, http://www.washingtonpost.com/wp-dyn/content/article/2007/09/16/AR2007091601300.html.

259. 5 U.S.C. § 9902(e)(8) (amended by National Defense Authorization Act for Fiscal Year 2008, SEC. 1106).

260. SRA International, *Program Executive Office (PEO)*, 3-13.

261. National Security Personnel System, *Managing Compensation under NSPS: A Guide for Managers and Supervisors*, 21.

262. SRA International, *Program Executive Office (PEO)*, 3-15.

263. SRA International, 3-10–3-11.

264. SRA International, 3-11.

265. SRA International, 3-15.

266. Crain, "The Brief, Eventful History of the National Security Personnel System," 31–32.

267. SRA International, *Program Executive Office (PEO)*, 4-15 (55–75 percent agree, 15–25 percent disagree).

268. SRA International, 4-16.

269. SRA International, 4-5.

270. SRA International, 4-6.

271. SRA International, 4-13.

272. SRA International, 4-14.

273. SRA International, 3-10.

274. SRA International, 2-24.

275. SRA International, 5-8–5-9.

276. SRA International, 3-10–3-11, 5-5.

277. SRA International, 4-23, 5-5.

278. SRA International, 3-2, 3-10.

279. SRA International, 3-5.

280. SRA International, 5-1.

281. SRA International, 3-9.

282. SRA International, 4-36.

283. SRA International, 3-16, 3-20.

284. SRA International, 3-11.

285. SRA International, 5-2.

286. SRA International, 4-33, 5-5–5-6.

287. SRA International, 4-30–4-33.

288. Stephen Losey, "GAO Worries about Growing Contempt for NSPS," *Federal Times*, September 15, 2008, 4; SRA International, *Program Executive Office (PEO)*, 4-43.

289. Dr. Chu, interview by Putney and Beck, 53; *The National Security Personnel System—Is It Really Working?* (statement of Max Stier, president and CEO, Partnership for Public Service), 60.

290. Michael Dominguez, interview by author, April 19, 2017.

291. Michael Dominguez, interview by author. See also *Improving Performance: A Review of Pay-for-Performance Systems in the Federal Government* (statement of AFGE President John Gage), 46.

292. Dr. Sanders, interview by Putney, 48.

293. Dr. Sanders, interview by Putney, 39.

294. DOD, "National Security Personnel System; Proposed Rule," *Federal Register* 70, no. 29 (February 14, 2005): 7597 section 9901.910 (a), https://www.gpo.gov/fdsys/pkg/FR-2005-02-14/pdf/FR-2005-02-14.pdf.

295. DOD, 7570.

296. DOD, 7601 section 9901.917(d)(1).

297. DOD, 7595 section 9901.903.

298. DOD, 7596 section 9901.905; 7599 section 9901.914(d)(3).

299. DOD, "Department of Defense Human Resources Management and Labor Relations Systems; Final Rule," 66128.

300. *Implementation by the Department of Defense of the National Security System* (statement of AFGE President John Gage), 56–57.

301. Don Hale, "To All DoD Employees: The Valentine's Day Slaughter of DoD Civilians," memorandum (Washington, DC: American Federation of Government Employees), http://www.afge171.org/DEFCON/Docs/NSPS/20050214TOALLDODEMPLOYEES.pdf.

302. DOD, "Department of Defense Human Resources Management and Labor Relations Systems; Final Rule," 66128. See also "UDoDWC Proposal on Emergencies and Post-Implementation Bargaining," http://www.afge171.org/DEFCON/Docs/NSPS/20050509UDWCscope_of_bargaining.pdf.

303. DOD, "Department of Defense Human Resources Management and Labor Relations Systems; Final Rule," 66128.

304. DOD, 66129.

305. DOD, 66181, 66123. See also Stephen Barr, "Pentagon and Union Officials Differ on Progress, But Will Keep Talking," *Washington Post*, May 20, 2005. http://www.washingtonpost.com/wp-dyn/content/article/2005/05/19/AR2005051901711.html.

306. 5 U.S.C. § 9902(h) (as codified National Defense Authorization Act for Fiscal Year 2004, SEC. 1101).

307. DOD, "National Security Personnel System; Proposed Rule," 7593 section 9901.807(b)(2).

308. DOD, 7593 section 9901.807(c).

309. DOD, 7594 section 9901.807(k)(8)(i) and (ii).

310. DOD, 7594 section 9901.807(k)(8)(iii). See also *Implementation by the Department of Defense of the National Security System* (statement of Derek B. Stewart, director, military and Department of Defense civilian personnel issues, GAO), 52.

311. DOD, "National Security Personnel System; Proposed Rule," 7594 section 9901.807(k)(9).

312. DOD, 7594 section 9901.807(k)(6).

313. DOD, 7594 section 9901.807(k)(6).

314. *Implementation by the Department of Defense of the National Security System* (statement of Senator Levin), 4–5.

315. DOD, "Department of Defense Human Resources Management and Labor Relations Systems; Final Rule," 66192 section 9901.107(a)(2), 66209 section 9901.807(f)(2)(ii), 66209 section 9901.807(g).

316. *American Federation of Government Employees, AFL-CIO et al. v. Donald H. Rumsfeld et al.*, Complaint for Declaratory and Injunctive Relief, Civil Action No. 05CV2183 (EGS), United States District Court for the District of Columbia, November 7, 2005, http://www.afge171.org/DEFCON/Docs/NSPS/2005_11_07NSPSLawsuit.pdf.

317. *American Federation of Government Employees, AFL-CIO v. Rumsfeld*, 422 F. Supp.2d, 16, (D.D.C. 2006), https://www.courtlistener.com/opinion/2573489/american-fed-of-gov-empl-afl-cio-v-rumsfeld/.

318. *National Treasury Employees Union v. Chertoff*, 452 F.3d 839 (D.C. Cir. 2006), http://www.kentlaw.edu/faculty/mmalin/classes/PublicSectorSp09/CourseDocs/NTEUvChertoff.pdf.

319. Management Rights, 5 C.F.R. Pt. 9701.511(a); 9701.515(d)(5) (2006).

320. *National Treasury Employees Union v. Chertoff*, 452 F.3d 839 (D.C. Cir. 2006).

321. *The National Security Personnel System—Is It Really Working?* (statement of Representative Walter Jones), 19.

322. *The Status of Federal Personnel Reform*, Serial No. 110–12 (statement of Representative Kenny Marchant), 114.

323. *Status of Federal Personnel Reform* (statement of Robert Tobias, director, public sector executive programs, School of Public Affairs, American University; Joseph Swerdzewski, former general counsel, Federal Labor Relations Authority; Hannah Sistare, vice president, NAPA; and Kevin Simpson, executive vice president, Partnership for Public Service), 114–16.

324. *Status of Federal Personnel Reform* (statement of Charles Tiefer, former House counsel and professor at University of Baltimore School of Law), 115–16, (statement of Mr. Simpson, executive vice president of the Partnership for Public Service), 116

325. *American Federation of Government Employees, AFL-CIO v. Gates*, 486 F.3d 1316 (D.C. Cir. 2007), http://www.afgelocal1345.org/NSPS_Decision.html.

326. *American Federation of Government Employees, AFL-CIO v. Gates.*

327. *American Federation of Government Employees, AFL-CIO v. Gates.*

328. National Defense Authorization Act for Fiscal Year 2008, H.R. 1585, 110th Cong. (2008), § 1106(a)(1), § 1106 (a)(2), § 1106 (a)(5), and § 1106 (a)(9), as reported by HASC.

329. National Defense Authorization Act for Fiscal Year 2008, § 1106(a)(3), § 1106 (a)(5), and § 1106 (a)(9).

330. National Defense Authorization Act for Fiscal Year 2008, S. 1547, 110th Cong. (2008), § 1104(b)(1), as reported by SASC.

331. National Defense Authorization Act for Fiscal Year 2008, § 1104(a).

332. National Defense Authorization Act for Fiscal Year 2008, § 1104(b)(2) and § 1104(b)(3).

333. 5 U.S.C. § 9902(b) (as amended by the National Defense Authorization Act for Fiscal Year 2008, § 1106).

334. 5 U.S.C. § 9902(b)(7) and § 9902(i)(1) (as amended by the National Defense Authorization Act for Fiscal Year 2008, SEC. 1106).

335. Stephen Barr, "Compromise on Pentagon Pay System, Union Rights," *Washington Post*, December 10, 2007, http://www.washingtonpost.com/wp-dyn/content/article/2007/12/09/AR2007120900897.html.

336. Stephen Barr, "Compromise on Pentagon Pay System, Union Rights" (quoting Ron Ault, president of the Metal Trades Department of the AFL-CIO, and Gregory J. Junemann, president of the International Federation of Professional and Technical Engineers); National Federation of Federal Employees, "Bush Signs Defense Authorization, NSPS Reform into Law," press release, January 29, 2008, http://www.nffe.org/local178/ht/d/ReleaseDetails/i/5360.

337. Brittany Ballenstedt, "Bush Signs Bill That Sends Unions Back to Bargaining Table at Defense," *Government Executive*, January 29, 2008, http://www.govexec.com/defense/2008/01/bush-signs-bill-that-sends-unions-back-to-bargaining-table-at-defense/26180/.

338. Dr. Chu, interview by Putney and Beck, 22.

339. DOD, "National Security Personnel System; Proposed Rule," *Federal Register* 73, no. 100 (May 22, 2008): 29905 (section 9901.305), https://www.gpo.gov/fdsys/pkg/FR-2008-05-22.

340. DOD, 29888.

341. *Improving Performance: A Review of Pay-for-Performance Systems in the Federal Government*, S. Hrg. 110–814 (statement of AFGE president John Gage), 31, 44.

342. Letter from Secretary England to Senator Levin and Representative Skelton (September 29, 2008) (see Brook, Schroeder, and King, *National Security Personnel System*, 29; Brittany Ballenstedt, "Pentagon Drops Plans to Convert Union Employees to NSPS," *Government Executive*, September 30, 2008, http://www.govexec.com/defense/2008/09/pentagon-drops-plans-to-convert-union-employees-to-nsps/27783/).

343. Letter from Barack Obama to Gregory Junemann (see Brook, Schroeder, and King, *National Security Personnel System*, 31); Letter from Barack Obama to John Gage (September 9, 2008), http://www.afge171.org/DEFCON/Docs/NSPS/NSPSObama.pdf.

344. Joe Davidson, "Pay-For-Performance Goes on the Defensive," *Washington Post*, April 2, 2009, http://www.washingtonpost.com/wp-dyn/content/article/2009/04/01/AR2009040103985.html.

345. Joe Davidson, "Pentagon's Personnel System Under Fire," *Washington Post*, February 20, 2009, http://www.washingtonpost.com/wp-dyn/content/article/2009/02/19/AR2009021903211.html.

346. Joe Davidson, "Pentagon to Review Pay-for-Performance System," *Washington Post*, March 17, 2009, http://www.washingtonpost.com/wp-dyn/content/article/2009/03/16/AR2009031603087.html.

347. Joe Davidson, "Performance Pay for Federal Employees Still a Matter of Debate," *Washington Post*, June 23, 2009, http://www.washingtonpost.com/wp-dyn/content/article/2009/06/22/AR2009062202978.html.

348. National Defense Authorization Act for Fiscal Year 2010, H.R. 2647, 111th Cong. (2010), § 1112, https://www.congress.gov/bill/111th-congress/house-bill/2647/text; Joe Davidson, "Death Knell for NSPS?" *Washington Post*, June 19, 2009, http://www.washingtonpost.com/wp-dyn/content/article/2009/06/18/AR2009061804055_2.html.

349. National Defense Authorization Act for Fiscal Year 2010, S. 1390, 111th Cong. (2010), § 1101(g), https://www.congress.gov/bill/111th-congress/senate-bill/1390/text.

350. National Defense Authorization Act for Fiscal Year 2010, § 1101(a)(2) and § 1101(c).

351. Defense Business Board, *Review of National Security Personnel System*, 10–15.

352. Defense Business Board, 6.

353. Joe Davidson, "Findings on Pay Structure Leave Some Cold," *Washington Post*, July 17, 2009.

354. Joe Davidson, "Rebuild Pay-For-Performance System, Panel Says," *Washington Post*, August 26, 2009.

355. National Defense Authorization Act for Fiscal Year 2010, Pub. L. 111–84, 123 Stat. 2190 (2009), SEC. 1113(b).

356. National Defense Authorization Act for Fiscal Year 2010, SEC. 1113(d).

357. DOD, "DOD Civilian Personnel Management System: Performance Management and Appraisal Program," DoD Instruction 1400.25, Volume 431 (Washington, DC: Office of the Under Secretary of Defense for Personnel and Readiness, February 4, 2016), 7, https://www.esd.whs.mil/Portals/54/Documents/DD/issuances/140025/1400.25_vol%2043I.pdf?ver=2018-11-13-103735-597.

358. Andy Medici, "DoD to Roll Out 'New Beginnings' Performance Appraisal System," *Federal Times*, May 14, 2015; Stephen Losey, "DoD Task Force: Rate Civilian Employees on Pass-Fail Basis," *Federal Times*, November 1, 2011.

359. Joe Davidson, "Lessons Learned from Pay-For-Performance," *Washington Post*, June 9, 2010, http://www.washingtonpost.com/wp-dyn/content/article/2010/06/08/AR2010060804980.html.

360. Defense Business Board, *Review of National Security Personnel System*, 6.

361. Dr. Sanders, interview by Putney, 44.

362. DOD, *Force of the Future, Final Report: Reform Proposals*, report circulated for comment (Washington, DC: Office of the Secretary of Defense, August 3, 2015), 52.

363. DOD, 52–53; DOD, *Force of the Future* (Washington, DC: Office of the Secretary of Defense), 3, posted online by *Government Executive*, September 16, 2015, https://www.govexec.com/media/gbc/docs/pdfs_edit/091515cc1.pdf.

364. Charles Clark, "Pentagon Plan to Move Civilian Workers Outside the Civil Service System Draws Fire," *Government Executive*, September 15, 2015, http://www.govexec.com/management/2015/09/pentagon-plan-move-civilian-workers-outside-civil-service-system-draws-fire/121043/. See also American Federation of Government Employees, "2016 Issue Papers" (papers presented at the AFGE 2016 Legislative and Grassroots

Mobilization Conference, Washington, DC, February 7–10, 2016), 9–12, 49–55, https://www.afge.org/globalassets/documents/issue-papers/2016-issue-papers.pdf.

365. Gregory Junemann (International Federation of Professional & Technical Workers), letter to Paige Hinkle-Bowles, deputy assistant secretary of defense for civilian personnel policy (September 9, 2015).

366. Byron Charlton (UDWC chair), letter to Secretary of Defense Ashton Carter (September 10, 2015).

367. DOD, *Force of the Future, Final Report: Reform Proposals*, ver. 5.0 (Washington, DC: Office of the Secretary of Defense, February 16, 2016), 58.

368. Edwin Dorn et al., *The Defense Civilian Intelligence Personnel System: An Independent Assessment of Design, Implementation, and Impact* (Washington, DC: National Academy of Public Administration, June 2010), 94–95, https://www.napawash.org/uploads/Academy_Studies/FINAL-DCIPS-REPORT-June-2010.pdf.

369. Dorn et al., 97–98.

370. Dorn et al., 84–88.

371. Dorn et al., 86.

372. Dorn et al., xiii.

373. Jennifer Lamping Lewis et al., *2016 Assessment of the Civilian Acquisition Workforce Demonstration Project*, RR1783 (Santa Monica, CA: RAND, 2017), xx, 53–67, https://www.rand.org/content/dam/rand/pubs/research_reports/RR1700/RR1783/RAND_RR1783.pdf.

374. Lamping Lewis et al., 107–11.

375. Lamping Lewis et al., 117–20.

376. National Defense Authorization Act for Fiscal Year 2017, Pub. L. 114–328, 130 Stat. 2000 (2016), SEC. 1121 and SEC. 1122, https://www.congress.gov/114/plaws/publ328/PLAW-114publ328.pdf; National Defense Authorization Act for Fiscal Year 2016, Pub. L. 114–92, 129 Stat. 726 (2015), SEC 846 and SEC. 1107, https://www.congress.gov/114/plaws/publ92/PLAW-114publ92.pdf.

377. Ashton Carter, "Remarks on 'The Next Two Links to the Force of the Future'" (Washington, DC: Pentagon Courtyard, June 9, 2016), https://www.defense.gov/News/Speeches/Speech-View/Article/795341/remarks-on-the-next-two-links-to-the-force-of-the-future/.

378. National Defense Authorization Act for Fiscal Year 2016, SEC. 1109, SEC. 1110, SEC. 1111, SEC. 1112, and SEC. 1113; National Defense Authorization Act for Fiscal Year 2017, SEC. 1105, SEC. 1106, SEC. 1110, SEC. 1124, and SEC. 1125.

379. National Defense Authorization Act for Fiscal Year 2016, SEC. 1101.

380. National Defense Authorization Act for Fiscal Year 2016, SEC. 1105.

381. National Defense Authorization Act for Fiscal Year 2016, SEC. 1106.

CHAPTER 2

1. *The Acquisition of Major Weapons Systems by the Department of Defense: Hearing Before the Committee on Armed Services, United States Senate*, S. Hrg. 110–639, 110th Cong.

(June 3, 2009) (statement of Senator Levin), 2, https://www.gpo.gov/fdsys/pkg/CHRG
-110shrg45699/pdf/CHRG-110shrg45699.pdf.

2. *Acquisition of Major Weapons Systems by the Department of Defense and S. 454, the Weapon Systems Acquisition Reform Act of 2009: Hearing Before the Committee on Armed Services, United States Senate*, S. Hrg. 111-149, 111th Cong. (March 3, 2009) (statement of Senator Levin), 3, https://www.gpo.gov/fdsys/pkg/CHRG-111shrg53267/pdf/CHRG
-111shrg53267.pdf.

3. John McCain, "Statement on Markup of S. 454, 'The Weapon Systems Acquisition Reform Act of 2009,'" April 2, 2009, https://www.mccain.senate.gov/public/index.cfm/floor-statements?ID=6742F50E-043A-B5AF-DB88-98B82439D8B6.

4. GAO, *Defense Acquisitions: Assessments of Selected Weapon Programs*, GAO-13-294SP (Washington, DC: GAO, March 2013), Highlights, https://www.gao.gov/assets/660/653379.pdf.

5. GAO, 8, 21, https://www.gao.gov/assets/690/683838.pdf.

6. *Case Studies in DOD Acquisition: Finding What Works: Hearing Before the Committee on Armed Services, House of Representatives*, H.A.S.C. No. 113-113, 113th Cong. (June 24, 2014) (statement of Representative Howard P. "Buck" McKeon), 1, https://ia801901.us
.archive.org/9/items/gov.gpo.fdsys.CHRG-113hhrg89506/CHRG-113hhrg89506.pdf.

7. John McCain, "Remarks by Senator John McCain on the Continuing Need for Defense Acquisition Reform," (press/floor statements, May 5, 2014), https://www.mccain
.senate.gov/public/index.cfm/floor-statements?ID=D4A92C50-43A4-462B-9C99
-80B4B9B31908.

8. President's Blue Ribbon Commission on Defense Management, *A Quest for Excellence: Final Report to the President*, Packard Commission Report (Washington, DC: Office of the President of the United States, June 1986), 60, https://babel.hathitrust.org/cgi/pt?id
=pur1.32754078697772;view=1up;seq=3.

9. National Defense Authorization Act for Fiscal Year 1987, Pub. L. 99-661, 99th Cong. (1986), SEC. 907, https://www.gpo.gov/fdsys/pkg/STATUTE-100/pdf/STATUTE-100
-Pg3816.pdf.

10. William J. Perry, "Specifications & Standards—A New Way of Doing Business" (Washington, DC: Office of the Secretary of Defense, June 24, 1994), https://www.sae.org/standardsdev/military/milperry.htm.

11. President's Blue Ribbon Commission on Defense Management, *A Quest for Excellence*, Packard Commission Report, 44.

12. J. Ronald Fox, *Defense Acquisition Reform 1960–2000: An Elusive Goal* (Washington, DC: Center of Military History, United States Army, 2011), 13, https://history.army.mil/html/books/051/51-3-1/CMH_Pub_51-3-1.pdf. See also Jacques S. Gansler, *Affording Defense* (Cambridge, MA: MIT Press, 1989), 158–65.

13. Office of Management and Budget, "Total Government Expenditures by Major Category of Expenditure as Percentages of GDP: 1948–2016" (Washington, DC: Office of Management and Budget, 2018), https://www.whitehouse.gov/sites/whitehouse.gov/files/omb/budget/fy2018/hist14z5.xls.

14. Thomas L. McNaugher, *New Weapons, Old Politics: America's Military Procurement Muddle* (Washington, DC: Brookings Institution Press, 1989), 46.

15. McNaugher, 49.

16. Gilbert W. Fitzhugh et al., *Report to the President and the Secretary of Defense on the Department of Defense by the Blue Ribbon Defense Panel*, Fitzhugh Commission Report, in United States Congress, *Defense Acquisition: Major Commission Reports (1949–1988) Volume 1* (Washington, DC: Government Printing Office, 1988), 218–19, https://babel.hathitrust.org/cgi/pt?id=umn.31951002964783;view=1up;seq=1.

17. Fitzhugh et al., 210.

18. McNaugher, *New Weapons, Old Politics*, 43–44; see DOD, *Performance of the Defense Acquisition System: 2014 Annual Report* (Washington, DC: Under Secretary of Defense for Acquisition, Technology, and Logistics, June 13, 2014), 47, https://www.defense.gov/Portals/1/Documents/pubs/Performance-of-Defense-Acquisition-System-2014.pdf.

19. Fox, *Defense Acquisition Reform 1960–2000*, 40.

20. Fox, 39.

21. Edmund Dews et al., *Acquisition Policy Effectiveness: Department of Defense Experience in the 1970s*, R-2516-DR&E (Santa Monica, CA: RAND, October 1979), 2, https://www.rand.org/content/dam/rand/pubs/reports/2006/R2516.pdf). See also Shannon A. Brown and Walton S. Moody, "Defense Acquisition in the 1970s: Retrenchment and Reform," in *Providing the Means of War: Perspectives on Defense Acquisition, 1945–2000*, ed. Shannon A. Brown (Washington, DC: United States Army Center of Military History and Industrial College of the Armed Forces, 2005), 146–50, https://history.army.mil/html/books/070/70-87-1/CMH_Pub_70-87-1.pdf.

22. Dews et al., *Acquisition Policy Effectiveness*, 52.

23. Peter J. Grace et al., *The President's Private Sector Survey on Cost Control: Report of the Office of the Secretary of Defense Task Force*, Grace Commission Report, in United States Congress, *Defense Acquisition: Major U.S. Commission Reports (1949–1988) Volume 1* (Washington, DC: Government Printing Office, 1988), 812–13, https://babel.hathitrust.org/cgi/pt?id=umn.31951002964783;view=1up;seq=1. See also David L. McNicol, *Cost Growth, Acquisition Policy, and Budget Climate*, IDA Document NS D-5180 (Revised) (Alexandria, VA: Institute for Defense Analyses, September 2014), 3.

24. Donald Atwood, "Keynote Address" (presented at the 20th Annual Financial Management Conference, Washington, DC, March 18, 1991).

25. Ronald T. Kadish et al., *Defense Acquisition Performance Assessment Report* (Washington, DC: Office of the Deputy Under Secretary of Defense, January 2006), 25, http://www.dtic.mil/docs/citations/ADA459941.

26. GAO, *Acquisition Reform: DOD Should Streamline Its Decision-Making Process for Weapon Systems to Reduce Inefficiencies*, GAO-15-192 (Washington, DC: GAO, February 2015), 6, https://www.gao.gov/assets/670/668629.pdf.

27. GAO, *Defense Acquisitions: Department of Defense Actions on Program Manager Empowerment and Accountability*," GAO-08-62R (Washington, DC: GAO, November 9, 2007), 8, https://www.gao.gov/assets/100/95239.pdf; Defense Business Board, *Review of*

DoD's Program Managers, Report FY 11-03 (Washington, DC: Defense Business Board, Defense Pentagon, April 2011), 2, http://dbb.defense.gov/Portals/35/Documents/Reports/2011/FY11-3_Review_Of_DOD%27s_Program_Managers_2011-4.pdf.

28. President's Blue Ribbon Commission on Defense Management, *A Quest for Excellence*, Packard Commission Report, 66.

29. BENS Task Force on Defense Acquisition Law and Oversight, *Getting to Best: Reforming the Defense Acquisition Enterprise—A Business Imperative for Change from the Task Force on Defense Acquisition Law and Oversight* (Washington, DC: Business Executives for National Security, July 2009), 31, https://www.bens.org/document.doc?id=44.

30. National Performance Review, "Reinventing Federal Procurement," September 14, 1993, https://govinfo.library.unt.edu/npr/library/nprrpt/annrpt/sysrpt93/reinven.html.

31. Advisory Panel on Streamlining and Codifying Acquisition Regulations, "Section 809 Panel Interim Report," May 2017, https://section809panel.org/wp-content/uploads/2017/05/Sec809Panel_Interim-Report_May2017_FINAL-for-web.pdf, 2.

32. David McNicol, *Cost Growth in Major Weapon Procurement Programs*, IDA Paper P-3832 (Alexandria, VA: Institute for Defense Analyses, 2004), S-2–S-3, 11.

33. McNicol, S-5–S-6.

34. For example, Gene Porter et al., *The Major Causes of Cost Growth in Defense Acquisition*, vol. I, *Executive Summary*, IDA Paper P-4531 (Alexandria, VA: Institute for Defense Analyses, December 2009), ES-1–ES-2, ES-7; Mark A. Lorell, Robert S. Leonard, and Abby Doll, *Extreme Cost Growth: Themes from Six U.S. Air Force Major Defense Acquisition Programs*, RR-630-AF (Santa Monica, CA: RAND, 2015), xiii, https://www.rand.org/content/dam/rand/pubs/research_reports/RR600/RR630/RAND_RR630.pdf; Richard Diehl, Brandon Gould, and Tzee-Nan Lo, *Root Causes of Nunn-McCurdy Breaches—A Survey of PARCA Root Causes Analyses, 2010–2011*, IDA Paper P-4911 (Alexandria, VA: Institute for Defense Analyses, August 2012), viii.

35. GAO, *Weapons Acquisition: A Rare Opportunity for Lasting Change*, GAO/NSIAD-93015 (Washington, DC: GAO, December 1992), 39, https://www.gao.gov/assets/160/152880.pdf.

36. GAO, 2.

37. Paul Francis, "The Acquisition Culture: Complicated, Inefficient, and in Equilibrium," in *Defense Acquisition Reform: Where Do We Go From Here? A Compendium of Views by Leading Experts*, S. Prt. 113-28, 113th Cong. (2014), 74, https://www.gpo.gov/fdsys/pkg/CPRT-113SPRT90719/pdf/CPRT-113SPRT90719.pdf.

38. Ronald Reagan, "Inaugural Address," January 20, 1981, http://www.presidency.ucsb.edu/ws/?pid=43130.

39. DOD, *National Defense Budget Estimates for FY 2018* (Washington, DC: Office of the Under Secretary of Defense (Comptroller), Revised August 2017), 84–85, http://comptroller.defense.gov/Portals/45/Documents/defbudget/fy2018/FY18_Green_Book.pdf.

40. *Defense Procurement Policies and Procedures: Cost Management and Control: Hearings Before the Special Panel on Defense Procurement Procedures of the Committee on Armed Services, House of Representatives*, H.A.S.C. No. 97-31, 97th Cong.

41. *Defense Procurement Policies and Procedures*, H.A.S.C. 97-31, October 22, 1981 (statement of Walton H. Sheley Jr., director, Mission Analysis and Systems Acquisition Division, GAO), 1008.

42. *Defense Procurement Policy and Management: Hearing Before the Committee on Armed Services, United States Senate*, SAS-0036, 97th Cong. (July 28, 1981); *Acquisition Process in the Department of Defense: Hearings Before the Committee on Governmental Affairs, United States Senate*, SGA-0058, 97th Cong. (October 21, 27; November 5, 1981).

43. *Defense Procurement Policy and Management*, SAS-0036 (statement of Senator Tower), 3.

44. *Acquisition Process in the Department of Defense*, SGA-0058, October 21, 1981 (statement of Senator Cohen), 8.

45. Frank Carlucci, "Improving the Acquisition Process," The Carlucci Memorandum (memorandum for the Secretaries of the Military Departments, April 30, 1981), in *Defense Procurement Policy and Management*, SAS-0036.

46. *Defense Procurement Policies and Procedures*, H.A.S.C. 97-31, October 28, 1981 (statement of Deputy Secretary of Defense Frank C. Carlucci), 1085.

47. Carlucci, "Improving the Acquisition Process," Recommendation 1 through Recommendation 8, 21–25.

48. *Defense Procurement Policies and Procedures*, H.A.S.C. No. 97-31, October 28, 1981 (statement of Deputy Secretary Carlucci), 1087.

49. *Acquisition Process in the Department of Defense*, SGA-0058, October 21, 1981 (statement of Comptroller General Charles A. Bowsher), 16.

50. *Acquisition Process in the Department of Defense*, 16.

51. *Defense Procurement Policies and Procedures*, H.A.S.C. 97-31, July 30, 1981 (statement of Representative Dave McCurdy), 132.

52. *Acquisition Process in the Department of Defense*, SGA-0058, October 21, 1981 (statement of Norman I. Augustine, chair, Defense Science Board, and vice president, Martin Marietta Corp.), 89. See also Weapons Acquisition Policy and Procedures: Curbing Cost Growth, Committee Print No. 13, 24, 28–29.

53. Carlucci, "Improving the Acquisition Process," 18, 19, 21.

54. O'Neil and Porter, *What to Buy?*, 96, 124.

55. Carlucci, "Improving the Acquisition Process," 33.

56. Fox, *Defense Acquisition Reform 1960–2000*, 117.

57. Carlucci, "Improving the Acquisition Process," 24.

58. GAO, *Navy Contracting: Cost Overruns and Claims Potential on Navy Shipbuilding Contracts*, GAO/NSIAD-88-15 (Washington, DC: GAO, October 1987), 7–14, https://www.gao.gov/assets/210/209736.pdf; GAO, *Navy Contracting: Status of Cost Growth and Claims on Shipbuilding Contracts*, GAO/NSIAD-89-189 (Washington, DC: GAO, August 1989), 1–4, 9–12, https://www.gao.gov/assets/220/211517.pdf; GAO, *Navy Contracting: Cost Growth Continues on Ship Construction Contracts*, GAO/NSIAD-92-218 (Washington, DC: GAO, August 1992), 1–3, 8–19, https://www.gao.gov/assets/220/216563.pdf.

59. *Defense Procurement Policies and Procedures*, H.A.S.C. No. 97-31, October 27, 1981 (statement of Norman Augustine, vice president, operations, Martin Marietta Aero-

space), 1063; *Acquisition Process in the Department of Defense*, SGA-0058, October 21, 1981 (statement of Robert Hale, assistant director for national security, Office of Management and Budget), 56–57. See also Fitzhugh et al., *Report to the President and the Secretary of Defense*, 220; E. Perkins McGuire et al., *Report of the Commission on Government Procurement*, in United States Congress, *Defense Acquisition: Major U.S. Commission Reports (1949–1988)*, 403.

60. Grace et al., *President's Private Sector Survey on Cost Control*, 753.

61. Dr. David S. Chu (former director of program analysis and evaluation), interview with author, February 13, 2018.

62. Dr. Chu, interview with author, February 13, 2018; David Berteau (former assistant to the deputy secretary of defense and deputy assistant secretary of defense), interview with author, September 21, 2017.

63. Walter Isaacson, "The Winds of Reform," *Time*, March 7, 1983, http://content.time.com/time/magazine/article/0,9171,953733,00.html (quoting Under Secretary of Defense Richard Delauer).

64. Wesley G. Pippert, "Study Shows Pentagon Cost Overruns," *UPI*, February 18, 1983, https://www.upi.com/Archives/1983/02/18/Study-shows-Pentagon-cost%20-overruns/2206414392400/.

65. *Department of Defense Authorization for Appropriations for Fiscal Year 1984: Hearings Before the Committee on Armed Services, United States Senate*, S. Hrg. 98-49, Pt. 2, 98th Cong. (February 25, 1983), 629–789.

66. Isaacson, "The Winds of Reform."

67. Acquisition Improvement Task Force, *Final Report of the Task Force on Acquisition Improvement* (Washington, DC: DOD, December 23, 1981), 3, http://www.dtic.mil/dtic/tr/fulltext/u2/a124531.pdf.

68. Acquisition Improvement Task Force, 3.

69. Acquisition Improvement Task Force, 4.

70. Acquisition Improvement Task Force, 5.

71. Fox, *Defense Acquisition Reform 1960–2000*, 115.

72. Berteau, interview with author, September 21, 2017.

73. *Hearings on H.R. 2545, Defense Procurement Reform Act of 1983: Hearings Before the Investigations Subcommittee of the Committee on Armed Services, House of Representatives*, H.A.S.C. No. 98-31, 98th Cong. (April 27, 1983) (statement of Representative Bill Nichols), 22.

74. *Department of Defense Authorization for Appropriations for Fiscal Year 1984*, S. Hrg. 98-49, Pt. 2, February 25, 1983 (statement of Senator Metzenbaum quoting Deputy Under Secretary William Long), 770.

75. GAO, *Acquisition: DOD's Defense Acquisition Improvement Program: A Status Report*, GAO/NSIAD-86-148 (Washington, DC: GAO, July 1986), 12, https://www.gao.gov/assets/210/208701.pdf.

76. GAO, *Acquisition: Status of the Defense Acquisition Improvement Program's 33 Initiatives*, GAO/NSIAD-86-176BR (Washington, DC: GAO, September 1986), 5, 10, 19–20, https://www.gao.gov/assets/80/76045.pdf.

77. GAO, *Acquisition: DOD's Acquisition Improvement Program—Program Managers' Views*, GAO/NSIAD-86-193FS (Washington, DC: GAO, September 1986), 7, https://www.gao.gov/assets/90/87419.pdf. Although the data are sparse, some evidence suggests that programs initiated in the early 1980s experienced less cost growth than those initiated in the 1970s. Mark V. Arena et al., *Historical Costs Growth of Completed Weapon System Programs*, TR-343-AF (Santa Monica, CA: RAND, 2006), 33, https://www.rand.org/content/dam/rand/pubs/technical_reports/2006/RAND_TR343.pdf; J. A. Drezner et al., *An Analysis of Weapon System Cost Growth*, MR-291-AF (Santa Monica: CA: RAND, 1993), 30–32, https://www.rand.org/pubs/monograph_reports/MR291.html); McNicol, *Cost Growth, Acquisition Policy, and Budget Climate*, 3–4; O'Neil and Porter, *What to Buy?*, 113–14; Raymond W. Reig et al., *Department of Defense Acquisition Management Metrics*, Technical Report TR 1-99 (Fort Belvoir, VA: DSMC Press, 1999), http://www.dtic.mil/dtic/tr/fulltext/u2/a375748.pdf.

78. Grace et al., *President's Private Sector Survey on Cost Control*, 746.

79. Grace et al., 753.

80. John J. Fialka, "Embattled Weapon," *Wall Street Journal*, February 17, 1982, in Dina Rasor, ed., *More Bucks, Less Bang: How the Pentagon Buys Ineffective Weapons* (Washington, DC: Fund for Constitutional Government, 1983), 28; William Boly, "The $13 Billion Dud," *California Magazine*, February 1983, in Rasor, *More Bucks, Less Bang*, 13.

81. Morton Mintz, "Depth Charge: Cost Overruns on New Trident Sub Leave a Muddied Wake," *Washington Post*, October 4, 1981, in Rasor, *More Bucks, Less Bang*, 212, 219.

82. Gregg Easterbrook, "All Aboard Air Oblivion," *Washington Monthly*, September 1981, in Rasor, *More Bucks, Less Bang*, 55.

83. Alexander Cockburn, "The Real AWACS Secret: It Doesn't Work," *Wall Street Journal*, September 24, 1981, in Rasor, *More Bucks, Less Bang*, 126, 127.

84. Patrick Oster and Bruce Ingersoll, "M-1," *Chicago Sun-Times*, April 26, 1981, in Rasor, *More Bucks, Less Bang*, 37, 34.

85. Frank Greve, "Dream Weapon a Nightmare," *Knight-Ridder Newspapers*, May 2, 1982, in Rasor, *More Bucks, Less Bang*, 70.

86. Gregg Easterbrook, "Divad," *The Atlantic Monthly*, October 1982, in Rasor, *More Bucks, Less Bang*, 104.

87. Easterbrook, "All Aboard Air Oblivion," 51.

88. Isaacson, "The Winds of Reform," (citing Heritage Foundation analysts John Boyd, Pierre Sprey, and George Kuhn). See also John T. Correll, "The Reformers," *Air Force Magazine*, February 2008, http://www.airforcemag.com/magazinearchive/pages/2008/february%202008/0208reformers.aspx?signon=false.

89. Knut Royce, "'Stealth' Bomber Called 'A Joke,'" *Hearst Newspapers*, December 5, 1982, in Rasor, *More Bucks, Less Bang*, 192.

90. Oster and Ingersoll, "M-1," 37.

91. William Greider, "The Education of David Stockman," *The Atlantic*, December 1981, https://www.theatlantic.com/magazine/archive/1981/12/the-education-of-david-stockman/305760/.

92. Robert S. Hancock, "Contractor Purchasing System Review (DAR Sup. No. 1)" (memorandum, Tinker Air Force Base, OK: Headquarters Oklahoma City Air Logistics Center [AFLC], July 12, 1982), in *Examination of Armed Services Policies and Procedures in the Procurement of Spare and Repair Parts, and the Pricing Thereof of These Items: Hearings Before the Subcommittee on Investigations, Committee on Armed Services, House of Representatives*, H.A.S.C. No. 98-26, 98th Cong. (April 19, 1983), 16. See also Daniel Wirls, *Buildup: The Politics of Defense in the Reagan Era* (Ithaca, NY: Cornell University Press, 1992), 99; Andrew J. Butrica, "An Overview of Acquisition, 1981–1990," in *Providing the Means of War: Perspectives on Defense Acquisition, 1945–2000*, ed. Shannon A. Brown (Washington, DC: United States Army Center of Military History and Industrial College of the Armed Forces, 2005), 207–8, https://history.army.mil/html/books/070/70-87-1/CMH_Pub_70-87-1.pdf.

93. *Examination of Armed Services Policies and Procedures.*

94. *Examination of Armed Services Policies and Procedures* (statement of Edward Lawton, Directorate of Contracting and Manufacturing, Oklahoma City Air Logistics Center), 26.

95. *Examination of Armed Services Policies and Procedures* (statement of Robert S. Hancock, "Contractor Purchasing System Review [DAR Sup. No. 1] [memorandum]), 16; (statement of Ira Kemp, associate director, contracting and manufacturing policy, headquarters, U.S. Air Force), 93. See also S*pare Parts Procurement for the Department of Defense: Hearings Before the Committee on Armed Services, United States Senate*, S. Hrg. 98-531, 98th Cong. (October 26, 1983) (statement of Joseph H. Sherick, inspector general, DOD), 5.

96. *Examination of Armed Services Policies and Procedures* (statement of Gerard Mignano, chief, Cost and Price Analysis Branch, Defense Industrial Supply Center, Philadelphia, PA), 55.

97. *Hearings on H.R. 2545, Defense Procurement Reform Act of 1983*, H.A.S.C. No. 98-31, October 19, 1983 (statement of Representative John R. Kasich), 211.

98. *Examination of Armed Services Policies and Procedures* (statement of Gerard Mignano), 55, 58; June 9, 1983 (statement of Vice Admiral Eugene Grinstead, director, Defense Logistics Agency), 359. See also S*pare Parts Procurement for the Department of Defense*, S. Hrg. 98-531, October 26, 1983 (statement of Mr. Sherick), 59.

99. *Examination of Armed Services Policies and Procedures* (colloquy between Representative Nichols and Mr. Mignano), 58; (statement of Admiral Grinstead), 358.

100. *Examination of Armed Services Policies and Procedures* (statement of John Melchner, assistant inspector general for auditing, Inspector General, DOD), 420.

101. S*pare Parts Procurement for the Department of Defense*, S. Hrg. 98-531, October 26, 1983 (colloquy between Senator Levin and Mr. Sherick), 26; October 27, 1983 (colloquy between Senator Levin and Arthur Wegner, president, Pratt & Whitney Group, United Technologies), 164–65.

102. *Examination of Armed Services Policies and Procedures* (statement of Representative Kasich), 108.

103. *Examination of Armed Services Policies and Procedures* (statement of Mr. Melchner), 403; (letter from Mr. Stewart Storms of Lemoore, CA, to Representative Charles Pashayan Jr.), 412–13.

104. *Examination of Armed Services Policies and Procedures* (statement of Representative James G. Martin), 37.

105. Casper Weinberger, "Spare Parts Procurement" (memorandum to Secretaries of the Military Departments . . . Directors of the Defense Agencies, Washington, DC: The Secretary of Defense, July 25, 1983), in S*pare Parts Procurement for the Department of Defense*, S. Hrg. 98-531, October 27, 1983, 262–64.

106. Casper Weinberger, "Spare Parts Acquisition" (memorandum to Secretaries of the Military Departments . . . Directors of the Defense Agencies, Washington, DC: The Secretary of Defense, August 29, 1983), in S*pare Parts Procurement for the Department of Defense*, S. Hrg. 98-531, October 27, 1983, 79–80.

107. *Management of the Department of Defense: Hearing Before the Committee on Governmental Affairs, United States Senate*, S. Hrg. 98-150, Pt. 6, 98th Cong. (November 2, 1983) (statement of Paul Thayer, deputy secretary of defense), 123.

108. *Management of the Department of Defense* (statement of Major General David Stallings, director for procurement and production, Army Materiel Development and Readiness Command), 22.

109. *Management of the Department of Defense* (statement of Rear Admiral Joseph Sansone Jr., deputy chief of navy materiel [contracts and business management]), 55–56.

110. *Management of the Department of Defense* (statement of Major General Alfred Hansen, director of air force logistics plans and programs), 25.

111. DOD Inspector General, *Audit Report: The Spare Parts Breakout Program*, No. 90-056 (Washington, DC: DOD, April 5, 1990), 6, https://media.defense.gov/1990/Apr/05/2001714349/-1/-1/1/90-056.pdf.

112. S*pare Parts Procurement for the Department of Defense*, S. Hrg. 98-531, October 26, 1983 (statement of Senator Nunn), 2; James Barron, "High Cost of Military Parts," *New York Times*, September 1, 1983, http://www.nytimes.com/1983/09/01/business/high-cost-of-military-parts.html?pagewanted=all; James Kilpatrick, "$1,118.26 Each—For Want of a Plastic Cup," *Philadelphia Inquirer*, August 30, 1983.

113. *Management of the Department of Defense: Hearing Before the Committee on Governmental Affairs, United States Senate*, S. Hrg. 98-150, Pt. 6 (statement of Senator Cohen), 18.

114. *Management of the Department of Defense* (statement of Senator Roth), 3.

115. *Management of the Department of Defense* (statement of Senator Roth), 3.

116. *Management of the Department of Defense*, 26.

117. Defense Contract Audit Agency, *Report on Aerospace Ground Equipment (AGE), Acquisition Practices, United Technologies Corp., Pratt & Whitney Aircraft Group (P&WAG), Government Products Division (GPD), West Palm Beach, Fla.*, Audit Report No. 1481-4A120042 (West Palm Beach, FL: September 30, 1983), in *Management of the Department of Defense*, 85.

118. Charles Mohr, "Military Price on Coffee Cited as $7,622," *New York Times*, September 20, 1984, http://www.nytimes.com/1984/09/20/us/military-price-on-coffee-cited

-as-7622.html; Tim Carrington, "Politics '84—Congress Is Stonewalled: Pentagon Frustrates Reform Efforts," *Wall Street Journal*, December 26, 1984; Dina Rasor, *The Pentagon Underground*, 1st ed. (New York: Times Books, 1985), 149–50, 157, 159, 169; William Hartung, *Prophets of War: Lockheed Martin and the Making of the Military-Industrial Complex* (New York: Nation Books, 2011), 139–40.

119. Wayne Biddle, "Price of Toilet Seat Is Cut for Navy," *New York Times*, February 6, 1985, http://www.nytimes.com/1985/02/06/us/price-of-toilet-seat-is-cut-for-navy.html; "DOD and the Toilet Seats," *Washington Post*, April 20, 1985; Herblock, "Joy to the World," *Washington Post*, December 17, 1985.

120. "House Accord May Clear Way for Vote on Defense Measure," *Congressional Quarterly Weekly Report*, September 14, 1985, 1799, quoted in Brown and Moody, "Defense Acquisition in the 1970s," 208.

121. *Defense Week*, April 1984, quoted in Wirls, *Buildup: The Politics of Defense*, 169.

122. Ronald O'Rourke, "Alleged Fraud, Waste, and Abuse: General Dynamics Corp.," Issue Brief (Washington, DC: Congressional Research Service, Foreign Affairs and National Defense Division, July 12, 1985), 3, https://digital.library.unt.edu/ark:/67531/metacrs9051/m1/1/high_res_d/IB85067_1985Jul12.pdf.

123. "U.S. Rejects Offer to Talk by Veliotis," *Boston Globe*, January 18, 1984.

124. O'Rourke, "Alleged Fraud, Waste, and Abuse," 8.

125. O'Rourke, 9.

126. O'Rourke, 10.

127. Don Shannon, "Pentagon Probe Halts General Dynamics Pay," *Los Angeles Times*, March 6, 1985, http://articles.latimes.com/1985-03-06/news/mn-26228_1_general-dynamics.

128. *Management of the Department of Defense* (statement of Senator Levin), 20.

129. Department of Defense Authorization Act, 1982, Pub. L. 97-86, 95 Stat. 1099 (1981), SEC. 917, http://uscode.house.gov/statutes/pl/97/86.pdf (subsequently codified by Department of Defense Authorization Act, 1983, Pub. L. 97-252, 96 Stat. 718 (1982), SEC. 1107, http://uscode.house.gov/statutes/pl/97/252.pdf.

130. Department of Defense Authorization Act, 1983, SEC. 1117.

131. Department of Defense Authorization Act, 1984, Pub. L. 98-94, 97 Stat. 614 (1983), SECs. 1203, 1211, 1215, and 1216, https://www.gpo.gov/fdsys/pkg/STATUTE-97/pdf/STATUTE-97-Pg614.pdf.

132. Deficit Reduction Act of 1984, Pub. L. 98-369, 98 Stat. 494 (1984), SECs. 2701–2753.

133. "Hill Enacts Pentagon Procurement 'Reforms,'" in *CQ Almanac 1985*, 41st ed. (Washington, DC: Congressional Quarterly, 1986), 164–72.

134. Jon Etherton, "Overcoming Obstacles in Acquisition Reform," Testimony before the Committee on Armed Services, United States House of Representatives (Arlington, VA: National Defense Industrial Association, February 12, 2014), 4, https://www.ndia.org/-/media/sites/ndia/policy/documents/acquisition-reform/acquisition-reform-initiative-2014/etherton-hasc-2-12-14-1.ashx?la=en; Jon Etherton (former SASC professional staff member), interview with author, August 30, 2017; Colleen Preston (former HASC staff member and deputy under secretary of defense for acquisition reform), interview with author, October 5, 2017.

135. E.g., Program Fraud Civil Remedies Act of 1986, Sections 6103 and 6014 of the Omnibus Budget Reconciliation Act of 1986 (Pub. L. 99-501); Major Fraud Act of 1988, Pub. L. 100-700; Office of Federal Procurement Policy Act Amendments of 1988, Pub. L. 100-679, SEC. 8, "Procurement Integrity."

136. Defense Procurement Reform Act of 1984, Department of Defense Authorization Act, 1985, Pub. L. 98-525, 98 Stat. 2492 (1984), Title XII, https://www.gpo.gov/fdsys/pkg/STATUTE-98/pdf/STATUTE-98-Pg2492.pdf, SECs. 1216, 1231, 1233, 1234, and 1245; Defense Procurement Improvement Act of 1985, Department of Defense Authorization Act, 1986, Pub. L. 99-145, 99 Stat. 583 (1985), Title IX, https://www.gpo.gov/fdsys/pkg/STATUTE-99/pdf/STATUTE-99-Pg583.pdf, SECs. 913, 914, 931, and 934; Defense Acquisition Improvement Act of 1986, Department of Defense Authorization Act, 1987, title IV, SECs. 926 and 927.

137. GAO, *Procurement: Defense Logistics Agency Implementation of the Spare Parts Initiatives*, GAO/NSIAD-87-143 (Washington, DC: GAO, June 1987), 13–17, https://www.gao.gov/assets/210/209374.pdf.

138. Preston, interview with author, October 5, 2017.

139. GAO, *Procurement: Defense Logistics Agency Implementation*, GAO/NSIAD-87-143, 2. See also GAO, *Procurement: Navy Implementation of the Spare Parts Initiatives*, GAO/NSIAD-87-149 (Washington, DC: GAO, June 1987), 1–2, https://www.gao.gov/assets/210/209372.pdf; GAO, *Procurement: Spare Parts Initiatives Air Force Implementation*, GAO/NSIAD-87-28 (Washington, DC: GAO, February 1987), 1–2, https://www.gao.gov/assets/210/209101.pdf; GAO, *Procurement: Army Implementation of Spare Parts Initiatives*, GAO/NSIAD-87-148 (Washington, DC: GAO, June 1987), 2–3, https://www.gao.gov/assets/210/209388.pdf.

140. DOD Inspector General, "Audit Report: The Spare Parts," i, 11.

141. Jon Etherton (former SASC staffer), interview with author, August 30, 2017.

142. Department of Defense Authorization Act for Fiscal Year 1999, S. Rep. No. 105-189, 105th Cong. (1998), 316, https://www.congress.gov/105/crpt/srpt189/CRPT-105srpt189.pdf.

143. GAO, *Defense Acquisition: Price Trends for Defense Logistics Agency's Weapon System Parts*, GAO-01-22 (Washington, DC: GAO, November 2000), https://www.gao.gov/assets/230/229803.pdf; GAO, *Defense Acquisition: Status of Defense Logistics Agency's Efforts to Address Spare Part Price Increases*, GAO-02-505 (Washington, DC: GAO, April 2002), https://www.gao.gov/assets/240/234041.pdf.

144. GAO, *Defense Acquisition: Navy Needs Plan to Address Rising Prices in Aviation Parts*, GAO-02-565 (Washington, DC: GAO, May 2002), https://www.gao.gov/assets/240/234770.pdf.

145. GAO, *Defense Acquisition: Prices of Marine Corps Spare Parts Have Increased*, GAO/NSIAD-00-123 (Washington, DC: GAO, July 2000), https://www.gao.gov/assets/230/229384.pdf.

146. DOD Inspector General, *Acquisition: Commercial Contract for Noncompetitive Spare Parts with Hamilton Sundstrand Corporation*, D-2006-122 (Washington, DC: DOD), September 29, 2006, 3, https://media.defense.gov/2006/Sep/29/2001712572/-1/-1/1/06-122

.pdf; DOD Inspector General, *Summary of DOD Office of Inspector General Spare-Parts Pricing Audits: Additional Guidance Is Needed*, DODIG-2015-103 (Washington, DC: DOD, March 31, 2015), 4, https://media.defense.gov/2015/Mar/31/2001713487/-1/-1/1/DODIG-2015-104.pdf; Richard Van Atta et al., *Department of Defense Access to Intellectual Property for Weapon Systems Sustainment*, IDA Paper P-8266 (Alexandria, VA: Institute for Defense Analyses, May 2017), vi.

147. Department of Defense Authorization Act, 1985, SEC. 1234.

148. Department of Defense Authorization Act, 1986, SEC. 912.

149. Department of Defense Authorization Act, 1986, SEC. 917. See also GAO, *Defense Procurement: Work Measurement Programs at Selected Contractor Locations*, GAO/NSIAD-88-43BR (Washington, D.C., GAO, November 1987), 6, https://www.gao.gov/assets/80/76846.pdf.

150. GAO, *DOD Warranties: Improvements Needed in Implementation of Warranty Legislation*, GAO/NSIAD-87-122 (Washington, DC: GAO, July 1987), 22, https://www.gao.gov/assets/150/145497.pdf; GAO, *DOD Warranties: Effective Administration Systems Are Needed to Implement Warranties*, GAO/NSIAD-89-57 (Washington, DC: GAO, September 1989), https://www.gao.gov/assets/150/148140.pdf.

151. Defense Systems Management College, *Streamlining Defense Acquisition Laws*, Report of the Law Advisory Panel to the United States Congress, Section 800 Report (Fort Belvoir, VA: Defense Systems Management College, January 1993), 2–115, http://www.dtic.mil/dtic/tr/fulltext/u2/a262699.pdf.

152. GAO, *Weapons Acquisition: Warranty Law*, GAO/NSIAD-96-88, 4.

153. National Defense Authorization Act for Fiscal Year 1998, Pub. L. 105-85, 111 Stat. 1629, 105th Cong. (1997), SEC. 847, https://www.congress.gov/105/plaws/publ85/PLAW-105publ85.pdf.

154. Eleanor Spector (former director of defense procurement), interview with author, September 13, 2017.

155. National Defense Authorization Act for Fiscal Year 1993, Pub. L. 102-484, 111 Stat. 1629, 102nd Cong. (1992), SEC. 821, https://www.gpo.gov/fdsys/pkg/STATUTE-106/pdf/STATUTE-106-Pg2315.pdf.

156. Defense Systems Management College, *Streamlining Defense Acquisition Laws*, Section 800 Report, 3-65–3-66.

157. Federal Acquisition Streamlining Act of 1994, Pub. L. 103-355, SEC.3007.

158. *Acquisition Reform–1986: Hearings Before the Acquisition and Procurement Policy Panel of the Committee on Armed Services, House of Representatives*, H.A.S.C. 99-63, 99th Cong. (April 10, 1986), 261.

159. National Defense Authorization Act for Fiscal Year 1987, Pub. L. 99-661, SEC. 934.

160. Defense Systems Management College, *Streamlining Defense Acquisition Laws*, Section 800 Report, 2-86.

161. Federal Acquisition Streamlining Act of 1994, Pub. L. 103-355, SEC. 2201(b).

162. In the late 1980s, RAND and the GAO independently reported that the cost performance of 1980s systems appeared to be slightly better than that of 1970s systems,

but discounted the improvement because 1980s systems were only now "entering a period in their acquisition cycles during which significant cost growth or schedule slippages have historically occurred." GAO, *Major Acquisitions: Summary of Recurring Problems and Systemic Issues: 1960–1987*, GAO/NSIAD-88-135BR (Washington, DC: GAO, September 1988), 5, 13, 22. https://www.gao.gov/assets/80/77194.pdf. See also Michael Rich and Edmund Dews, *Improving the Military Acquisition Process: Lessons from Rand Research*, R-3373-AF/RC (Santa Monica, CA: RAND, February 1986), viii–ix, 30, 48 https://www.rand.org/content/dam/rand/pubs/reports/2005/R3373.pdf.

163. James R. Locher, III, *Victory on the Potomac: The Goldwater-Nichols Act Unifies the Pentagon*, Military History Series (College Station: Texas A&M University Press, 2002), 285.

164. Letter from Senator William Roth Jr. to Caspar Weinberger (March 27, 1985) and letter from Representative William Dickinson to President Reagan (April 1, 1985), quoted in Locher, *Victory on the Potomac*, 285–86.

165. Fox, *Defense Acquisition Reform 1960–2000*, 121–22.

166. Berteau, interview with author, September 21, 2017.

167. "Hicks Leaves Key Post at Defense Department," *New York Times*, October 11, 1986, http://www.nytimes.com/1986/10/11/us/hicks-leaves-key-post-at-defense-department.html?mcubz=3.

168. Locher, *Victory on the Potomac*, 292.

169. Bill Keller, "Weinberger Backs New Buying Rules," *New York Times*, August 16, 1985.

170. Bill Keller, "Panel Set to Propose Major Overhaul for Pentagon," *New York Times*, October 11, 1985.

171. President's Blue Ribbon Commission on Defense Management, *A Quest for Excellence*, Packard Commission Report, 44.

172. President's Blue Ribbon Commission on Defense Management, xxii, 42.

173. President's Blue Ribbon Commission on Defense Management, 44–47.

174. *The Acquisition Findings in the Report of the President's Blue Ribbon Commission on Defense Management: Hearing Before the Subcommittee on Defense Acquisition Policy of the Committee on Armed Services, United States Senate*, S. Hrg. 99-805, 99th Cong. (April 8, 1986) (statement of Dr. William Perry, member, President's Blue Ribbon Commission on Defense Management), 34.

175. President's Blue Ribbon Commission on Defense Management, *A Quest for Excellence*, Packard Commission Report, xxiii.

176. President's Blue Ribbon Commission on Defense Management, 55–57.

177. President's Blue Ribbon Commission on Defense Management, 57–59.

178. President's Blue Ribbon Commission on Defense Management, 59–60.

179. *The Acquisition Findings in the Report of the President's Blue Ribbon Commission*, S. Hrg. 99-805, 45.

180. President's Blue Ribbon Commission on Defense Management, *A Quest for Excellence*, Packard Commission Report, xxiv. David Berteau reports that the commission's views on this issue were crystalized by the testimony of senior DOD officials at a

closed November meeting of the commission. In the morning, Secretary of the Navy John Lehman testified that the DOD needed a strong central acquisition executive to extend to the other services successful acquisition initiatives like the ones that he was pursuing in the Navy. In the afternoon, Air Force General Larry Skantze also testified that the department needed a strong central acquisition executive—to stop the services from carrying out misguided acquisition initiatives like those advocated by Secretary Lehman (Berteau, interview with author, September 21, 2017).

181. President's Blue Ribbon Commission on Defense Management, 53. See also *The Acquisition Findings in the Report of the President's Blue Ribbon Commission on Defense Management*, S. Hrg. 99-805, 59–60, 62–63 (colloquy between Senator Levin and Commission Chair David Packard, Acquisition Task Force Chair William Perry, and senior consultant Jacques Gansler). The commission endorsed the authority of the new under secretary to direct the service secretaries (*Acquisition Findings*, 67).

182. President's Blue Ribbon Commission on Defense Management, *A Quest for Excellence*, Packard Commission Report, 57–58.

183. President's Blue Ribbon Commission on Defense Management, 54.

184. President's Blue Ribbon Commission on Defense Management, 54.

185. President's Blue Ribbon Commission on Defense Management, 50.

186. McNicol, *Cost Growth in Major Weapon Procurement Programs*, 41.

187. McNicol, 41.

188. Richard Halloran, "President's Commission Criticizes Military Structure and Suppliers," *New York Times*, March 1, 1986.

189. "Implementation of the Recommendations of the President's Commission on Defense Management," National Security Decision Directive Number 219 (Washington, DC: The White House, April 1, 1986), https://fas.org/irp/offdocs/nsdd/23-2755a.gif.

190. Military Retirement Reform Act of 1986, Pub. L. 99-348, 100 Stat. 682 (1986), SEC. 501, https://www.gpo.gov/fdsys/pkg/STATUTE-100/pdf/STATUTE-100-Pg682.pdf.

191. National Defense Authorization Act for Fiscal Year 1987, Title IX.

192. Halloran, "President's Commission Criticizes Military."

193. *Acquisition Reform–1986*, HASC No. 99-63, April 9, 1986 (Secretary of the Navy John Lehman), 186, 193.

194. Preston, interview with author, October 5, 2017.

195. DOD, "Major and Non-Major Defense Acquisition Process," DODD 5000.1 (Washington, DC: USD[A], September 1, 1987), 2 (para. D.7.a.), in *Report on the Duties and Authority of the Under Secretary of Defense (Acquisition) of the Committee on Armed Services, House of Representatives*, Committee Print No. 15, 100th Cong. (November 16, 1987), 186.

196. DOD, "Under Secretary of Defense (Acquisition)," DODD 5134.1 (Washington, DC: OSD, February 10, 1987), para. E.4, in *Oversight of Legislation Establishing the Position of Under Secretary of Defense for Acquisition*, S. Hrg. 100-581, 12. See also colloquies between Senator Levin, Deputy Secretary Taft, and Under Secretary Godwin, 158–59, 169–70.

197. DOD, "Major and Non-Major Defense Acquisition Process," DODD 5000.1, para. F.1.a., in Report on the Duties and Authority of the Under Secretary of Defense

(Acquisition), Committee Print No. 15, 189. See also *Oversight of Legislation Establishing the Position of Under Secretary of Defense for Acquisition*, S. Hrg. 100-581 (colloquy between Senator Bingaman and Under Secretary Godwin), 141.

198. DOD, "Defense Acquisition Program Procedures, DODI 5000.2 (Washington, DC: USD[A], September 1, 1987), 6, http://www.whs.mil/library/mildoc/DODI%205000.2,%201%20September%201987.pdf.

199. Berteau, interview with author, September 21, 2017. See also Fox, *Defense Acquisition Reform 1960–2000*, 224. Some of these provisions were later modified as a result of pressure from Congress. Report on the Duties and Authority of the Under Secretary of Defense (Acquisition), Committee Print No. 15, 28–29.

200. Fox, *Defense Acquisition Reform 1960–2000*, 143.

201. *Oversight of Legislation Establishing the Position of Under Secretary of Defense for Acquisition*, S. Hrg. 100-581 (statement of Under Secretary Godwin), 23.

202. *Oversight of Legislation Establishing the Position of Under Secretary of Defense for Acquisition*, 115.

203. *Oversight of Legislation Establishing the Position of Under Secretary of Defense for Acquisition*, 116. See also *Report on the Duties and Authority of the Under Secretary of Defense (Acquisition)*, Committee Print No. 15, 29–30.

204. *Oversight of Legislation Establishing the Position of Under Secretary of Defense for Acquisition*, 113.

205. Karen Tumulty, "Military Thwarted Him, Ex-Pentagon Purchasing Czar Testifies," *Los Angeles Times*, September 23, 1987, http://articles.latimes.com/1987-09-23/news/mn-6360_1_military-purchasing.

206. President's Blue Ribbon Commission on Defense Management, *A Quest for Excellence*, Packard Commission Report, 54.

207. *Oversight of Legislation Establishing the Position of Under Secretary of Defense for Acquisition*, S. Hrg. 100-581, 122, 131–32, 153.

208. Fox, *Defense Acquisition Reform 1960–2000*, 145–46 (citing Frank Conahan of the GAO).

209. David Graham et al., *Defense Acquisition: Observations Two Years after the Packard Commission*, vol. I, *Main Report*, IDA Report R-347 (Alexandria, VA: Institute for Defense Analyses, November 1988), III-14.

210. Report on the Duties and Authority of the Under Secretary of Defense (Acquisition), Committee Print No. 15, 37.

211. Tumulty, "Military Thwarted Him." See also Fox, *Defense Management Challenge*, 147.

212. Graham et al., *Defense Acquisition*, II-11; *Report on the Duties and Authority of the Under Secretary of Defense (Acquisition)*, Committee Print No. 15, 44, 47–48.

213. Peter Grier, "Pentagon's Purchasing Chief Resigns, Frustrated with Pace of Reform," *Christian Science Monitor*, September 21, 1987, https://www.csmonitor.com/1987/0921/awin.html.

214. Report on the Duties and Authority of the Under Secretary of Defense (Acquisition), Committee Print No. 15, 18–19. See also Graham et al., *Defense Acquisition*, VII-2–VII-3.

215. Graham et al., *Defense Acquisition*, II-11–II-12.
216. Graham et al., II-12.
217. Graham et al., IV-11.
218. George H. W. Bush, "Address on Administration Goals Before a Joint Session of Congress," February 9, 1989, http://www.presidency.ucsb.edu/ws/index.php?pid=16660.
219. *Nominations Before the Senate Armed Services Committee, First Session, 101st Congress: Hearings Before the Committee on Armed Services, United States Senate*, S. Hrg. 101-537, 101st Cong. (March 14, 1989) (statement of Richard B. Cheney), 23, 34.
220. Berteau, interview with author, September 21, 2017.
221. Dick Cheney, *Defense Management: Report to the President* (Washington, DC: Office of the Secretary of Defense, July 1989), 3–4, http://www.dtic.mil/dtic/tr/fulltext/u2/a216011.pdf.
222. Letter from Donald Atwood to Senator Sam Nunn (April 10, 1989), in *Nominations Before the Senate Armed Services Committee, First Session, 101st Congress: Hearings Before the Committee on Armed Services, United States Senate*, S. Hrg. 101-537, 101st Cong. (April 5, 1989), 133.
223. *Nominations Before the Senate Armed Services Committee, First Session*, S. Hrg. 101-537 (August 3, 1989) (statement of John A. Betti), 492.
224. Molly Moore, "Pentagon Weapons Acquisition Chief, Under Fire Over Cost, Quits Post," *Washington Post*, December 13, 1990.
225. GAO, *Navy A-12: Cost and Requirements*, GAO/NSIAD-91-98 (Washington, DC: GAO, December 1990) 3, https://www.gao.gov/assets/220/213440.pdf. See also *A-12 Acquisition: Hearings Before the Investigations Subcommittee of the Committee on Armed Services, House of Representatives*, H.A.S.C. No. 102-29, 102nd Cong. (April 9, 1991) (statement of Representative Andy Ireland), 3.
226. *Department of Defense Authorization for Appropriations for Fiscal Year 1991: Hearings Before the Committee on Armed Services, United States Senate*, S. Hrg. 101-986, Pt. 1, 101st Cong. (April 26, 1990) (statement of Secretary Cheney), 781–82, 799–800, 806–7, 832.
227. DOD Inspector General, *Review of the A-12 Aircraft Program*, Audit Report No. 91-059 (Washington, DC: DOD, February 28, 1991), 2, https://media.defense.gov/1991/Feb/28/2001714477/-1/-1/1/91-059.pdf; *A-12 Acquisition*, H.A.S.C. No. 102-29, April 9, 1991 (statement of Representative Ireland), 3. Letter from Susan Crawford, inspector general, to the Honorable Andy Ireland, November 29, 1990, in DOD Inspector General, *Review of the A-12 Aircraft Program*, Audit Report No. 91-059 (Washington, DC: DOD, February 28, 1991), 36 (Appendix C), https://media.defense.gov/1991/Feb/28/2001714477/-1/-1/1/91-059.pdf; Eric Schmitt, "Pentagon Official Resigns After Criticism About Overruns on Plane," *New York Times*, December 13, 1990, https://www.nytimes.com/1990/12/13/us/pentagon-official-resigns-after-criticism-about-overruns-on-plane.html; Eric Schmitt, "Pentagon Scraps $57 Billion Order for Attack Plan," *New York Times*, January 8, 1991, https://www.nytimes.com/1991/01/08/us/pentagon-scraps-57-billion-order-for-attack-plane.html?pagewanted=all.
228. DOD, "Defense Acquisition," DODD 5000.1 (Washington, DC: Office of the Secretary of Defense, February 23, 1991), 1-2-1-3 (Part 1, B.3.c.), http://www.whs.mil/library/mildoc/DODD%205000.1,%2023%20February%201991.pdf.

229. Steven Pearlstein, "Incoming at Pentagon: A 'Czar,'" *Washington Post*, May 22, 1991, https://www.washingtonpost.com/archive/politics/1991/05/22/incoming-at-pentagon-a-czar/38fe9a70-df78-486a-92ea-ee8ddb1693ed/?utm_term=.bf15c99210_1f.

230. Even with Cheney's intervention, however, the Packard recommendation that the USD(A) help lead the review of military requirements was never implemented. Berteau, interview with author, September 21, 2017.

231. David L. McNicol and Linda Wu, *Evidence on the Effect of DOD Acquisition Policy and Process on Cost Growth of Major Defense Acquisition Programs*, IDA Paper P-5126 (Alexandria, VA: Institute for Defense Analyses, September 2014), iv–v. Other studies show conflicting results. Davis and Anton, "Annual Growth of Contract Costs," 5; Mark Arena et al., *Historical Cost Growth*, 32–33; Raymond Reig et al., *Department of Defense Acquisition Management Metrics*, 5-3–5-4); David S. Christensen, David A. Stearle, and Caisse Vickery, "The Impact of the Packard Commission's Recommendations on Reducing Cost Overruns on Defense Acquisition Contracts," *Acquisition Review Quarterly* (Summer 1999): 256–57, http://www.dtic.mil/get-tr-doc/pdf?AD=ADA372859).

232. McNicol and Wu, *Evidence on the Effect*, vi–vii.

233. DOD, *National Defense Budget Estimates for FY 2017* (Washington, DC: Office of the Under Secretary of Defense [Comptroller], March 2016), 83–84 (Table 6-1), http://comptroller.defense.gov/Portals/45/Documents/defbudget/fy2017/FY17_Green_Book.pdf. An exceptionally high percentage (40.7 percent) of programs initiated in the 1987 to 1989 (pre-Packard) period were terminated, presumably because of the end of the Cold War (David L. McNicol, *Influences on the Timing and Frequency of Cancellations and Truncations of Major Defense Acquisition Programs*, IDA Paper P-8280 [Alexandria, VA: Institute for Defense Analyses, March 2017], 7).

234. McNicol and Wu, *Evidence on the Effect*, v.

235. McNicol and Wu, v.

236. Wendy Kirby, "Expanding the Use of Commercial Products and 'Commercial-Style' Acquisition Techniques in Defense Procurement: A Proposed Legal Framework," President's Blue Ribbon Commission on Defense Management, *A Quest for Excellence*, Packard Commission Report, app. H.

237. President's Blue Ribbon Commission on Defense Management, *A Quest for Excellence*, Packard Commission Report, 61.

238. President's Blue Ribbon Commission on Defense Management, 55.

239. National Defense Authorization Act for Fiscal Year 1987, SEC. 907.

240. Jeff Bingaman, "The Twelfth Annual Gilbert A. Cuneo Lecture: The Origins and Development of the Federal Acquisition Streamlining Act," *Military Law Review* 146 (Summer 1994): 152, https://www.loc.gov/rr/frd/Military_Law/Military_Law_Review/pdf-files/276875~1.pdf. See also DOD's Inadequate Use of Off-the-Shelf Items, Committee Print S. Prt. 101-62, 101st Cong. (October 30, 1989); *Department of Defense Authorization for Appropriations for Fiscal Year 1994 and the Future Years Defense Program: Hearings Before the Committee on Armed Services, United States Senate*, S. Hrg. 103-303, Pt. 5, 103rd (Cong.) (June 28, 1993) (statement of Senator Levin), 461.

241. National Defense Authorization Act for Fiscal Year 1991, Pub. L. 101-510, 104 Stat. 1485, 101st Cong. (1990), SEC. 800, https://www.gpo.gov/fdsys/pkg/STATUTE-104/pdf/STATUTE-104-Pg1485.pdf.

242. Defense Systems Management College, *Streamlining Defense Acquisition Laws*, Section 800 Report, vii, 6. See also *Department of Defense Authorization for Appropriations for Fiscal Year 1994*, S. Hrg. 103-303, Pt. 5, June 28, 1993 (statement of Senator Bingaman), 430.

243. Etherton, "Overcoming Obstacles," 7–8.

244. Federal Acquisition Streamlining Act of 1994, S. 1587, 103rd Cong. (1994), https://www.congress.gov/103/bills/s1587/BILLS-103s1587enr.pdf.

245. Ann Devroy and Stephen Barr, "Gore Heads Latest Government Evaluation; Clinton Orders 'National Performance Review' to Identify What Works and What Doesn't," *Washington Post*, March 4, 1993.

246. Thomas Rosenstiel, "Gore on 'Letterman'? It's No Joke, Media," *Los Angeles Times*, September 10, 1993, http://articles.latimes.com/1993-09-10/entertainment/ca-33466_1_vice-president. See also National Performance Review, "Reinventing Federal Procurement."

247. Preston, interview with author, October 5, 2017.

248. Federal Acquisition Streamlining Act of 1994, Pub. L. 103-355, Title IV.

249. Federal Acquisition Streamlining Act of 1994, SEC. 4301.

250. *Department of Defense Authorization for Appropriations for Fiscal Year 1994*, S. Hrg. 103-303, Pt. 5, June 28, 1993 (statement of Colleen Preston, deputy under secretary of defense for acquisition reform), 441–43.

251. William Perry, "Acquisition Reform: A Mandate for Change" (Washington, DC: Office of the Secretary of Defense, February 4, 1994), 3–4, https://www.dau.mil/policy/PolicyDocuments/the1781Acquistion%20Reform%20a%20Mandate%20for%20Change.pdf.

252. Perry, "Specifications & Standards."

253. Perry, "Specifications & Standards."

254. GAO, *Acquisition Reform: DOD Begins Program to Reform Specifications and Standards*, GAO/NSIAD-95-14 (Washington, DC: GAO, October 1994), https://www.gao.gov/archive/1995/ns95014.pdf; Defense Systems Management College, *Streamlining Defense Acquisition Laws*, Section 800 Report, 8-3–8-5; DOD's Inadequate Use of Off-the-Shelf Items, Committee Print S. Prt. 101-62, 2–5.

255. Preston, interview with author, October 5, 2017. See also Fox, *Defense Acquisition Reform 1960–2000*, 172.

256. Mark A. Lorell, Jeffrey A. Drezner, and Julia F. Lowell, *Reforming Mil-Specs: The Navy Experience with Military Specifications and Standards Reform*, DB-312-NAVY (Santa Monica, CA: RAND, 1999), 8–10, https://www.rand.org/content/dam/rand/pubs/documented_briefings/2005/RAND_DB312.pdf; Richard H. Shertzer, "MIL-SPEC & MIL-STD Reform" (Troy, MI: Society of Automotive Engineers, 1998), 6–7, http://www.wise-intern.org/journal/1998/shertzer.pdf.

257. Jared Serbu, "Buying Commercial in DoD: 15 Years After Acquisition Reform," *Federal News Radio*, May 21, 2012, https://federalnewsradio.com/federal-drive/2012/05/buying-commercial-in-dod-15-years-after-acquisition-reform/.

258. Etherton, "Overcoming Obstacles," 9–10, 12.

259. *Acquisition Reform: Fact or Fiction: Hearing Before the Military Acquisition Subcommittee of the Committee on Armed Services, House of Representatives*, H.A.S.C. No. 103-26, 103rd Cong. (June 15, 1993) (statement of Deputy Secretary of Defense William Perry), 3.

260. Coopers & Lybrand, *The DOD Regulatory Cost Premium: A Quantitative Assessment* (Fort Belvoir, VA: Defense Technical Information Center, December 1994), https://apps.dtic.mil/dtic/tr/fulltext/u2/a295799.pdf.

261. Coopers & Lybrand, 18–18a.

262. Perry, "Acquisition Reform: A Mandate for Change," 2–3.

263. Perry, 6.

264. Perry, 8.

265. "Tank Parts, Off the Shelf," *New York Times*, April 6, 1993, https://www.nytimes.com/1993/04/06/opinion/tank-parts-off-the-shelf.html. See also Warren Wetmore, "Trouble with Off-the-Shelf Tank Parts," *New York Times*, April 22, 1993.

266. GAO, *Acquisition Reform: Efforts to Reduce the Cost*, GAO/NSIAD-96-106, 3.

267. Christopher H. Hanks et al., *Reexamining Military Acquisition Reform: Are We There Yet?* MG-291-A (Santa Monica, CA: RAND, 2005), 10–11, https://www.rand.org/content/dam/rand/pubs/monographs/2005/RAND_MG291.pdf.

268. George Cahlink, "Fallen Star," *Government Executive*, February 1, 2004, http://www.govexec.com/magazine/2004/02/fallen-star/15929/.

269. Eleanor Spector (former director of defense procurement), interview with author, September 13, 2017.

270. Beck, Brokaw, and Kelmar, *A Model for Leading Change*, 7–8.

271. Hanks et al., *Reexamining Military Acquisition Reform*, 48, 108.

272. Hanks et al., 26–30.

273. GAO, *Acquisition Reform: Efforts to Reduce the Cost to Manage and Oversee DOD Contracts*, GAO/NSIAD-96-106 (Washington, DC: GAO, April 1996), 5, https://www.gao.gov/archive/1996/ns96106.pdf.

274. Mark A. Lorell et al., "Acquisition Reform and the Evolution of the U.S. Weapons Market," in *Cheaper, Faster, Better? Commercial Approaches to Weapons Acquisition*, MR-1147-AF (Santa Monica, CA: RAND, 2000), 35, https://www.rand.org/content/dam/rand/pubs/monograph_reports/MR1147/MR1147.chap2.final.pdf.

275. GAO, *Acquisition Reform: Efforts to Reduce the Cost*, GAO/NSIAD-96-106, 5.

276. GAO, *Acquisition Reform: DOD Faces Challenges in Reducing Oversight Costs*, GAO/NSIAD-97-48 (Washington, DC: GAO, January 1997), 4, https://www.gao.gov/archive/1997/ns97048.pdf.

277. Mark Lorell and John C. Graser, *An Overview of Acquisition Reform Cost Savings Estimates*, MR-1329-AF (Santa Monica, CA: RAND, 2001), xvi, https://www.rand.org/content/dam/rand/pubs/monograph_reports/2009/MR1329.pdf.

278. Lorell and Graser, xvi.

279. Lorell and Graser, xvi–xvii

280. Lorell and Graser, xvii.

281. William J. Clinton, "Streamlining the Bureaucracy" (memorandum, Washington, DC: The White House, September 11, 1993), https://govinfo.library.unt.edu/npr/library/direct/memos/230a.html.

282. DOD Inspector General, *DOD Acquisition Workforce Reduction Trends and Impacts*, Report No. D-2000-088 (Washington, DC: DOD, February 29, 2000), i, 4, https://media.defense.gov/2000/Feb/29/2001713980/-1/-1/1/00-088.pdf.

283. Michael H. Powell, *The Defense Acquisition Workforce Growth Initiative: Changing Workforce Characteristics and the Implications for Workforce Retention*, RGSD-383 (Santa Monica, CA: RAND, 2017), 11, https://www.rand.org/pubs/rgs_dissertations/RGSD383.html.

284. Frank Kendall (former under secretary of defense for acquisition, technology, and logistics), interview with author, October 30, 2017.

285. DOD Inspector General, *DOD Acquisition Workforce Reduction*, ii.

286. Commission on Army Acquisition and Program Management in Expeditionary Operations, *Urgent Reform Required*, 21.

287. Acquisition Advisory Panel, *Report of the Acquisition Advisory Panel to the Office of Federal Procurement Policy and the United States Congress*, Section 1423 Report (Washington, DC: Acquisition Advisory Panel, January 2007), 365, https://www.acquisition.gov/sites/default/files/page_file_uploads/ACQUISITION-ADVISORY-PANEL-2007-Report_final.pdf.

288. Jacques Gansler, "Establishment of a Study Group to Analyze Implementation of Price-Based Acquisition within the Department of Defense," Memorandum for the Secretaries of the Military Departments, October 15, 1998, http://www.secnav.navy.mil/rda/Policy/1998%20Policy%20Memoranda/abm9846a.pdf. See also Gansler, "The Road Ahead: Accelerating the Transformation of Department of Defense Acquisition and Logistics Processes and Practices" (Washington, DC: DOD, June 2000), 6, 12, http://www.dtic.mil/dtic/tr/fulltext/u2/a387387.pdf).

289. Defense Science Board, *Report of the Defense Science Board Task Force on Defense Acquisition Reform (Phase III): A Streamlined Approach to Weapons Systems Research, Development and Acquisition. The Application of Commercial Practices* (Washington, DC: Office of the Under Secretary of Defense for Acquisition and Technology, May 1996), vi, 12–13, I-1, https://www.acq.osd.mil/dsb/reports/1990s/1996DefenseAcquisitionReform-PhaseIII.pdf. See also Defense Science Board, *Report of the Defense Science Board Task Force on Defense Acquisition Reform* (Washington, DC: Office of the Under Secretary of Defense for Acquisition, July 1993), i, http://www.dtic.mil/dtic/tr/fulltext/u2/a268734.pdf; Defense Science Board, *Report of the Defense Science Board Task Force on Defense Acquisition Reform (Phase II)* (Washington, DC: Office of the Under Secretary of Defense for Acquisition and Technology, August 1994), C-8, http://www.dtic.mil/dtic/tr/fulltext/u2/a286410.pdf.

290. Lorell, Drezner, and Cook, *Price-Based Acquisition*, xvi, 56–70. One order of magnitude estimate put the savings at 0.006 percent of contract value (64).

291. Lorell, Drezner, and Cook, xvi. 133.

292. Lorell, Drezner, and Cook, xvii, 128–30.

293. Lorell, Drezner, and Cook, xiv, 15.

294. Henry Pandes, *A Quest for Efficiencies: Total System Performance Responsibility*, Research Report AU/ACSC/094/2001-04 (Maxwell Air Force Base, AL: Air Command and Staff College, Air University, April 2001), 14, http://www.dtic.mil/get-tr-doc/pdf?AD =ADA407267.

295. Lorell, Drezner, and Cook, *Price-Based Acquisition*, 85–125.

296. GAO, *Depot Maintenance: Air Force Faces Challenges in Managing to 50–50 Ceiling*, statement of David R. Warren, director, defense management issues, National Security and International Affairs Division, GAO/T-NSIAD-00-112 (Washington, DC: GAO, March 3, 2002), 12, https://www.gao.gov/assets/110/108264.pdf.

297. *Department of Defense Authorization for Appropriations for Fiscal Year 2003: Hearings Before the Committee on Armed Services, United States Senate*, S. Hrg. 107-696, Pt. 7, 107th Cong. (March 20, 2002) (statement of Peter Teets, under secretary of the air force and director, National Reconnaissance Office), 150–151, https://www.gpo.gov/fdsys/pkg/CHRG-107shrg81928/pdf/CHRG-107shrg81928.pdf; Debra Werner, "Reputation on the Line," *C4ISR Journal*, April 1, 2011, 18.

298. GAO, *Global Positioning System*, GAO-09-325 (Washington, DC: GAO, April 2009), 10, https://www.gao.gov/new.items/d09325.pdf.

299. Tom Christie, "What Has 35 Years of Acquisition Reform Accomplished?" *U.S. Naval Institute Proceedings* 132, no. 2 (February 2006): 30–35, http://connection.ebscohost .com/c/articles/19774584/what-has-35-years-acquisition-reform-accomplished.

300. Office of the Under Secretary of Defense for Acquisition, Technology, and Logistics, *Report of the Defense Science Board/Air Force Scientific Advisory Board Joint Task Force on Acquisition of National Security Space Programs* (Washington, DC: DOD, May 2003), 3, http://www.dtic.mil/dtic/tr/fulltext/u2/a429180.pdf.

301. Lorell, Leonard, and Doll, *Extreme Cost Growth*, 38.

302. Werner, "Reputation on the Line," 18 (quoting Lt. Gen. Michael Hamel, commander, Space and Missile Systems Center, Air Force Space Command).

303. Lorell, Drezner, and Cook, *Price-Based Acquisition*, 61.

304. Hanks et al., *Reexamining Military Acquisition Reform*, 113–15.

305. Donald Rumsfeld, "DOD Acquisition and Logistics Excellence Week Kickoff— Bureaucracy to Battlefield," https://agovernmentofthepeople.com/2001/09/10/donald -rumsfeld-speech-about-bureaucratic-waste/.

306. Rumsfeld.

307. Rogers and Birmingham, "A Ten-Year Review," 46.

308. National Defense Authorization Act for Fiscal Year 2003, S. Rep. No. 107-151, 107th Cong. (2002), 336, https://www.congress.gov/107/crpt/srpt151/CRPT-107srpt151.pdf.

309. *Department of Defense Acquisition Policy: Hearing Before the Subcommittee on Readiness and Management Support of the Committee on Armed Services, United States Senate*, S. Hrg. 107–118, 107th Cong. (February 27, 2002) (statement of Principal Deputy Under Secretary Michael Wynne), 68, https://www.gpo.gov/fdsys/pkg/CHRG-107shrg82253/ pdf/CHRG-107shrg82253.pdf.

310. *Department of Defense Acquisition Policy* (statement of Assistant Secretary of the Air Force Marvin R. Sambur), 42.

311. Hanks et al., *Reexamining Military Acquisition Reform*, xix–xx, 17–20.

312. Edward W. Rogers and Robert P. Birmingham, "A Ten-Year Review of the Vision for Transforming the Defense Acquisition System," *Defense Acquisition Review Journal* (January–April 2004): 55, http://www.dtic.mil/dtic/tr/fulltext/u2/a423544.pdf.

313. McNicol, *Cost Growth in Major Weapon Procurement Programs*, 54.

314. Porter et al., *Major Causes of Cost Growth*, vol. I, *Executive Summary*, ES-1–ES-2, ES-8.

315. Porter et al., ES-9–ES-13.

316. Porter et al., ES-9–ES-10.

317. Lorell, Leonard, and Doll, *Extreme Cost Growth*, xi.

318. Lorell, Leonard, and Doll, xiii.

319. Lorell, Leonard, and Doll, xiii–xiv.

320. GAO, *Joint Strike Fighter Acquisition: Mature Critical Technologies Needed to Reduce Risks*, GAO-02-39 (Washington, DC: GAO, October 2001), 3, https://www.gao.gov/assets/240/232918.pdf.; National Defense Authorization Act for Fiscal Year 2001, S. Rep. No. 106-292, 106th Cong. (2000), 137–38, https://www.gpo.gov/fdsys/pkg/CRPT-106srpt292/pdf/CRPT-106srpt292.pdf.

321. GAO, *Tactical Aircraft: Opportunity to Reduce Risks in the Joint Strike Fighter Program with Different Acquisition Strategy*, GAO-05-271 (Washington, DC: GAO, March 2005), 2–3, https://www.gao.gov/assets/250/245629.pdf.

322. *The Joint Strike Fighter: Hearing Before the Committee on Armed Services, United States Senate*, S. Hrg. 111-823, 111th Cong. (March 11, 2001), 11, 35, https://www.gpo.gov/fdsys/pkg/CHRG-111shrg63688/pdf/CHRG-111shrg63688.pdf; Porter et al., *Major Causes of Cost Growth*, vol. I, *Executive Summary*, ES-25; *Budget Request on Departments of the Navy and Air Force Tactical Aviation Programs: Hearing on the National Defense Authorization Act for Fiscal Year 2009 and Oversight of Previously Authorized Programs Before the Committee of Armed Services, House of Representatives*, H.A.S.C. No. 110-128, 110th Cong. (March 11, 2008), 9, https://ia801901.us.archive.org/11/items/gov.gpo.fdsys.CHRG-110hhrg43685/CHRG-110hhrg43685.pdf; GAO, *F-35 Joint Strike Fighter: Assessment Needed to Address Affordability Changes*, GAO-15-364 (Washington, DC: GAO, April 2015), 1, https://www.gao.gov/assets/670/669619.pdf.

323. Lee Ferran, "U.S. Weapons Man: F-35 Fighter Plan Was 'Acquisition Malpractice,'" *ABC News*, February 7, 2012, http://abcnews.go.com/Blotter/35-fighter-plan-acquisition-malpractice-pentagon-official/story?id=15530008.

324. *Department of Defense Authorization for Appropriations for Fiscal Year 2017 and the Future Years Defense Program: Hearings Before the Committee on Armed Services, United States Senate*, S. Hrg. 114-658, Pt. 1, 114th Cong. (April 26, 2015) (statement of Senator McCain), 561, https://www.gpo.gov/fdsys/pkg/CHRG-114shrg26098/pdf/CHRG-114shrg26098.pdf.

325. Department of Defense and Emergency Supplemental Appropriations for Recovery from and Response to Terrorist Attacks on the United States Act, 2002, Pub. L. 107-117, 115 Stat. 2230 (2002), SEC. 8159, https://www.hsdl.org/?view&did=467869.

326. DOD Inspector General, *Acquisition: Acquisition of the Boeing KC-767A Tanker Aircraft*, D-2004-064 (Washington, DC: DOD, March 29, 2004), iii, https://media

.defense.gov/2004/Mar/29/2001712733/-1/-1/1/04-064.pdf; *Proposed Lease of Boeing 767 Tankers by USAF: Hearing before the Committee on Commerce, Science, and Transportation, United States Senate*, S. Hrg. 108-991, 108th Cong. (September 3, 2003) 31, 43, 57 https://www.gpo.gov/fdsys/pkg/CHRG-108shrg91376/pdf/CHRG-108shrg91376.pdf; John McCain, "Investigation into Air Force Leasing of Boeing Aerial Refueling Tankers," 108th Cong., 2nd sess., *Congressional Record* 150, no. 134 (November 19, 2004): S11536–S11542, https://www.congress.gov/crec/2004/11/19/CREC-2004-11-19-senate.pdf.

327. Jeffrey Smith and Renae Merle, "Roche, Top Aide Plan to Resign Air Force Posts: Secretary, Acquisitions Chief Are Criticized on Boeing Deal," *Washington Post*, November 17, 2004, http://www.washingtonpost.com/wp-dyn/articles/A55154-2004Nov16.html.

328. Leslie Wayne, "Ex-Pentagon Official Gets 9 Months for Conspiring to Favor Boeing," *New York Times*, October 2, 2004, http://www.nytimes.com/2004/10/02/business/expentagon-official-gets-9-months-for-conspiring-to-favor-boeing.html.

329. Johnathan Karp and Andy Pasztor, "Pentagon Takes Away Authority of Air Force Over 21 Programs," *Wall Street Journal*, March 29, 2005; Renae Merle, "Defense Depart. to Supervise Acquisitions for Air Force," *Washington Post*, March 29, 2005, http://www.washingtonpost.com/wp-dyn/articles/A8065-2005Mar28.html.

330. Porter et al., *Major Causes of Cost Growth*, vol. I, *Executive Summary*, ES-22; Frank Kendall, "Adventures in Defense Acquisition," in *Getting Defense Acquisition Right* (Fort Belvoir, VA: Defense Acquisition University Press, 2017), 213, https://www.defense.gov/Portals/1/Documents/pubs/Getting-Acquisition-Right-Jan2017.pdf. See also GAO, *Defense Acquisitions: Future Combat Systems Challenges and Prospects for Success*, statement of Paul L. Francis, director, acquisition and sourcing management, GAO-05-428T (Washington, DC: GAO, March 16, 2005), 2, https://www.gao.gov/assets/120/111419.pdf.

331. GAO, *Defense Acquisitions: Role of Lead Systems Integrator on Future Combat Systems Program Poses Oversight Challenges*, GAO-07-380 (Washington, DC: GAO, June 2007), 10–15, https://www.gao.gov/new.items/d07380.pdf; GAO, *Defense Acquisitions: Future Combat Systems Challenges and Prospects for Success*, statement of Paul L. Francis, director, acquisition and sourcing management, GAO-05-422T (Washington, DC: GAO, March 16, 2005), 10, https://www.gao.gov/assets/120/111403.pdf.

332. GAO, *Defense Acquisitions: Future Combat Systems Risks Underscore the Importance of Oversight*, statement of Paul L. Francis, director, acquisition and sourcing management, GAO-07-672T (Washington, DC: GAO, March 27, 2007), 4–8, https://www.gao.gov/new.items/d07672t.pdf.

333. Christopher Drew and Elisabeth Bumiller, "Military Budget Reflects a Shift in U.S. Strategy," *New York Times*, April 7, 2009, http://www.nytimes.com/2009/04/07/us/politics/07defense.html; Greg Jaffe and Shalilagh Murray, "Gates Seeks Sharp Turn in Spending," *Washington Post*, April 7, 2009, http://www.washingtonpost.com/wp-dyn/content/article/2009/04/06/AR2009040601784.html; Christopher Drew, "Conflicting Priorities Endanger High-Tech Army Program," *New York Times*, July 19, 2009, https://mobile.nytimes.com/2009/07/20/business/20combat.html.

334. Porter et al., *Major Causes of Cost Growth*, vol. I, *Executive Summary*, ES-27; GAO, *Defense Acquisitions: Plans Need to Allow Enough Time to Demonstrate Capability of First*

Littoral Combat Ships, GAO-05-255 (Washington, DC: GAO, March 2005), 6–28, https://www.gao.gov/assets/250/245521.pdf.

335. Philip Taubman, "Lesson on How Not to Build a Navy Ship," *New York Times*, April 25, 2008, http://www.nytimes.com/2008/04/25/us/25ship.html.

336. Porter et al., *Major Causes of Cost Growth*, vol. I, *Executive Summary*, ES-27.

337. Hope Hodge Seck, "Acquisition Chief: LCS Program 'Broke' the Navy," *Military.com*, December 2, 2016, https://www.military.com/daily-news/2016/12/02/acquisition-chief-lcs-program-broke-navy.html.

338. John McCain, "Littoral Combat Ship Program," 113th Cong., 2nd sess., *Congressional Record* 160, no. 58 (April 9, 2014): S2319, https://www.congress.gov/crec/2014/04/09/CREC-2014-04-09-senate.pdf. See also Ronald O'Rourke, *Navy Littoral Combat Ship/Frigate (LCS/FFGX) Program: Background and Issues for Congress*, RL33741 (Washington, DC: Congressional Research Service, August 11, 2017), 10–15, https://digital.library.unt.edu/ark:/67531/metadc1020877/m2/1/high_res_d/RL33741_2017Aug11.pdf.

339. Lorell, Leonard, and Doll, *Extreme Cost Growth*, 25.

340. Lorell, Leonard, and Doll, 12.

341. Lorell, Leonard, and Doll, 28.

342. Porter et al., *Major Causes of Cost Growth*, vol. I, *Executive Summary*, ES-30.

343. *The Acquisition of Major Weapons Systems by the Department of Defense*, S. Hrg. 110-639 (statement of Senator Levin), 3.

344. Lorell, Leonard, and Doll, *Extreme Cost Growth*, 5.

345. Lorell, Leonard, and Doll, 9, 17.

346. Gary E. Christle, Dan Davis, and Gene Porter, *CNA Independent Assessment: Air Force Acquisition Return to Excellence*, CRM D0019891.A2/Final (Alexandria, VA: Center for Naval Analyses, 2009), 19, https://www.cna.org/CNA_files/PDF/D0019891.A2.pdf.

347. GAO, *Best Practices: High Levels of Knowledge at Key Points Differentiate Commercial Shipbuilding from Navy Shipbuilding*, GAO-09-322 (Washington, DC: GAO, May 2009), 28, https://www.gao.gov/assets/290/289531.pdf.

348. GAO, x.

349. Gordon England, "Acquisition Action Plan" (memorandum for secretaries of the military departments, June 7, 2005), in Ronald T. Kadish et al, *Defense Acquisition Performance Assessment Report* (Washington, DC: Deputy Under Secretary of Defense, January 2006), v, http://www.dtic.mil/docs/citations/ADA459941.

350. Kadish et. al, *Defense Acquisition Performance Assessment Report*, 45, 74–75.

351. McNicol and Wu, *Evidence on the Effect*, v.

352. Davis and Anton, "Annual Growth of Contract Costs," 11.

353. *Department of Defense Authorization for Appropriations for Fiscal Year 2006: Hearings Before the Committee on Armed Services, United States Senate*. S. Hrg. 109-22, Pt. 4, 109th Cong. (March 16; April 6, 14, 2005), https://www.gpo.gov/fdsys/pkg/CHRG-109shrg21105/pdf/CHRG-109shrg21105.pdf.

354. *Department of Defense Authorization for Appropriations for Fiscal Year 2006*, March 16, 2005 (statement of Senator McCain), 2.

355. *Department of Defense Authorization for Appropriations for Fiscal Year 2006*, 679–80, 701.

356. GAO, *Defense Acquisitions: Assessments of Major Weapon Programs*, GAO-03-476 (Washington, DC: GAO, May 2003), https://www.gao.gov/new.items/d03476.pdf; GAO, *Defense Acquisitions: Assessments of Major Weapon Programs*, GAO-04-248 (Washington, DC: GAO, March 2004), https://www.gao.gov/assets/250/241798.pdf.

357. GAO, *Defense Acquisitions: Assessments of Selected Major Weapon Programs*, GAO-05-301 (Washington, DC: GAO, March 2013), 5, https://www.gao.gov/new.items/d05301.pdf.

358. GAO, 6.

359. *Nominations Before the Senate Armed Services Committee, First Session, 109th Congress: Hearings Before the Committee on Armed Services, United States Senate*, S. Hrg. 109-487, 109th Cong. (April 19, 2005) (statement of Senator Levin), 115–16, https://www.gpo.gov/fdsys/pkg/CHRG-109shrg34348/pdf/CHRG-109shrg34348.pdf.

360. *Nominations Before the Senate Armed Services Committee* (statement of Secretary England), 120.

361. *Nominations Before the Senate Armed Services Committee* (statement of Secretary England), 121.

362. England, "Acquisition Action Plan," v.

363. *Needed Improvement to Defense Acquisition Processes and Organizations: Hearing Before the Committee on Armed Services, United States Senate*, S. Hrg. 109-469, 109th Cong. (September 27, 2005) (statement of Senator Warner), 2, https://www.gpo.gov/fdsys/pkg/CHRG-109shrg28576/pdf/CHRG-109shrg28576.pdf.

364. *Needed Improvement to Defense Acquisition Processes and Organizations* (statement of Senator Levin), 3–4.

365. *Defense Acquisition Issues Related to Tactical Aviation and Army Programs: Hearing Before the Subcommittee on Airland of the Committee on Armed Services, United States Senate*, S. Hrg. 109-468, 109th Cong. (November 15, 2005) (statement of John Hamre, president and CEO, Center for Strategic and International Studies; Katherine Schinasi, managing director, acquisition and sourcing management, GAO; Gene Porter, research analyst, Institute for Defense Analyses; Frank Anderson, president, Defense Acquisition University; and Gary Christle, senior project director, Center for Naval Analyses), 60–62, https://www.gpo.gov/fdsys/pkg/CHRG-109shrg28575/pdf/CHRG-109shrg28575.pdf.

366. GAO, *Defense Acquisitions: Assessments of Selected Major Weapon Programs*, GAO-06-391 (Washington, DC: GAO, March 2006), 12, https://www.gao.gov/assets/250/249468.pdf.

367. Major Defense Acquisition Programs: Determination Required before Milestone B Approval, 10 U.S.C. § 2366b (as codified by SEC. 801 of the John Warner National Defense Authorization Act for Fiscal Year 2007, Pub. L. 109-364).

368. Major Defense Acquisition Programs, 10 U.S.C. § 2366b.

369. Major Defense Acquisition Programs, SEC. 805; John Warner National Defense Authorization Act for Fiscal Year 2007, Pub. L. 109-364, SEC. 807; National Defense Authorization Act for Fiscal Year 2008, Pub. L. 110-181, 122 Stat. 3, 110th Cong. (2008), SEC. 802, https://www.gpo.gov/fdsys/pkg/PLAW-110publ181/pdf/PLAW-110publ181.pdf.

370. *Nominations Before the Senate Armed Services Committee, First Session, 110th Congress: Hearings Before the Committee on Armed Services, United States Senate*, S. Hrg. 110-370, 110th Cong. (October 4, 2007) (statement of Under Secretary John J. Young Jr.), 1096, https://www.gpo.gov/fdsys/pkg/CHRG-110shrg42309/pdf/CHRG-110shrg42309.pdf.

371. *Nominations Before the Senate Armed Services Committee* (answer to prepared questions submitted to Under Secretary Young, by Senator Levin), 1119–20.

372. *Nominations Before the Senate Armed Services Committee* (statement of Under Secretary Young), 1096.

373. DOD, *Performance of the Defense Acquisition System: 2016 Annual Report* (Washington, DC: Under Secretary of Defense for Acquisition, Technology, and Logistics [USD(AT&L)], October 24, 2016), xxiv–xxv, https://www.acq.osd.mil/fo/docs/Performance-of-Defense-Acquisition-System-2016.pdf.

374. GAO, *Defense Acquisitions: Assessments of Selected Weapon Programs*, GAO-07-406SP (Washington, DC: GAO, March 2007), 11, https://www.gao.gov/assets/260/258416.pdf.

375. GAO, *Defense Acquisitions: Assessments of Selected Weapon Programs*, GAO-08-467SP (Washington, DC: GAO, March 2008), 7, https://www.gao.gov/new.items/d08467sp.pdf. The GAO reiterated that the DOD was failing to live up to its own policies for program initiation, largely because of "unrealistic cost estimates" based on "limited knowledge and optimistic assumptions about system requirements and critical technologies." GAO, *Defense Acquisitions: A Knowledge-Based Funding Approach Could Improve Major Weapon System Program Outcomes*, GAO-08-619 (Washington, DC: GAO, July 2008), 3, https://www.gao.gov/assets/280/277905.pdf.

376. *Acquisition of Major Weapons Systems by the Department of Defense*, S. Hrg. 110-639 (statement of Under Secretary Young), 11.

377. *Acquisition of Major Weapons Systems*, 11, 36.

378. *Acquisition of Major Weapons Systems* (statement of Katherine V. Schinasi, managing director, acquisition and sourcing management, GAO), 22–23.

379. National Research Council, *Pre-Milestone A and Early-Phase Systems Engineering: A Retrospective Review and Benefits for Future Air Force Systems Acquisition* (Washington, DC: National Academies Press, 2008), 9, https://www.nap.edu/catalog/12065/pre-milestone-a-and-early-phase-systems-engineering-a-retrospective.

380. Defense Science Board, *Report of the Defense Science Board Task Force on Test and Evaluation* (Washington, DC: Office of the Under Secretary of Defense for Acquisition and Technology, May 2008), 1–3, 4–7, 9, 15, 24, http://www.dtic.mil/dtic/tr/fulltext/u2/a482504.pdf.

381. Weapon Systems Acquisition Reform Act of 2009, S. 454, 111th Cong. (2009), https://www.congress.gov/bill/111th-congress/senate-bill/454/text/is.

382. Carl Levin, "Statements on Introduced Bills and Joint Resolutions," 111th Cong., 1st sess., *Congressional Record* 155, no. 31 (February 23, 2009): S2366, https://www.congress.gov/crec/2014/05/05/CREC-2014-05-05.pdf.

383. *Acquisition of Major Weapons Systems by the Department of Defense*, S. Hrg. 111-149 (statement of Senator McCain), 5.

384. *Nominations Before the Senate Armed Services Committee, First Session, 111th Congress: Hearings Before the Committee on Armed Services, United States Senate*, S. Hrg. 111-362, 111th Cong. (March 26, 2009) (statement of Ashton Carter), 192, 197, https://www.gpo.gov/fdsys/pkg/CHRG-111shrg55953/pdf/CHRG-111shrg55953.pdf.

385. Weapon Systems Acquisition Reform Act of 2009, S. 454, https://www.congress.gov/bill/111th-congress/senate-bill/454/actions.

386. Weapon Systems Acquisition Reform Act of 2009, Pub. L. 111-23, 123 Stat. 1704, 111th Cong. (2009), SEC. 101, https://www.gpo.gov/fdsys/pkg/PLAW-111publ23/pdf/PLAW-111publ23.pdf.

387. Weapon Systems Acquisition Reform Act of 2009, SEC. 102.

388. Weapon Systems Acquisition Reform Act of 2009, SEC. 104.

389. Weapon Systems Acquisition Reform Act of 2009, SEC. 201.

390. Frank Kendall, "Real Acquisition Reform (or Improvement) Must Come From Within," in *Getting Defense Acquisition Right* (Fort Belvoir, VA: Defense Acquisition University Press, 2017), 33–35, https://www.defense.gov/Portals/1/Documents/pubs/Getting-Acquisition-Right-Jan2017.pdf.

391. *Acquisition of Major Weapons Systems by the Department of Defense*, S. Hrg. 111-149 (statement of Jacques S. Gansler, chair, Defense Science Board Task Force on Industrial Structure for Transformation), 49.

392. *Acquisition of Major Weapons Systems by the Department of Defense* (statement of Paul G. Kaminski, chair, Committee on Pre-Milestone A Systems Engineering Air Force Studies Board, National Research Council), 51.

393. *Administration Perspectives on Managing the Defense Acquisition System and the Defense Acquisition Workforce: Hearing Before the Panel on Defense Acquisition Reform of the Committee on Armed Services, House of Representatives*, H.A.S.C. No. 111-134, 111th Cong. (March 11, 2010) (statement of Under Secretary Ashton B. Carter), 5–6, https://www.gpo.gov/fdsys/pkg/CHRG-111hhrg58104/pdf/CHRG-111hhrg58104.pdf. See also Ashton B. Carter, "Memorandum for Secretaries of the Military Departments, Implementation of the Weapon Systems Acquisition Reform Act of 2009," Directive-Type Memorandum 09-927 (Washington, DC: Under Secretary of Defense, December 4, 2009). See also David J. Berteau, Joachim Hofbauer, and Stephanie Sanok, *Implementation of the Weapon Systems Acquisition Reform Act of 2009: A Progress Report* (Washington, DC: Center for Strategic and International Studies, May 26, 2010), https://csis-prod.s3.amazonaws.com/s3fs-public/legacy_files/files/publication/20100528%20WSARA%20Progress%20Report.pdf.

394. Frank Kendall, "The Original Better Buying Power—David Packard Acquisition Rules 1971," in *Getting Defense Acquisition Right* (Fort Belvoir, VA: Defense Acquisition University Press, 2017), 17, https://www.defense.gov/Portals/1/Documents/pubs/Getting-Acquisition-Right-Jan2017.pdf.

395. Kendall, 18.

396. Ashton Carter, "The Defense Industry Enters a New Era" (Washington, DC: Under Secretary of Defense, February 9, 2011), https://www.acq.osd.mil/fo/docs/USD_AT&L__Cowen_Speech_020911.pdf.

397. *Administration Perspectives on Managing the Defense Acquisition System*, H.A.S.C. No. 111-134 (statement of Ashton B. Carter), 5–6. See also *Department of Defense Authorization for Appropriations for Fiscal Year 2015 and the Future Years Defense Program: Hearings Before the Committee on Armed Services, United States Senate*, S. Hrg. 113-465, Pt. 1, 113th Cong. (April 30, 2014) (statement of Under Secretary Frank Kendall), 1045–46, https://www.gpo.gov/fdsys/pkg/CHRG-113shrg91186/pdf/CHRG-113shrg91186.pdf.

398. Frank Kendall (former under secretary of defense for acquisition, technology, and logistics), interview with author, October 30, 2017.

399. Heidi Shyu (former assistant secretary of the army), interview with author, October 12, 2017.

400. GAO, *Defense Acquisitions: Assessments of Selected Weapon Programs*, GAO-11-233SP, 2.

401. GAO, *Defense Acquisitions: Assessments of Selected Weapon Programs*, GAO-12-400SP, 34.

402. GAO, 29.

403. GAO. *Defense Acquisitions: Assessments of Selected Weapon Programs*, GAO-13-294SP, 23.

404. GAO, 24. See also *Department of Defense Authorization for Appropriations for Fiscal Year 2015*, S. Hrg. 113-465, Pt. 1 (statement of Michael J. Sullivan, director, acquisition and sourcing management, GAO), 1062.

405. GAO, *Defense Acquisitions: Assessments of Selected Weapon Programs*, GAO-14-340SP (Washington, DC: GAO, March 2014), 5, https://www.gao.gov/assets/670/662184.pdf.

406. GAO, *Defense Acquisitions: Assessments of Selected Weapon Programs*, GAO-16-329SP (Washington, DC: GAO, March 2016), 14, https://www.gao.gov/assets/680/676281.pdf.

407. GAO, *Defense Acquisitions: Assessments of Selected Weapon Programs*, GAO-17-333SP, 8.

408. GAO, 21.

409. Davis and Anton, "Annual Growth of Contract Costs," 5.

410. DOD, *Performance of the Defense Acquisition System*, 14 (Figure 2.2).

411. National Defense Authorization Act for Fiscal Year 2016, Pub. L. 114-92, 129 Stat. 726, 114th Cong. (2015), SEC. 828, https://www.gpo.gov/fdsys/pkg/PLAW-114publ92/pdf/PLAW-114publ92.pdf.

412. Kendall, "Real Acquisition Reform," 37. See also Jason Sherman, "Pentagon's Big-Ticket Programs Again Pass Muster in Audit, Avoid Statutory 'Penalty Tax,'" *Inside Defense*, November 21, 2017, https://insidedefense.com/daily-news/pentagons-big-ticket-programs-again-pass-muster-audit-avoid-statutory-penalty-tax.

413. For example, Drezner et al., *An Analysis of Weapon System Cost Growth*, 32–34.

414. William Swank et al., *Acquisition Trend Metrics in the Department of Defense*, Technical Report TR 1-00 (Fort Belvoir, VA: Defense Acquisition University, Defense Systems Management College, October 2000), 4, http://www.dtic.mil/dtic/tr/fulltext/u2/a460218.pdf; Lorell and Graser, *Overview of Acquisition Reform*, 120.

415. GAO, *Defense Acquisitions: Assessments of Selected Weapon Programs*, GAO-15-342SP, 26.

416. GAO, *Defense Acquisitions: Assessments of Selected Weapon Programs*, GAO-16-329SP, 1.

417. GAO, *Defense Acquisitions: Assessments of Selected Weapon Programs*, GAO-17-333SP, 2.

418. *Twenty-Five Years of Acquisition Reform: Where Do We Go From Here? Hearing Before the Committee on Armed Services, House of Representatives*, H.A.S.C. No. 113-66, 113th Cong. (October 29, 2013), 1–2, https://www.gpo.gov/fdsys/pkg/CHRG-113hhrg85330/pdf/CHRG-113hhrg85330.pdf.

419. *Case Studies in DOD Acquisition*, H.A.S.C. 113-113; *Defense Reform: Empowering Success in Acquisition: Hearing Before the Committee on Armed Services, House of Representatives*, H.A.S.C. No. 113-115, 113th Cong. (July 10, 2014), https://www.gpo.gov/fdsys/pkg/CHRG-113hhrg89508/pdf/CHRG-113hhrg89508.pdf; *A Case for Reform: Improving DOD's Ability to Respond to the Pace of Technological Change: Hearing Before the Committee on Armed Services, House of Representatives*, H.A.S.C. No. 114-2, 114th Cong. (January 28, 2015), https://www.gpo.gov/fdsys/pkg/CHRG-114hhrg94089/pdf/CHRG-114hhrg94089.pdf; *Acquisition Reform: Experimentation and Agility: Hearing Before the Committee on Armed Services, House of Representatives*, H.A.S.C. No. 114-76, 114th Cong. (January 7, 2016), https://www.gpo.gov/fdsys/pkg/CHRG-114hhrg98885/pdf/CHRG-114hhrg98885.pdf; *Acquisition Reform: Starting Programs Well: Hearing Before the Committee on Armed Services, House of Representatives*, H.A.S.C. No. 114-83, 114th Cong. (February 3, 2016), https://www.gpo.gov/fdsys/pkg/CHRG-114hhrg98892/pdf/CHRG-114hhrg98892.pdf.

420. *Twenty-Five Years of Acquisition Reform*, H.A.S.C. No. 113-66, 18.

421. Agile Acquisition to Retain Technological Edge Act, H.R. 1597, 114th Cong. (2015), https://www.congress.gov/114/bills/hr1597/BILLS-114hr1597ih.pdf (introduced March 25, 2015); Acquisition Agility Act, H.R. 4741, 114th Cong. (2016), https://www.congress.gov/114/bills/hr4741/BILLS-114hr4741ih.pdf (introduced March 15, 2016).

422. National Defense Authorization Act for Fiscal Year 2017, H.R. 4909, 114th Cong. (2016), SECs. 1701–1705, https://www.congress.gov/114/bills/hr4909/BILLS-114hr4909pcs.pdf (reported in House, May 4, 2016).

423. National Defense Authorization Act for Fiscal Year 2017, Pub. L. 114-328, SECs. 805–809.

424. Dana Milbank, "John McCain Sees a World on Fire," *Washington Post*, February 10, 2015, https://www.washingtonpost.com/opinions/john-mccain-sees-a-world-on-fire/2015/02/10/17024dbc-b172-11e4-854b-a38d13486ba1_story.html?utm_term=.cdb2dd25627e.

425. John McCain and Carl Levin, "Sample Letter to Contributors," in *Defense Acquisition Reform: Where Do We Go From Here? A Compendium of Views by Leading Experts*, S. Prt. 113-28, 113th Cong. (2014), 235–40, https://www.gpo.gov/fdsys/pkg/CPRT-113SPRT90719/pdf/CPRT-113SPRT90719.pdf.

426. *Defense Acquisition Reform*, statement of David Oliver, former principal deputy USD(AT&L), 142. See also statement of John Lehman, former secretary of the navy, 142; statement of Dov Zakheim, former DOD comptroller, 227.

427. *Defense Acquisition Reform*, statement of David Berteau, former assistant secretary of defense, 20. See also statement of Daniel Gordon, associate dean for procurement law, George Washington University Law School, 100; statement of Christine Fox, former D/CAPE, 61; statement of Frank Kendall, USD(AT&L), 133; statement of Jamie Morin, former air force comptroller, 158; statement of Michael Sullivan, director, Acquisition and Sourcing Management Team, GAO, 208.

428. *Defense Acquisition Reform*, statement of Tom Christie, former director, DOT&E, 41; statement of Mike Gilmore, director, DOT&E, 92; statement of Paul Kaminski, former USD(AT&L), 126; statement of Dov Zakheim, former DOD comptroller, 228.

429. *Defense Acquisition Reform*, statement of Dr. Jack Gansler, former USD(AT&L), 83; statement of Gary Roughead, former chief of naval operations, 176; statement of Sean Stackley, assistant secretary of the navy (research, development, and acquisition), 205.

430. *Defense Acquisition Reform*, statement of Dr. Jack Gansler, former USD(AT&L), 81–82; statement of John Lehman, former secretary of the navy, 140.

431. *Defense Acquisition Reform*, statement of Todd Harrison, Center for Strategic and Budgetary Assessments, 118.

432. *Defense Acquisition Reform*, statement of Norman Augustine, former DSB chair, 15; statement of David Oliver, former principal deputy USD(AT&L), 168; statement of Gary Roughead, former chief of naval operations, 175–76; statement of Norton Schwarz, former air force chief of staff, 193.

433. *Defense Acquisition Reform*, statement of James Cartwright, former vice chair of the Joint Chiefs of Staff, 35; statement of Paul Kaminski, former USD(AT&L), 126–27.

434. *Defense Acquisition Reform*, statement of Dr. Jack Gansler, former USD(AT&L), 85; statement of William C. Greenwalt, former SASC staffer, 108.

435. *Defense Acquisition Reform*, statement of Tom Christie, former DOT&E, 43.

436. John McCain, "Remarks by Senator John McCain on Defense Acquisition Reform at the U.S. Chamber of Commerce Today," July 29, 2015, https://www.mccain.senate.gov/public/index.cfm/speeches?ID=EEE8DD42-DEFE-4E09-87B6-66352A0B3820.

437. National Defense Authorization Act for Fiscal Year 2016, S. 1376, SEC. 801.

438. National Defense Authorization Act for Fiscal Year 2016, SEC, 843.

439. National Defense Authorization Act for Fiscal Year 2017, S. 2943, SEC. 901.

440. *Department of Defense Authorization for Appropriations for Fiscal Year 2016*, S. Hrg. 114-204, Pt. 3 (Assistant Secretary of the Army Heidi Shyu), 165.

441. *Department of Defense Authorization for Appropriations for Fiscal Year 2016*, 166.

442. GAO, *Acquisition Reform: DOD Should Streamline Its Decision-Making Process*, GAO-15-192, 6.

443. GAO, 12–14.

444. Sydney J. Freedberg Jr., "'If We Fail, Fire Us': CSA Gen. Milley on Acquisition Changes," *Breaking Defense*, October 25, 2015, https://breakingdefense.com/2015/10/if-we-fail-fire-us-csa-gen-milley-on-acquisition-changes/.

445. *Acquisition Reform: Next Steps*, S. Hrg. 114-394, 1.

446. *Acquisition Reform: Next Steps*, 2.

447. McCain, "Remarks by Senator John McCain on Defense Acquisition Reform."

448. Bill Greenwalt (former SASC professional staff member), interview with author, October 31, 2017.

CHAPTER 3

1. *Waste, Fraud, and Abuse: Hearing Before the Committee on Governmental Affairs, United States Senate*, S. Hrg. 100-41, Pt. 1, 100th Cong. (February 18, 1987), 6.

2. *Waste, Fraud, and Abuse*, 7–8.

3. GAO, *Managing the Cost of Government, Building an Effective Financial Management Structure*, vol. I, *Major Issues*, GAO/AFMD-85-35 (Washington, DC: Comptroller General of the United States, February 1985), https://www.gao.gov/assets/290/287200.pdf; GAO, *Managing the Cost of Government, Building an Effective Financial Management Structure*, vol. II, *Conceptual Framework*, GAO/AFMD-85-35-A (Washington, DC: Comptroller General of the United States, February 1985), http://archive.gao.gov/d1ot2/126342.pdf.

4. GAO, *Managing the Cost of Government*, vol. I, *Major Issues*, 5.

5. Chief Financial Officers Act of 1990, Pub. L. 101-576, 104 Stat. 2838, 101st Cong. (1990), https://www.gpo.gov/fdsys/pkg/STATUTE-104/pdf/STATUTE-104-Pg2838.pdf.

6. Government Management Reform Act of 1994, Pub. L. 103-356, 108 Stat. 3410, 103rd Cong. (1994), SEC. 405, https://www.gpo.gov/fdsys/pkg/STATUTE-108/pdf/STATUTE-108-Pg3410.pdf.

7. DOD Inspector General, *Summary of DOD Office of the Inspector General Audits of DOD Financial Management Challenges*, Report No. DODIG-2015-144 (Alexandria, VA: DOD, July 7, 2015), 1, https://comptroller.defense.gov/Portals/45/documents/micp_docs/Reference_Documents/DODIG-2015-144.pdf.

8. Aaron Gregg, "First Full Audit of Pentagon Notes Compliance Issues," *Washington Post*, November 26, 2018, A14.

9. Jill Aitoro, "So We're Celebrating the Pentagon's Failed Audit?" *Defense News*, November 20, 2018, https://www.defensenews.com/opinion/2018/11/20/so-were-celebrating-the-pentagons-failed-audit/.

10. Paul Ketrick et al., *Assessment of DOD Enterprise Resource Planning Business Systems*, IDA Paper P-4691 (Alexandria, VA: Institute for Defense Analyses, February 2011), 18; Christopher Hanks, "Business Sense," *Government Executive*, May 28, 2008, https://www.govexec.com/excellence/management-matters/2008/05/business-sense/26954/; Edward G. Keating et al., "The Defense Finance and Accounting Service, the Chief Financial Officers Act, and Improving Management of the Department of Defense," *Armed Forces Comptroller* 46, no. 2 (Spring 2001): 20–23; Cornelius E. Tierney, "Cost for Government: What Costs: How Much Accounting," *Government Accountants Journal* 43, no. 1 (Spring 1994): 5; Christopher Hanks, "Financial Accountability at the DoD: Reviewing the Bidding," *Defense AR Journal* 16, no. 2 (July 2009): 185, https://www.dau.mil/library/arj/ARJ/arj51/ARJ51.pdf.

11. Edward Keating et al., *Improving the Defense Finance and Accounting Service's Interactions with Its Customers*, RAND Monograph Report MR-1261-DFAS (Santa Monica, CA: RAND, 2001), 40, https://www.rand.org/content/dam/rand/pubs/monograph

_reports/2007/MR1261.pdf. See also Hanks, "Financial Accountability at the DOD," 188; Hanks, "Business Sense"; Hanks, "A Proposal to Emphasize Managerial Cost Accounting in the Department of Defense," *Armed Forces Comptroller* 57, no. 2 (Spring 2012): 35.

12. Zack Gaddy (former DFAS director), interview with author, February 21, 2018; Douglas Brook, "Audited Financial Statements in the Federal Government: Intentions, Outcomes, and On-Going Challenges for Management and Policy-Making," *Journal of Public Budgeting, Accounting & Financial Management* 22, no. 1 (2010): 71.

13. Robert Speer (former Army comptroller), interview with author, February 5, 2018. (Speer remembers finding a ten-foot-long stack of the financial reports that he had produced in the hallway of a customer facility in the 1990s. "We have to produce them," he was told, but "nobody ever reads them.")

14. Robert N. Anthony, "The FASAB's Dilemma," *Government Accountants Journal* 45, no. 1 (Spring 1996). See also Brook, "Audited Financial Statements in the Federal Government," 74; L. R. Jones, "Counterpoint Essay: Nine Reasons Why the CFO Act May Not Achieve Its Objectives," *Public Budgeting & Finance* 13, no. 1 (March 1993): 89, https://doi.org/10.1111/1540-5850.00968; Hanks, "Financial Accountability at the DOD," 183–84; Elaine Chao, "Keynote Address," in *Improving Program Delivery and Stewardship through Modern Financial Management*, Proceedings of the 20th Annual Financial Management Conference, Washington, DC, March 18, 1991, 25, https://www.gao.gov/assets/680/676819.pdf; *Chief Financial Officers Act Oversight: Hearing Before the Subcommittee on Government Management, Information, and Technology of the Committee on Government Reform and Oversight, House of Representatives*, HRG-1995-GRO-0050, 104th Cong. (July 25, 1995) (statement of Gerald Riso, former associate director for management in the Office of Management and Budget), 93–102.

15. *Financial Management Problems in the U.S. Air Force: Hearing Before the Committee on Governmental Affairs, United States Senate*, S. Hrg. 101-732, 101st Cong. (February 23, 1990) (statement of Comptroller General Charles A. Bowsher), 14.

16. Thomas Spoehr, "Bad Idea: Counting on the Pentagon Audit to Find Waste and Inefficiency," *Defense 360*, December 6, 2018, https://defense360.csis.org/bad-idea-counting-on-the-pentagon-audit-to-find-waste-and-inefficiency/.

17. *DOD Financial Management: Hearing Before the Committee on Governmental Affairs, United States Senate*, S. Hrg. 103-855, 103rd Cong. (April 12, 1994), 49; David Morrison, "Green-Eyeshade Blues," *National Journal* 26, no. 50 (December 10, 1994): 2898–901.

18. Office of Management and Budget, "Historical Tables: Table 5.4–Discretionary Budget Authority by Agency: 1976–2022 and Table 5.5–Percentage Distribution of Discretionary Budget Authority by Agency: 1976–2022," https://www.whitehouse.gov/omb/historical-tables/.

19. DOD, *Financial Improvement and Audit Readiness (FIAR) Plan Status Report* (Washington, DC: Office of the Undersecretary of Defense (Comptroller)/Chief Financial Officer, November 2013), ES-4, https://comptroller.defense.gov/Portals/45/documents/fiar/FIAR_Plan_November_2013.pdf.

20. "The World's Largest Public Companies in 2017," *Forbes*, https://www.forbes.com/sites/corinnejurney/2017/05/24/the-worlds-largest-public-companies-2017/.

21. GAO, *DOD Financial Management: Improved Controls, Processes, and Systems Are Needed for Accurate and Reliable Financial Information*, GAO-11-933T (Washington, DC: GAO, September 23, 2011), 5, https://www.gao.gov/assets/590/585372.pdf; Mark Easton and Joe Quinn, "Auditing Our Budgetary Resources ... An Opportunity and a Responsibility," *Armed Forces Comptroller* 57, no. 3 (Summer 2012): 18; House Armed Services Committee, *Panel on Defense Financial Management and Auditability Reform: Findings and Recommendations* (Washington, DC: House of Representatives, January 24, 2012), 4, https://armedservices.house.gov/sites/republicans.armedservices.house.gov/files/wysiwyg_uploaded/Defense%20Financial%20Management%20and%20Auditability%20Reform%20Panel%20Report%20%28FINAL%29.pdf; Kathleen Noe, "DOD's Future Integrated Financial Systems Architecture," *Armed Forces Comptroller* 44, no. 1 (Winter 1999): 18–19.

22. *DOD Financial Management*, S. Hrg. 103-855 (statement of DOD Comptroller John J. Hamre), 66.

23. GAO, *Financial Management: Examples of Weaknesses*, GAO/AFMD-88-35BR (Washington, DC: GAO, February 1988), https://www.gao.gov/assets/80/76989.pdf.

24. Jay F. Williams, "The Evolution of DOD Financial Management, or Chronicles of a Sojourn Through DOD's Books," *Armed Forces Comptroller* 40, no. 2 (Spring 1995): 18.

25. Williams, 18.

26. GAO, *Management Report: Improvements Needed in Controls over the Processes Used to Prepare the U.S. Consolidated Financial Statements*, GAO-17-524 (Washington, DC: GAO, July 2017), 4–6, https://www.gao.gov/assets/690/685744.pdf; GAO, *Financial Audit: Fiscal Years 2016 and 2015 Consolidated Financial Statements of the U.S. Government*, GAO-17-283R (Washington, DC: GAO, January 2017), 2–3, https://www.gao.gov/assets/690/682081.pdf; GAO, *Fiscal Year 2015 U.S. Government Financial Statements: Need to Address the Government's Remaining Financial Management Challenges and Long-Term Fiscal Path*, GAO-16-541T (Washington, DC: GAO, April 6, 2016) (statement of Gene L. Dodaro, comptroller general of the United States), 13, https://www.gao.gov/assets/680/676377.pdf.

27. Mary L. Kemp, "Improving DOD's Inter/Intra-Governmental Financial Reporting: Phase I—Campaign Plan to Improve the End-to-End Process for Reimbursable Activity," *Armed Forces Comptroller* 59, no. 1 (Winter 2014): 30.

28. Mary L. Kemp, "Improving DOD's Intragovernmental Financial Reporting: Phase II—Project Plan to Improve the End-to-End Process for Reimbursable Activity," *Armed Forces Comptroller* 61, no. 2 (Spring 2016): 9.

29. *Federal Consolidated Financial Statements: Can the Federal Government Balance Its Books? Hearings Before the Subcommittee on Government Management, Information, and Technology of the Committee on Government Reform and Oversight, House of Representatives*, Serial No. 105-158, 105th Cong. (April 16, 1998) (statement of DOD Inspector General Eleanor Hill), 288.

30. GAO, *DOD Financial Management: Integrated Approach, Accountability, and Incentives Are Keys to Effective Reform*, GAO-01-681T (Washington, DC: Comptroller General of the United States, May 8, 2001) (statement of Gregory D. Kutz, director, Financial Management and Assurance), 7, https://www.gao.gov/assets/110/108812.pdf.

31. GAO, *Department of Defense: Progress in Financial Management Reform*, GAO/T-AIMD-NSIAD-00-163 (Washington, DC: GAO, May 9, 2000) (statement of Jeffrey C. Steinhoff, acting assistant comptroller general, Accounting and Information Management Division), 46, https://www.gao.gov/assets/110/108425.pdf.

32. GAO, 46–47.

33. GAO, *Continuing and Widespread Weaknesses in Internal Controls Result in Losses Through Fraud, Waste, and Abuse*, FGMSD-80-65 (Washington, DC: Comptroller General of the United States, August 28, 1980), https://www.gao.gov/assets/140/130279.pdf.

34. Elmer Staats, "Accurate Information—Government Managers Cannot Do Without It," in *A New Decade—The Outlook for Financial Management*, 22–33, Proceedings of Ninth Financial Management Conference, Washington, DC, March 3, 1980, https://www.gao.gov/assets/680/676125.pdf.

35. GAO, *Financial Management: Examples of Weaknesses*, GAO/AFMD-88-35BR, 7.

36. President's Private Sector Survey on Cost Control, *Report on the Office of the Secretary of Defense* (Washington, DC: Government Printing Office, 1983), 310, https://babel.hathitrust.org/cgi/pt?id=mdp.39015015456794;view=1up;seq=4.

37. J. P. Bolduc, "The President's Private Sector Survey on Cost Controls," in *Financial Management Reform*, 3, Proceedings of the Twelfth Annual Financial Management Conference, Washington, DC, March 30, 1983, https://www.gao.gov/assets/680/676728.pdf.

38. Joseph Wright Jr., "Reform '88," in *Financial Management Reform*, Proceedings of the Twelfth Annual Financial Management Conference, Washington, DC, March 30, 1983, 18, https://www.gao.gov/assets/680/676728.pdf.

39. Wright, 19.

40. Federal Managers' Financial Integrity Act of 1982, Pub. L. 97-255, 96 Stat. 814 (1982).

41. GAO, *Financial Integrity Act: Continuing Efforts Needed to Improve Internal Control and Accounting Systems*, GAO/AFMD-88-10 (Washington, DC: GAO, December 1987), 4, 13, https://www.gao.gov/assets/150/145978.pdf; GAO, *Department of Defense's Progress in Implementing the Federal Managers' Financial Integrity Act*, GAO/NSIAD-85-147 (Washington, DC: GAO, September 27, 1985), 2, https://www.gao.gov/assets/150/143480.pdf.

42. GAO, *Financial Integrity Act: The Government Faces Serious Internal Control and Accounting Systems Problems*, GAO/AFMD-86-14 (Washington, DC: GAO, December 1985), 52, https://www.gao.gov/assets/150/143993.pdf.

43. *Bringing Modern Financial Management to the Federal Government: The Role of Treasury's Financial Management Service: Hearing Before a Subcommittee of the Committee on Government Operations, House of Representatives*, HRG-1988-OPH-0037, 100th Cong. (October 13, 1988) (statement of Marcus W. Page, deputy fiscal assistant secretary, Department of the Treasury), 46.

44. GAO, *Financial Management: Examples of Weaknesses*, GAO/AFMD-88-35BR, 5.

45. *Management of the Department of Defense Automated Information Systems Acquisitions: Hearing Before the Legislation and National Security Subcommittee of the Committee on Government Operations, House of Representatives*, HRG-1989-OPH-0046, 101st Cong. (May 18, 1989) (statement of Comptroller General Charles Bowsher), 9.

46. *Management of the Department of Defense Automated Information Systems Acquisitions*, HRG-1989-OPH-0046, May 18, 1989, 2; GAO, *Financial Integrity Act: Inadequate Controls Result in Ineffective Federal Programs and Billions in Losses*, GAO/AFMD-90-10 (Washington, DC: GAO, December 1985), 28, https://www.gao.gov/assets/150/148414.pdf.

47. GAO, *Managing the Cost of Government*, vol. I, *Major Issues*, GAO/AFMD-85-35, 1.

48. GAO, *Managing the Cost of Government*, vol. II, *Conceptual Framework*, GAO/AFMD-85-35-A, 1, 11–14.

49. GAO, 2–3.

50. GAO, 4.

51. GAO, *Managing the Cost of Government*, vol. I, *Major Issues*, GAO/AFMD-85-35, 3.

52. GAO, *Managing the Cost of Government*, vol. II, *Conceptual Framework*, GAO/AFMD-85-35-A, 13.

53. GAO, 16.

54. *DOD's Plans for Financial Management Improvement and Achieving Audit Readiness: Hearing Before the Panel on Defense Financial Management and Auditability Reform of the Committee on Armed Services, House of Representatives*, H.A.S.C. No. 112-59, 112th Cong. (July 28, 2011) (statement of DOD Comptroller Robert Hale), 18, https://www.gpo.gov/fdsys/pkg/CHRG-112hhrg68167/pdf/CHRG-112hhrg68167.pdf.

55. Robert Hale (former DOD comptroller), interview with author, January 24, 2018.

56. Federal Management Reorganization and Cost Control Act of 1986, S. 2230, 99th Cong. (1986), https://www.congress.gov/bill/99th-congress/senate-bill/2230; Federal Financial Management Reform Act of 1987, S. 1529, 100th Cong. (1987), https://www.congress.gov/bill/100th-congress/senate-bill/1529.

57. *Federal Management Reorganization, Cost Control, and Loan Accounting Reform: Hearings Before the Committee on Governmental Affairs, United States Senate, on S. 2230 and S. 2142*, S. Hrg. 99-879, 99th Cong. (May 13, 1986) (statement of Comptroller General Charles A. Bowsher), 20–31; *Waste, Fraud, and Abuse*, S. Hrg. 100-41, Pt. 1, (February 18, 1987) (statement of Comptroller General Charles A. Bowsher), 5–21; *Financial Management*, S. Hrg 100-562 (July 23, 1987), 3–15.

58. *Federal Management Reorganization, Cost Control, and Loan Accounting Reform*, S. Hrg. 99-879, May 13, 1986) (statement of Comptroller General Charles A. Bowsher), 21.

59. GAO, *The Federal Financial Management Reform Act of 1987*, GAO/T-AFMD-87-18 (Washington, DC: GAO, July 23, 1987) (statement of Charles A. Bowsher, Comptroller General of the United States), 9, https://www.gao.gov/assets/110/101807.pdf.

60. After Bowsher's testimony, GAO reports continued to call for auditable financial statements but omitted any reference to accrual-based budgeting. See, e.g., GAO, *Financial Integrity Act: Inadequate Controls Result in Ineffective Federal Programs and Billions in Losses*, GAO/AFMD-90-10, 6, 35, 54.

61. GAO, *The Federal Financial Management Reform Act of 1987*, GAO/T-AFMD-87-18, 14.

62. Frank Hodsoll, "Keynote Address," in *Implementing the Administration's Plan for Audited Financial Statements in the Federal Government* (Arlington, VA: Joint Financial Management Improvement Program, September 18, 1990), 4.

63. *Chief Financial Officers Act Oversight*, HRG-1995-GRO-0050 (statement of Harold I. Steinberg, former deputy controller/acting controller, Office of Federal Financial Management, Office of Management and Budget), 132.

64. *Chief Financial Officers Act Oversight*, HRG-1995-GRO-0050. See Pat Wechsler, "Lost in the Ledger: Lack of Audits Leads to Federal Waste, Abuse," *Newsday*, August 6, 1989; Alison Leigh Cowan, "Accountants Group Urges a Financial Officer for U.S.," *New York Times*, September 12, 1989; Charley Reese, "Fiscal Mess Can Be Eased by Going Back to Basic Accounting," *Orlando Sentinel*, November 2, 1989; Glenn Hall, "Federal Mismanagement Could Cost Taxpayers up to $150 Billion, GAO Says," *Wall Street Journal*, November 30, 1989; Robert Rankin, "Government's Accounting Systems Faulty, CPAs Say," *Philadelphia Inquirer*, December 12, 1989; David Dirks, "Viewpoint: Does the U.S. Government Keep Its Accounts Straight? Senate Bill Would Untangle Financial Mess," *Denver Post*, May 21, 1990; Dick Marlowe, "What Government Needs Is a Good Overhauling," *Orlando Sentinel*, July 29, 1990; Reed Pew, "U.S. Government Needs Financial Overseer," *Salt Lake Tribune*, October 7, 1990; Ronald Rogozinski, "Letter to the Editor: Strengthen Federal Financial Reform," *Allentown Morning Call*, October 30, 1990.

65. Chief Financial Officers Act of 1990, H.R. 5687, 101st Cong. (November 15, 1990), https://www.congress.gov/bill/101st-congress/house-bill/5687/actions.

66. Jones, "Counterpoint Essay: Nine Reasons Why," 88.

67. Chief Financial Officers Act of 1990, Pub. L. 101-576, SECs. 303(a) and (d).

68. Government Management Reform Act of 1994, Pub. L. 103-356.

69. Anthony, "The FASAB's Dilemma."

70. Anthony.

71. Anthony.

72. Don Shycoff, *The Businesses of Defense* (Bowie, MD: JKS Publishing, 1995), 11.

73. Shycoff, 16. See also Robert Anthony, "The Fatal Defect in the Federal Accounting System," *Public Budgeting & Finance* 20, no. 4 (Winter 2000): 1–10.

74. Balanced Budget and Emergency Deficit Control Act of 1985, Pub. L. 99-177, 99 Stat. 1037, 99th Cong. (1985), https://www.gpo.gov/fdsys/pkg/STATUTE-99/pdf/STATUTE-99-Pg1037.pdf.

75. See, for example, William Safire, "Essay; Is Peace Bullish?" *New York Times*, June 21, 1989, https://www.nytimes.com/1989/06/08/opinion/essay-is-peace-bullish.html; Robert Samuelson, "Don't Look for Any Big 'Peace Dividend,'" *Washington Post*, June 21, 1989; Paul Blustein and John Berry, "Deep Pentagon Cuts Could Boost Economy's Fortunes," *Washington Post*, November 22, 1989; "The Elusive Peace Dividend," *Washington Post*, November 27, 1989; Stephen Rosenfeld, "Looking for a Peace Dividend," *Washington Post*, December 15, 1989; Seymour Melman, "What to Do with the Cold War Money," *New York Times*, December 17, 1989, http://economicreconstruction.org/sites/economicreconstruction.com/static/SeymourMelman/archive/published/what_to_do_with_the_cold_war.pdf.

76. George H. W. Bush, "Address on Administration Goals Before a Joint Session of Congress," February 9, 1989, http://www.presidency.ucsb.edu/ws/index.php?pid=16660.

77. DOD, *Defense Management: Report to the President* (Washington, DC: Office of the Secretary of Defense, July 1989), i, http://www.dtic.mil/dtic/tr/fulltext/u2/a216011.pdf.

78. Stephen Engelberg, "Pentagon Plans $2.3 Billion Saving in '91 by Cutting 16,000 Jobs," *New York Times*, January 12, 1990, https://www.nytimes.com/1990/01/12/us/pentagon-plans-2.3-billion-saving-in-91-by-cutting-16000-jobs.html.

79. DOD, *Defense Science Board Task Force Report: FY 1994-99 Future Years Defense Plan*, Odeen Panel Report (Washington, DC: Office of the Secretary of Defense, May 1993), 8, https://www.acq.osd.mil/dsb/reports/1990s/FY1994-99FutureYearsDefensePlan.pdf.

80. Shycoff, *The Businesses of Defense*, 13–15; *Pentagon Financial Management Problems: Hearing Before the Committee on Governmental Affairs, United States Senate*, S. Hrg. 103-705, 103rd Cong. (July 1, 1993) (statement of Alvin Tucker, acting chief financial officer, DOD), 46.

81. GAO, *Defense Management: Impediments Jeopardize Logistics Corporate Information Management*, GAO/NSIAD-95-28 (Washington, DC: GAO, October 1994), 10, https://www.gao.gov/assets/160/154732.pdf.

82. DOD, *Department of Defense Corporate Information Management* (Washington, DC: Assistant Secretary of Defense (Command, Control, Communications and Intelligence), April 1991), 4, http://www.dtic.mil/dtic/tr/fulltext/u2/a251456.pdf.

83. DOD, 4–6.

84. DOD, 8.

85. DOD, 10.

86. DOD, 17–20.

87. William Schwabe and Leslie Lewis, "Linking the Corporate Information Management (CIM) Initiative to Strategy-to-Tasks," DB-112-OSD (Santa Monica, CA: RAND, 1994) https://www.rand.org/content/dam/rand/pubs/documented_briefings/2007/DB112.pdf, 19; GAO, *Defense ADP: Corporate Information Management Must Overcome Major Problems*, GAO/IMTEC-92-77 (Washington, DC: GAO, September 1992), 7, https://www.gao.gov/assets/220/216897.pdf.

88. GAO, *Defense ADP: Corporate Information Management Initiative Faces Significant Challenges*, GAO/IMTEC-91-35 (Washington, DC: GAO, April 1991), 4, https://www.gao.gov/assets/220/214036.pdf.

89. DOD, *Status of the Department of Defense Corporate Information Management (CIM) Initiative* (Washington, DC: Office of the Assistant Secretary of Defense, October 1992), 4, http://www.dtic.mil/dtic/tr/fulltext/u2/a257774.pdf.

90. *Waste and Financial Management Problems at the Air Force: Hearing Before the Committee on Governmental Affairs, United States Senate*, S. Hrg. 102-757, 102nd Cong. (February 19, 1992) (statement of Senator Glenn), 30.

91. GAO, *Defense ADP: Corporate Information Management Savings Are Not Supported*, GAO/IMTEC-91-18 (Washington, DC: GAO, February 1991), 3, https://www.gao.gov/assets/220/213801.pdf.

92. *Waste and Financial Management Problems at the Air Force*, S. Hrg. 102-757 (statement of Air Force Comptroller Michael B. Donley), 21–22.

93. GAO, *Defense ADP: Corporate Information Management Initiative Faces Significant Challenges*, GAO/IMTEC-91-35, 4.

94. *The Department of Defense's Financial Management Problems*, HRG-1995-GRO-0084 (statement of Navy Comptroller Deborah P. Christie), 79. See also *Pentagon Financial Management Problems*, S. Hrg. 103-705, 54 (statement of John W. Beach, principal deputy assistant secretary for financial management, US Air Force).

95. GAO, *Defense Management: Impediments Jeopardize Logistics*, GAO/NSIAD-95-28, 20–21.

96. *Waste and Financial Management Problems at the Air Force*, S. Hrg. 102-757 (statement of DOD Comptroller Sean O'Keefe), 30–31.

97. Gary W. Amlin, "Standardizing Policy and Systems in the Defense Finance and Accounting Services," *Armed Forces Comptroller* 37, no. 3 (Summer 1992): 38.

98. GAO, *Defense ADP: Corporate Information Management Must Overcome Major Problems*, GAO/IMTEC-92-77, 14–15; GAO, *DOD's FMFIA Assertions*, GAO-AFMD-93-61R (Washington, DC: GAO, April 27, 1993), 12, https://www.gao.gov/assets/90/83065.pdf; GAO, *Defense IRM: Management Commitment Needed to Achieve Defense Data Administration Goals*, GAO/AIMD-94-14 (Washington, DC: GAO, January 1994), 2, https://www.gao.gov/assets/220/219139.pdf; GAO, *Defense Management Initiatives: Limited Progress in Implementing Management Improvement Initiatives*, GAO/T-AIMD-94-105 (Washington, DC: GAO, April 14, 1994) (statement of David O. Mellemann, director, Information Resources Management/National Security and Internal Affairs Accounting and Information Management Division), 21–22, https://www.gao.gov/assets/110/105494.pdf; GAO, *Defense IRM: Poor Implementation of Management Controls Has Put Migration Strategy at Risk*, GAO/AIMD-98-5 (Washington, DC: GAO, October 1997), 4, https://www.gao.gov/assets/160/156018.pdf.

99. GAO, *Defense ADP: Corporate Information Management Must Overcome Major Problems*, GAO/IMTEC-92-77, 1–2. See also February 1994 Booz-Allen Report on CIM, quoted in GAO, *Defense Management: Stronger Support Needed for Corporate Information Management Initiative to Succeed*, GAO-AIMD/NSIAD-94-101 (Washington, DC: GAO, April 1994), 8, https://www.gpo.gov/fdsys/pkg/GAOREPORTS-AIMD-NSIAD-94-101/html/GAOREPORTS-AIMD-NSIAD-94-101.htm.

100. GAO, *Defense Management: Impediments Jeopardize Logistics*, GAO/NSIAD-95-28, 12.

101. Shycoff, *The Businesses of Defense*, 106.

102. GAO, *Defense Management: Impediments Jeopardize Logistics*, GAO/NSIAD-95-28, 4, 15.

103. Shycoff, *The Businesses of Defense*, 106, 125.

104. GAO, *Defense Management: Impediments Jeopardize Logistics*, GAO/NSIAD-95-28, 3.

105. Shycoff, *The Businesses of Defense*, 96.

106. Shycoff, 90–91.

107. Shycoff, 54.

108. GAO, *DEFENSE: Health Care*, GAO-IMTEC-93-29R (Washington, DC: GAO, June 3, 1993), 1, https://www.gao.gov/assets/90/83132.pdf.

109. *DOD Financial Management*, S. Hrg. 103-855 (statement of DOD Comptroller John Hamre), 76. See also Richard F. Keevey, "DOD's Financial Management Initiatives: A Blueprint for Reform," *Armed Forces Comptroller* 40, no. 1 (Winter 1995): 10.

110. *DOD Financial Management*, S. Hrg. 103-855 (statement of DOD Comptroller John Hamre), 64.

111. *DOD Financial Management*, S. Hrg. 103-855, 72.

112. *DOD Financial Management*, S. Hrg. 103-855, 73.

113. GAO, *Defense IRM: Management Commitment Needed to Achieve Defense Data Administration Goals*, GAO/AIMD-94-14, 10–12.

114. GAO, 24.

115. DOD Inspector General, *Acquisition of the Defense Joint Accounting System*, Report No. D-2000-151 (Arlington, VA: DOD, OAIG-AUD), June 16, 2000, 5–8, https://media.defense.gov/2000/Jun/16/2001712386/-1/-1/1/00-151.pdf.

116. *Department of Defense Authorization for Appropriations for Fiscal Year 2005*, S. Hrg. 108-440, Pt. 3, (March 23, 2004) (statement of Comptroller General David M. Walker), 160.

117. *Department of Defense Authorization for Appropriations for Fiscal Year 2005* (statement of Comptroller General David M. Walker), 160–61.

118. *Department of Defense Financial Management*, S. Hrg. 107-803 (statement of Comptroller General David M. Walker), 7.

119. *Department of Defense Financial Management* (statement of Comptroller General David M. Walker), 7.

120. *Results of the Department of Defense's Fiscal Year 1999 Financial Statements Audit: Hearing Before the Subcommittee on Government Management, Information, and Technology of the Committee on Government Reform, House of Representatives*, Serial No. 106-200, 106th Cong. (May 9, 2000) (statement of DOD Comptroller William J. Lynn), 83. See also William J. Lynn III, "The Military Financial Management Agenda," *Armed Forces Comptroller* 43, no. 3 (Summer 1998): 9–12.

121. *Results of the Department of Defense's Fiscal Year 1999 Financial Statements Audit*, Serial No. 106-200 (statement of DOD Comptroller William J. Lynn), 84.

122. *Waste and Financial Management Problems at the Air Force*, S. Hrg. 102-757 (statement of DOD Comptroller Sean O'Keefe), 30.

123. GAO, *Defense's Planned Implementation of the $77 Billion Defense Business Operations Fund*, GAO/T-AFMD-91-5 (Washington, DC: GAO, April 30, 1991) (statement of Donald H. Chapin, assistant comptroller general, Accounting and Financial Management), 2, https://www.gao.gov/assets/110/103780.pdf.

124. *Department of Defense Authorization for Appropriations for Fiscal Year 1991: Hearings Before the Committee on Armed Services, United States Senate, on S. 2884*, S. Hrg. 101-986, Pt. 6, 101st Cong. (April 24, 1990) (statement of Donald J. Atwood, deputy secretary of defense), 253.

125. Donald Atwood, "Keynote Address," in *Improving Program Delivery and Stewardship through Modern Financial Management*, Proceedings of the 20th Annual Financial Management Conference, Washington, DC, March 18, 1991, 13, https://www.gao

.gov/assets/680/676819.pdf. See also *The CFO Act and the Army Audit: Persistent Pentagon Financial Management Problems: Hearing Before the Committee on Governmental Affairs, United States Senate*, S. Hrg. 102-1107, 102nd Cong. (August 7, 1992) (statement of DFAS Director Albert Conte), 31.

126. Albert V. Conte, "Consolidation of DOD Accounting and Finance Operations," *Armed Forces Comptroller* 37, no. 4 (Fall 1992): 41; "Defense Financial Management: A Pictorial History," *Armed Forces Comptroller* 53, no. 4 (Fall 2008): 8.

127. GAO, *DOD Financial Management: An Overview of Finance and Accounting Activities at DOD*, GAO/NSIAD/AIMD-97-61 (Washington, DC: GAO, February 1997), 2–3, https://www.gao.gov/assets/230/223630.pdf.

128. *Oversight of the Financial Management Practices at the Department of Defense: Hearing Before the Subcommittee on Government Management, Information, and Technology of the Committee on Government Reform, House of Representatives*, Serial No. 106-80, 106th Cong. (May 4, 1999) (statement of DOD Comptroller William Lynn), 73–74.

129. Ed Kufeldt, "Balanced Scorecard Briefing for NAPA BaSIG," (Indianapolis, IN: Defense Finance and Accounting Service, February 2004) 15, http://unpan1.un.org/intradoc/groups/public/documents/ASPA/UNPAN015178.pdf.

130. Teresa McKay, *DFAS FY17–21 Strategic Plan* (Indianapolis, IN: Defense Finance and Accounting Service, August 21, 2017), 3.

131. Speer, interview with author, February 6, 2018. See also *The Department of Defense's Financial Management Problems*, HRG-1995-GRO-0084 (statement of Gene Dodaro, assistant comptroller general, Accounting and Information Division, GAO), 39.

132. GAO, *DOD Financial Management: An Overview of Finance and Accounting Activities at DOD*, GAO/NSIAD/AIMD-97-61 (Washington, DC: GAO, February 1997), 10, https://www.gao.gov/assets/230/223630.pdf.

133. *Chief Financial Officers Act Oversight*, HRG-1995-GRO-0050, letter from John Hamre to Bill Young, chair, Subcommittee on National Security, Committee on Appropriations, House of Representatives, May 22, 1995, 255–58. See also *The Department of Defense's Financial Management Problems*, HRG-1995-GRO-0084 (statement of DOD Comptroller John J. Hamre), 10.

134. *Department of Defense Authorization for Appropriations for Fiscal Years 1992 and 1993: Hearings Before the Committee on Armed Services, United States Senate, on S. 1507*, S. Hrg. 102-255, Pt. 3, 102nd Cong. (May 15, 1991) (statement of Principal Deputy Comptroller Donald B. Shycoff), 332.

135. Shycoff, *The Businesses of Defense*, 14, 39–40.

136. When the funds experienced losses they either raised prices or received direct appropriations to make up the difference (GAO, *Defense Business Operations Fund: Improved Pricing Practices and Financial Reports Are Needed to Set Accurate Prices*, GAO/AIMD 94-132 (Washington, DC: GAO, June 1994), 3, https://www.gao.gov/assets/220/219787.pdf).

137. Shycoff, *The Businesses of Defense*, 34–39.

138. *Department of Defense Authorization for Appropriations for Fiscal Years 1992 and 1993*, S. Hrg. 102-255, Pt. 3 (statement of Principal Deputy Comptroller Donald B. Shycoff), 333.

139. *Department of Defense Authorization for Appropriations for Fiscal Years 1992 and 1993* (statement of Principal Deputy Comptroller Donald B. Shycoff), 341.

140. GAO, *Financial Management: Defense Business Operations Fund Implementation Status*, GAO/AFMD-92-8, 1.

141. GAO, *Defense's Planned Implementation of the $77 Billion Defense Business Operations Fund*, GAO/T-AFMD-91-5, 2.

142. GAO, 11.

143. GAO, *Financial Management: Defense Business Operations Fund Implementation Status*, GAO/T-AFMD-92-8, 1.

144. Shycoff, *The Businesses of Defense*, 14.

145. *Department of Defense Authorization for Appropriations for Fiscal Years 1992 and 1993*, S. Hrg. 102-255, Pt. 3 (statement of Principal Deputy Comptroller Donald B. Shycoff), 335.

146. GAO, *Defense's Planned Implementation of the $77 Billion Defense Business Operations Fund*, GAO/T-AFMD-91-5, 9. See also *Department of Defense Authorization for Appropriations for Fiscal Years 1992 and 1993*, S. Hrg. 102-255, Pt. 3 (statement of Principal Deputy Comptroller Donald B. Shycoff), 335.

147. GAO, *Financial Management: Defense Business Operations Fund Implementation Status*, GAO/T-AFMD-92-8, 4.

148. GAO, *Defense Business Fund*, GAO/AFMD-93-52R (Washington, DC: GAO, March 1, 1993), 6, https://www.gao.gov/assets/90/82910.pdf.

149. GAO.

150. GAO, 7.

151. GAO, *Defense Management Initiatives: Limited Progress in Implementing Management Improvement Initiatives*, GAO/T-AIMD-94-105, 15.

152. GAO, *Financial Management: Challenges Confronting DOD's Reform Initiatives*, GAO/T-AIMD-95-146 (Washington, DC: GAO, May 23, 1995) (statement of Charles A. Bowsher, comptroller general of the United States), 4, https://www.gao.gov/assets/110/106036.pdf.

153. GAO.

154. GAO, *Defense Business Fund*, GAO/AFMD-93-52R, 2.

155. GAO, 4.

156. GAO, *Defense Management Initiatives: Limited Progress in Implementing Management Improvement Initiatives*, GAO/T-AIMD-94-105, 6.

157. GAO, *Defense Business Fund*, GAO/AFMD-93-52R, 9.

158. GAO, *DOD's FMFIA Assertions*, GAO-AFMD-93-61R, 8; GAO, *Financial Management: Status of the Defense Business Operations Fund*, GAO/AFMD-94-80 (Washington, DC: GAO, March 1994), 8, https://www.gao.gov/assets/220/219267.pdf; GAO, *Financial Management: Challenges Confronting DOD's Reform Initiatives*, GAO/T-AIMD-95-146, 10; GAO, *CFO Act Financial Audits: Increased Attention Must Be Given to Preparing Navy's Financial Reports*, GAO/AIMD-96-7 (Washington, DC: GAO, March 1996), 8, https://www.gao.gov/assets/230/222265.pdf.

159. GAO, *Financial Management: Challenges Confronting DOD's Reform Initiatives*, GAO/T-AIMD-95-146, 10.

160. Richard H. P. Sia, "Finances of Pentagon in Disarray: Auditors Discover Quagmire that Puts Budget Plan at Risk," *Baltimore Sun*, April 18, 1993, http://articles.baltimoresun.com/1993-04-18/news/1993108012_1_pentagon-fund-financial-reports-business-operations.

161. Sia.

162. Sia.

163. GAO, *Defense Business Fund*, GAO/AFMD-93-52R, 8–9.

164. Shycoff, *The Businesses of Defense*, 14–15.

165. Shycoff.

166. GAO, *Defense Business Operations Fund: Improved Pricing Practices and Financial Reports Are Needed to Set Accurate Prices*, GAO/AIMD-94-132, 2, 5.

167. William Gregory, "Depot Dilemma," *Government Executive* 26, no. 6 (June 1994): 61.

168. *Pentagon Financial Management Problems*, S. Hrg. 103-705, 14. See also Phyllis Jordan, "Defense Fund Isn't Saving as Intended; Congress Wants It Corrected, and Defense Secretary Less Aspin Has Called for a Review," *Virginia Pilot*, May 17, 1993.

169. Alice Maroni, "Smarter Defense Financial Management: It's the Real Thing; It's the Right Thing," *Navy Comptroller* 4, no. 1 (October 1993): 46, http://www.dtic.mil/dtic/tr/fulltext/u2/a269432.pdf.

170. DOD, *Defense Science Board Task Force Report: FY 1994-99 Future Years Defense Plan*, 11.

171. GAO, *Financial Management: Status of the Defense Business Operations Fund*, GAO/AFMD-94-80, March 1994, 4.

172. GAO, *DOD Financial Management: An Overview of Finance and Accounting Activities at DOD*, GAO/NSIAD/AIMD-97-61. See also Strom Thurmond National Defense Authorization Act for Fiscal Year 1999, Pub. L. 105- 261, 112 Stat. 1920, 105th Cong. (1998), SEC. 1008, https://www.congress.gov/105/plaws/publ261/PLAW-105publ261.pdf.

173. *Financial Management Problems in the U.S. Air Force*, S. Hrg. 101-732 (statement of Senator Glenn), 1, 4.

174. GAO, *Financial Audit: Air Force Does Not Effectively Account for Billions of Dollars of Resources*, GAO/AFMD-90-23 (Washington, DC: GAO, February 1990), 4, https://www.gao.gov/assets/150/148671.pdf; *Financial Management Problems in the U.S. Air Force*, S. Hrg. 101-732 (statement of Senator Glenn), 2.

175. GAO, *Financial Audit: Air Force Does Not Effectively Account for Billions of Dollars of Resources*, GAO/AFMD-90-23, 3, 27.

176. GAO, 37.

177. GAO, 38.

178. GAO, 5.

179. GAO, 3, 80.

180. *Financial Management Problems in the U.S. Air Force*, S. Hrg. 101-732 (letter from Donald Rice, Air Force secretary, to Charles A. Bowsher, comptroller general of the United States), 170.

181. *Financial Management Problems in the U.S. Air Force*, S. Hrg. 101-732 (letter from Donald Rice, Air Force secretary, to Charles A. Bowsher, comptroller general of the United States), 170.

182. *Financial Management Problems in the U.S. Air Force*, S. Hrg. 101-732 (letter from Donald Rice, Air Force secretary, to Charles A. Bowsher, comptroller general of the United States), 170.

183. *Financial Management Problems in the U.S. Air Force*, S. Hrg. 101-732 (letter from Donald Rice, Air Force secretary, to Charles A. Bowsher, comptroller general of the United States), 171–72.

184. *Financial Management Problems in the U.S. Air Force*, S. Hrg. 101-732, (statement of Senator Glenn), 1, 3.

185. *Financial Management Problems in the U.S. Air Force*, S. Hrg. 101-732, (statement of Senator Glenn), 2.

186. *Financial Management Problems in the U.S. Air Force*, S. Hrg. 101-732 (statement of Senator Lieberman), 7–8.

187. Joint Financial Management Improvement Program, "Panel Session Summaries," chap. 3 in *Improving Program Delivery and Stewardship through Modern Financial Management*, Proceedings of the 20th Annual Financial Management Conference, Washington, DC, March 18, 1991, 44.

188. *Waste and Financial Management Problems at the Air Force*, S. Hrg. 102-757 (statement of Comptroller General Charles Bowsher), 5.

189. *Waste and Financial Management Problems at the Air Force* (statement of Air Force Comptroller Michael B. Donley), 20–21.

190. *Waste and Financial Management Problems at the Air Force* (statement of Air Force Comptroller Michael B. Donley), 20.

191. *Waste and Financial Management Problems at the Air Force* (statement of Senator Glenn), 21.

192. *Waste and Financial Management Problems at the Air Force* (statement of Air Force Comptroller Michael B. Donley), 15.

193. *Waste and Financial Management Problems at the Air Force* (statement of Air Force Comptroller Michael B. Donley), 15.

194. *The CFO Act and the Army Audit: Persistent Pentagon Financial Management Problems*, S. Hrg. 102-1107 (August 7, 1992) (statement of Senator Glenn), 1.

195. GAO, *Financial Audit: Examination of the Army's Financial Statements for Fiscal Year 1991*, GAO/AFMD-92-83, 1, 8–10 (Washington, DC: GAO, August 1992), 10, https://www.gao.gov/assets/220/216471.pdf.

196. GAO.

197. *The CFO Act and the Army Audit*, S. Hrg. 102-1107 (statement of Senator Glenn), 7.

198. GAO, *Financial Audit: Examination of the Army's Financial Statements for Fiscal Years 1992 and 1991*, GAO/AIMD-93-1 (Washington, DC: GAO, June 1993), 7, https://www.gao.gov/assets/220/218041.pdf.

199. GAO, 8.

200. GAO, *Financial Management: Strong Leadership Needed to Improve Army's Financial Accountability*, GAO/AIMD-94-12 (Washington, DC: GAO, December 1993), 2–3, https://www.gao.gov/assets/160/153959.pdf.

201. GAO, *Financial Audit: Examination of the Army's Financial Statements for Fiscal Years 1992 and 1991*, GAO/AIMD-93-1, 13.

202. GAO, *Financial Management: DOD Has Not Responded Effectively to Serious, Long-standing Problems*, GAO/T-AIMD-93-1, 1–2. See also Morrison, "Green-Eyeshade Blues," 2898.

203. *Pentagon Financial Management Problems*, S Hrg. 103-705 (statement of Senator Glenn), 2.

204. *Pentagon Financial Management Problems*, (statement of Senator Glenn), 19.

205. *Pentagon Financial Management Problems*, 41–42.

206. *Pentagon Financial Management Problems*, (statement of Comptroller General Charles A. Bowsher) 23–24.

207. *Pentagon Financial Management Problems* (statement of Deputy DOD Comptroller Alvin Tucker), 47.

208. *Pentagon Financial Management Problems* (statement of Deputy DOD Comptroller Alvin Tucker), 47–48.

209. *Pentagon Financial Management Problems* (statement of Lt. Gen. Merle Freitag, Comptroller of the Army), 56.

210. Albert Gore Jr., *Improving Financial Management: Accompanying Report of the National Performance Review* (Washington, DC: Office of the Vice President, September 1993), "Adopt Good Business Practices—FM09: Simplify The Financial Reporting Process," https://govinfo.library.unt.edu/npr/library/reports/fm.html.

211. Gore, "Build a Strong Financial Management Infrastructure—FM05: Use the Chief Financial Officers (CFO) Act to Improve Financial Services."

212. Government Management Reform Act of 1994, Pub. L. 103-356. See *Federal Consolidated Financial Statements: Can the Federal Government Balance Its Books?* Serial No. 105-158, 105th Cong. (April 1, 1998) (statement of Edward DeSeve, acting deputy director for management, Office of Management and Budget), 37.

213. GAO, *Financial Management: FFMIA Implementation Necessary to Achieve Accountability*, GAO-03-31 (Washington, DC: GAO, October 2002), 16–17, https://www.gao.gov/assets/240/236045.pdf.

214. *Can the Federal Government Balance Its Books? A Review of the Federal Consolidated Financial Statements: Hearing Before the Subcommittee on Government Management, Information, and Technology of the Committee on Government Reform, House of Representatives*, Serial No. 106-73, 106th Cong. (March 31, 1999) (statement of Comptroller General David Walker), 16. See also *Are the Financial Records of the Federal Government Reliable? Hearing Before the Subcommittee on Government Efficiency, Financial Management and Intergovernmental Relations of the Committee on Government Reform, House of Representatives*, Serial No. 107-31, 107th Cong. (March 30, 2001) (statement of Mr. Walker), 4–5.

215. Harold I. Steinberg, "The Chief Financial Officers Act: A Ten Year Progress Report," *Government Accountants Journal* 49, no. 4 (Winter 2000): 52.

216. GAO, *Financial Management: Federal Financial Management Improvement Act Results for Fiscal Year 1999*, GAO/AIMD-00-307 (Washington, DC: GAO, September 2000), 20, https://www.gao.gov/assets/230/229654.pdf.

217. *DOD Financial Management*, S. Hrg. 103-855 (statement of DOD Comptroller John J. Hamre), 70.

218. *DOD Financial Management* (statement of Comptroller General Charles A. Bowsher), 18.

219. *DOD Financial Management* (statement of DOD Comptroller John J. Hamre), 70.

220. Dana Priest, "Losing Control: Defense Department Billions Go Astray, Often Without a Trace," *Washington Post*, May 14, 1995.

221. Priest.

222. Priest.

223. *Chief Financial Officers Act Oversight*, HRG-1995-GRO-0050, letter from John Hamre to Bill Young, May 22, 1995, 255–58.

224. *Chief Financial Officers Act Oversight*, HRG-1995-GRO-0050 (statement of Representative Stephen Horn), 1.

225. Keevey, "DOD's Financial Management Initiatives."

226. Keevey.

227. Keevey.

228. *The Department of Defense's Financial Management Problems*, HRG-1995-GRO-0084 (statement of Alvin Tucker), 18; Sandra G. Lyons, "Department of Defense Implementation Strategies for Audited Financial Statements," *Armed Forces Comptroller* 45, no. 2 (Summer 2000): 12–14; *Pentagon Financial Management Problems*, S Hrg. 103-705 (statement of Senator Glenn), 1; *DOD Financial Management*, S. Hrg. 103-855 (statement of DOD Comptroller John J. Hamre), 70; *Oversight of the Financial Management Practices at the Department of Defense*, Serial No. 106-80 (statement of DOD Comptroller William Lynn), 75, 93; Lynn, "The Military Financial Management Agenda"; James Speer, "Achieving Auditable Financial Statements within the Air Force," *Armed Forces Comptroller* 45, no. 2 (Summer 2000): 23–25.

229. *The Department of Defense's Financial Management Problems*, HRG-1995-GRO-0084 (statement of Deputy Comptroller Alvin Tucker), 17.

230. *Department of Defense's Financial Management Problems*, HRG-1995-GRO-0084 (statement of DOD Comptroller John Hamre), 24.

231. *Department of Defense's Financial Management Problems*, HRG-1995-GRO-0084 (statement of Mr. Tucker), 14. See also GAO, *Financial Management: Challenges Confronting DOD's Reform Initiatives*, GAO/T-AIMD-95-146, 5; *Oversight of the Financial Management Practices at the Department of Defense*, Serial No. 106-80 (statement of Robert Lieberman, assistant DOD inspector general for audit), 97.

232. *Oversight of the Financial Management Practices at the Department of Defense*, Serial No. 106-80 (statement of Gene Dodaro, assistant comptroller general for accounting and information management), 96–97.

233. *Oversight of the Financial Management Practices at the Department of Defense* (statement of Mr. Lieberman), 97.

234. *The Department of Defense's Financial Management Problems*, HRG-1995-GRO-0084 (colloquy between Air Force Comptroller Robert F. Hale and Representative Stephen Horn), 124–25.

235. GAO, *CFO Act Financial Audits: Increased Attention Must Be Given to Preparing Navy's Financial Reports*, GAO/AIMD-96-7, 3, 11.

236. GAO, 3, 15, 17.

237. *Federal Consolidated Financial Statements: Can the Federal Government Balance its Books?* Serial No. 105-158 (April 1, 1998) (statement of Gene L. Dodaro, assistant comptroller general), 18–19.

238. *Federal Consolidated Financial Statements* (April 16, 1998) (statement of Gene L. Dodaro, assistant comptroller general), 307–38.

239. *Federal Consolidated Financial Statements* (statement of DOD Inspector General Eleanor Hill), 286.

240. *Can the Federal Government Balance Its Books? A Review of the Federal Consolidated Financial Statements* Serial No. 106-73 (statement of Comptroller General David Walker), 14; *Are the Financial Records of the Federal Government Reliable?* Serial No. 107-31 (statement of Representative Stephen Horn), 1.

241. *Are the Financial Records of the Federal Government Reliable?* Serial No. 107-31 (statement of Comptroller General David Walker), 5; *Results of the Department of Defense's Fiscal Year 1999 Financial Statements Audit*, Serial No. 106-200 (statement of Representative Stephen Horn), 1.

242. *Oversight of the Financial Management Practices at the Department of Defense*, Serial No. 106-80 (statement of Acting DOD Inspector General Donald Mancuso), 8.

243. GAO, *Department of Defense: Progress in Financial Management Reform*, GAO/T-AIMD-NSIAD-00-163, 37, 47.

244. *Department of Defense Financial Management*, S. Hrg. 107-803 (statement of Comptroller General David M. Walker), 6.

245. *Results of the Department of Defense's Fiscal Year 1999 Financial Statements Audit*, Serial No. 106-200 (statement of Robert J. Lieberman, assistant inspector general for auditing, DOD), 3.

246. *Making the Pentagon Accountable: Financial Problems and Progress*, S. Hrg. 103-934 (statement of Deputy DOD Inspector General Derek J. Vander Schaff), 71.

247. *Federal Consolidated Financial Statements: Can the Federal Government Balance Its Books?* Serial No. 105-158 (April 16, 1998) (statement of DOD Inspector General Eleanor Hill), 296.

248. *Oversight of the Financial Management Practices at the Department of Defense*, Serial No. 106-80, 99–101.

249. National Defense Authorization Act for Fiscal Year 2002: Report to Accompany S. 1416, S. Rep. No. 107-62, 107th Cong. (2001), https://www.congress.gov/107/crpt/srpt62/CRPT-107srpt62.pdf.

250. National Defense Authorization Act for Fiscal Year 2002, Pub. L. 107-107, 115 Stat. 1012, 107th Cong. (2001), SEC. 1008, https://www.gpo.gov/fdsys/pkg/PLAW-107publ107/pdf/PLAW-107publ107.pdf.

251. *Department of Defense Financial Management*, S. Hrg. 107-803 (statement of Deputy DOD Inspector General Robert J. Lieberman), 17.

252. *The Department of Defense: What Is Being Done to Resolve Longstanding Financial Management Problems? Hearing Before the Subcommittee on Government Efficiency, Financial Management and Intergovernmental Relations of the Committee on Government Reform, House of Representatives*, Serial No. 107-157, 107th Cong. (March 20, 2002) (statement of Mr. Lieberman, deputy inspector general, DOD), 65.

253. GAO, *Financial Management: Analysis of DOD's First Biennial Financial Management Improvement Plan*, GAO/AIMD-99-44, 11, 17. See also GAO, *Executive Guide: Measuring Performance and Demonstrating Results of Information Technology Investments*, GAO/AIMD-98-89 (Washington, DC: GAO, March 1998), 42, https://www.gao.gov/assets/80/76378.pdf; GAO, *Major Management Challenges and Program Risks: A Governmentwide Perspective*, GAO/OCG-99-1 (Washington, DC: GAO, January 1, 1999), 79–83, https://www.gao.gov/assets/200/199564.pdf.

254. GAO, *Department of Defense: Implications of Financial Management Issues*, GAO/T-AIMD/NSIAD-00-264 (Washington, DC: GAO, July 20, 2000) (statement of Jeffrey C. Steinhoff, assistant comptroller general, Accounting and Information Management Division), 28–29, https://www.gao.gov/assets/110/108579.pdf; GAO, *Department of Defense: Progress in Financial Management Reform*, GAO-AIMD/NSIAD-00-163, 49; GAO, *Information Technology: Architecture Needed to Guide Modernization of DOD's Financial Operations*, GAO-01-525 (Washington, DC: GAO, May 2001), 9–10, 20, https://www.gao.gov/assets/240/231440.pdf.

255. GAO, *Information Technology: Architecture Needed to Guide Modernization of DOD's Financial Operations*, GAO-01-525, 28. See also GAO, *DOD Financial Management: Integrated Approach, Accountability, and Incentives Are Keys to Effective Reform*, GAO-01-681T, 15; GAO, *Department of Defense: Progress in Financial Management Reform*, GAO-AIMD/NSIAD-00-163, 48.

256. GAO, *Information Technology: Architecture Needed to Guide Modernization of DOD's Financial Operations*, GAO-01-525, 30.

257. *Nominations Before the Senate Armed Services Committee, First Session, 107th Congress: Hearings Before the Committee on Armed Services, United States Senate*, S. Hrg. 107-749, 107th Cong. (January 11, 2001) (statement of Senator Byrd), 68, https://www.gpo.gov/fdsys/pkg/CHRG-107shrg75903/pdf/CHRG-107shrg75903.pdf.

258. *Nominations Before the Senate Armed Services Committee* (statement of Senator Byrd), 69.

259. *Nominations Before the Senate Armed Services Committee* (statement of Donald Rumsfeld), 69–70.

260. The IDA Study Group, composed of experienced business people and supported by a private sector professional services firm under separate contract, was tasked to develop the framework for an effective transformation of DOD financial management (DOD, *Transforming Department of Defense Financial Management: A Strategy for Change*, Final Report [Washington, DC: DOD, April 13, 2001], 1, http://archive.defense.gov/news/Jul2001/d20010710finmngt.pdf).

261. *Transforming the Department of Defense for Financial Management: A Strategy for Change: Hearing Before the Subcommittee on National Security, Veterans Affairs and International Relations of the Committee on Government Reform, House of Representatives*, Serial No. 107-198, 107th Cong. (June 4, 2002) (statement of Stephen Friedman, chairman, DOD Financial Management Study Group), 8–10.

262. DOD, *Transforming Department of Defense Financial Management*, i.

263. DOD, 22.

264. DOD, 15.

265. DOD, 13.

266. Donald Rumsfeld, "Memorandum to Secretaries of the Military Departments, July 19, 2001," in *Fiscal Year 2001 Department of Defense Overview* (Washington, DC: The Office of the Secretary of Defense), 1–20, https://comptroller.defense.gov/Portals/45/documents/cfs/fy2001/04_Overview-Agency-Wide-FY2001.pdf.

267. DOD Inspector General, *Development of the Defense Finance and Accounting Service Corporate Database and Other Financial Management Systems*, Report No. D-2002-014 (Washington, DC: DOD, November 7, 2001), 10, https://media.defense.gov/2001/Nov/07/2001715804/-1/-1/1/02-014.pdf.

268. Catherine Santana, "Department of Defense Financial Management Modernization," *Armed Forces Comptroller* 47, no. 1 (Winter 2002): 10; *Transforming the Department of Defense for Financial Management: A Strategy for Change*, Serial No. 107-198 (statement of Deputy DOD Comptroller Tina Jonas), 48; GAO, *DOD Business Systems Modernization: Limited Progress in Development of Business Enterprise Architecture and Oversight of Information Technology Investments*, GAO-04-731R (Washington, DC: GAO, May 17, 2004), 6, https://www.gao.gov/assets/100/92616.pdf.

269. Santana, "Department of Defense Financial Management Modernization," 10.

270. *Department of Defense Financial Management*, S. Hrg. 107-803 (statement of DOD Comptroller Dov S. Zakheim), 17.

271. *Department of Defense Financial Management*, S. Hrg. 107-803, 28.

272. *Department of Defense Financial Management*, S. Hrg. 107-803, 22.

273. *Department of Defense Financial Management*, S. Hrg. 107-803, 41.

274. *Department of Defense Financial Management*, S. Hrg. 107-803, 46.

275. *Department of Defense Financial Management*, S. Hrg. 107-803, 17.

276. *Transforming the Department of Defense for Financial Management: A Strategy for Change*, Serial No. 107-198 (statement of Representative Christopher Shays), 2.

277. *Transforming the Department of Defense for Financial Management* (statement of Representative John Tierney), 45–46. See also *Department of Defense Financial Management*, S. Hrg. 107-803 (statement of Senator Akaka), 2, 29.

278. *Transforming the Department of Defense for Financial Management* (statement of Deputy DOD Comptroller Larry Lanzillotta), 46. See also HCGR, "Winning the War on Financial Management—Status of Department of Defense Reform Efforts," Serial No. 108-64 (June 25, 2003) (statement of Mr. Lanzillotta), 81.

279. Bob Stump National Defense Authorization Act for Fiscal Year 2003, Pub. L. 107-314, 116 Stat. 2458, 107th Cong. (2002), https://www.gpo.gov/fdsys/pkg/PLAW-107publ314/pdf/PLAW-107publ314.pdf.

280. National Defense Authorization Act for Fiscal Year 2003: Conference Report to Accompany H.R. 4546, H. Rep. No. 107-772, 107th Cong. (2002), 682, https://www.congress.gov/107/crpt/hrpt772/CRPT-107hrpt772.pdf.

281. "In His Own Words: An Interview with the Honorable Dr. Dov S. Zakheim," *Armed Forces Comptroller* 46, no. 4 (Fall 2001): 7.

282. *Department of Defense Financial Management*, S. Hrg. 107-803 (statement of DOD Comptroller Dov Zakheim), 28.

283. *The Department of Defense: What Is Being Done to Resolve Longstanding Financial Management Problems?* Serial No. 107-157 (statement of Deputy DOD Comptroller Tina W. Jonas), 22–23.

284. *DOD Financial Management: Following One Item Through the Maze: Hearing Before the Subcommittee on National Security, Veterans Affairs and International Relations of the Committee on Government Reform, House of Representatives*, Serial No. 107-208, 107th Cong. (June 25, 2002) (statement of Gregory Kutz, director, Financial Management and Assurance Team, GAO), 10.

285. GAO, *DOD Business Systems Modernization: Continued Investment in Key Accounting Systems Needs to Be Justified*, GAO-03-465 (Washington, DC: GAO, March 2003), 2, https://www.gao.gov/assets/240/237687.pdf.

286. GAO, *Business Systems Modernization: Summary of GAO's Assessment of the Department of Defense's Initial Business Enterprise Architecture*, GAO-03-877R (Washington, DC: GAO, July 7, 2003), 6, https://www.gao.gov/assets/100/92066.pdf.

287. *Department of Defense Authorization for Appropriations for Fiscal Year 2005: Hearings Before the Committee on Armed Services, United States Senate, on S. 2400*, S. Hrg. 108-440, Pt. 3, 108th Cong. (March 23, 2004) (statement of DOD Comptroller Dov S. Zakheim), 146.

288. *Department of Defense Authorization for Appropriations for Fiscal Year 2005*, S. Hrg. 108-440, Pt. 3 (March 23, 2004) (statement of Comptroller General David M. Walker), 138.

289. Robert Jennings, "BMMP—A Progress Report," *Armed Forces Comptroller* 49, no. 1 (Winter 2004): 11.

290. *Winning the War on Financial Management—Status of Department of Defense Reform Efforts: Hearing Before the Subcommittee on Government Efficiency and Financial Management of the Committee on Government Reform, House of Representatives*, Serial No. 108-64, 108th Cong. (June 25, 2003) (statement of Deputy DOD Comptroller Larry Lanzillotta), 49.

291. *Winning the War on Financial Management* (statement of Deputy DOD Comptroller Larry Lanzillotta), 48.

292. GAO, *Business Systems Modernization: Summary of GAO's Assessment of the Department of Defense's Initial Business Enterprise Architecture*, GAO-03-877R, 4. See also *The Federal Government's Financial Statement and Accountability of Taxpayer Dollars at the Departments of Defense and Homeland Security: Hearing Before the Financial Management, The Budget, and International Security Subcommittee of the Committee on Governmental Affairs,*

United States Senate, S. Hrg. 108-660, 108th (July 8, 2004) (statement of Acting DOD Comptroller Larry Lanzillotta), 39.

293. Hale, interview with author, January 24, 2018.

294. GAO, *Business Systems Modernization: Summary of GAO's Assessment of the Department of Defense's Initial Business Enterprise Architecture*, GAO-03-877R, 5–6; GAO, *DOD Business Systems Modernization: Important Progress Made to Develop Business Enterprise Architecture, but Much More Work Remains*, GAO-03-1018 (Washington, DC: GAO, September 2003), 4–5, https://www.gao.gov/assets/240/239717.pdf.

295. GAO, *Business Systems Modernization: Summary of GAO's Assessment of the Department of Defense's Initial Business Enterprise Architecture*, GAO-03-877R, 6–7.

296. GAO, 5. See also *Department of Defense Authorization for Appropriations for Fiscal Year 2005*, S. Hrg. 108-440, Pt. 3, (March 23, 2004) (statement of DOD Comptroller Dov Zakheim), 146; *Business Process Modernization at the Department of Defense: Joint Hearing Before the Subcommittee on Government Efficiency and Financial Management and the Subcommittee on National Security, Emerging Threats and International Relations of the Committee on Government Reform, House of Representatives*, Serial No. 108-229, 108th Cong. (July 7, 2004) (statement of Acting DOD Comptroller Larry Lanzillotta), 80; *The Federal Government's Financial Statement and Accountability of Taxpayer Dollars at the Departments of Defense and Homeland Security*, S. Hrg. 108-660 (statement of Mr. Lanzillotta), 25.

297. *The Status of Financial Management Reform within the Department of Defense and the Individual Services*, S. Hrg. 108-859 (statement of Comptroller General David M. Walker), 16.

298. *Status of Financial Management Reform* (statement of Comptroller General David M. Walker), 16.

299. *Department of Defense Authorization for Appropriations for Fiscal Year 2005*, S. Hrg 108-440, Pt. 3 (statement of Senator Akaka), 127. See also *Department of Defense Business Transformation and Financial Management Accountability: Hearing Before the Subcommittee on Readiness and Management Support of the Committee on Armed Services, United States Senate*, S. Hrg. 109-364, 109th Cong. (November 9, 2005) (statement of Senator Akaka), 3, https://www.gpo.gov/fdsys/pkg/CHRG-109shrg27089/pdf/CHRG-109shrg27089.pdf.

300. *The Status of Financial Management Reform within the Department of Defense and the Individual Services*, S. Hrg. 108-859 (statement of Senator Levin), 3. See also *Business Systems Modernization at the Department of Defense: Hearing Before the Subcommittee on Government Management, Finance, and Accountability of the Committee on Government Reform, House of Representatives*, Serial No. 109-52, 109th Cong. (June 8, 2005) (statement of Gregory D. Kutz, director, Financial Management and Assurance, GAO), 6, 59; *Department of Defense Business Transformation and Financial Management Accountability*, S. Hrg. 109-364 (statement of Randolph C. Hite, director of information technology, architecture and system issues, GAO), 14.

301. *Department of Defense Authorization for Appropriations for Fiscal Year 2005*, S. Hrg. 108-440, Pt. 3 (statement of DOD Comptroller Dov Zakheim), 146.

302. *Business Process Modernization at the Department of Defense*, Serial No. 108-229 (statement of Acting DOD Comptroller Larry Lanzillotta), 60–61.

303. *Department of Defense Authorization for Appropriations for Fiscal Year 2006: Hearings Before the Committee on Armed Services, United States Senate, on S. 1042*, S. Hrg. 109-22, Pt. 3, 109th Cong. (April 13, 2005) (statement of Under Secretary Michael Wynne), 136.

304. *Department of Defense Authorization for Appropriations for Fiscal Year 2006*, 120, 132.

305. *Department of Defense Authorization for Appropriations for Fiscal Year 2006*, 128.

306. *The Status of Financial Management Reform within the Department of Defense and the Individual Services*, S. Hrg. 108-859 (statement of DOD Comptroller Tina Jonas), 127. See also GAO, *Defense Business Transformation: A Comprehensive Plan, Integrated Efforts, and Sustained Leadership Are Needed to Assure Success*, GAO-07-229T (Washington, DC: GAO, November 16, 2006) (statement of Comptroller General David M. Walker), 8–19, https://www.gao.gov/assets/120/115058.pdf; *Business Systems Modernization at the Department of Defense*, Serial No. 109-52 (statement of Randolph Hite, director, Information Technology Architecture and Systems Issues, GAO), 59.

307. *Business Systems Modernization at the Department of Defense*, Serial No. 109-52 (statement of Paul Brinkley, special assistant to the under secretary of defense, acquisition technology and logistics [business transformation]), 61.

308. *Business Systems Modernization at the Department of Defense* (statement of Paul Brinkley, special assistant to the under secretary of defense, acquisition technology and logistics [business transformation]), 61.

309. *Business Systems Modernization at the Department of Defense* (statement of Thomas Modly, deputy under secretary of defense for financial management, Office of the Under Secretary of Defense [Comptroller]), 36–37.

310. Paul Brinkley, "Taking Business Transformation to the Next Level," *Armed Forces Comptroller* 51, no. 1 (Winter 2006): 8.

311. *Department of Defense Business Transformation and Financial Management Accountability*, S. Hrg. 109-364 (statement of Randolph C. Hite, director of information technology, architecture and system issues, GAO), 22.

312. Christine Wenrich, "We're Talking SFIS: Introducing the Common Business Language of DOD," *Armed Forces Comptroller* 50, no. 2 (Spring 2005): 20 (quoting David Wabeke, acting director of the BMMP Financial Management Domain). See also Christine Wenrich, "Implementing Standards in DOD Business Systems for Improved Financial Visibility," *Armed Forces Comptroller* 50, no. 4 (Fall 2005): 22–24.

313. *Department of Defense Authorization for Appropriations for Fiscal Year 2006*, S. Hrg. 109-22, Pt. 3, (April 13, 2005) (statement of Comptroller General David M. Walker), 133.

314. *Department of Defense Business Transformation and Financial Management Accountability*, S. Hrg. 109-364 (statement of Randolph C. Hite, GAO), 22.

315. *Department of Defense Business Transformation and Financial Management Accountability*, 15, 21.

316. *Department of Defense Business Transformation and Financial Management Accountability*, 15, 21.

317. *Department of Defense Business Transformation and Financial Management Accountability*, 23.

318. *Department of Defense Business Transformation and Financial Management Accountability*, 23–24.

319. GAO, *Defense Business Transformation: A Comprehensive Plan, Integrated Efforts, and Sustained Leadership Are Needed to Assure Success*, GAO-07-229T, 8.

320. *Department of Defense Business Transformation and Financial Management Accountability*, S. Hrg. 109-364 (statement of Under Secretary Kenneth Krieg), 38.

321. *Department of Defense Business Transformation and Financial Management Accountability* (statement of Under Secretary Kenneth Krieg), 38.

322. GAO, *Defense Business Transformation: A Comprehensive Plan, Integrated Efforts, and Sustained Leadership Are Needed to Assure Success*, GAO-07-229T, 18–19.

323. GAO, *Defense Business Transformation: A Full-time Chief Management Officer with a Term Appointment Is Needed at DOD to Maintain Continuity of Effort and Achieve Sustainable Success*, GAO-08-132T (Washington, DC: GAO, October 16, 2007) (statement of Comptroller General David M. Walker), 23, https://www.gao.gov/assets/120/118074.pdf.

324. GAO, *Defense Business Transformation: Sustaining Progress Requires Continuity of Leadership and an Integrated Approach*, GAO-08-462T (Washington, DC: GAO, February 7, 2008) (statement of Comptroller General David M. Walker), 21, https://www.gao.gov/assets/120/118870.pdf.

325. GAO, 4. See also GAO, *DOD Business Systems Modernization: Military Departments Need to Strengthen Management of Enterprise Architecture Programs*, GAO-08-519 (Washington, DC: GAO, May 2008), https://www.gao.gov/new.items/d08519.pdf. Members of Congress echoed the GAO view (*Department of Defense Business Systems Modernization and Financial Management Accountability Efforts: Hearing Before the Subcommittee on Readiness and Management Support of the Committee on Armed Services, United States Senate*, S. Hrg. 109-915, 109th Cong. (November 16, 2006) (statement of Senator Ensign), 2; *Business Transformation and Financial Management at the Department of Defense: Hearing Before the Subcommittee on Readiness and Management Support of the Committee on Armed Services, United States Senate*, S. Hrg. 110-533, 110th Cong. (February 7, 2008) (statement of Senator Akaka), 2, (statement of Senator Thune), 3.

326. GAO, *DOD Business Systems Modernization: Further Actions Needed to Address Challenges and Improve Accountability*, GAO-13-557 (GAO, May 2013), 10, 15–19, https://www.gao.gov/assets/660/654733.pdf.

327. GAO, *DOD Financial Management: Effect of Continuing Weaknesses on Management and Operations and Status of Key Challenges*, GAO-14-576T (Washington, DC: GAO, May 13, 2014) (statement of Asif A. Khan, director, Financial Management and Assurance), 28, https://www.gao.gov/assets/670/663157.pdf.

328. Ketrick et al., *Assessment of DOD Enterprise Resource Planning*, E-4–E-7.

329. Gaddy, interview with author, February 21, 2018.

330. GAO, *DOD Business Systems Modernization: Continued Investment in Key Accounting Systems Needs to be Justified*, GAO-03-465, 21.

331. DOD Inspector General, *Development of the Defense Finance and Accounting Service Corporate Database*, 6.

332. Mohammad Rashid, Liaquat Hossain, and Jon David Patrick, "The Evolution of ERP Systems: A Historical Perspective," in *Enterprise Resource Planning: Global Opportunities & Challenges*, ed. Mohammad Abdur Rashid (Hershey, PA: IDEA Group Publishing, 2002), 2, https://faculty.biu.ac.il/~shnaidh/zooloo/nihul/evolution.pdf.

333. Rashid, Hossain, and Patrick, 5–6.

334. Christopher Koch, "Supply Chain: Hershey's Bittersweet Lesson," *CIO*, November 15, 2002, https://www.cio.com/article/2440386/supply-chain---hershey-s-bittersweet-lesson.html.

335. Christopher Koch, "Nike Rebounds: How (and Why) Nike Recovered from Its Supply Chain Disaster," *CIO*, June 15, 2004, https://www.cio.com/article/2439601/nike-rebounds--how--and-why--nike-recovered-from-its-supply-chain-disaster.html.

336. Koch.

337. Richard Oliver, "ERP Is Dead! Long Live ERP!" *Management Review*, November 1999, 12–13; David Stodder, "Roll Over, ERP," *Intelligent Enterprise*, July 17, 2000, 14; Tom Stein, "ERP's Fight for Life," *Information Week*, April 12, 1999, 59–66.

338. Harold Carver and William Jackson, *A Case Study of the United States Navy's Enterprise Resource Planning System*, MBA Professional Report (Monterey, CA: Naval Postgraduate School, June 2006), 4–5, http://www.dtic.mil/dtic/tr/fulltext/u2/a451388.pdf. See also Brian Kilcourse, "ERP Is Dead; Long Live 'Enterprise Enablement,'" *RSR*, September 24, 2013, https://www.rsrresearch.com/research/erp-is-dead-long-live-enterprise-enablement; Thomas Wailgum, "Why ERP Is Still So Hard," *CIO*, September 9, 2009, 3, https://www.cio.com/article/2424944/enterprise-software/why-erp-is-still-so-hard.html.

339. Wailgum, "Why ERP Is Still So Hard," 1. See also Ketrick et al., *Assessment of DOD Enterprise Resource Planning*, A-2–A-3.

340. Cindy Jutras, "Sage Says ERP Is Dead. What (I Think) They Really Mean Is," *Mint Jutras*, July 31, 2015, http://www.mintjutras.com/sage-says-erp-is-dead-what-i-think-they-really-mean-is/.

341. Laura Odell et al., *Beyond Enterprise Resource Planning (ERP): The Next Generation Enterprise Resource Planning Environment*, IDA Paper P-4852 (Alexandria, VA: Institute for Defense Analyses, February 2012), 20; Carver and Jackson, *A Case Study*, 12.

342. GAO, *DOD Financial Management: Challenges in the Implementation of Business Systems Could Impact Audit Readiness Efforts*, GAO-12-177T (Washington, DC: GAO, October 27, 2011) (statement of Asif A. Khan, director, Financial Management and Assurance), 4–6, https://www.gao.gov/assets/590/585958.pdf.

343. Gary R. Bliss, "PARCA Root Cause Analysis for Enterprise Resource Planning Systems," (memorandum for the principal deputy under secretary of defense (AT&L), Washington, DC: Office of the Under Secretary of Defense, February 23, 2011), https://www.acq.osd.mil/parca/docs/2011-02-23-parca-rca-erp.pdf.

344. DOD Inspector General, *Development of the Defense Finance and Accounting Service Corporate Database*, 7, 11.

345. GAO, *DOD Business Systems Modernization: Billions Continue to be Invested with Inadequate Management Oversight and Accountability*, GAO-04-615 (Washington, DC: GAO, May 2004), 48–49, https://www.gao.gov/assets/250/242540.pdf.

346. GAO, 35–36.

347. GAO, 39–42.

348. GAO, 62.

349. GAO, *DOD Business Systems Modernization: Navy ERP Adherence to Best Business Practices Critical to Avoid Past Failures*, GAO-05-858 (Washington, DC: GAO, September 2005), 3, https://www.gao.gov/new.items/d05858.pdf.

350. Henry S. Kenyon, "Business Transformation Agency Hits the Ground Running," *SIGNAL*, September 2006, https://www.afcea.org/content/?q=business-transformation-agency-hits-ground-running.

351. Brinkley, "Taking Business Transformation," 10.

352. GAO, *DOD Business Transformation: Lack of an Integrated Strategy Puts the Army's Asset Visibility System Investments at Risk*, GAO-07-860 (Washington, DC: GAO, July 2007), 7, 32, https://www.gao.gov/assets/270/264676.pdf.

353. GAO, *DOD Business Systems Modernization: Important Management Controls Being Implemented on Major Navy Program, but Improvements Needed in Key Areas*, GAO-08-896 (Washington, DC: GAO, September 2008), 26, https://www.gao.gov/assets/290/280049.pdf.

354. *Nominations Before the Senate Armed Services Committee, Second Session, 111th Congress: Hearings Before the Committee on Armed Services, United States Senate*, S. Hrg. 111-896, 111th Cong. (March 23, 2010) (statement of Elizabeth A. McGrath), 62. See also GAO, *DOD Systems Modernization: Management of Integrated Military Human Capital Program Needs Additional Improvements*, GAO-05-189 (Washington, DC: GAO, February 2005), 4, https://www.gao.gov/assets/250/245300.pdf.

355. GAO, *Defense Business Transformation: A Comprehensive Plan, Integrated Efforts, and Sustained Leadership Are Needed to Assure Success*, GAO-07-229T, 26.

356. *Nominations Before the Senate Armed Services Committee, First Session, 111th Congress: Hearings Before the Committee on Armed Services, United States Senate*, S. Hrg. 111-362, 111th Cong. (November 19, 2009) (statement of Dr. Clifford L. Stanley), 1483. See GAO, *DOD Systems Modernization: Maintaining Effective Communication Is Needed to Help Ensure the Army's Successful Deployment of the Defense Integrated Military Human Resources System*, GAO-08-927R (Washington, DC: GAO, September 8, 2008), 3, https://www.gao.gov/assets/100/95723.pdf.

357. *Department of Defense Authorization for Appropriations for Fiscal Year 2011: Hearings Before the Committee on Armed Services, United States Senate, on S. 3454. Part 1*, S. Hrg. 111-701, Pt. 1, 111th Cong. (February 2, 2010) (statement of Secretary of Defense Robert Gates), 55, https://www.gpo.gov/fdsys/pkg/CHRG-111shrg62155/pdf/CHRG-111shrg62155.pdf.

358. Thom Shanker, "Pentagon Plans Steps to Reduce Budget and Jobs," *New York Times*, August 10, 2010; David S. Cloud, "Gates Calls for Cuts at Pentagon," *Los Angeles Times*, August 10, 2010.

359. GAO, *DOD Business Transformation: Lack of an Integrated Strategy Puts the Army's Asset Visibility System Investments at Risk*, GAO-07-860, 21–22.

360. GAO, *DOD Business Transformation: Air Force's Current Approach Increases Risk that Asset Visibility Goals and Transformation Priorities Will Not Be Achieved*, GAO-08-

866 (Washington, DC: GAO, August 2008), 18–22, https://www.gao.gov/assets/280/279477.pdf.

361. GAO, *DOD Business Systems Modernization: Important Management Controls Being Implemented on Major Navy Program, but Improvements Needed in Key Areas*, GAO-08-896, 46–47.

362. DOD Inspector General, *Navy Enterprise Resource Planning System Does Not Comply with the Standard Financial Information Structure and U.S. Government Standard General Ledger*, Report No. DODIG-2012-051 (Alexandria, VA: DOD, February 13, 2012), 4–6, https://media.defense.gov/2012/Feb/13/2001713323/-1/-1/1/DODIG-2012-051.pdf; GAO, *DOD Financial Management: Ongoing Challenges in Implementing the Financial Improvement and Audit Readiness Plan*, GAO-11-932T (Washington, DC: GAO, September 15, 2011) (statement of Asif A. Khan, director, Financial Management and Assurance), 1–2, https://www.gao.gov/assets/130/126969.pdf; GAO, *DOD Financial Management: Implementation Weaknesses in Army and Air Force Business Systems Could Jeopardize DOD's Auditability Goals*, GAO-12-134 (Washington, DC: GAO, February 2012), 9–11, https://www.gao.gov/assets/590/588902.pdf. See also DOD Inspector General, *General Fund Enterprise Business System Did Not Provide Required Financial Information*, Report No. DODIG-2012-066 (Alexandria, VA: DOD, March 26, 2012), i, http://www.dtic.mil/dtic/tr/fulltext/u2/a559121.pdf; Jordana Mishory, "DOD IG: Army Enterprise Business System May Not Resolve Weaknesses," *Inside the Pentagon* 28, no. 13 (March 29, 2012): 6–7.

363. GAO, *DOD Business Transformation: Improved Management Oversight of Business System Modernization Efforts Needed*, GAO-11-53 (Washington, DC: GAO, October 2010), Highlights, https://www.gao.gov/assets/320/311118.pdf. In addition, a 2009 survey confirmed that ERPs were a "keep me awake at night" issue throughout the DOD financial community (Lewis W. Crenshaw, "Top Concerns of Defense Financial Managers," *Armed Forces Comptroller* 54, no. 4 (Fall 2009): 38.

364. GAO, *DOD Business Systems Modernization: Important Management Controls Being Implemented on Major Navy Program, but Improvements Needed in Key Areas*, GAO-08-896, 5.

365. *Department of Defense Authorization for Appropriations for Fiscal Year 2005*, S. Hrg. 108-440, Pt. 3, (March 23, 2004) (statement of Comptroller General David M. Walker), 128.

366. *The Status of Financial Management Reform within the Department of Defense and the Individual Services*, S. Hrg. 108-859 (statement of Mr. Walker), 6.

367. A Bill to Amend Title 10, United States Code, to Establish the Position of Deputy Secretary of Defense for Management, and for Other Purposes, S. 780, 109th Cong. (April 14, 2005), https://www.gpo.gov/fdsys/pkg/BILLS-109s780is/pdf/BILLS-109s780is.pdf.

368. Robert Byrd, "SA 2442," *Congressional Record* 151, no. 147 (November 8, 2005): S12536, https://www.congress.gov/crec/2005/11/08/CREC-2005-11-08-senate.pdf.

369. Robert Byrd, "Amendment 2442—Purpose: To Establish the Position of Deputy Secretary of Defense for Management," *Congressional Record* 151, no. 147 (November 8, 2005): S12484, https://www.congress.gov/crec/2005/11/08/CREC-2005-11-08-senate.pdf.

370. *Department of Defense Authorization for Appropriations for Fiscal Year 2006*, S. Hrg. 109-22, Pt. 3, (April 13, 2005) (statement of Under Secretary Michael W. Wynne), 109. See also *Improving Financial and Business Management at the Department of Defense: Hearing Before the Federal Financial Management, Government, Federal Services, and International Subcommittee of the Committee on Homeland Security and Governmental Affairs, United States Senate*, S. Hrg. 110-500 110th Cong. (October 16, 2007) (statement of Paul A. Brinkley, deputy under secretary of defense for business transformation), 16, https://www.gpo.gov/fdsys/pkg/CHRG-110shrg38850/pdf/CHRG-110shrg38850.pdf.

371. Byrd, "Amendment 2442—Purpose: To Establish the Position," 12484. See also National Defense Authorization Act for Fiscal Year 2006, Pub. L. 109-163, 110 Stat. 3136, 109th Cong. (2006), SEC. 907, https://www.gpo.gov/fdsys/pkg/PLAW-109publ163/pdf/PLAW-109publ163.pdf.

372. Defense Business Board, "Creating a Chief Management Officer in the Department of Defense: Task Group Report," Report FY06-4 (Washington, DC: Defense Business Board, May 2006), 3–5, https://dbb.defense.gov/Portals/35/Documents/Reports/2006/FY06-4_Creating_Chief_Management_Officer_2006-5.pdf; National Defense Authorization Act for Fiscal Year 2008, Report to Accompany S. 1547, S. Rep. No. 110-77, 110th Cong. (2007), https://www.congress.gov/110/crpt/srpt77/CRPT-110srpt77.pdf), citing Jason Dechant et al., *Does DOD Need a Chief Management Officer?* IDA Paper P-4169 (Alexandria, VA: Institute for Defense Analyses, December 2006), DRAFT FINAL (Not Cleared for Public Release).

373. GAO, *Defense Business Transformation: A Full-Time Chief Management Officer with a Term Appointment Is Needed at DOD to Maintain Continuity of Effort and Achieve Sustainable Success*, GAO-08-132T, 5, 17–18.

374. National Defense Authorization Act for Fiscal Year 2008, Conference Report to Accompany H.R. 1585, H. Rep. No. 110-477, 110th Cong. (2007), 970, https://www.congress.gov/110/crpt/hrpt477/CRPT-110hrpt477.pdf.

375. National Defense Authorization Act for Fiscal Year 2008, Pub. L. 100-181, 122 Stat. 3, 110th Cong. (2008), SEC. 904, https://www.congress.gov/110/plaws/publ181/PLAW-110publ181.pdf.

376. *Nominations Before the Senate Armed Services Committee, First Session, 111th Congress*, S. Hrg. 111-362, (January 15, 2009) (statement of William J. Lynn III), 60.

377. GAO, *Fiscal Year 2008 U.S. Government Financial Statements: Federal Government Faces New and Continuing Financial Management and Fiscal Challenges*, GAO-09-805T (Washington, DC: GAO, July 9, 2009) (statement of Gene L. Dodaro, acting comptroller general of the United States), 8, https://www.gao.gov/assets/130/122929.pdf.

378. *Nominations Before the Senate Armed Services Committee, Second Session, 111th Congress*, S. Hrg. 111-896, (March 23, 2010) (statement of Elizabeth A. McGrath), 60.

379. *Nominations Before the Senate Armed Services Committee*, S. Hrg. 111-896, 59.

380. *Nominations Before the Senate Armed Services Committee*, S. Hrg. 111-896, 54.

381. Defense Business System Management Committee Approval. 10 U.S.C. § 186b (2008). https://www.gpo.gov/fdsys/pkg/USCODE-2006-title10/pdf/USCODE-2006-title10-subtitleA-partI-chap7-sec186.pdf.

382. Ketrick et al., *Assessment of DOD Enterprise Resource Planning*, 24.

383. Joe Westphal (former under secretary of the army), interview with author, February 26, 2018.

384. GAO, *DOD Business Systems Modernization: Further Actions Needed to Address Challenges and Improve Accountability*, GAO-13-557, 35, 37–38. See also DOD Inspector General, *Enterprise Resource Planning Systems Schedule Delays and Reengineering Weaknesses Increase Risks to DOD's Auditability Goals*, Report No. DODIG-2012-111 (Alexandria, VA: DOD, July 13, 2012), 11, https://media.defense.gov/2012/Jul/13/2001712150/-1/-1/1/DODIG-2012-111.pdf.

385. GAO, *DOD Business Systems Modernization: Further Actions Needed to Address Challenges and Improve Accountability*, GAO-13-557, 35.

386. Bliss, "PARCA Root Cause Analysis."

387. GAO, *DOD Business Systems Modernization: Important Management Controls Being Implemented on Major Navy Program, but Improvements Needed in Key Areas*, GAO-08-896, 4–5.

388. *Financial Management and Business Transformation at the Department of Defense: Hearing Before the Subcommittee on Readiness and Management Support of the Committee on Armed Services, United States Senate*, S. Hrg. 112-658, 112th Cong. (April 18, 2012) (statement of Navy Under Secretary Robert O. Work), 20, https://www.gpo.gov/fdsys/pkg/CHRG-112shrg77485/pdf/CHRG-112shrg77485.pdf; *Department of Defense Update on the Financial Improvement and Audit Readiness Plan: Hearing Before the Committee on Armed Services, House of Representatives*, H.A.S.C. No. 114-126, 114th Cong. (June 15, 2016) (statement of Navy Comptroller Susan J. Rabern), 6–7, https://www.gpo.gov/fdsys/pkg/CHRG-114hhrg20793/pdf/CHRG-114hhrg20793.pdf; DOD, *Financial Improvement and Audit Readiness (FIAR) Plan Status Report* (Washington, DC: Office of the Undersecretary of Defense [Comptroller]/Chief Financial Officer, May 2017), VI-17, https://comptroller.defense.gov/Portals/45/documents/fiar/FIAR_Plan_May_2017.pdf.

389. Speer, interview with author, February 5, 2018. See also Kristyn Jones and Frank A. Distasio, "Army Moving to Compliance with the Chief Financial Officers Act," *Armed Forces Comptroller* 56, no. 2 (Spring 2011): 8–10.

390. Ketrick et al., *Assessment of DOD Enterprise Resource Planning*, A-4; Speer, interview with author, February 5, 2018.

391. DOD, *Financial Improvement and Audit Readiness (FIAR) Plan Status Report* (May 2017), VI-2, VI-5, VI-9, VI-12.

392. Percell Group, LLC, "Executive Summary: Expeditionary Combat Support System Acquisition Incident Review Team Final Report" (Centerville, GA: Percell Group, LLC, 2013), 5, http://www.thepercellgroup.com/home/wp-content/uploads/2013/12/ecss_publicly_releasable.pdf.

393. Percell Group, 7.

394. United States Senate, *The Air Force's Expeditionary Combat Support System (ECSS): A Cautionary Tale on the Need for Business Process Reengineering and Complying with Acquisition Best Practices*, Staff Report (Washington, DC: Permanent Subcommittee on Investigations, Committee on Homeland Security and Government Affairs, July 7, 2014),

29–30, http://www.defensedaily.com/wp-content/uploads/2014/07/Senate-Permanent-Subcommittee-on-Investigations-Air-Force-ECSS.pdf.

395. Ketrick et al., *Assessment of DOD Enterprise Resource Planning*, A-5.

396. Ketrick et al., A-5. RICE objects refer to unique factors that complicate the implementation of new business systems: reports, interfaces, conversions, and enhancements.

397. DOD, *Financial Improvement and Audit Readiness (FIAR) Plan Status Report* (Washington, DC: Office of the Undersecretary of Defense [Comptroller]/Chief Financial Officer, May 2016), VII-26, https://comptroller.defense.gov/Portals/45/documents/fiar/FIAR_Plan_May_2016.pdf.

398. *Financial Management and Business Transformation at the Department of Defense*, S. Hrg. 112-297 (statement of Air Force Comptroller Jamie Morin), 64.

399. Gary Bliss, "Root Cause Analysis of the Expeditionary Combat Support System Program," memorandum for the under secretary of defense (AT&L) (Washington, DC: Office of the Under Secretary of Defense, August 28, 2013), 2, https://www.acq.osd.mil/parca/docs/2013-08-28-parca-rca-ecss.pdf.

400. Percell Group, "Executive Summary: Expeditionary Combat Support System," 1–4.

401. Bliss, "Root Cause Analysis of the Expeditionary Combat Support System," 3.

402. Bliss, 1.

403. *Financial Management and Business Transformation at the Department of Defense*, S. Hrg. 112-297 (statement of Senator McCaskill), 70–71. Six months later, the Air Force claimed to have reduced the number of planned interfaces to 230 but had managed to implement only two, on a pilot basis (GAO, *DOD Financial Management: Implementation Weaknesses in Army and Air Force Business Systems Could Jeopardize DOD's Auditability Goals*, GAO-12-134, 16).

404. *Financial Management and Business Transformation at the Department of Defense*, S. Hrg. 112-658 (statement of Air Force Comptroller Jamie M. Morin), 23–25.

405. GAO, *DOD Major Automated Information Systems: Improvements Can Be Made in Applying Leading Practices for Managing Risk and Testing*, GAO-17-322 (Washington, DC: GAO, March 2017), 46, https://www.gao.gov/assets/690/683831.pdf.

406. Bliss, "Root Cause Analysis of the Expeditionary Combat Support System," 3.

407. United States Senate, *The Air Force's Expeditionary Combat System (ECSS): A Cautionary Tale*, 7.

408. *Financial Management and Business Transformation at the Department of Defense*, S. Hrg. 112-658 (statement of Air Force Comptroller Jamie M. Morin), 25.

409. DOD, *Transforming Department of Defense Financial Management*, 13.

410. *Department of Defense Financial Management*, S. Hrg. 107-803 (statement of DOD Comptroller Dov Zakheim), 47.

411. *Winning the War on Financial Management—Status of Department of Defense Reform Efforts*, Serial No. 108-64 (statement of Deputy DOD Comptroller Larry Lanzillotta), 83.

412. *Winning the War on Financial Management* (statement of Mr. Granetto, director, Defense Financial Auditing Service, DOD Inspector General), 91.

413. Executive Office of the President of the United States, *A Blueprint for New Beginnings: A Responsible Budget for America's Priorities* (Washington, DC: Government Printing Office, 2001), 180, https://www.gpo.gov/fdsys/pkg/BUDGET-2002-BLUEPRINT/pdf/BUDGET-2002-BLUEPRINT.pdf.

414. Executive Office of the President of the United States, 180.

415. Office of Management and Budget, *The President's Management Agenda: Fiscal Year 2002* (Washington, DC: Government Printing Office, 2002), 20, https://georgewbush-whitehouse.archives.gov/omb/budget/fy2002/mgmt.pdf; Everson, "Financial Management and the President's Management Agenda," 11–12.

416. GAO, *Financial Management: Further Actions Are Needed to Establish Framework to Guide Audit Opinion and Business Management Improvement Efforts at DOD*, GAO-04-910R (Washington, DC: GAO, September 20, 2004), 2, https://www.gao.gov/assets/100/92890.pdf.

417. *Department of Defense Authorization for Appropriations for Fiscal Year 2005*, S. Hrg. 108-440, Pt. 3 (March 23, 2004) 166–67. Dr. Zakheim acknowledged that "at least one Service" signed up "quite reluctantly" (167).

418. *Business Process Modernization at the Department of Defense*, Serial No. 108-229 (statement of Deputy DOD Comptroller Larry Lanzillotta), 85.

419. *The Federal Government's Financial Statement and Accountability of Taxpayer Dollars at the Departments of Defense and Homeland Security*, S. Hrg. 108-660 (statement of Mr. Lanzillotta), 42.

420. GAO, *Financial Management: Further Actions Are Needed to Establish Framework to Guide Audit Opinion and Business Management Improvement Efforts at DOD*, GAO-04-910R, 3–4.

421. *The Status of Financial Management Reform within the Department of Defense and the Individual Services*, S. Hrg. 108-859 (statement of Comptroller General David M. Walker), 5, 108.

422. *Waging War on Waste: An Examination of DOD's Business Practices: Hearing Before the Oversight of Government Management, the Federal Workforce and the District of Columbia Subcommittee of the Committee on Homeland Security and Governmental Affairs, United States Senate*, S. Hrg. 109-172, 109th Cong. (April 28, 2005) (statement of Mr. Walker), 23.

423. Ronald W. Reagan National Defense Authorization Act for Fiscal Year 2005, Pub. L. 108-375, 118 Stat. 1811, 108th Cong. (2004), SEC. 352, https://www.gpo.gov/fdsys/pkg/PLAW-108publ375/pdf/PLAW-108publ375.pdf. See also National Defense Authorization Act for Fiscal Year 2005: Report of the Committee on Armed Services, House of Representatives, on H.R. 4200, H. Rep. No. 108-491, 108th Cong. (May 14, 2004), 292, https://www.gpo.gov/fdsys/pkg/CRPT-108hrpt491/pdf/CRPT-108hrpt491.pdf.

424. National Defense Authorization Act for Fiscal Year 2006, Pub. L. 109-163, SEC. 376.

425. National Defense Authorization Act for Fiscal Year 2006: Report to Accompany S. 1042, S. Rep. No. 109-60, 109th Cong. (2005), 282, https://www.congress.gov/109/crpt/srpt69/CRPT-109srpt69.pdf.

426. Gordon England, "Moving Forward with Improving Financial Management," memorandum for secretaries of the military departments (Washington, DC: Office of the Deputy Secretary of Defense, November 8, 2005).

427. *Financial Management at the Department of Defense: Hearing Before the Federal Financial Management, Government Information, and Internal Security Subcommittee of the Committee on Homeland Security and Governmental Affairs, United States Senate*, S. Hrg. 109-971, 109th Cong. (August 3, 2006) (statement of Deputy DOD Comptroller J. David Patterson), 18.

428. DOD, *Defense Financial Improvement and Audit Readiness Plan* (Washington, DC: Office of the Under Secretary of Defense Comptroller, December 2005), 27–65, https://comptroller.defense.gov/Portals/45/documents/fiar/FIAR_Plan_Dec_2005Complete.pdf.

429. GAO, *Defense Business Transformation: A Comprehensive Plan, Integrated Efforts, and Sustained Leadership Are Needed to Assure Success*," GAO-07-229T, 31.

430. DOD, *Defense Financial Improvement and Audit Readiness Plan* (Washington, DC: Office of the Under Secretary of Defense [Comptroller], September 30, 2007), https://comptroller.defense.gov/Portals/45/documents/fiar/FIAR_Plan_Sept_2007.pdf.

431. GAO, *Financial Management: Achieving Financial Statement Auditability in the Department of Defense*, GAO-09-373 (Washington, DC: GAO, May 2009), 4, https://www.gao.gov/assets/290/289253.pdf.

432. Gaddy, interview with author, February 21, 2018. Former DOD comptroller Bob Hale says that the initial FIAR plans were "just an accumulation of whatever the Services were working on anyway" (Hale, interview with author, January 24, 2018).

433. DOD, *Defense Financial Improvement and Audit Readiness Plan* (2007), v, 2.

434. Tina W. Jonas, "Reforming Financial Management at the Department of Defense," *Journal of Government Financial Management* 57, no. 3 (Fall 2008): 22.

435. Jonas, 2–4.

436. DOD, *Agency Financial Report for Fiscal Year 2009* (Washington, DC: Office of the Under Secretary of Defense [Comptroller], November 16, 2009), 22, https://comptroller.defense.gov/Portals/45/Documents/afr/fy2009/Fiscal_Year_2009_Department_of_Defense_Agencywide_Agency_Financial_Report.pdf. See also DOD Inspector General, *Summary of DOD Office of the Inspector General Audits of Financial Management*, Report No. D-2010-002 (Alexandria, VA: DOD, October 19, 2009), 113, http://www.dtic.mil/dtic/tr/fulltext/u2/a512880.pdf; Mary L. Ugone, "Financial Management Should Be Every Manager's Concern," *Armed Forces Comptroller* 55, no. 1 (Winter 2010): 16.

437. *Improving Financial and Business Management at the Department of Defense*, S. Hrg. 110-500, (October 16, 2007) (statement of Senator Coburn), 4.

438. *Nominations Before the Senate Armed Services Committee, First Session, 111th Congress*, S. Hrg. 111-362, January 15, 2009, 33.

439. GAO, *Department of Defense: Financial Management Improvement and Audit Readiness Efforts Continue to Evolve*, GAO-10-1059T (Washington, DC: GAO, September 29, 2010) (statement of Asif A. Khan, director, Financial Management and Assurance), 9–11, https://www.gao.gov/assets/130/125319.pdf.

440. *Improving Financial Accountability at the Department of Defense: Hearing Before the Federal Financial Management, Government Information, Federal Services, and International Security Subcommittee of the Committee on Homeland Security and Governmental Affairs, United States Senate*, S. Hrg. 111-1066, 111th Cong. (September 29, 2010) (statement of DOD Comptroller Robert F. Hale), 26, https://www.gpo.gov/fdsys/pkg/CHRG-111shrg63833/pdf/CHRG-111shrg63833.pdf.

441. *Improving Financial Accountability at the Department of Defense*, S. Hrg. 111-1066 (statement of DOD Comptroller Robert F. Hale), 8.

442. Hale, interview with author, January 24, 2018. See also Mark E. Easton, "DOD's Financial Audit Strategy: The Way Ahead," *Armed Forces Comptroller* 55, no. 1 (Winter 2010): 13–14.

443. Sam Stein, "Obama Deficit Commission Member Calls for Pentagon Audit," *Huffington Post*, May 26, 2010, https://www.huffingtonpost.com/2010/05/26/obama-deficit-commission_n_591111.html; HSGAC, *Improving Financial Accountability at the Department of Defense*, S. Hrg. 111-1066 (statement of Senator McCain), 3.

444. National Defense Authorization Act for Fiscal Year 2010, Report on H.R. 2647, H.R. No. 111-166, 111th Cong. (2009), SEC. 1052, https://www.congress.gov/111/crpt/hrpt166/CRPT-111hrpt166.pdf.

445. National Defense Authorization Act for Fiscal Year 2010, Pub. L. 111-84, 123 Stat. 2190, 111th Cong. (2009), SEC. 1003, https://www.congress.gov/111/plaws/publ84/PLAW-111publ84.pdf.

446. *Nominations Before the Senate Armed Services Committee, First Session, 112th Congress: Hearings Before the Committee on Armed Services, United States Senate*, S. Hrg. 112-149, 112th Cong. (June 9, 2011) (statement of Leon Panetta), 211, https://www.gpo.gov/fdsys/pkg/CHRG-112shrg74537/pdf/CHRG-112shrg74537.pdf.

447. Hale, interview with author, January 24, 2018.

448. *The Future of National Defense and the United States Military Ten Years After 9/11: Perspectives of Secretary of Defense Leon Panetta and Chairman of the Joint Chiefs of Staff General Martin Dempsey: Hearing Before the Committee on Armed Services, House of Representatives*, H.A.S.C. No. 112-76, 112th Cong. (October 13, 2011) (statement of Secretary of Defense Leon E. Panetta), 7, https://www.gpo.gov/fdsys/pkg/CHRG-112hhrg71447/pdf/CHRG-112hhrg71447.pdf.

449. DOD, *Financial Improvement and Audit Readiness (FIAR) Plan Status Report* (Washington, DC: Office of the Under Secretary of Defense [Comptroller]/CFO, May 2011), I-7–I-10, https://comptroller.defense.gov/Portals/45/documents/fiar/FIAR_Plan_May_2011.pdf.

450. *The Future of National Defense and the United States Military*, H.A.S.C. No. 112-76, (statement of Secretary of Defense Leon Panetta), 86–87.

451. *Financial Management and Business Transformation at the Department of Defense*, S. Hrg. 112-658 (statement of Air Force Comptroller Jamie M. Morin), 43.

452. National Defense Authorization Act for Fiscal Year 2012, Pub. L. 112-81, 125 Stat. 1298, 112th Cong. (2011), SEC. 1003, https://www.gpo.gov/fdsys/pkg/PLAW-112publ81/pdf/PLAW-112publ81.pdf.

453. GAO, *DOD Financial Management: Improvement Needed in DOD Components' Implementation of Audit Readiness Effort*, GAO-11-851. (Washington, DC: GAO, September 2011), 15, https://www.gao.gov/assets/330/323172.pdf; GAO, *DOD Financial Management: Ongoing Challenges in Implementing the Financial Improvement and Audit Readiness Plan*, GAO-11-932T, 8–9.

454. GAO, *DOD Financial Management: Ongoing Challenges with Reconciling Navy and Marine Corps Fund Balance with Treasury*, GAO-12-132 (Washington, DC: GAO, December 2011), 10–13, https://www.gao.gov/assets/590/587213.pdf; GAO, *DOD Financial Management: Ongoing Challenges in Implementing the Financial Improvement and Audit Readiness Plan*, GAO-11-932T, 13–14.

455. *Financial Management and Business Transformation at the Department of Defense*, S. Hrg. 112-658 (statement of Navy Comptroller Gladys Commons), 107.

456. John Chadwick, "Lead, Follow, or Get Out of the Way," *Armed Forces Comptroller* 51, no. 1 (Winter 2006): 19.

457. *DOD's Plans for Financial Management Improvement and Achieving Audit Readiness*, H.A.S.C. No. 112-59 (statement of DOD Comptroller Robert Hale), 13.

458. GAO, *DOD Financial Management: Marine Corps Statement of Budgetary Resources Audit Results and Lessons Learned*, GAO-11-830 (Washington, DC: GAO, September 2011), Highlights, https://www.gao.gov/assets/330/323281.pdf.

459. GAO, 9.

460. GAO, 31.

461. John A. Knubel, "The CFO Act Financial Audit Process: A Unique Tool in DOD's Efficiency Toolbox," *Armed Forces Comptroller* 56, no. 3 (Summer 2011): 32. See also Alex Hardisson, "Marine Corps Audit Journey: A Look Back and a Leap Forward," *Armed Forces Comptroller* 56, no. 2 (Spring 2011): 16–18.

462. Knubel, "The CFO Act Financial Audit Process," 32–33.

463. GAO, *DOD Financial Management: Marine Corps Statement of Budgetary Resources Audit Results and Lessons Learned*, GAO-11-830, 10.

464. GAO, *DOD Financial Management: Ongoing Challenges in Implementing the Financial Improvement and Audit Readiness Plan*, GAO-11-932T, 12; *Financial Management and Business Transformation at the Department of Defense*, S. Hrg. 112-658 (statement of Asif Khan of GAO), 38.

465. GAO, *DOD Financial Management: Actions Are Needed on Audit Issues Related to the Marine Corps' 2012 Schedule of Budgetary Activity*, GAO-15-198, 8–9.

466. Audit the Pentagon Act of 2012, S. Rep. No. 3487, 112th Cong. (introduced August 2, 2012), https://www.gpo.gov/fdsys/pkg/BILLS-112s3487is/pdf/BILLS-112s3487is.pdf.

467. Tom Coburn, "Why We Must Audit the Pentagon," *Washington Examiner*, August 18, 2012, https://www.washingtonexaminer.com/why-we-must-audit-the-pentagon.

468. National Defense Authorization Act for Fiscal Year 2013, Pub. L. 112-239, SEC. 1007.

469. National Defense Authorization Act for Fiscal Year 2013, Conference Report to Accompany H.R. 4310, H. Rep. 112-705, 112th Cong. (2012), 845, https://www.congress.gov/112/crpt/hrpt705/CRPT-112hrpt705.pdf.

470. Speer, interview with author, February 5, 2018. See also DOD, *Financial Improvement and Audit Readiness (FIAR) Plan Status Report* (Washington, DC: Office of the Undersecretary of Defense (Comptroller)/Chief Financial Officer, May 2013), A4-4, https://comptroller.defense.gov/Portals/45/documents/fiar/FIAR_Plan_May_2013.pdf.

471. *Improving Financial Management at the Department of Defense: Hearing Before the Committee on Homeland Security and Governmental Affairs, United States Senate*, S. Hrg. 113-753, 113th Cong. (May 13, 2004), 23, https://www.gpo.gov/fdsys/pkg/CHRG-113shrg89683/pdf/CHRG-113shrg89683.pdf.

472. Hale, interview with author, January 24, 2018.

473. GAO, *DOD Financial Management: Actions Are Needed on Audit Issues Related to the Marine Corps' 2012 Schedule of Budgetary Activity*, GAO-15-198, 53.

474. DOD Inspector General, "Statement of the Honorable Jon T. Rymer Inspector General, Department of Defense Before the Senate Homeland Security and Governmental Affairs Committee on 'Improving Financial Accountability at the Department of Defense'" (Washington, DC: DOD, May 13, 2014), 3, https://media.defense.gov/2017/Apr/18/2001734039/-1/-1/1/DODIGTESTIMONYHSGAC-FINANCIAL ACCOUNTABILITY.PDF.

475. DOD, "Secretary of Defense Speech: Audit Recognition Ceremony," speech of Chuck Hagel (Washington, DC: The Pentagon, February 6, 2014), http://archive.defense.gov/Speeches/Speech.aspx?SpeechID=1829.

476. GAO, *DOD Financial Management: Actions Are Needed on Audit Issues Related to the Marine Corps' 2012 Schedule of Budgetary Activity*, GAO-15-198, 50.

477. Hope Hodge Seck, "Pentagon Withdraws Marine Corps Audit Approval," *Marine Times*, March 23, 2015, https://www.marinecorpstimes.com/news/pentagon-congress/2015/03/23/pentagon-withdraws-marine-corps-audit-approval/.

478. GAO, *DOD Financial Management: Actions Are Needed on Audit Issues Related to the Marine Corps' 2012 Schedule of Budgetary Activity*, GAO-15-198, 18, 65.

479. Charles Grassley, "Marine Corps Audit," *Congressional Record* 161, no. 125 (August 4, 2015): S6254, https://www.congress.gov/crec/2015/08/04/CREC-2015-08-04-senate.pdf.

480. *Department of Defense Auditability Challenges: Hearing Before the Subcommittee on Oversight and Investigations of the Committee on Armed Services, House of Representatives*, H.A.S.C. No. 112-157, 112th Cong. (September 14, 2012) (statement of Army Comptroller Mary Sally Matiella), 7, https://www.hsdl.org/?view&did=740918.

481. *Department of Defense Auditability Challenges* (statement of Navy Comptroller Gladys J. Commons), 8.

482. *Department of Defense Auditability Challenges* (statement of Marilyn M. Thomas, principal deputy assistant secretary for financial management and comptroller, Department of the Air Force), 10.

483. Jimaye Sones and Barbara Crawford, "Takeaways from a Successful Audit," *Armed Forces Comptroller* 57, no. 3 (Summer 2012): 24–27; Doug Bennett, "FIAR in Seven Easy Steps (or Abandon Hope, All Ye Who Enter—NOT!)," *Armed Forces Comptroller* 57, no. 3 (Summer 2012): 33–35; Richard Gustafson, "Audit Ready Every Day!" *Armed Forces Comptroller* 57, no. 3 (Summer 2012): 38–41.

484. Robert Maitner, "Department of Defense—Moving Toward Financial Statement Auditability: Will It Happen?" *Armed Forces Comptroller* 58, no. 1 (Winter 2013): 44, (quoting Army director of audit readiness Jim Watkins).

485. DOD Inspector General, "Statement of the Honorable Jon T. Rymer Inspector General, Department of Defense," 7. See also DOD Inspector General, *Summary of DOD Office of the Inspector General Audits*, 2–4.

486. GAO, *DOD Financial Management: Effect of Continuing Weaknesses on Management and Operations and Status of Key Challenges*, GAO-14-576T, 19.

487. GAO, 20.

488. GAO, 26. See also GAO, *DOD Financial Management: The Defense Finance and Accounting Service Needs to Fully Implement Financial Improvements for Contract Pay*, GAO-14-10 (Washington, DC: GAO, June 2014), https://www.gao.gov/assets/670/664318.pdf. See also DOD Inspector General, *Army Financial Improvement Plans Generally Managed Effectively, but Better Contract Management Needed*, Report No. DODIG-2014-056 (Alexandria, VA: DOD, April 8, 2014), 6, https://media.defense.gov/2014/Apr/08/2001713362/-1/-1/1/DODIG-2014-056.pdf. See also DOD Inspector General, *Improvements Needed in the General Fund Enterprise Business System Budget-to-Report Business Process*, Report No. DODIG-2014-090 (Alexandria, VA: DOD, July 2, 2014), 4, https://media.defense.gov/2014/Jul/02/2001713378/-1/-1/1/DODIG-2014-090.pdf.

489. DOD Inspector General, "Statement of the Honorable Jon T. Rymer Inspector General, Department of Defense," 7. See also DOD Inspector General, *Summary of DOD Office of the Inspector General Audits*, 8. See also GAO, *DOD Financial Management: Effect of Continuing Weaknesses on Management and Operations and Status of Key Challenges*, GAO-14-576T, 24, 28–29. See also GAO, *DOD Financial Management: Actions Under Way Need to Be Successfully Completed to Address Long-Standing Funds Control Weaknesses*, GAO-14-94 (Washington, DC: GAO, April 2014), https://www.gao.gov/assets/670/662798.pdf.

490. *Improving Financial Management at the Department of Defense*, S. Hrg. 113-753 (statement of Senator Coburn), 5.

491. *Improving Financial Management at the Department of Defense* (statement of Senator Johnson), 26.

492. *Improving Financial Management at the Department of Defense* (statement of Acting Army Comptroller Robert Speer), 36. See also Al Runnels, "Interview of the Honorable Lisa S. Disbrow, Assistant Secretary of the Air Force (Financial Management & Comptroller) (SAF/FM)," *Armed Forces Comptroller* 59, no. 4 (Fall 2014): 22–25.

493. Speer, interview with author, February 5, 2018.

494. For example, Department of the Army, *Fiscal Year 2016 United States Army General Fund Schedule of Budgetary Activity Report* (Washington, DC: Office of the Assistant Secretary of the Army [Financial Management & Comptroller]), 2016), 7–8, https://media.defense.gov/2016/Nov/14/2001714291/-1/-1/1/DODIG-2017-021.pdf. See also Department of the Navy, *United States Navy: Fiscal Year 2016 Schedule of Budgetary Activity* (Washington, DC: Assistant Secretary of the Navy Financial Management and Comptroller, 2016), 32–33, http://www.secnav.navy.mil/fmc/fmo/Documents/FY16-SBA-AFR.pdf; Department of the Air Force, *United States Air Force Schedule of Budgetary Activity*, FY

2015 (Washington, DC: Principal Deputy Assistant Secretary of the Air Force [Financial Management and Comptroller], 2015), 22–23, http://www.saffm.hq.af.mil/Portals/84/documents/financial_statements/AFD-151123-039.pdf?ver=2016-08-09-091637-697.

495. DOD, *Financial Improvement and Audit Readiness (FIAR) Plan Status Report* (May 2016), II-3 (Army), III-3 (Navy), IV-3 (Air Force). See also *Department of Defense Update on the Financial Improvement and Audit Readiness Plan*, H.A.S.C. No. 114-126 (statement of Navy Comptroller Susan J. Rabern), 6–7.

496. DOD, *Financial Improvement and Audit Readiness (FIAR) Plan Status Report* (Washington, DC: Office of the Undersecretary of Defense [Comptroller]/Chief Financial Officer, November 2016), ES-7, ES-8, I-1, I-2, I-3, https://comptroller.defense.gov/Portals/45/documents/fiar/FIAR_Plan_November_2016.pdf.

497. *Department of Defense Update on the Financial Improvement and Audit Readiness Plan*, H.A.S.C. No. 114-126 (statement of DOD Comptroller Michael McCord), 24.

498. DOD Inspector General, *Army General Fund Adjustments Not Adequately Documented or Supported*, Report No. DODIG-2016-113 (Alexandria, VA: DOD, July 26, 2016), 4, https://media.defense.gov/2016/Jul/26/2001714261/-1/-1/1/DODIG-2016-113.pdf.

499. Scot J. Paltrow, "U.S. Army Fudged Its Accounts by Trillions of Dollars, Auditor Finds," *Reuters*, August 19, 2016, https://www.reuters.com/article/us-usa-audit-army/u-s-army-fudged-its-accounts-by-trillions-of-dollars-auditor-finds-idUSKCN10U1IG. The article quoted a former Defense IG official, who stated, "They don't know what the heck the balances should be."

500. Jamie Crawford, "Audit Reveals Army's Trillion-Dollar Accounting Gaffes," *CNN*, August 23, 2016, https://www.cnn.com/2016/08/23/politics/us-army-audit-accounting-errors/index.html.

501. Charles Grassley, "Auditing the Books of the Department of Defense," *Congressional Record* 162, no. 109 (July 7, 2016): S4841–S4843, https://www.congress.gov/crec/2016/07/07/CREC-2016-07-07-senate.pdf.

502. Grassley, S4843.

503. Tony Bertuca, "Pentagon Comptroller: Massive DOD Audit Effort to Drive Reform," *Inside Defense*, October 30, 2017, https://insidedefense.com/daily-news/pentagon-comptroller-massive-dod-audit-effort-drive-reform.

504. David Norquist, "Nomination Hearing—Under Secretary of Defense (Comptroller): Opening Statement" (Washington, DC: United States Congress, Senate Armed Services Committee, May 9, 2017), 3, https://www.armed-services.senate.gov/imo/media/doc/Norquist_05-09-17.pdf.

505. David Norquist, "Advanced Policy Questions for David Norquist" (May 9, 2017), 3–4, https://www.armed-services.senate.gov/imo/media/doc/Norquist_APQs_05-09-17.pdf.

506. Bertuca, "Pentagon Comptroller: Massive DOD Audit." See also Norquist, "Pentagon Comptroller: Using the Audit"; Charles S. Clark, "Pentagon IG Offers Details of Biggest Audit Ever," *Government Executive*, January 8, 2018, https://www.govexec.com/management/2018/01/pentagon-ig-offers-details-biggest-audit-ever/145045/; Tony Bertuca, "Lawmakers Welcome New DOD Audit, but Say It 'Will Not Be Pretty.'" *Inside De-*

fense, January 10, 2018, https://insidedefense.com/inside-navy/lawmakers-welcome-new-dod-audit-say-it-will-not-be-pretty.

507. David Norquist, Letter to Michael Enzi, Chairman, Senate Budget Committee (March 6, 2018), https://www.budget.senate.gov/imo/media/doc/OSD002067-18%20USDC%20Norquist%20Response%20to%20Sen%20Enzi%208%20Feb%202018%20Ltr%20on%20DLA%20Au....pdf.

508. For example, a limited SBA audit of the Army "triggered more than 17,500 formal auditor requests, requiring the Army to provide over 26,000 documents" in 2015 (DOD, *Financial Improvement and Audit Readiness (FIAR) Plan Status Report* (Washington, DC: Office of the Undersecretary of Defense [Comptroller]/Chief Financial Officer, November 2015), ES-2, https://comptroller.defense.gov/Portals/45/documents/fiar/FIAR_Plan_November_2015.pdf.

509. Senate Budget Committee, "Hearing on the Pentagon Audit and Business Operations Overhaul" (Washington, DC: United States Senate, March 7, 2018), http://www.cq.com/doc/congressionaltranscripts-5277809?0.

510. Aitoro, "So We're Celebrating the Pentagon's Failed Audit?"

511. *Independent Auditor's Report on the Department of Defense FY 2018 and FY 2018 Basic Financial Statements*, November 15, 2018, in *Department of Defense Annual Financial Report, Fiscal Year 2018*, 126–37, https://comptroller.defense.gov/Portals/45/Documents/afr/fy2018/DoD_FY18_Agency_Financial_Report.pdf.

512. See Thomas Spoehr, "The Unaffordable Pentagon Audit," *National Interest*, December 27, 2017, http://nationalinterest.org/feature/the-unaffordable-pentagon-audit-23784.

513. Anti-Deficiency Act, Pub. L. 97-258, 96 Stat. 877, 97th Cong. (1982), https://www.gpo.gov/fdsys/pkg/STATUTE-96/pdf/STATUTE-96-Pg877.pdf.

AFTERWORD

1. Jared Serbu, "DoD Stands Up 9 Teams to Look for Cost Savings via Shared Services, Business Reforms," *Federal News Network*, March 8, 2018, https://federalnewsnetwork.com/defense-main/2018/03/dod-stands-up-9-teams-to-look-for-cost-savings-via-shared-services-business-reforms/.

2. *FY 2018-FY2022 National Defense Business Operations Plan Appendices*, April 9, 2018, A-47–A-66, https://cmo.defense.gov/Portals/47/Documents/Publications/NBDOP/TAB%20B%20FY18-22%20NDBOP%20Appendices.pdf?ver=2018-05-25-131454-683.

3. Gordon Lubold, "Mattis Plans to Remove Pentagon's Chief Management Officer," *Wall Street Journal*, September 5, 2018, https://www.wsj.com/articles/mattis-plans-to-remove-pentagons-chief-management-officer-1536181817.

4. Jared Serbu, "Congress Creates New DoD Chief Management Officer, Punts on Role of CIO," *Federal News Network*, December 12, 2016, https://federalnewsnetwork.com/defense/2016/12/congress-creates-new-dod-chief-management-officer-punts-role-cio/.

INDEX

A-12 program (Navy), 114
Abell, Charles, 41
accrual-based accounting, 153, 161–63, 172, 288n60
Acquisition Agility Act (HASC), 143
Acquisition Demonstration (Acq Demo) project, 35–37, 45, 56, 66, 77–78
"Acquisition Excellence," 124
Acquisition Executive, 109, 113, 145
Acquisition Improvement Program (Carlucci Initiatives), 23, 85, 94–99, 109, 128, 137, 139–40
acquisition system: "contract definition" phase, 90; formal process of, 88–89; fraud in, 89, 102; need for reform, 87; oversight and review, 91, 96, 119, 128, 137, 147; reforms of, 24, 101, 113; review by Gordon England, 128, 129–30
Acquisition Task Force, 108
acquisition workforce: development fund for, 157; downsizing of, 6, 20, 87, 121–22, 142; pay-banding approach to, 35–36; rightsizing of, 147; understaffed, undertrained, 91–92, 105; unrealistic expectations for, 141
across-the-board cuts, 3
AEHF (Advanced Extremely High Frequency) Satellite System, 127
"affordability caps," 134
AFGE (American Federation of Government Employees), 47, 61, 68, 72, 77, 241n143
AIP (Acquisition Improvement Program) (Carlucci Initiatives), 23, 85, 94–99, 109, 128, 137, 139–40

Air Force, Department of the, 204; accountant theft from, 180; auditable financial statement attempts, 150, 159, 163, 177–79, 183, 213–14; DEAMS program, 196, 203; and DIMHRS software, 198; and DJAS, 168; ECSS program, 196, 202–4; ERPs, 198, 202–4; hiring, retention issues, 33–34, 132, 225; immature technology funding, 124; independent review of, 127; intra-agency transactions, 157–58; legacy system interfaces, 203, 311n403; "lightning bolt" initiatives, 120; McCain hearings, 129; MDAPs, 125–26; military equipment plan, 210; no configuration management system, 193; reliance on obsolete systems, 210; Space-Based Infrared System, 123; spare parts prices, 100–101; tanker leases, 126; TSPR contracts, 122–23
Akaka, Daniel, 190, 199
alternative source requirements, 105–6, 141
American Federation of Government Employees (AFGE), 47, 61, 68, 72, 77, 241n143
Analyses of Alternatives (AoAs), 127, 133, 147
Anthony, Robert, 153, 163
Anti-Deficiency Act, 183, 218
Anton, Philip S., 128
AoAs (analyses of alternatives), 127, 133, 147
appointee turnover, 92
Army, Department of the: accounting code example, 159; architectural framework issues, 193; asserting audit

Army (*continued*)
readiness, 213; auditable financial statement attempts, 150, 159, 163, 179–81, 210, 213–15; and DIMHRS software, 198; ERPs, 198, 204, 220; FCS (Future Combat Systems), 126, 129, 131, 146; GCSS-A, 196; GFEBS (General Fund Enterprise Business System), 196, 202; "ghost" soldier fraud, 180; Heidi Shyu testimony, 145; incomplete specs for architectural environment, 193; IPPS-A, 202; legacy systems, 202; LMP (Logistics Modernization Program), 196–97; Mark Milley statement, 145; McCain hearings, 129; MDAPs termination, 128; Office of Business Transformation, 202; outside audit of, 179–80; questioning audit goal, 154; recruitment issues, 33; spare parts issue, 101; Terminal High-Altitude Area Defense, 123; useless software, 160–61; Wedtech scandal, 11
"as-is" structures, 187–90, 193
Atwood, Donald, 20, 114, 165, 170–72
auditable financial statements, 151–54, 204, 216–19; 2002 attempt, 208; 2004 attempt, 206; 2007 attempt, 205–6; 2010 attempt, 210–11; 2014 goal, 210; 2017 goal, 209; 2018 attempt disclaimers, 150; Air Force attempts, 150, 159, 163, 177–79, 183, 213–14; for all federal agencies, 181–82; alternative to, 223; Alvin Tucker on, 181; Army attempts, 150, 159, 163, 179–81, 210, 213–15; versus balance sheets, 178–79; billions-of-dollars discrepancies, 178; Bob Hale on, 208–9; Bob Speer on, 214; calls for, 162–63; CFO Act (1990) requiring, 150, 154, 163; Clinton administration, 181; DOD as "unauditable," 150, 155–56, 181–83, 186; FIAR (Financial Improvement and Audit Readiness) plan, 207–9, 213–14, 313n432; as GAO goal, 149; G. W. Bush administration, 205; legislation mandating, 163; linked problems impeding, 151; manual record reviews, 183; Michael Donley on, 179; Navy attempts, 150, 183–84, 210–11, 213–14; partial solutions approach to, 151; Patrick Shanahan on, 216; questionable value of, 220–22; Ron Johnson on, 214; separate budget and accounting, 163; separate systems' issue, 163; trillions-of-dollars adjustments, 185; "try harder" approaches to, 152; wide support for, 162–63; as wrong goal, 153–55, 185, 223
auditing for auditability, 18, 151, 177–86, 204–16, 219
Audit the Pentagon Act (2012), 211
Augustine, Norman, 95
author: as DCMO, 2–4; in Senate, 5–7, 13, 18
Authorization for Use of Military Force (2001), 37
AWACS aircraft, 99

balanced budget requirement, 164
BBP (Better Buying Power) initiative, 134–37, 144, 146
BCA (Budget Control Act of 2011), 2
BEA (Business Enterprise Architecture), 151, 186–94, 201, 219, 223
BENS (Business Executives for National Security), 92
Berteau, David, 113, 266–67n180
"best customer pricing," 104
Betti, John, 114
"big bang" approach to reform, 76, 77, 79
bipartisan efforts, 138–39; breakdown of, 13–14; civilian personnel reforms, 23, 29; Collins-Levin bill, 14, 41–44; FASA (Federal Acquisition Streamlining Act of 1994), 12, 117–18, 120–21, 139; Goldwater-Nichols Act (1986), 7–10, 130; Lobbying Disclosure Act (1995), 12; NSPS attempts, 27, 40–44, 48, 71–72; Packard Commission, 139; in SASC, 13;

WSARA-era reforms, 138–39. *See also* consensus building
bite-sized reforms, 24
"blank check" concerns, 19
BMMP (Business Management Modernization Program), 189, 192
Bowsher, Charles, 95, 149, 161–62, 288n60
BPR (business process reengineering), 155, 169, 200–201, 220
Bradley Fighting Vehicle, 99
Brinkley, Paul, 191, 197
broadbanding, 57
BSM (Business Systems Modernization program), DLA, 196–97
BTA (Business Transformation Agency), 153, 197–98, 220
Budget Control Act of 2011 (BCA), 2
budgeting and accounting systems, 161–64
"Budgeting to Likely Cost," 96
Bush, (George W.) administration: BEA grand design, 186–87; *Blueprint for New Beginnings,* 205; deregulating acquisition system, 123–24; improved audit opinions under, 207–8; and NSPS, 22–23, 26, 29, 45, 52, 76–77; and pay-banding approach, 38; rejecting bipartisanship, 14, 23, 42–44; weapons systems acquisition issues, 18
Bush (George H. W.) administration, 6, 113, 163–65
Business Enterprise Architecture (BEA), 151, 186–94, 201, 219, 223
Business Executives for National Security (BENS), 92
Business Management Modernization Program (BMMP), 189, 192
business process reengineering (BPR), 155, 169, 200–201, 220
business rules, 58, 65, 73–74, 78, 191–92, 198
Business Systems Modernization program (BSM), DLA, 196–97
Business Transformation Agency (BTA), 153, 197–98, 220

Byrd, Robert, 187, 199

C-5A aircraft, 99
C-130J program, 129
CAIG (Cost Analysis Improvement Group), 139
calendar-driven goals, 51, 209, 218–19
California National Guard, 20
"capability gap analysis" need, 192
CAPE (Director of Cost Assessment and Performance Evaluation), 139
"Cap the Knife." *See* Weinberger, Caspar
Carlucci Initiatives (Acquisition Improvement Program), 23, 85, 94–99, 109, 128, 137, 139–40
Carson, Brad, 16, 77
Carson, Johnny, 102
Carter, Ashton, 15–16, 20, 77–78, 133–34
case studies, 22–25
CFO Act (Chief Financial Officers Act of 1990), 18, 150, 154–55, 163, 178–79, 181, 205
Chapter 71 (Title 5, United States Code), 41–42, 44
chart of Pentagon information systems, 189
charts of accounts, 160, 162
checklist mentality, 145
Cheney, Dick, 40, 113–14, 172, 270n230
China Lake Project, 32–35
Chu, David, 38–40, 45, 48–49
CICA (Competition in Contracting Act of 1984), 18, 103, 137
CIM (Corporate Information Management) program: abandoned, 188, 191, 219; compared to BEA, 188, 194; compared to BMMP, 189; compared to DIMHRS, 198; DMRD 925 establishing, 165; Don Shycoff on, 167–68; focusing on "migratory" solutions, 166–67; as ground-up solution, 151–52, 165, 223; John Hamre on, 168–69; mixed record of, 169–70; Zakheim and Lanzillotta on, 191

CIO Digital Magazine, 195–96
Civil Service Reform Act of 1978 (CSRA), 6, 31–32, 54–55
civil service system: Brad Carson on, 77–78; China Lake alternative to, 32–34; criticisms of, 27, 31–32, 77; CSRA (Civil Service Reform Act of 1978), 6, 31–32, 54–55; Homeland Security Act waivers of, 37; job protections in, 37, 79; Lab Demo (laboratory demonstration) program, 32–37, 45, 56, 66–67, 77–78; necessary complexity of, 28; NSPS versus, 40–41, 63, 74; pay-for-performance versus seniority in, 16, 36; reforms within, 22–24, 78–80; replacement of, 36; role of, 30–31; transparency and regularity in, 80; waiving of statutes, 37, 41–42. *See also* NSPS; pay banding
clean audit: 1990s attempt, 204; 2006 FIAR attempt, 207; 2018 attempt, 150; BEA approach, 188; David Norquist on, 216; DHS successful, 215; Dov Zakheim on, 205; as goal, 156–64, 216, 223; as questionable goal, 220–22. *See also* auditable financial statements
Clinton administration: bipartisanship under, 12; and CIM program, 168–69; DSB Task Force, 176; National Performance Review, 32, 55, 117; reform efforts of, 20, 86
CMO (chief management officer), 200–203, 211, 224, 226
Coburn, Tom, 208, 211–12, 214
coffee pots ($6,000), 102
Cohen, William, 94
COLAs (cost of living increases), 60, 63, 72
Cold War end, 106, 115, 176, 270n233
collective bargaining: in Collins bill, 41–44; versus "consultation," 49; G. W. Bush administration and, 29, 40–42; labor relations paper (2004), 46–47; NSPS and, 50, 67–73, 76; Obama administration and, 73–74
Collins, Susan, 14, 29, 41–44, 48, 71
Combating Terrorism, Office of, 37
command, chain of, 9, 14, 109, 112–14, 144
commercial items purchases: "best customer pricing" for, 104; contrasted with weapons systems, 141; delayed implementation of, 85–86, 131, 138; FASA exemptions for, 117–18; limiting, 131; military bias against, 116; military specifications for, 6, 17, 24, 85–86; PBA and, 122; savings from use of, 118–19; Section 800 Panel, 116–17
commercial off-the-shelf (COTS) products, 7, 17, 84, 195, 198, 203–4
commissary reform, 4
Commons, Gladys, 210
Competition in Contracting Act of 1984 (CICA), 18, 103, 137
concurrent development, testing, manufacturing, 125–26
consensus building, 8, 10–11, 15, 27, 130, 226. *See also* bipartisan efforts
consolidated financial statements, 179, 184
"Conspiracy of Hope," 128
consultation versus collective bargaining, 3, 41, 47, 49
Coopers & Lybrand study, 119–20
Corporate Information Management program. *See* CIM
corporate jets, 102
cost accounting system goal, 173
Cost Analysis Improvement Group (CAIG), 139
cost assessment and program evaluation (D/CAPE), 133
Costello, Robert, 113
cost estimates: in early 80s, 99–107; Grace Commission, 91, 96; improvements in, 97, 109, 124–25, 131, 216; independent (ICE), 96, 132, 134; McNicol on, 92, 124; Norquist on, 215–16; overly optimistic,

125, 127, 139, 141; Packard Commission on, 24, 85, 108–9; Tinker Air Force Base issues, 100
cost of living increases (COLAs), 60, 63, 72
COTS (commercial off-the-shelf) products, 7, 17, 84, 195, 198, 203–4
counterfeit parts, 6
country club, resort fees, 102
Critical Infrastructure Protection Board, 37
cross-functional teams, 4, 10–11, 150, 200
CSRA (Civil Service Reform Act of 1978), 6, 31–32, 54–55
cyber workforce, 9, 24, 30, 78

DAB (Defense Acquisition Board), 91, 110–12
DAI (Defense Agencies Initiative), 197
DAPA (Defense Acquisition Performance Assessment of 2006), 91
data calls, 155, 190, 218
data definitions, 155, 217–18
Davis, Dan, 128
Davis, Tom, 40, 45
DBB (Defense Business Board), 1–5, 74–76
DBOF (Defense Business Operations Fund), 153, 165, 170–77, 220
DBSMC (Defense Business Systems Management Committee), 153, 201, 220
DCAA (Defense Contract Audit Agency), 89, 106
D/CAPE (cost assessment and program evaluation), 133
DC Circuit Court of Appeals, 70–71
DCD (DFAS Corporate Database), 194–95
DCIPS (Defense Civilian Intelligence Personnel System), 77–78
DCMO (Deputy Chief Management Officer), 2, 153, 199–201, 220, 224–26, viii
Deadeye program, 111
DEAMS (Defense Enterprise Accounting and Management System), 196, 203
"death spiral," 176
Defense Acquisition Board (DAB), 91, 110–12
Defense Acquisition Performance Assessment of 2006 (DAPA), 91
Defense Agencies Initiative (DAI), 197
Defense Business Board (DBB), 1–5, 74–76
Defense Business Operations Fund (DBOF), 153, 165, 170–77, 220
Defense Business Systems Management Committee (DBSMC), 153, 201, 220
Defense Civilian Emerging Leader Program, 75
Defense Civilian Intelligence Personnel System (DCIPS), 77–78
Defense Contract Audit Agency (DCAA), 89, 106
Defense Contract Management Agency, 21
Defense Enterprise Accounting and Management System (DEAMS), 196, 203
Defense Finance and Accounting Service. *See* DFAS
Defense Integrated Military Human Resources System (DIMHRS), 197–98
Defense Joint Accounting System (DJAS), 168–69
defense laboratories, 24, 27, 33–35
Defense Logistics Agency (DLA), 24, 104–5, 157, 167, 196–97, 210, 220
Defense Management Review Decisions (DMRDs), 20, 164–65
Defense POW/MIA Accounting Agency, 21
Defense Science Board (DSB), 31, 34–36, 95, 123, 132, 176
Defense Security Cooperation Agency, 21
Defense Systems Acquisition Review Council (DSARC), 91

Defense Systems Management College, 120
Defense Threat Reduction Agency, 21
Defense Transformation for the 21st Century Act, 39
Defense Travel System (DTS), 197
Deficit Reduction Act (Gramm-Rudman-Hollings, 1985), 164
DeLauer, Richard, 102
demonstration projects, 30, 32; Acq Demo, 35–37, 45, 56, 66, 77–78; China Lake, 32–35; defense laboratories, 27; Force of the Future, 77; Lab Demo, 34–37, 45, 56, 66–67, 77–78; pay banding in, 38
Department of Homeland Security (DHS), 28, 37, 70, 215
Deputy Chief Management Officer (DCMO), 2, 153, 199–201, 220, 224–26; viii
deputy secretary (DOD), 14–15, 199, 226
Deputy's Management Action Group (DMAG), 15, 231n38
deregulation of acquisitions, 123
DFAS (Defense Finance and Accounting Service): consolidating responsibilities, 155, 167, 220; DCD (DFAS Corporate Database), 194–95; and DJAS, 168–69; establishment of, 170–72; financial management review on, 165; initial resistance to, 177; and loss of institutional knowledge, 172; partial successes of, 182, 204; purchase of services from, 157; reducing unmatched disbursements, 182; transfer to Department of Treasury, 211; use of transitional systems, 219–20; work on DBOF suspended, 174
DHS (Department of Homeland Security), 28, 37, 70, 215
DIMHRS (Defense Integrated Military Human Resources System), 197–98
direct hire authority, 79
Director of Cost Assessment and Performance Evaluation (CAPE), 139

Director of Operational Test and Evaluation (DOT&E), 85, 137, 139
disclaimers of opinion on audits, 150, 210–11, 214, 216, 222
Divad air-defense system, 99
DJAS (Defense Joint Accounting System), 168–69
DLA (Defense Logistics Agency), 24, 104–5, 157, 167, 196–97, 210, 220
DMAG (Deputy's Management Action Group), 15, 231n38
DMRDs (Defense Management Review Decisions), 20, 164–65
DOD (Department of Defense), 224–25; can't close down for audit, 191; conflict with OPM, 38; congressional distrust of, 103; current state of business systems, 217–19; decision-making authority of, 14–15, 42; goals of not financial, 153; as its own economy, 156; waiving of laws by, 39; wasted efforts by, 218.
Dodaro, Gene, 185
DODD 5000.1, 114
DOD IG (DOD Inspector General): audits, 150, 184–86, 205, 211–15, 318n499; on "color of money," 158; on DFAS, 168–69; on ERP, 196; investigating contractors, 103; spare parts sourcing, 105; on workforce reductions, 121
Dominguez, Michael, 51, 67
Donley, Michael, 179
DOT&E (Director of Operational Test and Evaluation), 85, 137, 139
Douglass, John, 107
Druyun, Darleen, 120, 126
DSARC (Defense Systems Acquisition Review Council), 91
DSB (Defense Science Board), 31, 34–36, 95, 123, 132, 176
DTS (Defense Travel System), 197

Earned Value Management System, 202

ECSS (Expeditionary Combat Support System), 146, 196, 202–4, 210
"Edsel gap" comparison, 99
ELG (Executive Level Group), 165–66
employee appeals, 29, 39, 41–43, 66, 74, 79
employee motivation, 35, 53
employees as allies, 80
England, Gordon: acquisition review by, 128–30; as acting deputy secretary, 130, 197; BTA to address stovepipe issues, 197; as CMO, 200; FIAR plans, 207; Levin, Warner statements to, 129; and NSPS, 49–52, 54, 59, 67, 71, 73
Ensign, John, 199
enterprise licensing, 3
entertainment billing, 102–3
environmental law waivers, 37, 39
ERPs (Enterprise Resource Programs), 24, 308n363; in Air Force, 198, 202–4; in Army, 202–4, 220; consolidating responsibility, 220; "converged ERP" program, 196; DLA, 220; as "Expense, Regret, Pain," 196; implementation difficulties, declared dead, 195; improvements over legacy systems, 155, 217; lack of authority, 199; mixed success of, 204, 217, 220, 223; in Navy, 198, 201–2, 204, 220; technical and schedule difficulties, 197–99
Evolved Expendable Launch Vehicle, 132
Executive Level Group (ELG), 165–66
Expeditionary Combat Support System (ECSS), 146, 196, 202–4, 210

FAR (Federal Acquisition Regulation), 92
FASA (Federal Acquisition Streamlining Act of 1994), 12, 117–18, 121, 139
"father of DBOF," 164, 167, 173–75
Fat Leonard scandal, 89
FBWT (Fund Balance with Treasury) Initiative, 207, 210, 213
FCS (Future Combat Systems), 126, 129, 131, 146

Federal Acquisition Regulation (FAR), 92
Federal Acquisition Streamlining Act of 1994 (FASA), 12, 117–18, 121, 139
federal employee unions: and Acq Demo, 36, 77; Collins bill and, 41–42, 48; and Force of the Future, 77; and NSPS, 28–30, 46–48, 50–51, 74–76, 80, 238n90; and pay-banding, 38, 77; and pay-for-performance systems, 16, 29
Federal Managers' Financial Integrity Act of 1982 (FMFIA), 160
federated architecture concept, 191, 193–94
feeder systems, 172, 187, 194–96, 203, 217, 220
FIAR (Financial Improvement and Audit Readiness) plan, 207–9, 213–14, 313n432
financial management reform, 22
financial statements. *See* auditable financial statement
financial structure of DOD, 157–63. *See also* auditable financial statement
FIPs (financial improvement plans), 205–6
Fitzhugh Commission (1970), 90
fixed-price controls, 7, 86, 89, 95–96, 122, 131, 144
FMFIA (Federal Managers' Financial Integrity Act of 1982), 160
"Formula for Action," 108
FotF (Force of the Future Initiative), 16, 20, 77–78
four-way sign-off in committees, 13
Fox, J. Ronald, 90, 95
Francis, Paul, 92–93
front-end decisions, 6, 24–25; Ashton Carter on, 133–34; Carlucci on, 94–95; delegation of, 95; incentivizing unjustified optimism, 92, 108; Levin on, 130; McCain on, 130; MDAPs and, 128–29; need for OSD gate-keeping, 147; Packard Commission on, 108, 110; Perry on, 108; WSARA requirements, 132–33, 140–42

Fund Balance with Treasury (FBWT) Initiative, 207, 210, 213
Future Combat Systems (FCS), 126, 129, 131, 146

Gaddy, Zack, 207
Gage, John, 61, 72
Gansler, Jacques (Jack), 36, 133
Gantt charts, 207
GAO (Government Accountability Office or General Accounting Office), 161, 233n9; on acquisition workforce, 91; advocating integrated system architecture, 186–90; on AIP, 98; on Air Force test audit, 177–79; annual weapon programs assessments, 129–31; on appropriations coding, 159; on Army test audit, 179–80; on auditable financial statement goal, 149, 154, 178, 206, 221; on audits by "heroic efforts," 181; and BEA, 191–94; BTA response to, 197; on China Lake project, 33; on CIM, 167–70; citing improvements in acquisition process, 134–35; on contract payment adjustments, 184–85; on Coopers and Lybrand, 120; on cross-functional teams, 11; on DBMS, 174; and DBOF, 173–76; on DCMO, 200–201; on DFAS, 174; DOD audit attempts, 184; on enforcement backsliding, 136; on ERPs, 198–99; on FIAR, 207; on finance and accounting system, 159; on FMFIA, 160; on IG, 212–13; on IGTs, 158; improvements in cost performance, 265–66n162; on inappropriate billings, 103; on inefficient auditing, 185; on LMP and BSM, 197; on Marine Corps audit attempt, 210, 212–13; on MDAPs, 91–93, 134–36, 145; on Navy audit attempt, 183–84; on NSPS, 66; on oversight costs, 120; on pay-for-performance, 33, 36, 55; on "plugs," 213; and questionable value of audit attempts, 184–85, 221; on spare parts purchases, 104–5; supporting Carlucci initiatives, 95; on TSPR, 122; on warranties, 106; on widespread schedule slippage, 210, 212; on WSARA, 83
Gates, Robert, 4, 126, 198, 209
GCSS (Global Combat Support Systems), 196, 202, 210
GD (General Dynamics), 102
GFEBS (General Fund Enterprise Business System), 196, 202
Gibson, John, 224
Glenn, John, 25, 117, 162, 166, 178–80, 182
Global Hawk program, 127
Global Positioning System, 123
Godwin, Richard, 111–14
gold-plating of requirements, 24, 85, 109
Goldwater-Nichols Department of Defense Reorganization Act (1986), 7–10, 130
Gore, Al, 84, 92, 117, 138, 181
Government Management Reform Act (1994), 150, 163
Grace Commission (1983), 91, 96, 98, 159
grade inflation, 32, 55–56, 60
Graham, David, 112–13
Graham, Lindsey, 14
Gramm-Rudman-Hollings Deficit Reduction Act (1985), 164
"grand design" approaches, 151, 186–94, 201, 217–19, 223. *See also* Business Enterprise Architecture (BEA), CIM (Corporate Information Management) program
Grassley, Charles, 175, 213, 215
Greenwalt, Bill, 18, 146
"grunt work," management reform as, 25
GS (General Schedule) personnel system, 79–80; blue-collar employees not in, 72; and NSPS, 27, 59, 63–64, 66, 74; replaced by pay bands, 32, 35, 58–59, 63;

Senate on "practicable" pay levels, 43; as stable, predictable, 79
Guantánamo detainees, 13–14

Hagel, Chuck, 21, 212
Hale, Robert, 162, 183, 190, 208–10, 212, 214, 313n432
Hamre, John, 155, 168, 172, 176, 182
Hart, Gary, 103
HASC (House Armed Services Committee): Acquisition Agility Act, 143; and acquisition reform, 83; and auditability, 215; McCurdy hearings, 93; and NSPS, 40, 71–72, 74; and Packard Commission, 112–13; Thornberry as chair of, 143; William Perry and, 119
Herblock, 102
Hershey Foods ERP, 195
Hicks, Donald, 107
Hill, Eleanor, 158, 184–85
Hodsoll, Frank, 162
Homeland Security Act (2002), 37, 39
Horn, Stephen, 182–83
House Government Reform Committee, 40, 45
HQEs (highly qualified experts), 78
HSGAC (Homeland Security and Governmental Affairs Committee), 14
Hunter, Duncan, 40

IBM Center for the Business of Government, 57
ICE (independent cost estimate), 96, 132–34, 137, 141
IDA (Institute for Defense Analyses), 92, 112, 125, 130, 194, 201, 203, 300n260
IGTs (intergovernmental transactions), 158
Ill Wind scandal, 89, 104
immature technologies, 85, 124–27, 130, 133, 135, 141
implementation struggles, failures, 17–23, 84–85, 95
incremental acquisition concept, 18–19

incremental reforms, 30, 80–81, 202–4, 207, 210, 223
independent cost estimate (ICE), 96, 132–34, 137, 141
independent study groups, 187, 199, 204–5
individual right of action, 6
"industrial funds," 172, 174
inefficiency, finding in budget, 3
influence-peddling, 12
Inhofe, Jim, 13
inspectors general, 100, 103, 150
Institute for Defense Analyses (IDA), 92, 112, 125, 130, 194, 201, 203, 300n260
institutional knowledge, 31, 172
institutional resistance, 4, 38, 45, 138, 201, 225
integrated system architecture goal, 186–87, 193–94
intelligence workforce, 24, 78
interfaces, improved or eliminated, 170, 197–98, 203–4, 217, 311n403
intergovernmental transactions (IGTs), 158
interim migratory systems, 174
International Federation of Professional and Technical Engineers (IFPTE), 77
intra-agency transactions, 158, 177, 183–84, 219, 222
inventory, excess, 6
investment control system, 190
IPPS-A (Integrated Personnel and Pay System-Army), 202

James, Kay Cole, 49. *See also* OPM (Office of Personnel Management)
Johnson, Ron, 214
"jointness," 8
Joint Requirements and Management Board, 109, 111
Jonas, Tina, 191, 208
journal vouchers, 214–16, 218–19
JROC (Joint Requirements Oversight Council), 111, 147
JSF (Joint Strike Fighter), 125–26, 131

Kaminski, Paul, 133
Kasich, John, 100
Kendall, Frank, 126, 134
Ketrick, Paul, 194
Knight, Phil, 195
KPPs (key performance parameters), 50, 53

Lab Demo (laboratory demonstration) projects, 34–37, 45, 56, 66–67, 77–78
labor relations. *See* civil service system
Lacey, Mary, 51–52, 67. *See also* NSPS
Lanzillotta, Larry, 188, 191, 206
LCS (Littoral Combat Ship), 126–27
lead system integrators, 126, 131, 144
leases of aircraft, 126
legacy systems, 170, 193–94, 197–98, 201–4, 217, 220
Lehman, John, 110–11, 267n180
lessons learned, 219–23
Letterman, David, 117
Levin, Carl: on 2007 audit chances, 205–6; author and, 2, 6, 17; Collins-Levin bill, 14, 29, 41–42, 71; on cost overruns, 82, 129; foreword by, vii–viii; opposing NSPS, 40, 48; request to Secretary England, 129; in SASC, 13–14, 82–83; on undisciplined acquisition process, 130; Whistleblower Protection Act (1989), 6; and WSARA, 82–83, 144
Lieberman, Joseph, 178
"lightning bolt" initiatives, 120
LMP (Logistics Modernization Program), 196–97, 202
Lobbying Disclosure Act (1995), 12
"Losing Control" *(Washington Post)*, 182
Lynn, William III, 74, 169–70, 183, 185, 200

M-1 tank, 99
Major Defense Acquisition Programs. *See* MDAPs
management efficiencies savings, 3
Managing the Cost of Government, Building an Effective Financial Management Structure (GAO), 149
"managing up," 91
Mancuso, Don, 185
mandatory retirement, 7, 91
manpower cuts, 21–22
Marine Corps, 196–98, 210–13
Maroni, Alice, 176
material deficiencies, 184, 212, 214
Mattis, Jim, 224
McCain, John: acquisition reform work by, 126–27, 129–30; and BBP, 146; DOD reform, 9; and FCS and C-130J contracts, 129; importance of early program reviews, 132; as "man in a hurry," 143–44; and Military Commissions Act, 13–14; and University of Phoenix, 20; and USD(AT&L) split, 146; and WSARA, 82–83, 146
McCaskill, Claire, 203
McCurdy, Dave, 93, 95, 103, 127
McGrath, Elizabeth, 200
McKeon, Howard "Buck," 83
McNamara, Robert, 90
McNaugher, Thomas, 90
McNicol, David, 92, 109, 115–16, 128
MDA (Milestone Decision Authority), 111, 114, 131, 144–45
MDAPs (Major Defense Acquisition Programs), 89; Air Force, 125–26; Army, 128; cautions regarding, 136; centralizing control of, 83; Clinton reform effects, 86, 105; "Conspiracy of Hope" issue, 128; cost growth dropping, 136; cost overruns in, 93–94, 119, 127–29, 132, 136; FCS (Future Combat Systems), 126, 129, 131, 146; GAO on, 91–93, 134–36, 145; Godwin attempts regarding, 112; ICE on, 96, 137; incentive structure problems, 92–93; JSF (Joint Strike Fighter), 125–26, 131; LCS (Littoral Combat Ship), 126–27; McNicol on,

109–10, 115; milestone review process for, 91, 111, 130–32, 144–45, 147; premature initiation of, 128–31, 138; RAND review of, 125; role of service chiefs in, 144; spare parts and, 107–8; streamlining procedures, 119; successes within, 131, 135; terminations of, 128; USD(A) and, 111; "warranty" requirement, 105
merit principles in federal hiring, 31
Merit Systems Protection Board (MSPB), 33, 41–43, 53, 55, 69
metrics, need for, 98
"micromanagement" complaints, 94, 107
"micro-purchase" expedited procedures, 117
Milestone B certification, 130–31
Milestone Decision Authority (MDA), 111, 114, 131, 144–45
milestone review process for MDAPs, 91, 111, 130–32, 144–45, 147
Military Commissions Acts (2006, 2009), 14
Military Equipment Initiative, 207
military specifications and standards, 6, 17, 24, 84–85, 99, 116, 118–20
Milley, Mark, 145
Minuteman II missile parts, 100
Modly, Tom, 191
MSPB (Merit Systems Protection Board), 33, 41–43, 53, 55, 69

NAPA (National Academy of Public Administration), 57, 78
National Defense Authorization Act. *See* NDAA
National Defense Business Operations Plan, 224
National Guard, 20
National Performance Reviews (NPRs), 32, 55, 92, 117, 121, 181
National Polar-Orbiting Operational Environmental Satellite System (NPOESS), 127

National Security Council (NSC), 107
National Security Decision Directive 219 (NSDD), 110
National Security Personnel System. *See* NSPS
Naval Oceans Systems Center, 32
Naval Vessel Rules update, 126
Navy, Department of the, 204; A-12 program, 114; architectural performance requirements, 193; auditable financial statement attempts, 150, 183–84, 210–11, 213–14; civilian pay plan, 210; contract issues, 101, 127; cost overruns, 96; Deadeye program, 111; and DIMHRS, 198; ERP programs, 196–98, 201–2, 204, 220; FBWT statement, 210; financial system terminated, 161; LCS cost overruns, 126–27; no specs for architectural environment, 193; overpriced spare parts, 105; relations with USD(A), 111–15; scientist recruitment difficulties, 32–33; Sec. Lehman comments, 110–11, 267n180; Wedtech scandal, 11
NDAA (National Defense Authorization Act), 13, 24, 86, 142; fiscal year 1987, 85; fiscal year 2002, 185; fiscal year 2003, 19; fiscal year 2004, 26, 40; fiscal year 2006, 199; fiscal year 2008, 19; fiscal year 2010, 75, 209; fiscal year 2016, 9, 79, 136
NDIs (non-developmental items), 17
Nelson, Ben, 208
New York Times, 119
NFRs (notices of findings and recommendations), 211
Niehaus, Patricia, 76
Nike ERP, 195
Norquist, David, 215–16
NPOESS (National Polar-Orbiting Operational Environmental Satellite System), 127
NPR (National Performance Review), 32, 55, 92, 117, 121, 181

NSC (National Security Council), 107
NSDD (National Security Decision Directive) 219, 110
NSPS (National Security Personnel System): accusations of favoritism in, 36–37; application of pay bands, 57–58, 62–63, 65, 74; bipartisan opposition to, 48–49; bypassing OPM, 48; causing decrease in morale, 56; and collective bargaining rights, 67–68; Collins' alternative to, 41; compared to GS, 64; compromise bill passed (2008), 72–73; consequences of failure of, 76–77; David Chu on, 45; DBB report on, 74–75; DC Circuit Court ruling, 70–72; employee resistance and "union-busting" response, 65–67; G. W. Bush and, 22–23, 26, 29, 40, 76–77; hiring difficulties, 65; initial enactment of, 37–45; initial hearings, passage by House, 40; initial implementation, 26–27, 44–52; labor authority repealed, 72; lessons learned from, 79–81; military opposition to, 49; multiple objectives of, 54; Obama and, 66, 73–74; opaque rules, 58; pay-for-performance system under, 52–56; pay pools and other mechanisms, 59–63; prohibiting collective bargaining, 68; as "radioactive," 75; "rates of pay" definition, 73; reasons for failure, 23, 27–29; repeal of, 23, 27, 75, 77; replacing CSRA evaluations, 55; "Republican-only" approach to, 70–71; requiring too much time, 56; standards of review issues, 69–70; strategic review of, 49–50; termination of, 73–77; transparency concerns, 60–61; union-busting approach to, 67–72; union opposition to, 47–48, 67–70, 238n90; use of pay bands, 56–59, 62–63, 65, 74; weakening of union powers, 46–48; withholding public notice, 46

NSPS PEO (NSPS Program Executive Office), 50, 56, 61, 63–65, 109, 202
Nunn, Sam, 8
Nunn-McCurdy law, 103, 127

Obama administration, 20, 73–74, 82, 133, 139, 186, 200, 208
obligation and expenditure accounting, 162
off-the-shelf products, 7, 17, 84, 195, 198, 203
O'Keefe, Sean, 166–67
OMB (Office of Management and Budget): on accounting and management irregularities, 150, 159–60, 162, 205; David Stockman on Pentagon waste, 100; Kay Cole James on, 49; Marine Corps on timeline by, 211; Obama administration and, 74; Reagan administration and, 100; Ron Sanders on, 167.
one-size-fits-all solutions, 7, 28, 30, 86, 141, 225
operational testing, 24, 85, 103, 108, 137, 139
OPM (Office of Personnel Management): China Lake demonstration project, 32, 34; conflict with DOD, 38–39, 42, 48–49; and NSPS, 49, 51, 67, 74, 76; on performance appraisals, 55; success of Lab Demo programs, 34–37
"optimization" of service contracts, 4
Orszag, Peter, 74
"other transactions" authority, 126, 129, 131, 144
overhead cost, 142, 146; arbitrary assignment of, 100; author's experience with, 3, 7; consequences of reducing, 86–87; declining workload "death spiral," 176; determining dispensability, 22; oversight trade-off, 146, 158; price-based acquisition and, 122; from second-sourcing, 106; Weinberger's threat, 103; workforce size and, 142
over-optimistic cost estimates: Bill Lynn on, 169–70; Carlucci on, 94; as

"Conspiracy of Hope," 128; in era of acquisition reform, 141; incentives for, 108, 139; independent reviews, 127; Packard Commission and, 85, 109, 113; Perry on "huckster environment," 108; Rand on, 123, 125; in reform attempts, 24; TSPR and, 123; Young on, 131

P3I (pre-planned product improvements), 94, 97
Packard, David, 90–91, 108–16, 128–30, 134, 270n230
Packard Commission, 23–24, 90–91; on acquisition workforce, 91–92; as bipartisan effort, 139; Cheney's support for, 114; on China Lake project, 33; delegation of power and, 145; effects of, 87, 140–41; Gordon England and, 129; on "huckster environment," 108; implementation of recommendations, 164; as independent review, 107–8; purpose of, 107; recommendations, 84–85, 108–10, 138–40; response to, 110–11, 112–13; results of, 115–16, 142–43; risks of reforms, 145, 148; speed limit analogy, 109–10; supporting commercial item acquisition, 116; Warner on, 130
paddleboat analogy, 208
Panetta, Leon, 209–10
paperwork: contractor cost information, 106; and costs, 86–87; FMFIA adding to, 160; GAO report on, 91–92; reduction attempts, 36, 54, 86, 92, 117, 122, 164; reforms adding to, 92
"partial solutions" efforts, 151, 170–77, 194–204, 217, 219, 222
"passthrough" charges, 100, 104
patronage system, 31, 40, 47
Patterson, David, 207
pay banding: in Acq Demo program, 35–36, 56; China Lake approach to, 32–35; "Force of the Future" initiative, 77–78; NSPS application of, 57–58, 62–63, 65, 74; as one-size-fits-all-solution, 28, 56–57; overly broad categories, 58; and pay pools, 59–62
pay caps, 65, 78–79
pay comparability, 43
pay-for-performance, 52; Acq Demo program, 34–36, 77–78; after NSPS, 77–78; China Lake, 34; in Collins bill, 41; congressional opposition to, 37; David Walker on, 44–45; DCIPS program, 77–78; GAO on, 33; and inflated ratings, 55–56; Lab Demo program, 36; negative effects of, 53, 65–66; NSPS, 27–29, 50, 52–64, 72–74; objectives of, 54; versus pay-to-market, 62; positive effects of, 34, 52–53; SES program, 78; union opposition to, 29, 36, 50
pay pools, 59–63, 65, 73–74, 78
pay ranges, 246n210
PBA (price-based acquisition), 122
"peace dividend," 164
Pendleton Act (1883), 31
Pentagon information systems chart, 189
PEOs (program executive officers), 50–51, 56, 61, 63–66, 109, 145, 147, 202
performance management system. *See* NSPS
performance requirements, 114, 122, 136, 193
Perry, William: acquisition agenda of, 119; and commercial items exemptions, 117–19; on "huckster environment," 108; and RAND study, 121; and regulatory "cost premium," 119; replacing military specifications, 17, 24, 85; testimony to HASC, 112
'plug' adjustments, 213
"poison pill" in NSPS bill, 44
Porter, Gene, 125, 130
premature program initiation, 130
prevalidation, 183, 219
price-based acquisition (PBA), 122
"price-redeterminable" contracts, 100

private sector practices, 35, 88; accrual-based accounting, 161; audited financial statements, 153–54; ERPs (Enterprise Resource Programs), 195–96; goal of financial audit, 220–21; "Grace Commission," 159; G. W. Bush administration on, 205; pay banding, 28, 57–58; pay for performance, 52–53; pay levels, 60, 61, 62, 246n210; SASC on, 4
problem definition issue, 24, 85
procurement reforms (1984–1985), 84, 104–7, 138
procurement reforms (1989), 113, 119
procurement reforms (1990s), 119
program executive officers (PEOs), 50–51, 56, 61, 63–66, 109, 145, 147, 202
Project on Military Procurement, 99, 101
proprietary markings issues, 100
prototypes, 108, 110
Pryor, David, 103
public perceptions, 99–100

quantity discounts, 100

RAND, 20, 91, 120–23, 125, 265–66n162
Rasor, Dina, 99
Reagan administration, 93, 100, 107, 110
reductions in force (RIFs), 58, 72, 79
reenlistment bonuses, 20
Reinventing Government, 84, 116–29, 139
requirements development process, 127–30, 203
revolving funds, 163, 172
Rice, Donald, 178
Rickover, Hyman, 102
RIFs (reductions in force), 58, 72, 79
root cause analysis, 8, 158, 214
Roth, William, 162
Rumsfeld, Donald H.: DOD-wide Enterprise Architecture, 187; and NSPS, 26, 49, 71; opposing bipartisanship, 41–42; opposing OPM, 48–49; on over-engineering, 123; rejection of Collins bill, 41; Senate confirmation hearing, 187; study group on clean audit, 204–5; testimony before SGAC, 26; urging bold action, 38

SACS (standard accounting classification structure), 192
SAE (service acquisition executive), 109–10, 112, 126, 145
"salami slicing," 4
Sambur, Marv, 124
Sanders, Ron, 67
SASC (Senate Armed Services Committee), 2, viii; acquisition hearings, 129; Atwood testimony, 171; auditing to auditability issue, 185, 206; bipartisanship within, 12–14, 40–41, 48, 117; Byrd budget work, 187, 199; Cheney statement to, 113; Commons testimony, 210; "cross-functional mission teams," 10; England on employee compensation, 59; FASA passage, 12, 117; FY 2006 NDAA amendment, 199; Gates testimony, 198; Godwin testimony, 112; and Goldwater-Nichols reforms, 8–10; Hale testimony, 190; incremental acquisition concept, 18; Kreig testimony, 193; labor relations issues, 48, 69–72; Lanzillotta testimony, 206; Levin on cost overruns, 82; Levin on employee appeals rights, 69–70; Lynn testimony, 200; management and acquisition hearings, 93–94, 108; McCain as chair of, 143; McGrath testimony, 200; Norquist testimony, 215; NSPS proposals, 40–41, 74; Packard's reform efforts, 109; Panetta testimony, 209; requiring private sector practices, 4; Rumsfeld testimony, 187; Shyu testimony, 145; Wynne testimony, 191; Zakheim testimony, 188–89, 191, 205–6
SBA (schedule of budgetary activity), 212, 319n508

SBIRS (Space-Based Infrared System), 123, 132
SBR (Statement of Budgetary Resources), 207–10, 212–13
Schumer, Charles, 102
Science, Mathematics and Research for Transformation (SMART) scholarships, 78
Seawolf submarine, 115
Secretary of Defense, 10, 95; Carlucci, Frank, 95, 97; Carter, Ashton, 15–16, 20, 77–78, 133–34; Cheney, Dick, 40, 113–14, 172, 270n230; CIM and, 167; Gates, Robert, 4, 126, 198, 209; Grace Commission on, 98–99; Hagel, Chuck, 21, 212; JLSC and, 167; jurisdictional disputes involving, 197; Mattis, Jim, 224; McNamara, Robert, 90; micromanagement by, 94; Panetta, Leon, 209–10; program stability issue, 97, 145, 147; WSARA and, 141. *See also* Perry, William; Rumsfeld, Donald H.; Weinberger, Caspar
Section 800 Panel Report, 12, 106, 116–17
Senate Armed Services Committee. *See* SASC
Senate Governmental Affairs Committee. *See* SGAC
Senior Financial Management Oversight Council (SFMOC), 153, 183
seniority-based civil service, 36, 79
September 11, 2001 attacks, 27–28, 37
service acquisition executive (SAE), 109–10, 112, 126, 145
service-centric culture, 9
service contracts, 1–4, 221
SES pay-for-performance, 78
SFIS (Standard Financial Infrastructure System), 192, 217
SFMOC (Senior Financial Management Oversight Council), 153, 183
SGAC (Senate Governmental Affairs Committee), 2, viii; and Air Force financial management, 178–79; Alvin Tucker testimony to, 181; bipartisanship within, 12–13, 29, 48, 117, 162; Charles Bowsher testimony to, 95, 149, 162; David Walker's statement to, 38–39; Donald Rumsfeld's testimony to, 26, 42; hearings on Collins bill, 41–42; John Glenn as chair, 117, 162, 178–82; John Hamre testimony to, 168; John Tower testimony to, 93
Shanahan, Patrick, 151, 216
Shays, Christopher, 188
"should-cost" reviews, 134
Shycoff, Donald, 164, 167, 173–75
Shyu, Heidi, 145
"simplified acquisition threshold," 117
single-party legislative approach, 14, 29
Skantze, Larry, 267n180
SLC (Senior Leadership Council), 15, 231n37
SMART (Science, Mathematics and Research for Transformation) scholarships, 78
social engineering accusations, 16
"soda straw view," 207
software, 88, 161, 195, 198, 202–3
Space-Based Infrared System (SBIRS), 123, 132
spare parts procurement: issues with, 6, 100; public anger over, 84, 138; reform attempts, 23–24, 86, 101–2, 104–7, 137, 140
Spector, Eleanor, 120
speed limit analogy, 109–10
Speer, Robert, 214, 285n13
Spinney, Chuck, 97
spiral implementation approach, 18, 51–52
spoils system, 31
Staats, Elmer, 159
staff-driven legislation, 19
stair-step approach, 208, 223
standard accounting classification structure (SACS), 192

Standard Financial Infrastructure System (SFIS), 192, 217
Statement of Budgetary Resources (SBR), 207–10, 212–13
stealth technology, 99
Stein, Robert, 2
Stevens, Ted, 176
stock funds, 171–72
Stockman, David, 100
stovepiped legacy systems, addressing, 156, 189, 194, 197–99, 202, 220
Sullivan, Emmet, 70
supply chain, 6, 11

Taft, William, 111
tanker lease, 84, 126
"targeted local market supplements," 62–63, 65, 80
targeted solutions, 5–6, 10–11, 23, 28, 30, 78–79, 151, 219
technological maturity, 125, 129–30, 132–33, 135, 141
technology readiness levels (TRLs), 127–28, 131–33
Terminal High-Altitude Area Defense, 123
Thayer, Paul, 101
Thornberry, Mac, 83, 143
Thurmond, Strom, 13
Tierney, John, 188
Tinker Air Force Base, 100–101
Today Show, 102
toilet seats ($640), 102
Tonight Show, 102
top-down reform model, 152, 192–94, 218, 220
total system performance responsibility (TSPR), 122–23
Tower, John, 93
TRANSCOM (United States Transportation Command), 157
transgender service members, 20
Trident submarine, 99, 102

"trillion-dollar accounting gaffes," 215
TRLs (technology readiness levels), 127–28, 131–33
"trouble tickets," 198
Trump administration, 215
TSPR (total system performance responsibility), 122–23
Tucker, Alvin, 181

unions. *See* federal employee unions
United DOD Workers' Coalition, 77
universe of transactions, 210, 214–16, 222
unmatched disbursements, 172, 182–83, 218
unmatched transactions, 158, 183, 187
unqualified audit opinions: achieved, 181, 208, 213; as goal, 205, 207, 209, 212, 223
unrealistic performance expectations, 82, 108, 133, 141
unsupported adjustments, 178, 180, 185, 213, 219
"up-or-out" policy, 7, 16
USA Patriot Act (2001), 37
US Circuit Court of Appeals of DC, 70–71
USD (A) (Under Secretary of Defense for Acquisition), 109–15
USD (P&R) (Under Secretary of Defense for Personnel and Readiness), 7, 15, 20, 38, 77
USD (R&E) (Under Secretary for Research and Engineering), 102, 107, 147
USD(AT&L) (Under Secretary of Defense for Acquisition, Technology, and Logistics): certification required by, 131; Gansler, Jacques, 36; as judge, 110; Krieg, Ken, 193; splitting of, 9–10, 145–46; WSARA revamping of, 133, 138, 142; Wynne, Michael, 191, 199; Young, John, 131

V-22 Osprey, 132
Vander Schaaf, Derek, 185

Veliotis, Panagiotis Takis, 102
Viper anti-tank rocket, 99
vocabulary, common business, 192
Voinovich, George, 48
Volcker Commission on Public Service, 32

waivers and proposed waivers: of Chapter 71 (proposed), 42–44; of civil service laws, 32, 37, 41–42, 74; of collective bargaining rights, 41; of environmental laws, 39; of NSPS repeal, 75; performance specs and standards, 118; of technology readiness levels, 127
Walker, David, 31, 38, 44–45, 54, 169, 199
Wall Street Journal, 102
Warner, John, 13–14, 40, 48, 129–30, 199
Warner Robins Air Logistics Center, 177–78
warranty provisions, 7, 105–6
wartime contracting, 6, 131
Washington Post "Losing Control" article, 182
Weapon Systems Acquisition Reform Act. *See* WSARA
Wedtech, 11
Weinberger, Caspar: as "Cap the Knife," 93; delegating acquisition authority, 23, 95; on GD and Trident, 102; as MDA, 111; and Packard Commission, 107–8, 110–11; requiring overhead certification, 103; spare parts procurement, 101; toilet seat cartoon with, 102
Westphal, Joe, 201–2
"what the building thinks," 16
Whistleblower Protection Act (1989), 6
Whitlock, Craig, 2
Wikipedia information beating BEA's, 194
WIN-T (Warfighter Information Network-Tactical), 127
Wolfowitz, Paul, 124
Woodward, Bob, 2
Woolsey, James, 112
Work, Robert, 2, 201
"work measurement programs," 105
Wright, Joseph Jr., 159–60
WSARA (Weapon Systems Acquisition Reform Act of 2009), 146; bipartisan support for, 23, 138–39, 144; front-end review requirements, 132–33, 140–42; implementation issues, 85; McCain role, 132, 144; passage, signing of, 82–84, 133; positive results from, 24, 83, 135–38, 141–43, 146; Senate hearings on, 129–30, 132–34
Wynne, Michael, 191, 199

Yockey, Donald, 115
Young, John Jr., 131–32

Zakheim, Dov, 188–89, 191, 205–6

The authorized representative in the EU for product safety and compliance is:
Mare Nostrum Group
B.V Doelen 72
4831 GR Breda
The Netherlands